Metacognitive Interpersonal Therapy

Metacognitive Interpersonal Therapy (MIT) remains unique in providing instruments for dealing with clients with prominent emotional inhibition and suppression, a population for whom treatment options are largely lacking.

This book provides clinicians with techniques to treat this population, including guided imagery and re-scripting, two-chairs, role-play, body-oriented work and interpersonal mindfulness. *Metacognitive Interpersonal Therapy* is aimed at increasing clients' awareness of their inner world, fostering a sense of agency over their experience and dismantling the core, embodied aspects of the schemas. The techniques included also provide clients with fresh instruments to overcome pain and act creatively in their everyday life. Using an improved version of the MIT decision-making procedure, the authors have provided a set of techniques aimed at modifying mental imagery, body states and behaviour, as well as at steering attention to avoid falling prey to rumination. The book is structured to gently push clients towards change, but also to always prioritise the clients' goals and needs.

Metacognitive Interpersonal Therapy serves as an important guide for clinicians of any orientation.

Giancarlo Dimaggio, psychiatrist and psychotherapist, has published six books on psychotherapy for severe patients and around 200 scientific articles and book chapters. He is Editor-in-Chief of the *Journal of Clinical Psychology: In-Session*.

Paolo Ottavi, psychologist and psychotherapist, is the main developer of two published treatments with empirical support: Metacognition Oriented Social Skills Training and Metacognitive Interpersonal Mindfulness-Based Training.

Raffaele Popolo, psychiatrist and psychotherapist, has published many scientific papers and developed Metacognitive Interpersonal Therapy in Group which has already been tested in two randomised control trials and two pilot studies. It is currently applied in Norway, Spain and Australia.

Giampaolo Salvatore, psychiatrist and psychotherapist, has published many scientific papers and has adapted Metacognitive Interpersonal Therapy for psychosis and for borderline personality disorders.

Metacognitive Interpersonal Therapy

Body, Imagery and Change

Giancarlo Dimaggio, Paolo Ottavi,
Raffaele Popolo and Giampaolo Salvatore

LONDON AND NEW YORK

First published 2020
by Routledge
2 Park Square, Milton Park, Abingdon, Oxon OX14 4RN

and by Routledge
52 Vanderbilt Avenue, New York, NY 10017

Routledge is an imprint of the Taylor & Francis Group, an informa business

© 2020 Giancarlo Dimaggio, Paolo Ottavi, Raffaele Popolo and Giampaolo Salvatore

The right of Giancarlo Dimaggio, Paolo Ottavi, Raffaele Popolo and Giampaolo Salvatore to be identified as authors of this work has been asserted by them in accordance with sections 77 and 78 of the Copyright, Designs and Patents Act 1988.

All rights reserved. No part of this book may be reprinted or reproduced or utilised in any form or by any electronic, mechanical, or other means, now known or hereafter invented, including photocopying and recording, or in any information storage or retrieval system, without permission in writing from the publishers.

Trademark notice: Product or corporate names may be trademarks or registered trademarks, and are used only for identification and explanation without intent to infringe.

British Library Cataloguing-in-Publication Data
A catalogue record for this book is available from the British Library

Library of Congress Cataloging-in-Publication Data
Names: Dimaggio, Giancarlo, author. | Ottavi, Paolo, author. | Popolo, Raffaele, author. | Salvatore, Giampaolo, author.
Title: Metacognitive interpersonal therapy : body, imagery and change / Giancarlo Dimaggio, Paolo Ottavi, Raffaele Popolo, and Giampaolo Salvatore.
Description: Abingdon, Oxon ; New York, NY : Routledge, 2021. | Includes bibliographical references and index.
Identifiers: LCCN 2020014103 (print) | LCCN 2020014104 (ebook) | ISBN 9780367367022 (hardback) | ISBN 9780367367039 (paperback) | ISBN 9780429350894 (ebook)
Subjects: MESH: Personality Disorders—therapy | Psychotherapy—methods | Metacognition | Interpersonal Relations | Emotional Regulation
Classification: LCC RC554 (print) | LCC RC554 (ebook) | NLM WM 190 | DDC 616.85/81—dc23
LC record available at https://lccn.loc.gov/2020014103
LC ebook record available at https://lccn.loc.gov/2020014104

ISBN: 978-0-367-36702-2 (hbk)
ISBN: 978-0-367-36703-9 (pbk)
ISBN: 978-0-429-35089-4 (ebk)

Typeset in Minion Pro
by Apex CoVantage, LLC

Contents

	Introduction	1
1	Psychopathology of personality disorders: narratives, interpersonal schemas and mental states	9
2	Personality disorder psychopathology: metacognition, coping and emotional regulation, maintenance model	33
3	Use of imagery and bodily techniques in psychotherapy	71
4	The decision-making procedure and experiential techniques	105
5	Guided imagery and imagery rescripting	138
6	Drama techniques: Two-chairs, role-play and enactment	180
7	Body interventions	206
8	Behavioural exploration and activation	228
9	Techniques for restructuring attention and treating cognitive coping strategies	247
10	Metacognitive Interpersonal Therapy in Group (MIT-G)	272
11	Technique sequences	293
	References	312
	Index	327

Introduction

Life leaves marks on the body as well as in the psyche. Treating the mind often requires acting on a somatic level. Sequences of adverse events are engraved in the brain, stomach, skin and muscles, digging deep furrows, leaving memorised imprints resurfacing in adulthood as testimony of past suffering.

Patients with personality, anxiety, post-traumatic, dissociative and eating disorders sometimes clearly recall scenes triggering the distress for which they seek therapy. At other times, however, memory recall is not possible. It is then that the body recounts distressing events, in the same language in which these events were coded.

To be precise, these constitute implicit, tacit or procedural memories. A clinician witnesses these memories in the form of somatic symptoms concomitant with gaps in autobiographical memory and limited ability to describe what one feels in words. To give an example, a young adult with avoidant personality disorder (PD) fidgets on his chair, is restless, and only with difficulty manages to tell you he is anxious. In his body language you discern signs of fear of criticism and embarrassment, but this fear is not communicated through words.

A patient in his forties with narcissism has a racing heartbeat. He fears he is at risk of a heart attack, gets into a panic, but does not say out loud: "I'm afraid. I feel sad. My girlfriend has threatened to split and that's why my heart is beating." He cannot fully understand his experience, as he does not possess the language to describe these emotions.

A young woman with bulimia feels a nameless tension growing in her guts and the only way to soothe herself is to binge and then feel the shock of vomiting. Her mind is calm for a few hours, but the trigger of the tension remains unknown to her.

And naturally, someone suffering from the aftermath of a trauma demonstrates incessant hyperarousal through trembling, stress, being on edge, and the primeval fight-or-flight response is triggered. Children yelling at a family barbecue suffice to trigger the alert system once again, rekindling sensory and affective memories of the traumatic event that overwhelm the senses: the heart pumps blood to the muscles and awareness narrows, both being physical reactions of an animal presented with a limited range of possible options, among which the ones favoured the most are hiding in the depths of the forest or showing its claws.

Patients who do not recognise these distressing sensory experiences as part of their individual history represented through their body attempt to treat them directly through impulsive and/or compulsive behaviours, thus increasing the risk of further personal harm. For example, they consume alcohol and drugs, engage in excessive physical exercise, inflict cuts and burns on their body, binge on food as a medicine to soothe themselves or abstain from food to savour the pleasure of controlling one's hunger. Alternatively, they practice established protective automatisms performed at the speed of sound, such as avoidance, compliant submission and self-sacrifice.

Cognitive psychotherapists see loads of patients with such patterns of functioning. If they want to understand them they have to decode their non-verbal communication and somatic signals. They especially need to find a way to instil in them a sense of self-efficacy and the ability to regulate their emotions and behaviour when language does not provide them with sufficient information about either.

Modern psychotherapy has evolved, as has clinical cognitivism. The merit of classical cognitivism, centred on correcting presumed cognitive distortions, is currently under debate. The reason? Standard cognitive behaviour therapy (CBT) has turned out to be significantly less effective than it seemed in its early years. Many patients did not respond to treatment and the least functional patients were unable to access dysfunctional thoughts or, when they did, were not so willing to change their point of view if their therapist disputed them (Semerari, Carcione, Dimaggio, Falcone, Nicolò, Procacci, & Alleva, 2003). To summarise very briefly: The importance of bottom-up information-processing, whereby perception is driven by bodily, sensory information being integrated into mental representations, is currently increasing (Damasio, 1994; Greenberg, 2002; Ogden & Fisher, 2015; Van Der Kolk, 2014). You experience an effect, your body responds in a certain way, and this change in physiology influences your thoughts. Bottom-up processing can be subsumed under the concept of metacognition, which involves an awareness of the reciprocal influence between the body and the mind.

The result of this convergence of historical events? The cognitive psychotherapy map has been expanded and reformed. The so-called third wave cognitive therapies have emerged and, as a result, many psychotherapies have changed intervention targets. Some modalities, such as Schema therapy (Arntz & van Genderen, 2011), Acceptance and Commitment Therapy (Hayes, Strosahl, & Wilson, 2011) and Mindfulness Based Stress Reduction (Kabat-Zinn, 2003), remain in the cognitive therapy family. Others, such as EMDR, are thought to have moved beyond the boundaries of cognitive therapy, although in our opinion they are still part of the cognitive tradition. Yet others, such as sensorimotor therapy (Ogden & Fisher, 2015) or integrated trauma therapies (Van der Kolk, 2014), speak languages arising from historically different schools of thought. What do these modalities have in common? They all intervene in two elements of human experience that cognitive therapy has neglected: body and imagery. A new generation of therapists has made its appearance, including some with a background in CBT, who guide patients to relive their memories and plan their future through imagery work (Hackman, Bennett-Levy, & Holmes, 2011). They reconstruct patients' memories and fantasies, and are intently attuned to body signals while stories get re-enacted on stage, with the aim to identify and help rescript the dysfunctional narrative life has engraved in the body by means of the body itself.

This view of embodied cognition as processes experienced at gut level and occupying a core function in psychopathology requires a suitable treatment toolbox. The landscape opening up before us is rich; psychotherapy is today abuzz with tools for body-oriented and imagery-focused, mainly visual, work. If persons express the core idea of being weak and inept, ever fewer therapists engage in *disputing* these ideas as valid.

This was the cultural context we were moving in. What was the starting point?

MIT had one solid treatment tool: the decision-making procedure (Dimaggio, Montano, Popolo, Salvatore, 2015). Manualising MIT treatment facilitated empirical evaluation of its application. We started with a set of three individual cases treated at the Rome MIT Centre. Results were favourable: the patients benefitted by a great reduction in the number of personality disorder criteria endorsed and in reported subjective suffering (Dimaggio, Salvatore et al., 2017). This study was replicated in Brisbane, using a rigorous experimental design. Among the seven patients treated, six completed the treatment successfully, demonstrating significant improvements, and the patient who dropped out nevertheless reported symptom relief (Gordon-King, Schweitzer, & Dimaggio, 2018a). A case series also suggests that MIT is effective at treating Schizotypal PD (Cheli, Lysaker, & Dimaggio, 2019). Meanwhile we have developed a brief group approach (MIT-G), delivered in a mixed, psychoeducational and experiential, format (Popolo et al., 2019; Chapter 10). The goal was to design a time-effective and, if possible, cost-effective format. Application of the group format was tested in a pilot *randomised controlled trial* (RCT), also producing favourable results: among the 10 patients eight completed the treatment, and improvements in symptoms and social functioning were significantly greater compared to a control group (Popolo et al., 2019). The results of this study were replicated in a second non-controlled trial (Popolo et al., 2018) and outcomes will soon be available for a second larger RCT. Further studies in Spain, including patients with borderline features, yielded similar results with respect to low drop-out rates and levels of symptom improvement (Inchausti, Moreno-Campos, Prado-Abril, Sánchez-Reales, Fonseca-Pedrero, MacBeth, Popolo, & Dimaggio, 2020). An additional pilot MIT-G trial delivered to teenagers with PD is currently underway. We therefore wrote this book while emerging evidence placed MIT among the empirically supported therapies, although wider research is clearly needed.

We have continued to experiment by employing many useful tools, which we felt could enrich our therapeutic repertoire. We introduced imagery and body-oriented techniques, as well as various techniques drawn from mindfulness practice. We also encouraged the application of behavioural exposure and observed that we could activate patients early in therapy without betraying our theoretical principle that change should follow a shared formulation of functioning.

We realised that we were able to highlight healthy aspects of individual functioning even during the first sessions and bring them to the attention of almost all patients, including the least functional among them, laden with suffering. And that, if we asked patients to activate themselves behaviourally between one session and the next, including between the assessment session and the first treatment session, patients welcomed the idea! Or at least they took it into consideration. Our attempts worked: patients responded well. Hence, we asked ourselves: should we revise the decision-making procedure? We wanted to change its structure, at least partly, and introduce the new technical toolbox at full power.

The design we have outlined through our revisions over the years has evolved as follows. Patients see and feel themselves as inept, weak and incapable vis-à-vis an emotionally distant, powerful and disdainful Other. We do not attempt to convince them to the contrary. We try instead to trigger mental images of themselves as strong, capable and safe. Likewise, we do not attempt to convince them that these images, which lie beyond their awareness, exist; this is not our task. We rely on our clinical awareness and our fast reflexes to capture them as soon as they surface into consciousness, or we conduct the conversation with a view to making them emerge. Immediately thereafter we concentrate our efforts on preserving this imagery within patients' consciousness for as long as possible. We enable patients to experience these embodied ideas of self somatically, emotionally and cognitively. Once patients have sustained them long enough in their attentional space, we urge them to store them in memory and recall them at home. We politely and carefully negotiate that they commit to practising behaviours consistent with these benign ideas in their daily life and to actively retrieving them to master control over familiar phantoms encroaching upon them, in the form of old, recurring maladaptive automatisms.

Performed this way, cognitive restructuring assumes new value and, owing to these exercises, these planned, well-tried and practised steps, patients end up acknowledging that they are not weak, as they previously thought, and they can therefore try out activities they avoided before. In this book we shall describe every step of this journey.

Is our goal clear? We do not restrict ourselves to describing a set of techniques aimed at modifying mental imagery, body states and behaviour, as well as at steering attention to avoid falling prey to rumination. We wanted to design an improved version of the MIT decision-making procedure.

We have kept the therapy structure intact, what in conversation we call the "decision tree", which divides treatment into two macro-sections: *shared formulation of functioning* and *change promoting*. But we have modified these sections and grafted our repertoire of imagery-focused, body-oriented and attentional techniques within this revised framework.

This evolution in MIT required a revision of the theory. For some time we have been advocating the importance of *bottom-up* meaning attribution processes. In accordance with emotion psychology theories, it has always been clear that the relationship between cognition and emotion is reciprocal. On the one hand, there is the path to emotion generation emphasised by CBT: thought causes emotion. I change my thoughts to change my emotions.

On the other hand, there is an alternative path to emotion generation originating from the body and carried through thought, as described by embodied cognition theory. First, the body's reactions to the environment influence cognitive processes. Handling rigid objects leads to rigid judgements (Ackerman, Nocera, & Bargh, 2010). Feeling cold makes us ill-disposed towards others (Bargh, 2017). Our bodily state, posture, muscular tension and action tendencies influence cognitive processes. Second, the somatic component of emotion – arousal, expressive behaviour, actions – further influences thought (Bower, 1981; Damasio, 1994; Forgas, 2002; James, 1890). Physical sensations concomitant to joy lead to thinking positive thoughts, whereas physical concomitants to anxiety activate worried cognitions.

Therefore, to change cognitive-affective processes it is not enough to modify ideas engendering distress. It is also necessary to practice adaptive regulation of affect, for example by substituting one emotion with another emotion (Greenberg, 2002), and thus benefiting from the cognitive change deriving from the shift in affect.

Put in simple terms, should a patient feel sad, lifeless, fragile and powerless, a therapist would try to trigger mental images or bodily states through which she could experience herself as stronger and more active, and which could induce a pleasant hedonic state. In consequence, patients' ideation would be expected to change. Indeed, the power of emotions to generate congruent thoughts is a well-established fact, with positive emotions evidenced to prompt benevolent ideas (Fredrickson, 2001).

Expressed in yet another way: CBT uses *top-down* re-evaluation strategies of cognitions triggering emotions – "let's reason together differently" – to influence the latter. But this approach would not address the root cause of affective processes originating from bodily experience that influences cognition.

For example, part of the anger born from the conscious idea of having been cheated could be reduced, if the patient realises nobody is cheating her. But the emotional activation component arising from bodily states experienced prior to conscious valuation processes would not change on the basis of modifying cognitions.

Formalising the set of techniques used as part of the MIT decision tree in a consistent way has not been an abstract, conceptual exercise, but has rather evolved through consistent application and revision of the techniques over a considerable period of time.

Let us imagine Ilaria, a hypothetical patient combining features from various real patients described in this book. She is 32 and demonstrates tendencies to social avoidance, clinging dependency, paranoid attribution and passive-aggressive behaviour. She is sensitive to criticism to which she reacts by oscillating between a state of being fearful of annihilation and a predisposition to react angrily. Her husband scorns her while she is preparing their son for school. She reacts violently, thumping him.

She is astonished at herself, as this is the first time she has behaved violently. The therapist interprets the episode in light of her core wish to feel appreciated. Her expectation is that others will despise her and her usual reaction is embarrassment and feeling annihilated. Recently, however, her anger has been surfacing increasingly often. During a session with her therapist she admits being furious with her husband and says: "If I had him before me, I'd beat the hell out of him." And she would probably manage to do so, as she is a Thai boxing teacher. The therapist asks her to recall associated autobiographical episodes, similar memories from her past.

Ilaria remembers herself at 11. Her father thumping her in a corner of the kitchen. Herself on the ground and him towering over her and kicking her. The therapist suggests returning to that room using a guided imagery exercise. She manages to see her father and the therapist asks her if she is afraid, as she is trembling. The therapist then asks her to reopen her eyes and describe the room. In doing so she calms down. She returns to the scene, this time being instructed to have her adult self intervene. With the confidence that takes hold of her when doing martial arts, Ilaria enters the scene. The therapist guides her to tell her father to let go of the child. Initially her voice barely comes out. The therapist insists: "Breathe deeply. Concentrate on your diaphragm. Draw your voice out." Ilaria takes the child by the hand. "You've got to let her be", she says to her father. Ilaria has a strange reaction. The therapist asks what is happening to her. "My father ... is embarrassed." "And how do you feel?" "Guilty for causing him difficulties."

Ilaria finishes the exercise with a mixed feeling of relief and surprise. She thinks she understands the reason behind her anger attacks better, but her emotions have changed completely: her anger has disappeared and she feels astonished: "I didn't think I'd ever see my father vulnerable and that I'd have felt guilty."

The exercise lasts 10 minutes in total. The effect is an increase in self-awareness, gaining access to emotions she was previously unaware of, and a temporary increase in her capacity to regulate her distress. For anyone using imagery exercises the results are not surprising.

Which patients is this therapeutic model tailored to? Individuals with PDs remain the main target group, especially those with a tendency to behavioural inhibition, emotional over-regulation, and narrow social action (Dimaggio et al., 2018). Given, however, that these patients display significant, usually state-dependent and temporary, emotion dysregulation (Dimaggio, Popolo et al., 2017), we broaden the model's application to show how we tackle situations where emotions get out of hand (Salvatore et al., 2016). Throughout the book we describe patients with reference to PD diagnoses, as presented in the fifth edition of the

Diagnostic Statistical and Manual of Mental Disorders (DSM-5; American Psychiatric Association, 2013), and provide clinicians with easy clues to understanding patients' prototypical functioning (Westen & Shedler, 2000). The approach adopted here is, however, mostly based on individualised case formulation, tailoring treatment to each single individual's functioning. At the same time, the way we describe PD is consistent with the alternative model described in DSM-5 in the "Levels of Personality Functioning" section. This scale focuses on features largely consistent with our understanding of PD pathology, as involving a) maladaptive views of self and others; b) impaired capacity to understand and make sense of both self's and others' mental states; c) diminished agency or the capacity to set and sustain goal-directed actions.

Overall, the procedure described here can be applied to persons with symptom disorders, such as eating disorders, anxiety disorders, mood disorders, PTSD and so forth, and interpersonal difficulties. It should be noted that, when treating symptoms, we also adopt empirically validated and symptom-specific techniques.

In fact, for patients to improve it is necessary to work at the intersection of symptom and interpersonal dynamics (Gazzillo, Dimaggio, & Curtis, 2019): treating a woman with anorexia nervosa and avoidant traits is different from treating the same eating disorder symptoms in someone with a narcissistic personality.

We came to this experiential turning point in MIT by incorporating techniques coming from a myriad traditions. We describe those we have mastered through training or clinical practice in the last few years.

There is nothing stopping readers from incorporating this treatment framework, the decision-making procedure, in their own practice and using the rationale steering the choice of a technique at a specific moment in therapy with a specific patient, while using tools drawn from their therapeutic repertoire.

The practices described in this book are guided imagery, the two-chairs method, role-play, behavioural activation and experiments, mindfulness and attention regulation strategies, and sensorimotor work. We devote a chapter rich in clinical examples to each of these techniques.

We shall show how we reconstruct and re-inhabit memories and then rewrite them. We offer guidance on how to reduce metacognitive difficulties by helping patients access new self-knowledge produced through meditation and sensorimotor and imagery exercises, where the body is called into action. We elaborate upon how interpersonal schemas can be temporarily rewritten by involving patients in new forms of dialogue with relevant characters from their life histories or with problematic self-parts, which are given a name. We show how to help patients respond differently, instead of letting the characters poisoning their inner worlds spout critical, disdainful, diffident, or despairing monologues.

This book was born of many conversations among us, in the breaks between sessions or in the evening, often during dinner while we debate and drink wine or craft beer. By experimenting with new techniques, we enriched our wealth of knowledge and watched, with a ravenous and rapacious gaze, talented therapists performing actions different from those we were used to.

Dialogues conducted like lessons and meetings at the Rome Centre for Metacognitive Interpersonal Therapy gave rise to a group of friends and colleagues with whom it is easy to think while playing. However, the book was also born of the help that several patients offered by exposing themselves during sessions in the Centre's team's presence. We have benefitted from this as much as they have. Perhaps the biggest debt of gratitude is ours.

We shared our reflections with other colleagues in Italy, Norway, Denmark, Australia, Portugal, Spain and the US. MIT is now a model applied internationally.

We now share with you something that for a long time was no more than a flow of thoughts and dialogues between one session and the next. It did not amount to a book until the umpteenth time that, looking into each other's eyes, we detected surprise.

At that moment we suspended judgement and with childish enthusiasm told each other about seeing yet again one of our patients' suffering body revive and a mind stuck in rumination open up again to hope.

CHAPTER 1

Psychopathology of personality disorders
Narratives, interpersonal schemas and mental states

Personality disorders tend to self-perpetuation. A series of dysfunctional processes lead sufferers to remain trapped in forms of subjective experience and behaviours that cause symptoms and social dysfunctions. Over the years we developed a PD maintenance model (Dimaggio, Montano et al., 2002, 2015; Dimaggio, Semerari, Carcione, Procacci, & Nicolò, 2006) which we revise here. Interpersonal schemas and metacognitive dysfunctions are still at the core of dysfunction in PD, but we have added the role of maladaptive coping strategies, including various kinds of perseverative thought connected to interpersonal themes (Ottavi, Passarella, Pasinetti, Salvatore, & Dimaggio, 2016).

Maladaptive coping mechanisms are how people manage their distress in a way that contributes to its maintenance. Avoidance, perfectionism, compulsive self-care and so on are core to the persistence of suffering. In recent years, psychotherapists have been paying increasing attention to cognitive coping, especially repetitive thought, and it has been found to trigger or maintain symptoms and dysfunctional behaviours (Borkovec, Robinson, Pruzinsky, & DePree, 1983; Wells, 2008).

Patients with PD engage in repetitive thoughts about interpersonal relationships, rumination being a clear example. A patient with Dependent PD continuously thinks about what she could have done to avoid being dumped; a patient with Paranoid PD reverts to the episode in which he was made fun of to try and understand how he might have avoided it, and he always comes to the same conclusion that he would not have managed to. However, at the same time, he goes over what happened, seeking alternative endings in which he retaliates. His attention is then redirected to the negative outcome: others humiliating him. In this book we show how mental and behavioural coping contributes to maintaining PD.

We rendered the structure of interpersonal schemas clearer by showing that: a) they rest on procedural, automatic and unaware processes, which manifest themselves in the form of behaviours, bodily sensations and affects. We have always been attentive to the embodied component of such processes, but we now discuss it in detail (Chapter 3); b) the schema should include healthy and positive representations of the self and other; c) a schema is a relational test (Weiss, 1993) intending to evaluate whether the other confirms one's core negative self-image or instead one's core positive self-image.

The elements constituting the maintenance model in this new version are therefore the following:

1 Impoverished narratives/intellectualising
2 Pathogenic interpersonal schemas, in the form of both conscious beliefs and implicit procedures
3 Poor or fluctuating sense of *agency*
4 Recurrent mental states
5 Impaired metacognition
6 Dysfunctional coping, including poor affect regulation
7 Dysfunctional interpersonal cycles

Impoverished narratives/intellectualising

Patients propose theories about their way of being, how they function in society, and how the world ought to be functioning. But of most use to a therapist for extracting useful information are self-narratives, one's stories about one's own life. These stories have various names: narrative episodes and specific autobiographical memories (Conway & Pleydell-Pearce, 2000; Dimaggio, Montano et al., 2015) are the ones we prefer.

Self-narratives are fundamental for individuals' internal consistency, for them to know who they are and how to connect to others (Bruner, 1990). The stories we tell should include an awareness of our wishes, of what we expect from others, and of the difficulties we need to tackle while trying to satisfy these wishes. Stories help us make decisions: do I want to get married or not? Go to another town to change my job or stay attached to my roots, where I was born, to my own culture? Would I devote all my days and nights to a work project or find time for my partner and children? Having mental access to stories where significant characters replied to these questions, and especially to how I myself have in the past tackled such problems, provides a framework for decisions (Damasio, 1994). In fact, past episodes provide the springboard from which to imagine the future: "*future simulations* are built on *retrieved details* of *specific past experiences that* are recombined into novel events" (Schacter & Masore, 2016, p. 245).

A patient might treasure the memory of a superb basketball goal performed as a boy, which was accompanied by applause from his father. This memory becomes emblematic, a symbol of self-confidence that can be used as a springboard for future decisions requiring confidence in his skills. In a certain sense, negative memories can produce the same benefits: they make it possible to learn from experience and not repeat mistakes (Pillemer, 2003). Overall, people make sense of their lives and build an identity through continuously thinking about their personal story, which combines in a consistent manner what they recall of the past with the imagined future (McAdams, 1993). This produces a sense of unity, purpose and meaning (Conway & Pleydell-Pearce, 2000). According to Singer and colleagues (2013) certain autobiographical memories are linked to core events: *life story memories*. They are emotionally charged, detailed, precisely located timewise and more easily recalled than others. Some of these life stories become *self-defining memories*, that is, episodes people use to reflect on who they are; these memories are therefore linked to peoples' larger narrative scripts and their self-concept: "I'm the type of person that . . .". In fact, if a patient tells his therapist about himself while using his self-concept, he is intellectualising and blocking any access to raw experience.

For this reason, a clinician should not accept intellectualized statements and use them only as the starting point in search for specific narrative episodes. Narrating these episodes fosters a sense of closeness, and the narrative style is important. Anyone first relating generalised narratives and then supplying specific episodes regarding positive events is better at involving a listener (Brandon, Beike, & Cole, 2017).

In the case of PD, memories are usually negative. Charles suffered from Avoidant and Obsessive-Compulsive PD, chronic depression and recurring suicidal thoughts, and he was treated using MIT as part of an outcome study (Gordon-King, Schweitzer, & Dimaggio, 2018b). During Charles' therapy, personal memories, on which he based his core sense of self as being worthless and unlovable, emerged. A self-defining memory involved situations when he was a boy and his father, drunk, yelled at him and left him on his own in the car. One day Charles himself decided to go and hide in the car to take shelter from his parents' arguments. These memories were then joined by others in which he got physically and verbally bullied at school, which reinforced his sense of unworthiness. Charles' social avoidance was grounded explicitly on these memories. Every time he had to tackle a new situation, he was prey to images from his past in which his alcoholic father and depressed mother mistreated him and his father's face got mixed up with those of the bullies. He imagined the future as an infinite repetition of the past and consequently avoided it.

Many patients have problems regarding not only the contents of their narratives but also the quality of their autobiographical memories: they are *impoverished*. This indicates a difficulty in recalling detailed and specific narrative episodes regarding relationships. Instead patients resort to semantic memory, generalisations, abstractions, theories about human psychology, all of them being at the end of the day intellectualisations (Dimaggio, Montano et al., 2015; Lysaker & Lysaker, 2002; Neimeyer, 2000).

The specificity of the autobiographical memories of many patients with PD or symptom disorders is limited; this is typical in particular of Avoidant PD (Spinhoven, Bamelis, Molendijk, Haringsma, & Arntz, 2009), but of Obsessive-Compulsive, Narcissistic, Depressive and Passive-Aggressive PDs too (Dimaggio, Montano et al., 2015). Over-generalised autobiographical memories are typical in depression (Hermans et al., 2008) and eating disorders (Huber et al., 2015). Some scholars consider it a form of avoidant coping, with harmful effects on emotion regulation (Debeer, Raes, Williams, & Hermans, 2011). Patients with trauma histories often recall memories with limited specificity and avoid distressing triggers linked to the trauma (McNally, Lasko, Macklin, & Pitman, 1995). Generally, persons displaying a tendency to use generalised memories seem less interpersonally flexible (Dimaggio, Montano et al., 2015), and their sense of self and identity is poorly defined (Jørgensen, 2010).

When patients lack clear and specific autobiographical memories to guide them, they nevertheless act guided by implicit and automatic relational procedures, stories written in the body (van der Kolk, 2014). The mind cannot control these stories, because it is unaware of their power.

Semantic and episodic memory use different brain circuits (Klein & Loftus, 1993). This explains inconsistencies between the theory of self, on one hand, and the sense of self emerging from personally significant narratives, on the other. An Obsessive-Compulsive PD patient feels compelled to respect moral norms and rules. She might describe herself as a hard worker who does not enjoy relaxing. However, in the specific narratives she relates, it is not love for work that surfaces but irritation, depression and hostility towards others. She does not report experiences involving pleasure, relaxation, or playing. She has built an identity, on a semantic level, inconsistent with her specific memories, which point to frustration of other basic goals, such as autonomy and playful exploration.

Such a patient needs access to those memories where she would have liked to play, relax, freely explore her environment and enjoy herself, but met with others' punitive and prohibitive stance towards her wishes or their fear at the prospect of her growing independent. At this point she would grasp that her identity, expressed on a conceptual level, is based on a form of coping, moral perfectionism, while other wishes lie unexpressed and without any hope of being satisfied. But she has no access to these memories and consequently remains trapped in a state of obsessive conformity to moral rules in order to avoid punishments she does not recall she received.

Consequently, when we have to tackle a dearth of autobiographical memories, our therapeutic goal should be to draw them out, to give the patients a richer picture of what they think and feel in relational situations, over and above their abstract self-concept. We would therefore recall that an MIT clinician should look for circumstantiated and contextual descriptions of suffering and the factors making it arise and persist, which is what we refer to as *narrative episodes regarding interpersonal relationships*. A good narrative episode takes place within precise spatial (*where*) and temporal (*when*) boundaries. The actors on stage are recognisable (*who*) and there is dialogue between the actors. The topic covered (*what*) and the reason for which the story is being related (*why*) is communicated (Dimaggio, Montano et al., 2015).

Also typical are *disorganised narratives*, especially of Borderline and Histrionic PDs (Adler, Chin, Kolisetty, & Oltmanss, 2012) and often present in Dependent PD (Dimaggio, Semerari, Carcione, Nicolò, & Procacci, 2007). Some of the patients described in this book display such narratives, but generally the procedures depicted here are focused more on patients with impoverished narratives, rather than on those whose memories get jumbled together with each other and are accompanied by emotion dysregulation. With such patients the therapy goal is to first offer a safe environment, regulate affects, and then foster a more organised story-telling (Livesley, Dimaggio, & Clarkin, 2016). At this point one can apply the procedures described in this book.

Maladaptive interpersonal schemas

Maladaptive processes of ascribing meaning to interpersonal relationships lies at the core of PD. All human beings make sense of relational events with a set of tools, that is, interpersonal schemas, mostly developed and established during early developmental stages through the interaction of one's learning history and temperamental dispositions. They use these schemas for:

1 *Foreseeing* how others will react to their needs and demands. When needs are activated, they require maps making it possible to anticipate the conditions under which they will be met and the risks they run of being thwarted.
2 *Selecting* incoming information. Anyone with a fear of being judged pays selective attention to signs of criticism and scorn and ends up noticing even the most nuanced of them. Persons seeking care scrutinise their environment to see if others are willing to provide it.
3 *Decoding* what occurs in real relationships. When they interact with others, patients mix "realistic" readings of events with interpretations driven by their schemas. For example, someone fearing not being cared for by others at times of need and fragility is likely to interpret another's frowning expression as a refusal to care for her, whereas the person to whom the expectation or request is directed might, more reasonably, be worried or sad for reasons that have nothing to do with the subject.
4 *Guiding actions*. Schemas are world maps which also come with a sort of instruction manual about how to act with a view to triggering certain desired responses or how to react when we imagine that the plan we are following will not lead to our hoped for goal because we expect the other to react negatively. If I expect my wish to be met with tough criticism instead of appreciation, as a reaction I will decide to make the utmost effort to achieve at least a little of the appreciation I hope for and avoid the feeling of shame I would suffer if I were criticised.
5 *Steering* the recalling of memories and *structuring* them. When people think back on events, their minds tend to select those consistent with the structure of their schemas. This is why patients' narratives are not important so much because they accurately report facts, but because they show what the mind apprehends of the past, and how it organises and, consequently, communicates experience to others. Damasio (1994) notes that memories are not stored in the mind like films ready to appear on a screen. Starting from emotions, elements in multiple sensorial forms combine to produce narrative sequences in consciousness. The procedural component in schemas thus dictates the way the mind organises bits of experience in sequences that form predictable narrative patterns.

6 *Inducing emotional and behavioural reactions* in others. These reactions vary depending on the nature of the schema. If I expect my need for recognition to be satisfied by my boss, who is strict but just, my behaviour, whether conscious or automatic, will involve displaying my qualities but at the same time clearly signalling a respect of rank, in the sensible hope of achieving the desired appreciation. This respectful attitude is quite likely to conjure up a favourable attitude in the other.

Patients' schemas carry out all these functions, but with results varying from the unsatisfactory to the catastrophic. An example is the impact schema-driven actions have on others: they can steer them towards a negative response to a patient's wishes, and thus confirm the schema itself. A Paranoid PD patient, driven by a need for safety and afraid the other will attack and humiliate him, will demonstrate distrustful or aggressive behaviour and in turn trigger wary or aggressive reactions in the other. Both of these responses by the other will lead the relationship down a disagreeable path.

Schema structure is of capital importance in MIT for case formulation and planning effective treatment strategies. To define a schema we use an adapted form of the Core Conflictual Relational Theme concept (CCRT, Luborsky & Crits-Christoph, 1990).

The original CCRT structure is organised as follows: 1) Wish, corresponding in the most basic terms to the concept of goal; 2) "if . . . then" procedure, used for forecasting under what conditions the Wish could be achieved and for planning actions with this in mind; 3) the Other's response, followed by 4) the Self's response to the Other's response. As we shall demonstrate, we have elaborated on certain aspects of CCRT, so that in this book we shall refer to the wider concept of maladaptive or dysfunctional interpersonal schema. In particular, we shall clarify that a self-image is not simply how a person responds to another's response, but a core belief underlying a Wish. We will be talking interchangeably about "idea", "core" and "core-belief" for the sake of simplicity. At the same time, we shall address the embodied self-concept: thinking one is fragile is not merely a semantic abstraction with the self as its object, but also a way of feeling with bodily correlates: postural awareness and neurovegetative activation profiles. For this reason we shall not try to change self-concept by working mainly on a cognitive level, but by using a bottom-up approach to stimulate a sensory-informed self-experience that carries the cognitive component with it.

In this context a simple example of maladaptive schema structure is the following: "I am not lovable (*self-image underlying Wish*). I want to be comforted (*Wish: attachment*). If I display my suffering then (*Procedure*) the other will reject me (*the Other's response*). When this happens, I feel down and despondent and I close in on myself, seeing that my idea of not being lovable has been confirmed (*the Self's response to the Other's response*)."

Schemas: procedural component

Relationship quality in early development stages automatically shapes relational expectations and the attribution of meaning to current interpersonal events.

Bowlby (1988) showed how persons' early interactions with their environment during their development give rise to *Internal Working Models (IWMs)*, that is, procedural representations of the self and attachment figures, internalised *self-with-other* models.

IWMs are the basis for forecasts about the extent to which attachment figures will be available, accessible and responsive if turned to for help (Bowlby, 1988). Stern (1985) studied the recurring instances of pre-verbal attunement occurring between mother and child in the first two years of life. Underlying this attunement is the reference figure's ability to empathetically respond to a child's communicative behaviour as it manifests during the various stages of its life. In the first months after birth a reference figure responds with mimical expressions and vocalisations coordinated with the child's expressions and vocalisations. This coordination becomes ever richer and includes verbalisations. For example, if a mother sees her child is scared she will adopt a tender but worried expression and say: "Were you scared, poppet?"

Recurring interactions that foster attunement or lack thereof lead a child to construct *Representations of Interactions that Have been Generalised* (RIG), procedural representations involving a degree of abstraction. Several RIGs together form a network of experiences on which the sense of being with the other is grounded.

Even if they have similarities to IWMs, RIGs do not only concern attachment security but also an even earlier adaptive need for mirroring and intersubjective attunement selected during evolution (Tomasello, 2016). These generalised representations evolve from mental representations abstracted from recurring patterns of interactions following the activation of a given motivational system, organised around rank, autonomy, group inclusion and so on. They also form through the parallel embodied, sensory experience of recurring patterns of interactions, thus also presenting as sensory-motor memory traces that shape bodily experience. Recurring interactions where the other is uninterested when I show him the drawings I have done or the castles I have built, contribute to creating the core idea of a self with limited worth. In adult life this core idea gets activated every time the social rank motivation gets triggered, and steers forecasts about how an interaction will unfold, as we shall show later.

In any case, it is therefore a question of procedural recordings of past relational scripts that remain active throughout one's life and produce forecasts about interactions in the present that the person is unaware of. These theoretical observations help us to understand that in daily life we are steered by expectations about relationships operating on an implicit and procedural level and influencing relational behaviour automatically. The resigned voice and lowered gaze with which a subject greets a friend is the automatic and rapid expression of a Wish for affiliation combined with the expectation of being mocked. An irritated attitude towards a partner as soon as she comes home after a tiring day is the unconscious expression of a Wish for being cared for combined with the distressing representation of an uninterested other.

Some research shows how schemas in PD patients, in particular Borderline, function. In one laboratory study women suffering from this disorder were quicker to approach than to avoid aggressive faces and tended to react aggressively (Bertsch et al., 2018). These reactions occurred in the span of milliseconds, indicating that patients did not have time to think about their reactions. A sign therefore, in our view, of how their reactions were automatisms, indications of stories written in the past, scripts played out at the smallest signal of relational threats. Procedural schemas in action.

Wish and motivational systems

Schemas develop in order to understand if, and under what conditions, others will satisfy our Wishes in the relational world. To more quickly identify a Wish, clinicians should ask themselves what motivational system is steering their patients at a given moment. We follow the path of evolutionary psychology and therefore refer to Wishes or motivations that have been selected by human beings for pursuing certain needs (Bowlby, 1988; Gilbert, 2005; Lichtenberg, 1989; Liotti & Gilbert, 2011; Panksepp & Biven, 2012; Tomasello, 2016). Failure to achieve them inevitably leads to subjective suffering. The motivations are: 1) *attachment*. An individual wishes for care and protection; 2) *social rank/competition*. An individual fights to be recognised, win a challenge, be appreciated, valued or esteemed. This motivation gets activated when resources are limited or when an individual realises their worth is called into question; 3) *autonomy/exploration/agency*. An individual is driven by the intention to know the world, and discover his environment and territory, including knowing others' minds. To be able to explore, a person first needs to form an intention, a Wish to know a part of the physical and conceptual world that was previously unknown to him. Then he needs to validate the Wish and feel it is worth being pursued. A sense of personal efficacy is partly rooted in this motivation, as manifested in attempting to explore new states of the world and discovering that we are, at least in part, capable of doing so; 4) *belonging to the group/social inclusion*, namely the need to feel affiliated to a community on the basis of a sharing of values, rituals, beliefs and practices. Many patients suffer because they fear social exclusion and ostracism; 5) *caregiving*, complementary to attachment, a motivation to take care of and lend help to anyone seen as fragile, vulnerable and suffering; 6) *cooperation amongst equals* to achieve a joint and shared goal; 7) *sexuality/sensuality*, which is based on its reptilian equivalent, the motivation to mate, and is connected to the forming of stable affective ties in adulthood.

Some evolutionary psychotherapists include the motivation towards social play in this list (Panksepp & Biven, 2012). One can however consider play as not so much a motivation in itself, and if there is a drive to play it is more likely part of the exploratory system activation with concomitant excitement. Social play can be interpreted as the tendency to activate any motivational system in a pretend mode, on a *twin earth* (Lillard, 2001), with an "as if" function. We pretend to fight, to terrorise the other, who in turn simulates being afraid, courting us or cooperating. It is "as if" we had become cops and robbers, Scarlett Johansson, Batman, Jennifer Lawrence in *Hunger Games*, Julia Roberts trying on clothes in *Pretty Woman*, Cristiano Ronaldo scoring a spectacular goal. In the pretend play dimension, one can let actions and emotions connected to all motivational systems flow, without the story outcome being "true". One can simulate triumph, defeat, death, a narrow escape without this changing who one is for the other in a relationship.

In this reading the activation of the social play mode, of "as if", is at the root of therapeutic relationship transference and countertransference dynamics. Indeed therapy aims precisely to activate this mode in the relationship, so that a patient and clinician pass from: "She neglects me/criticises me/attacks me, and I'm attracted by her" to "it's as if my therapist was strict/ desirable/ cold and I react to him/her as if it were true".

There are more basic, non-interpersonal, motivations at the root of some individuals' behaviours. These are: 8) the *search for safety*, also termed *defence system* (Le Doux, 2015), which gets activated when subjects feel that physical integrity, both their own and those of people and objects they feel their own, is not secure. It is different from attachment because when faced with danger a subject does not turn to another seen as strong or competent, but tackles it directly by using strategies more primitive than the relational ones, for example the fight-or-flight response. It is thus a primitive, archaic system. The threat detection system linked to it (Gilbert, 2005) functions as an alert and scans the surroundings to find signs of threat to integrity. Just as basic a motive is 9) *predation*. This is based on the animal behaviour of searching for food and in humans it has been refined (Meloy, 1998) to include behaviours directed towards other humans. It includes aggressive actions towards a target, planned in a deliberate manner and often performed in cold blood. Catching a prey is a source of excitement. It is not to be confused with the desire for power and exultation when it is satisfied as part of the social rank motive. Here it is the feeling of strength, power and energy coming from catching a prey. If, however, the prey escapes or someone prevents it from being caught, this causes anger. A hypertrophy of this motivation is a feature of antisocial and psychopathic personalities and this should be borne in mind, differentiating it from competition. Another basic motivation is 10) *sexuality aimed at mating*. Unlike its interpersonal counterpart, which is interwoven with sensuality, affection and the idea of a stable bond, its only aim is to satisfy erotic pleasure; 11) lastly, the most basic of all motivations: homeostasis regulation, that is taking care to nourish and hydrate one's body and to keep it in suitable climatic conditions. However, this system is not given so much attention in therapeutic situations – except of course for the therapy room being at the right temperature (Lichtenberg, 1989).

A fundamental goal, whose accomplishment is dependent on satisfying several of the motives just described, is maintaining a good level of self-esteem. A parenthesis about a topic which we shall come back to later: self-esteem means a patient adopting the role of the other judging the self. "I esteem myself" means: I want to be appreciated and, if I put myself in an observer position (internalised other) I like what I am doing, I feel appreciated (by myself).

A lack of self-esteem can be born and grow entirely in the rank system: I want to win a competition, I am unable to, so poor self-esteem ensues. The latter however also feeds on the results of other motivations. It can be undermined if a Wish for attachment is unsuccessful: a person wanting to be loved imagines the other rejecting, feels unloved, deduces that it is because he is of little worth, and consequently experiences low self-esteem. It can erode too if we fail in providing care: a person who would like to care for a child or relative is unable to and, in addition to failing in fulfilling this motivation, she also harbours the idea that she is not a capable parent/relative, and accordingly her self-esteem collapses. An inability to satisfy the sexual motivation can also harm self-esteem: I have not managed to win over a girl I like, which in itself is disappointing, but on top of this, if my friends knew they would think me a loser. Lastly, feeling excluded from the group can harm self-esteem: they expel me because they consider me below them.

To sum up, a person can enter the rank system, and have poor self-esteem, as a result of failing to accomplish various other motivations: being loved, being capable of providing effective care, being successful at seducing or being accepted by a group's members.

Core self-representations

On the activation of every Wish there is also an accompanying set of core self-images, corresponding to *core beliefs* in cognitive psychotherapy. These images have a cognitive component, the self-concept or self-idea: lovable, effectual, unworthy, incapable and so on. At the same time, they also have an automatic, embodied and affectively charged component. An unlovable self-representation can therefore emerge both as an idea or concept, and as a self-state consisting of a combination of muscular and gut sensations linked to a worried anticipation of being abandoned by the other.

There are various self-representations underlying a Wish (Hermans & Dimaggio, 2004). For example, a person seeks attention based on a set of representations, some with a positive value – "lovable, deserving of attention" – and others with a negative value – "not lovable, deserving of rejection". These core representations can have various origins, being formed, for example, in the course of recurring interactions during early development (Bowlby, 1988; Stern, 1985), or in the face of trauma or adverse social experience occurring later in life, such as emigration or economic misfortunes. They can also be grounded in innate inclinations arising from temperament. What counts is that in adults these representations surface quickly, automatically and often without reflective effort when they are activated by a Wish.

Negative self-representations are usually dominant among patients; they are more likely to surface in consciousness and control forecasts about how others will respond. Positive and benign representations, on the contrary, most often remain in the shadows, unacknowledged. If they do surface in a subject's mind, he does not pay them any attention and does not let himself be guided by them.

If . . . then procedure

The Wish, underpinned by self-representations, motivates consideration of the procedures required for its fulfilment, namely the conditions under which a person hopes to obtain the desired response by the Other. A simple and adaptive procedure is: I am frightened, I need someone to protect me, *if I clearly show I am scared then* the other will care for me. This adaptive procedure can occur automatically, outside consciousness. A subject steered by a Wish behaves in a particular way, sensing, often in a preconscious manner, that a certain action will trigger a positive response. Within our conceptual framework "if . . . then" procedures aimed at triggering a hoped-for response are of a non-pathological nature.

As we have remarked, if one's *Wish* is to be cared for by another (attachment), one if . . . then procedure could be: "If I show I'm not OK and seek help . . . then the other will . . .". This part is functional, but at this point a patient may foresee – either consciously or implicitly – that he will meet with an unsatisfactory response from the Other, such as: "she will ignore me" or "he will criticise me for my weakness".

"If . . . then" procedures connecting a Wish to the Other's response are the most difficult part of schemas to reconstruct; great care has to be taken to ensure that the initial procedure as described by patients, yet which patients often do not allude to, is not confused with the coping procedures following the Other's response.

For example, the social rank motive may manifest in a person's Wish that his worth is acknowledged, fearful at the same time of being criticised, and consequently adopting perfectionist coping of the following type: if I get rejected for what I am, then I need to improve my performance so as to satisfy the other's standards. The procedure for satisfying the original Wish does not correspond to what was just described!

The latter is, instead, the procedure conceived in order to satisfy the Wish after activation of the representation of a critical other as connected to the schema. On the contrary, the primary "if . . . then" procedure represents a forecast about what type of behaviour will satisfy the basic Wish in the presence of a supportive other, with the confidence that this can be achieved. This procedure sounds like: "If I show my qualities for what they are, then . . ." and it foresees another who appreciates and values the self.

To fulfil the Wish, the primary procedure is: if I am spontaneous in my actions, applying the right degree of commitment, I hope the other will appreciate me. The other is, however, judgemental. The coping procedure is: if I raise my performance and do everything without any mistake, then perhaps the other will appreciate me.

The other's response

The primary goal of "if . . . then" procedures is to trigger *the Other's response*, a fundamental part of the schema. One should recall that the aim of a relational Wish is not an object or a symbol as such, but the other's favourable reaction. In the case of basic motivations, like getting food, the goal is to secure an object, for example, food. The impaired schemas found in PDs are of the relational type and rotate around the universal desires listed previously (e.g. social rank, attachment, exploration and so on). If they are not satisfied they invariably generate suffering.

A person therefore hopes for the other to respond in specific ways and expects certain responses on the basis of forecasts congruent to the underlying schema.

We would stress – and this is important when an MIT therapist tries to reconstruct a schema – that the Other's response, which is a behavioural indicator of the representation of the other, is often the part of the schema most likely to surface. Patients often ascribe the causes of their suffering to the ways others react. For example, patients expect a set of negative responses to thwart their Wishes, such as expecting others to display critical, dismissive or rejecting attitudes, to behave in a threatening, dominating or punitive manner, to obstruct or forsake them and to deny support.

The Other's response has two components. The first is the behaviour that a patient notices, the actions that the other performs and the patient records, remembers and recounts to his therapist. This component may very well be realistic. The most important element between the two is how a patient *represents* the other in his mind. For example, a patient in a situation of uneasiness might notice that the other has not been listening to him. He therefore concentrates on how the other acted. The patient interprets this on the basis of a more general representation of the other as *rejecting*. The patient therefore usually describes what the other did and ascribes some intentions to him. From this a clinician is able to deduce which part of the schema manifests in the way the patient constructs the other.

The term "Other's response" does not simply describe what the other does. In a patient's narrative what the other does is the key to grasping how the former *represents the Other* to himself in a consistent, schema-congruent manner. Importantly, when we think about the Other's response, we should not think of the other as a specific person, but of a position in a patient's mental space or imaginary world. The same position can be occupied by various characters: a critical father and a scornful husband, a nosy mother and a controlling wife. These are symbols used to interpret the other and respond accordingly, and do not necessarily correspond to reality.

Furthermore, what we need to understand is that the other's position always corresponds to an aspect of the schema structure. As in the self-esteem example, this means internalising the Other's responses to one's Wishes that are at least partly congruent with one's schemas. It means that, if one wants to be loved yet has an unlovable core image, one's point of view will coincide with the rejecting other's. Thus a part of the self adopts the rejecting other's position. This can surface in consciousness in the form of expressions such as: "I'm not worthy of being loved" or "I'm not worth anything". This distinction is fundamental in MIT. We do not focus therapeutic efforts on real others except, of course, for those involved in ongoing traumatising relationships. We instead steer patients towards an understanding of the way they construct the other and endorse, at least in part, negative attitudes about themselves in a schema-dependent way. Only at very advanced treatment stages do we concentrate on, so to speak, more realistic aspects of a person's experience. That is, one steers patients towards an understanding that their schemas direct their attention, attraction and interest towards people embodying the negative attitudes about themselves they have internalised during their learning history. They should therefore be assisted in shifting their attention towards people with less toxic features. However, if performed in initial therapy or in general before patients become aware of their schemas and are able to differentiate between them, the same operation would constitute a serious technical mistake.

Just like core self-images, the Other's responses can vary with regard to the same Wish. With their need to be appreciated, patients are inclined to construct the other as being critical and deprecating, but at the same time harbour the idea that the other appreciates and values them. In fact, as we shall show later, an interpersonal schema is a test of how a relationship is developing.

A patient, driven for example by a Wish to explore her surroundings, might wish that the other responds in a certain way, such as supporting her and backing her up. Christopher Columbus needed money for his voyage to Asia by the western route, which he was repeatedly denied. Isabel of Castile and Ferdinand of Aragon seemed willing to offer financial support but their response remained pending for years. Then in 1492, in the Alcazar Castle in Cordoba, Columbus received yet another rejection. He left on the back of a mule, in despair. King Ferdinand intervened and Isabel had him called back. They financed a voyage that would have many far-reaching consequences. Columbus was driven by the implicit forecast that the other would support him in his exploration and thanks to this he was able to persist in the face of a long succession of rejections, year after year. Patients manage challenging situations differently.

For example, a patient in need of support for his voyage would quickly foresee and believe the other as unwilling to grant the necessary means and resources and as likely to obstruct his endeavours. At this point, driven by the exploratory motive, a patient would try to evaluate if the Other's response will amount, as he fears, to obstructing the voyage or if there is scope for the support he hopes for (Weiss, 1993). He would like to set out on his voyage, yet fears, and is almost convinced, that nobody will supply him the necessary resources, and feebly hopes that somewhere there are Spanish sovereigns well-disposed towards his plans.

In the great majority of cases patients foresee others responding negatively to their Wishes. This is consistent with their problematic mode of constructing the other and their tendency to interpret the responses they receive in line with their maladaptive schemas. We shall come back to the concept of schema as a relational test later.

The self's response to the other's response

Once a patient perceives a specific response directed to her, thoughts and experiences will emerge that constitute *the Self's response to the Other's response*. If, for example, she considers that the other has criticised her, she will think she is of little worth and accordingly feel despondent.

This is one of the fundamental pivots around which the bulk of subjective suffering, symptoms and dysfunctional coping modes are located. A patient wishing to be cared for at a moment of weakness can be convinced that the other will reject him because he is undeserving of attention. He will consequently feel lonely and sad and isolate himself on the basis of the *foreseen* response by the Other, with a view to avoiding distress that would ensue from being rejected. If the schema is applied to an ongoing interaction the patient may interpret the other's communication signals as indicating an intention to "dump" him and will accordingly feel despondent, ashamed or sad.

Once again there are various potential responses that may be activated by the self, depending on the combination of the core self-idea with the other's response. An example can help illustrate this point. Let us imagine that a Wish of wanting to feel appreciated emerges following the activation of the social rank motive. If the active core self-idea revolves around feelings of *worthlessness* and the Other's response is *disapproving and deprecating*, the Self's response will manifest in thoughts such as "She's right. I'm worthless, as I feared" and will consequently involve feeling despondent or ashamed.

If the core self-image active at that moment is instead positive, anchored around feelings of worth and the other responds *in a disapproving and deprecating manner*, the Self's response will involve thinking that "Her criticism is unfair; she doesn't appreciate me as I deserve", consequently triggering anger.

The Self's response is therefore composed of cognitions and affects, which then activate coping procedures: for example, a patient asks for attention, perceives himself as being rejected, shifts from a Wish to be cared for to a Wish to ascend in social rank, and activates a procedure that constitutes the Self's response to the Other's response.

It is simpler than it appears. A patient's reasoning is:

> Given that if I seek help I will get criticised, to be appreciated I need to suppress my feelings of weakness (*switching off attachment-motivated proximity seeking and shifting to compulsive self-care*) and perform my duties flawlessly (*activation of the rank motivation in a perfectionist mode*). If I succeed the other will appreciate me.

The patient has, in this case, lost the chance to be cared for when he shows who he really is, but sees his secondary Wish satisfied.

Notes on schema formulation

During training therapists often confuse the two procedures and consider perfectionist type "if... then" procedures to be aimed at satisfying the initial Wish to be cared for. This is a misconception.

We would recall that in reality, primary, adaptive "if... then" procedures aimed at achieving a Wish are difficult to reconstruct because a patient does not relate them to his therapist. Probably because these mechanisms become established and are activated effortlessly as a result of one's learning history, he is no longer aware of them as he has completely broken the habit of consciously performing them.

To further clarify this we can present a procedure aimed at satisfying a Wish in an adaptive manner: "I wish to be comforted because I'm scared. If I tell my mother I'm afraid, then...". This procedure, of the type that assumes "If I'm afraid and need comforting, then I'll communicate this with the hope that the other will provide me care", is held up by a self-representation of being *lovable*.

However, this procedure is usually suppressed, with a subject not enacting it and no longer remembering that it could be useful to adopt it. What hinders OR obstructs its activation is the idea that if one dared to act driven by the conviction of being loved and therefore exposed oneself hoping to receive care, one could instead face a rejecting or deprecating other. Better then not to expose oneself.

What a clinician witnesses, therefore, is the coping procedure that is part of the Self's response to the Other's response. In a certain sense constructing, or bringing to light, functional adaptive "if . . . then" procedures, making it possible to pursue a *Wish* while expecting a satisfying *response* and feeling that expressing one's Wish is taking place in safe relational conditions, is a therapeutic goal (Weiss, 1993).

Put simply, we need to help patients to bring to light procedures like: "If I seek help then the other will rescue me" and "If I seek appreciation for what I've achieved the other will be curious and show interest and this will mean he holds me in esteem".

The Self's response includes information making it possible to understand what the core self-image within a particular schema is. The Wish is in fact supported by either conscious or implicit self-representations. A patient might be hesitant to seek help because she implicitly possesses a self-image of being "unlovable" or "of little worth" and her expectation is therefore that the other will justifiably reject her. The way patients react to the Other's response often provides clinicians the opportunity to become aware of the core self-image.

We anticipate that the Self's response to the Other's response is one of the most important processes to be analysed so as to facilitate correct and clinically useful assessments and clinician agreement on case formulations. Very often clinicians dwell on dysfunctional reaction modes: angry acting-out, self-harm, binge eating, substance abuse, relational avoidance, excessive physical exercise. In doing so, they neglect the core feelings the Other's response triggers in a patient, which are the most important target of therapeutic interventions and which need to be examined for treatment to be optimally effective.

A clinician should be very careful to explore in collaboration with patients if and how feelings like despondency and loneliness, fear, guilt or shame preceded other feelings, such as anger, or dysfunctional behaviours.

For an accurate formulation the Other's response should be considered the A (activating event) of an ABC sequence. A clinician can be satisfied when he has reconstructed with the patient what the latter thought of the Other's response (B) and what emotions and, consequently behaviours, these thoughts activated (C). As anticipated, one is able to understand the core element in the schema, the core self-image, thanks to this part of the formulation. A patient would be able to say that when he sees, imagines or mentally represents a critical other, he accepts the criticism because he considers himself as inept, and he consequently feels ashamed and despondent. This idea of the self and the accompanying emotion, "I'm inept and I'm ashamed of it", is the core image in the schema.

We now report the formulations of two relational episodes, one *incorrect* and the other *complete*.

The wrong formulation would sound like this:

> You asked your father to agree to your doing an internship abroad and paying for part of the trip. His reaction was judgemental and he told you it was not a good idea to go. You got angry and yelled at him. Then you shut yourself in

your room and thought that, as usual, your reaction was exaggerated and you don't know how to control your emotions.

In this case it is highly likely that the clinician neglected to sufficiently explore the *Self's response to the Other's response* and in particular the range of emotions experienced. A more detailed analysis of the episode would have made it possible to access those parts of the Self's response indicating that there are positive core-beliefs. In any case, without any positive core-belief the schema formulation is to be considered incomplete.

Consequently, the wrong formulation ends with the patient in a self-critical position. The clinician has not therefore shown the patient the healthy part, the positive self-representation underlying the Wish: autonomy and exploration. We would note that sometimes during assessment positive core-beliefs may not surface. If they do not, it is not necessarily a mistake on the part of the clinician. It could be that they are so feeble that the patient has almost totally lost the ability to notice them. Or else they are truly hypotrophic. In these cases the formulation should point out that they are lacking: "It is almost as if you were so dominated by the idea that others will undervalue you that you have lost all hope of being appreciated and there are no traces left of this possibility."

The correct formulation would instead sound like this:

> You asked your father to agree to your trip abroad for an internship and to pay for part of it. You looked forward to it; it could be heard in your words and your voice, and at the start you felt you would be successful. Then your father's reaction was judgemental and he told you it was not a good idea to go, showing himself to feel hurt and neglected. At that point you felt guilty at the idea of having hurt your father. At the same time, the thought that your father refused your request made you feel lonely and frightened at the idea of not being able to make the trip. As you felt lonely and frightened you thought that your father's approval was indispensable.
>
> Another part that struck me is that when you saw your father wouldn't support you, you got angry because you desperately needed this and felt his refusal to be unfair. It is as if this confirmed this internship is important to you and that you have the right to do it and feel ready for it. In the end, however, the hope of being able to make a trip you were convinced you deserved and looked forward to and the drive and enthusiasm spurred by this natural desire for autonomy and curiosity were frustrated. Shall we try and work on overcoming the feelings of loneliness, fear and guilt that stop you from achieving your independent plans?

As can be seen, a more comprehensive formulation includes various core self-images, various aspects of the Other's response, and various responses by the Self to the Other's response. Here the clinician highlights in particular the positive core-belief, namely of one being entitled to explore autonomously and enthusiastically, which exists in the narrative but is eclipsed by the negative representations of the self and the other.

Developing what seems to be a complex formulation is only a matter of training and practice. The ongoing practice of analysing in detail narrative episodes related by a patient facilitates formulations that are ever more accurate and similar in level of detail to the one described here.

Returning to the previous example, note that the therapist does not stop at the description of the other's behaviour ("he told you that") but concentrates on clarifying and communicating what the patient attributed to him. Subsequently the therapist does not dwell on the patient's angry reaction or self-criticism and especially does not question if these reactions were justified or realistic. He instead focuses on the primary feelings of guilt and fear and helps the patient to perceive how they come to obstruct an important Wish the latter intended to pursue.

When working with a patient driven by a schema like the one illustrated here, the aim of therapy is to help her reconnect with and pursue her primary Wishes, specifically those centred around autonomy, rather than systematically renouncing them in favour of coping behaviours aimed at protecting herself from feelings of judgement and guilt. This is achieved through the increasing awareness OR understanding that her attention towards a critical or vulnerable other is schema-dependent and does not necessarily correspond to reality.

The other fundamental therapeutic target is the set of negative self-images. A therapist should try to get the patient to spend less time ruminating over negative self-images; actually it is really about making them think less about the negative idea more than making them question its truth-like quality thus experiencing the concomitant embodied feelings as less intense and overpowering. At the same time the therapist should help the patient cultivate positive, benevolent self-images.

Let us further clarify the schema structure. What does it mean to examine the Self's response so as to identify the core self-image underlying the Wish? An interpersonal schema is grounded in the self-image that organises the Self's response to achieve the Wish. We would recall that a narrative episode is not important because it summarises events that actually occurred, but because it is a window to the person's interpersonal schemas, that is the way she constructs interpersonal relationships. The schema therefore tells us how a person foresees and expects events to unfold, how she interprets what has happened, how she organises and for how long she stores information in her memory. A schema is therefore literally a pre-concept, an idea that exists before a fact occurs.

When his *Wish* becomes activated, a person is already predisposed to expect events to occur OR unfold in a particular way. This is a function of core self-images, which are the main guide to his forecasts and interpretations. Put more simply, let us imagine a student suffering from Avoidant PD sitting a university exam. He is driven by a Wish to be appreciated (social rank motive) based on a core self-image of *limited worth*. This is a pre-existing idea! It is not the consequence of how the lecturer responds to him, but rather reflects the way he deep down thinks of and experiences himself.

Based on this self-idea he predicts that, if his performance reveals how much he has studied, which he considers insufficient, then the lecturer will despise him. This causes anticipatory anxiety. At the moment when the lecturer starts asking him questions, the student is likely to interpret his behaviour as judgemental and deprecating. At this point his response, from a cognitive point of view, is "He's quite right to criticise me; I'm not worth anything". This confirms the core negative self-image of inadequacy and inferiority. Emotionally he reacts with despondency at his failure or with shame at being publically proven unworthy. The two emotions often coexist.

As can be seen in this example, the Self's response to the Other's response is the part of the narrative episode supplying material to identify the core self-image activating the forecast and behaviours congruent to the interpersonal schema. Once again: the Self's response does not indicate a reaction to an environmental contingency – he criticised me therefore I'm not worth much – but is the path to identifying a stable personality aspect, the embodied self-concept: "There you are. See how I'm not worth much!"

Interpersonal schemas as a relational test

An interpersonal schema is not static but rather a dynamic process. In this regard we follow the concept of conditions of safety tests proposed in Control-Mastery Theory (Gazzillo, 2016; Weiss, 1993).

The concept signifies that human beings look for conditions of relational safety. Patients are steered by healthy, normal motivations but fear that pursuing their goals will engender negative consequences. Consequently, depending on their personal development history, they use various ways to test through their relationships whether their pathogenic beliefs are true, in the hope that they are not! To quote Gazzillo: "patients are deeply motivated to disconfirm, consciously and unconsciously, their pathogenic beliefs, because they are constrictive and a cause of distress" (2016, p. 29). He adds: "the suffering and constriction that pathogenic beliefs cause are such that these persons are strongly motivated to disconfirm them, so as to feel free and legitimized in the pursuit of their healthy goals" (p. 30).

In our language we say that patients try to evaluate whether the other might respond satisfactorily to their current Wish. If a subject is driven by the need for attention, he will try to discover whether the other will provide it, as he hopes, wishes and feels is right, or will reject him, as he fears. Of the two hypotheses he believes the second as more likely to be true, but would prefer that it were not so. The problem is that there is limited access to representations producing hope.

If a patient is driven by the competition motivation thus harbouring a Wish to be appreciated, she will try to discover whether she can display her creations in the hope of receiving a positive opinion, as she hopes and feels is right, but with the fear that she will receive harsh criticism. What surfaces in her consciousness is most likely and exclusively the fear of criticism. It is through parts of her narrative or aspects of her behaviours that the wished-for representations of self and the other surface.

Interpersonal relationships are therefore uncertain by definition and for this reason patients' approach is to carry out relational tests. As Gazzillo states (2016, p. 34): "*in all we do in our, more or less intimate, relationships, and therefore also during therapy, there can be at least one test dimension* . . . given that we want to feel safe to achieve our goals and disconfirm our pathogenic beliefs, each time we relate to another person we do all this and are careful to see whether and to what extent the Other's response is in line with our needs".

Let us more formally translate the concepts of Control-Mastery Theory into MIT schema formulation. Imagine that a person is driven by a very simple pathogenic schema structure associated to the social rank motivation and wishes to be appreciated. He harbours a core self-representation of *limited worth*. He thinks that, if he displays his qualities, then the Other's response will be *critical and contemptuous*. The Self's response to the Other's response is: *She criticised me. So I'm not worth much. I've grown despondent, I'm ashamed of having exposed myself, and now I feel humiliated.*

To protect himself from the distress of feeling shamed and humiliated, the patient now adopts a coping procedure of the behavioural avoidance type: *I'll close up and not expose any aspect of myself in order to protect myself from the distress that others' criticism, which is sure to follow, will cause me.*

Well, if his repertoire of representations of the self in relation to the other was limited to the above schema, he would not be able to access therapy or have any sort of social relationship, excluding instrumental ones or those not requiring practically any human contact. He would be likely to resort to using alcohol and drugs to tackle his feelings of despondency and humiliation. Schema structures of this kind leave no room for hope: everything is predetermined and it is inexorably certain that criticism will follow.

In day-to-day life and clinical situations things are more complex, as also emphasised in Control-Mastery Theory. Using our terminology, we have to imagine that for every motivational system there are at least two core self-images underlying the hope of a Wish being achieved. The first is a negative, pathogenic representation, similar to what was just described. This is the dominant image, which enters consciousness more easily and rapidly and drives the negative forecasts about how the other will react.

An alternative, more benign and positive image exists alongside the pathogenic representation, for example an image of the self as *effectual* and accordingly a benign representation of the other as attentive. Almost always the positive representation can be discerned at fleeting moments and as early as in the first sessions. Without being aware, a patient might describe moments during which she feels to be functioning well and confident, or else mention relationships where others react positively to her actions. She can describe and experience these events but is unable to recall them when under distress so as to feel comforted.

Let us go back. What happens every time a person enters a relationship, including the therapeutic relationship? A relational test becomes activated, consisting of procedures Control Mastery Theory has termed, as mentioned earlier, the conditions of safety test.

The person starts to collect data to examine whether the Other's response to his Wish to be appreciated will confirm his negative self-image. This is the hypothesis the patient believes more likely to be true. At the same time but often unconsciously, the patient hopes, even if unconvinced, that the other will appreciate him and therefore that the positive, effectual self-image will get reinforced: *gosh, the other appreciates me, which means I am worth something.*

These procedures demonstrate that patients are continuously evaluating if their forecasts, negative for the most part, will be confirmed or instead disproved by the facts, thus allowing room for a view of reality richer in alternatives, nuances and, especially, hope.

This complicates life a bit for a clinician, who needs to understand a schema with all its constituent components, including both positive and negative images of the self and other.

To explain the sense of using experiential techniques in this book it is fundamental to recall, as we pointed out at the start of this chapter, that schemas operate mainly on an automatic, procedural level. Therefore it is important to help patients improve their metacognitive skills in order for them to be able to comprehend the structure of their schemas. In fact, the cognitive and affective components of schemas often operate outside awareness as action and physical state sequences carried out automatically. In early therapy stages a clinician's work, as we shall see in Chapter 4, should be to decode body language and behaviour, supplementing information already collected verbally, so as to uncover these schemas.

Limited or fluctuating sense of *agency*

The sense of *agency* refers to the subjective awareness of being inhabited by Wishes, intentions and goals, and by the ability to initiate, carry out and monitor actions aimed at achieving them. It represents the conscious awareness of being the source of one's own actions and encompasses the idea that we are capable of altering our environment, which responds to our actions and intentions (Knox, 2011). The sensation of agency further involves regulating one's own mental states, which corresponds to the basic requirements of metacognitive mastery (Carcione et al., 2010). This is the awareness that we somehow have the power to examine and change our inner narratives, that we can regulate our attention, reasoning and behaviour to modify our affective state, for example to become angry, worried or sad, and also joyful. The DSM-5 personality functioning assessment scale places much importance on alterations to the sense of agency, and points out that the least functional patients have difficulty initiating actions on the basis of inner impulses and sustaining goal-directed behaviour even in the face of adversity. The idea that impairments in the sense of agency ought to be addressed in PD patients has been emerging in recent years (Dimaggio, Salvatore, Lysaker, Ottavi, & Popolo, 2015; Links, 2015).

Patients with limited sense of agency are passive and feel prey to external forces, for example another's will or the system of moral rules and duties to which they feel obliged to conform, and have difficulty launching behaviours born from their own ideas, Wishes and intentions. An impaired sense of agency can undermine a person's sense of identity. Anyone used to being steered by external forces perceived as overpowering or unmovable loses the sense of himself, his goals and values. We would anticipate that limited agency also depends on the capacity for metacognitive monitoring: patients have Wishes that could guide their actions, but a Wish that has not been acknowledged cannot serve as a guiding force for action.

An impaired sense of agency further prevents autonomous exploration. In its most pathological form patients are not even able to put together plans they recognise as their own. If they are, they think it is impossible to pursue them because they lack the resources or skills, or because, if they take action, they will be hit with catastrophic consequences such as failure, being forsaken by others or punished for breaking the rules. We would stress that, even if these ideas are congruent to a person's schemas, the sense of agency refers to a pre-verbal form of experience, which a patient perceives as a sense of energy, drive and initiative. He has difficulty forming autonomous ideas and plans in his mind and feels his body to be lacking in the energy and skills needed to take action. Sometimes he has the energy but is paralysed by the idea that other goals, which he feels he should adhere to, have priority. Adherence to moral goals is often prioritised in such processes (Mancini, 2018). A patient would like to relax or join in a recreational activity, but decides against it because she thinks it would be immoral or harmful to others.

> Anna Maria is 52 years old and is attending both individual and group therapy with two of the authors. She suffers from Dependent PD, dissociation and various somatisation disorders. We shall speak about her again in Chapter 8. She has been maintaining two romantic relationships for many years and cannot imagine breaking up with either of her partners. She leads a double life, split between two towns. Three years ago she experienced dissociative amnesia at the idea of breaking up with the partner she lives with. She woke up thinking she was 20 years in the past and she needed a month to recover her memories and locate herself in the present time. In therapy we reconstructed that the moment at which she awoke as she entered the dissociative state was a few months before her father's death.
>
> She currently manages only with great difficulty to think about parting with the partner she lives with and going to live on her own. Since thinking of moving away she has been waking every morning with the sensation that her mind is empty of ideas, unable to move and not knowing how to perform actions. The idea of living according to her own goals is alien to her. The therapists managed with difficulty to get her to acknowledge that she would like to attend gym and have her agree to set this as a therapeutic goal. But at the mere idea of attending gym Anna Maria freezes. She is not prey to images of being forsaken, as one might think in line with the common dependent schema: "If I move autonomously, the other will leave me or criticise me". Certainly, she has these ideas at other moments, but when she has to get dressed to go to the gym she is seized by a more basic sensation of physical weakness and mental void. She seems almost incapable of grasping how to get to a gym and what to do once enrolled. When she gets there, she feels her energy failing her and turns back. It should be noted that Anna Maria holds a position of responsibility at work and is appreciated by everybody for her energy, competence and efficiency. Her ability to act effectively is disrupted following activation of personal, internally generated goals.

Lack of agency is common in Dependent, Avoidant and Obsessive-compulsive PDs and in Narcissistic PD, especially in its vulnerable variant, and it is of course a feature of passive-aggressive traits.

There is also its opposite, which is hyperagentivity, which is frequent in narcissism. When patients are motivated by competitiveness to achieve a higher rank, either in real life or in their imagination, their actions are driven in the short-term by an unstoppable force, they become heedless of the risks or consequences for themselves or others, and have no fear of failure. They feel to be fully in control of things. There are some initial experimental findings showing a correlation between increased agentivity in the instrumental domain – perceiving that it is we who influence the movement of a physical object, for example it is we who cause a movement on a screen with a mouse – and narcissistic traits (Hascalovitz & Obhi, 2015). One may hypothesise that narcissism involves a sort of dissociation between hyperagentivity in the instrumental domain and poor agency in the relational domain. It could be that narcissistic patients have a sense that they can influence the world but this needs to be supported by the other's admiring gaze. When faced with responses involving rejection, criticism, or inattention, their sense of agency gets extinguished and they feel dead, emptied, impotent, devitalised and powerless. They consider the possibility of influencing others, involving them in their actions and animating them to the point they become attuned to their Wishes, as highly unlikely (Dimaggio & Lysaker, 2015a; Kohut, 1977).

Recurring mental states

PDs feature typical forms of subjective experience, consisting of ideas, emotions and somatic states alternating with each other in characteristic sequences (Dimaggio et al., 2007). PD patients' subjective experiences are not different from those of other human beings, but they tend to compulsively switch among a limited range of states. For example, when feeling exposed to a threat within a relationship, a patient might systematically switch from a sense of vulnerability, charged with anxiety, to one of anger at the idea that she has been unfairly hurt by the other. Another patient might oscillate between a feeling of guilt at the idea of having wronged his loved ones and serious worry at the idea that he might be abandoned if he acknowledges the need to be autonomous.

Again, an Avoidant PD patient might swing among states involving an anxious search for a relationship, shame at the idea of being judged, a search for isolation and self-consolation when he feels a depressive state accompanying his solitary condition, reverting back to anxious proximity-seeking. Once intimacy has been restored, he is likely to feel controlled and constrained and to react angrily. Meanwhile his ability to experience states involving confidence in himself, personal effectiveness, sharing with others, or recreation in company is limited.

The ability to react flexibly to a context is also limited in PD patients (Dimaggio et al., 2007). They mostly react on the basis of automatisms and schemas than what is happening at a given moment. If, during a dinner at the pub, the atmosphere becomes cheerful, with friends joking and poking fun, someone free from PD could become cheerful too and taunt the others, laugh at them and, while playing along, just blush a little if he becomes the subject of any jokes. All the while joining in with the group. A paranoid patient would instead feel humiliated and offended, a dependent one would fear saying things that could result in being neglected, and an avoidant patient would be strung up like a violin string in fear of looking ridiculous or would have great difficulty seeing herself joining in, to the point that she stops following the flow of conversation and cuts herself off.

We would distinguish three types of mental state: 1) *distressing* and *feared*, in which a patient experiences subjective suffering, which he tries to regulate in a maladaptive manner. Some typical distressing states are shame, unworthiness and limited worth, solitude and being forsaken, guilt, vulnerability and weakness; 2) *coping*, that is, states a patient actively seeks with a view to protecting himself from distressing experiences. Patients can rigidly and obsessively seek these states, which are not of an innately negative quality, in what constitutes a pathological response to stress. Examples of coping states are rebellious anger towards an oppressor, diffidence and suspiciousness, devitalised emptiness, workaholism and anxious avoidance; 3) *egosyntonic*, which have an intrinsic value of being pursued as goals in their own right, unlike the instrumental nature of coping states in preventing or managing distress. Examples of this are seeking to dominate others, aspiring to grandiosity, compulsive seduction and seeking pleasure/hedonism.

There is a list of the main states observed in PDs in Table 1.1 (taken from Dimaggio, Montano et al., 2015, to which the reader can refer for a complete list of states).

To understand a patient over and above diagnostic classifications, one needs to comprehend the forms of his subjective experience, by identifying which mental states he typically experiences. The best way to understand him is to reconstruct detailed autobiographical episodes and carefully listen to what he thinks, feels and experiences on a somatic level and how he describes others while talking of situations that caused him suffering or preceded symptoms and maladaptive behaviours. One should then investigate what precedes or activates the shift from one state to another. With this reconstruction a patient and a therapist can collaboratively develop an individualised formulation of the former's subjective experience, which can be used to inform the therapeutic plan.

Placing mental states inside pathogenic interpersonal schemas is at the core of MIT formulations. In fact, some states are experienced during the uncertain wait for a response from the other. However, in the majority of situations and in the most

Table 1.1 The states of mind typical of PDs

Type of state	State of mind	Personality disorder
Distressing or feared states	Abandonment, non-lovability, unworthiness	ALL PD
	Group exclusion, Outsiderness, alienation	AVOIDANT, NARCISSISTIC
	Vulnerability, weakness, perception of relational danger	PARANOID, AVOIDANT NARCISSISTIC, PASSIVE-AGGRESSIVE
	Unworthiness, fear of negative judgment, shame	ALL PD
	Moral guilt, survivor's guilt	OBSSESSIVE-COMPULSIVE, DEPENDENT, NARCISSISTIC, DEPRESSIVE
	Constriction, forced submission	AVOIDANT, DEPENDENT, PASSIVE-AGGRESSIVE, PARANOID, NARCISSISTIC

(*Continued*)

Table 1.1 (Continued)

Type of state	State of mind	Personality disorder
Coping states	Self-protective anger, opposition to an oppressor, rebellion against constriction	PARANOID, NARCISSISTIC, PASSIVE-AGGRESSIVE, AVOIDANT
	Mistrustfulness	PARANOID, COVERT NARCISSISM, AVOIDANT
	Devitalized Emptiness	NARCISSISTIC, DEPENDENT, AVOIDANT
	Avoidance, protective isolation	AVOIDANT, PARANOID, NARCISSISTIC
	Compliance, sought-for submission	DEPENDENT, AVOIDANT
	Workaholism, perfectionism; overload	OBSSESSIVE-COMPULSIVE, NARCISSISTIC, DEPENDENT, DEPRESSIVE
	Idealization of other, ideal protector	DEPENDENT
	Stupefaction	ASPECIFIC
Egosynthonic states	Grandiosity	NARCISISSTIC, PARANOID, AVOIDANT (TRANSITORY)
	Moral superiority, critical judgment, disdain	OBSSESSIVE-COMPULSIVE, NARCISSISTIC PASSIVE-AGGRESSIVE, DEPRESSIVE, PARANOID
	Seeking and maintaining of status, territoriality, consolidation of power	PARANOID, NARCISISSTIC
	Pleasure-Seeking, hedonism	NARCISSISTIC

Source: Dimaggio, Montano et al., 2015

symptomatic cases, states are experienced as part of the Self's response to the Other's response.

Let us consider an Obsessive-compulsive PD patient invited by friends to dinner. Initially the prospect seems pleasant, producing an agreeable state, and at this moment the patient is well functioning. However, an image immediately emerges of withholding from his family or work colleagues that he devoted time to this dinner. That same evening he could be finishing some pending chores, doing the housework, clearing the table, going over homework with his children. He remains briefly in this state of doubt and at this point feels anxious. If he tries telling his wife about the dinner, she is likely to interpret his facial expressions and his words as signs of worry and fatigue. He looks at his children and imagines that they are finding school tough or feel neglected. At this point he is convinced that the Other's response will signal fragility, suffering and need for help. He enters a state of mind involving guilt at the harm caused. He decides to not go. This leads him to swing between fleeting states of wellbeing where he thinks himself of high moral caliber, others where the world seems an interminable sequence of duties to be performed, and states of sadness caused by a prolonged lack of sources of pleasure.

CHAPTER 2

Personality disorder psychopathology
Metacognition, coping and emotional regulation, maintenance model

Metacognitive dysfunctions

PD patients have difficulty becoming aware of and comprehending their mental states, reflecting on them, and using the knowledge about what they themselves and others feel and think to lead a socially enriched life, resolve problems and conflicts, pursue and achieve goals, and reduce suffering (Fonagy, 1991). Operations that involve monitoring and introspecting about one's own mental states are collectively termed as metacognition (Carcione et al., 2010, 2011; Dimaggio et al., 2007; Dimaggio & Lysaker, 2010; Semerari et al., 2003).

We practice metacognition when we recognise the emotions we experience and the thoughts passing through our minds at particular moments. For example, when we realise we are anxious because we are waiting for the results of an exam on which our future career depends. Operations that enable us to perceive and attribute our wife's angry look to our having forgotten to buy milk are also metacognitive.

Metacognition involves aspects of awareness employed to navigate relational difficulties. If a young man is afraid he is not ready to sit an exam, he can commit himself to spending the whole night studying. If someone who cut in front us while driving is of large and heavy build, we would not expect ourselves to successfully confront him should he attack us, and would rather strategise to avoid conflict. In other words, we evaluate the prospect of ourselves insulting him and conclude that this is not a very good idea.

Metacognitive skills vary depending on the quality of the relational context within which one operates. Patients with schizophrenia, who typically experience more pervasive metacognitive impairment, display better functioning in a good psychotherapeutic relationship (Lysaker, Buck, & Ringer, 2007). Likewise, metacognitive functioning in PD patients greatly depends on the emotional context and relationship quality (Fonagy, Gergely, Jurist, & Target, 2002), making it fundamental to constantly regulate the therapeutic relationship, anticipating and repairing any relational ruptures that may occur (Semerari et al., 2003). An emotionally well-modulated environment that promotes co-operation provides patients with the ideal conditions for becoming increasingly aware of and able to interpret their inner states and their constituent emotional components. This makes it also possible to construct representations of the other's mind different from those usually activated by pre-existing schemas; in this case thinking about what passes through the therapist's mind offers patients a good opportunity to safely explore and put into practice adaptive metacognitive skills. If patients instead experience an interpersonal relationship as dangerous, for example perceiving the other as threatening or dominating, their metacognitive functioning will be disrupted and rigidly fixed to defensive interpretations of the other's mind (Liotti & Gilbert, 2011; Lysaker et al., 2011).

Metacognition is made of skills with which people can:

1   Perceive mental states and ascribe them to themselves or others
2   Think, reflect and reason about their own (self-reflectivity) and others' mental states (understanding other's mind)
3   Use this knowledge and reflectivity to make decisions, solve psychological and interpersonal problems and master subjective suffering (mastery)

(Carcione et al., 2010)

Let us consider the individual functions in detail (Figure 2.1), starting from the most fundamental, that is being aware of one's own thoughts and emotions, generated in one's own mind and not, in some way, introduced from outside of oneself. One needs to have the ability to ascribe this same sense of ownership of thoughts, emotions and intentions to others and realise that they, like us, are driven by their own goals and motivations and act on the basis of their beliefs and emotions (*Basic Requirements*).

These basic skills can malfunction in schizophrenic patients, who often fear there is a little machine in their head, manipulating and/or implanting thoughts in their mind or that they are surrounded by robots and androids (Lysaker et al., 2013).

Reflecting on one's own mind

Identification consists of recognising one's mental states and distinguishing between them. Identifying one's inner state makes it possible to define and describe the thoughts, beliefs, images and memories unfolding in the mind. It further involves reflecting on one's cognitive functioning related to memory, attention and so on: "Gosh, I'm not managing to concentrate today" (*Cognitive Identification*). Finally, identification also manifests through one's ability to recognise emotions

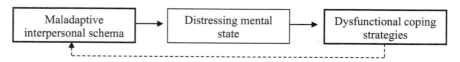

Figure 2.1 From schema to coping

experienced based on physical signals or behavioural reactions, what is termed as *Emotional Identification*.

Once we have defined what thoughts and emotions we experience at a certain moment, we can reason and think about these mental states and suggest links between behaviours and intentions, cognitions and emotions in psychological causality terms, a skill termed as *Relating Variables*, which is fundamentally disrupted in PDs. Patients have difficulty comprehending what ties a thought to an emotion, or how a behaviour is produced by an affect and not an automatism. For example, an avoidant patient, who starts feeling "uneasy" during a party, decides to go home; when asked what drove him to make this decision, he has difficulty articulating his thoughts, cannot explain the reason behind his decision, and chatters away as he is trying to justify his behaviour in an attempt to hide the embarrassment he feels towards his therapist: "It was late. I had to go home. I was tired."

Identification and Relating Variables processes together form *Metacognitive Monitoring*, which is very often impaired in PD patients (Semerari et al., 2014), who frequently resort to generic expressions like "I'm tense", "I feel uneasy", "It's annoying me", "I'm going running because I feel on edge" to cover their difficulties in identifying the emotions they feel. As a result, they have difficulty making themselves understood. In other cases they tend to describe their experiences in a detailed yet emotionless manner, or instead talk of what happened to them from the detached position of an observer, almost as if they had not experienced it themselves.

This difficulty in monitoring one's inner experience persists even when a therapist tries to reconstruct an exchange that took place in the episode the patient describes, with a view to pinpointing the interpersonal schema activated. When he asks the patient to explain what he means by feeling tense, the latter replies: "I don't know. I feel on edge. It makes me uneasy." A good level of monitoring capacity would instead allow the patient to mentalise, by synthesising elements from inner experience to reconstruct the schema: "I feel ashamed. I tend to blush in the presence of others. I feel all eyes on me, judging me . . . they must think I'm a cretin. . . . If she had said no, imagine the embarrassment! I'd so need to hide myself!"

Monitoring problems makes it difficult for patients to provide the information necessary for their therapist to form hypotheses about activated maladaptive interpersonal schemas. In a certain sense, one can state operationally that *monitoring difficulties is what prevents therapists from formulating schemas with all their detailed components*. If they try to formulate a schema, they find many undefined areas, full of question marks. When faced with a story recorded under limited monitoring capacity, a therapist asks himself: "So this patient wants . . . what? The other responded in a judgemental manner and the patient pulled back to himself. He did it because he thought . . . what? And felt . . . what?" Even core self-representations do not surface if patients display limited monitoring. A therapist finds himself thinking, "I've grasped that in vulnerable situations the patient would like the other to take care of him. OK. But what does this Wish reveal about how he perceives himself? As lovable or unlovable? As vulnerable and in danger or safe?"

This is an example of a schema reconstructed with a patient with good monitoring functioning; "I wish to feel appreciated (*Wish*). Although I think I'm not worth much, I am aware/I can acknowledge that I have some good qualities under certain situations (*Core self-images*). If I decide to show my qualities, I expect the *Other's responses to be judgemental and derogatory*. However, at other times I can see the other showing appreciation of me, which makes me feel happy and believe I'm worth something (*Self's response)*". If the image of the judgemental other is dominant, the *Self's response to the Other's response* may alternatively involve thoughts of being undeserving of others' appreciation, accompanied by feelings of shame and sadness.

This, on the other hand, is an example of a schema that is non-fully reconstructed, on account of monitoring difficulties. One's *Wish* is not clear, accompanied by under-defined *core self-images*, as the individual does not have a clear perception of oneself: "I don't know how I see myself. I don't feel good with myself. If others see what I've done *they will* criticise and judge me." As can be seen, in its behavioural component the *Other's response* is usually the easiest to reconstruct. The *Self's response to the Other's response* would be: "I feel tense and I close up. I'd like to flee. I'm not sure but I don't like contact with the other; I prefer to keep myself to myself." As can be seen in the Self's response to the Other's response, the action tendency is perceived, but the cognitive and emotional components of the response remain unidentified.

Self-reflectivity includes *Differentiation*, a skill enabling individuals to perceive the representational nature of thought. Differentiation is similar to other constructs in cognitive therapy, like defusion (Hayes, Strosahl, & Wilson, 2011), critical distance, or cognitive insight, and is broadly conceptualised as the degree of confidence one has in the validity of one's opinions (Beck, Baruch, Balter, Steer, & Warman, 2004).

Differentiation constitutes first and foremost the ability to perceive one's ideas as hypotheses and not as objective reflections of the outside world and, in particular, of relational reality. It includes the awareness that our evaluations of others' behaviour sometimes depend not on what they really think and feel, but on our own established maladaptive interpersonal schemas that manifest as a stable tendency to interpret behaviour in a particular, schema-congruent way.

The ability to differentiate further facilitates the distinction between dreams, imagination, hypotheses and beliefs. Let us imagine a patient narrating during a session: "I dreamt I was in a coffin. I was shouting with all my might but nobody came to my aid. When I woke up, I thought I was about to die. Something horrible is happening to me." Disruptions in the ability to differentiate result in limited awareness that thoughts, wishes, dreams, or forecasts about the future cannot in any way influence events or modify reality: "If I think about screaming at my daughter, it means I'm a potential killer."

There are various ways to differentiate and many of these require the interaction of several metacognitive functions (Carcione et al., 2010). The first type of differentiation, which is the one prioritised in MIT, is of the type *ideas as true vs. as learnt*. It involves the awareness that we interpret reality not so much for what it is but in line with patterns we have learnt during our development. One, thus progresses from a belief that "I think this, therefore it's true" to an awareness that "I think this, but I don't know if it's true; I realise that my thoughts have been influenced by my learning history".

Let us take a typical clinical situation: an avoidant patient grappling with his fear of failing an exam. The student is driven by the competition motivation, activated by an idea of oneself as inadequate. Before the exam he ruminates: "I'm a disaster. The exam will go badly. There's no hope for me." During the exam the teacher looks at the clock and makes a grimace; the student immediately starts thinking "That's it. It's over! I've said something really stupid! Now he's going to ask me to leave. . . . How embarrassing!"

He does not consider that perhaps the teacher is annoyed because there are too many students and the exam started late. Nor does it matter that, only a moment ago, he had given a good answer to a question and felt satisfied and confident the exam would go well.

Over the course of treatment this student comes to realise that in the past, when hoping for appreciation from others, he was used to receiving harsh, contemptuous replies, often accompanied by punitive silence. Accordingly, with his exam imminent, he fears he will go through these same experiences, to the extent of convincing himself that events will unfold negatively. The ability to differentiate would, instead, allow him to think "When I feel unsure and hesitant, I always think others will criticise and humiliate me. Now I understand I am used to thinking this way because of my parents' reactions when I expressed my worries at home, accusing me of being weak and fussy. I now realise the exam could go well or badly. I could cut a poor figure or do well. It's not all guaranteed in advance."

The second type of differentiation involves, what we call, *differentiation via access to healthy parts* (Dimaggio, Montano et al., 2015), or a differentiation of the type *ideas as always true* vs. *ideas as influenced by how I see myself and others depending on the context*. The student keeps repeating to himself, "I'm a disaster. I've always been a failure." However, when the therapist brings to the patient's attention that in previous sessions he had shared memories of being successful in other exams and sports events, the patient's eyes shine with happiness. In these cases differentiating means getting a patient to become aware that their views of oneself and others change depending on the context: "I've always thought I'm a dude who will be mocked by everybody. Now I realise it's not exactly like this, that I too sometimes have skills others appreciate."

We point out that this is a type of differentiation closely interwoven with another metacognitive function, integration, which we shall describe shortly (Carcione et al., 2011).

The third type of differentiation corresponds to Beck's cognitive *insight* concept (Beck et al., 2004), that is, the degree of conviction about the validity of a belief. Let us return to the example of the student who was convinced his exam would go badly before and during taking the exam. He would have willingly postponed it. His clinician asked him how convinced he was he would fail and he replied: "Completely. 100%."

Thinking back to the moment when the teacher looked at the clock and made a grimace, the patient did not have the slightest doubt this was a sign of boredom and contempt: "He was fed up with me and could not wait to get me out of his hair."

Often, if a therapist asks "How convinced are you now your idea was true?", the patient replies differently: "A bit less, in fact. Let's say 80%." If he starts to believe his idea is 80% true, it means he is starting to consider his representation as a hypothesis. This too is a start, even if momentary, to developing (capacity for) differentiation, arising from reduced certainty in one's conviction. Reality does not admit degrees of truth; if I am not certain, it means this is a hypothesis.

The fourth form of differentiation regards some very focal aspects of inner experience and is what MIT therapists focus on when other forms of differentiation, which require reviewing one's convictions, fail. It is a differentiation of the type *I believe my inner state completely depends on others* vs. *I have power and agency regarding my inner state*, which reflects an interweaving of differentiation and mastery (Carcione et al., 2010, 2011).

Patients are in this case profoundly convinced their suffering is entirely due to others' actions: "I can't go out because my mother is suffering and, if she doesn't stop suffering, how can I leave her alone? I'd be a bad daughter"; "My husband disapproves of my actions. He treats me like a prisoner. I've told him I want a separation, but he won't move and keeps coming to sleep in my bed. What can I do? I'm going crazy." These are patients who treat their sense of powerlessness and paralysis as a fact.

In these cases differentiating means coming to the realisation that one's own will determines one's mental state and actions: "When I see my husband get into my bed, I think about pushing him out. But then I see him suffering and feel a guilt I'm not able to overcome. This blocks me." It is thus a type of differentiation of ideas such as "I'm convinced of the fact that my inner state and actions depend on others" transforming into "I am thinking my actions depend on others, however I realise it's me that has difficulty regulating certain emotions". It is a type of differentiation depending, as stated previously, on the basic requirements of mastery, understanding one has power over one's inner world. We shall describe them later.

We have deliberately left for last the type of differentiation that standard cognitive therapy aims to promote, that is revising beliefs. This involves refuting one's conviction on a rational (Beck, 1976) or empirical level (Ellis, 1994) and, therefore, progressing from thoughts "I am convinced I'm a failure, this is a fact" to "I am thinking I'm a failure but this is incorrect, because I've realised I have done things right". In MIT we do not usually aim to establish this type of differentiation when working with PD patients (see Dimaggio, Montano et al., 2015).

At advanced stages of therapy, however, one can try to enable patients to engage in this kind of refutation. In her third year of therapy, an Obsessive-compulsive and Dependent PD patient said that, even if she tried to let herself be courted, nobody would find her attractive. Shortly afterwards she spoke of three men trying, in the last few weeks, to flirt with her. Her therapist confronted her jokingly because her belief of being unattractive did not reflect the reality of recent events and was clearly groundless, based on her schemas. In this book we will hardly ever propose examples where we promote this type of differentiation.

Lastly, self-reflectivity includes *integration*, namely the ability to maintain a coherent self-view, regardless of the flowing and alternating in consciousness of different, even contradictory, mental states, and irrespective of variations in our behaviour across different contexts. Integration also entails an awareness of how we have evolved, describing who we have become in comparison with our past selves: how, for example, we changed after experiencing life events with a profound personal meaning. Integration is a complex function that can be implemented on various levels. For example, a subject might recognise herself in her swings among mental states, maintaining a sense of consistency: I can be angry with my daughter in a certain situation but still remember and feel that I love her. A capacity for increasingly complex self-reflectivity enables us to recognise ourselves over the course of our lives, identify the ways in which we have stayed the same or changed, and understand what led us to become different (Carcione et al., 2010; Semerari et al., 2003).

Given disruptions in their capacity for integration, PD patients are generally unable to define the influences that drove changes over time in their subjective experience and levels of functioning: "I remember playing football and attending a youth club as a boy. Instead, now I'm timid and I spend my free time at home . . . I can't understand what happened to me." Capacity for integration makes it possible to simultaneously hold various positively and negatively valenced representations of oneself and the other within one's mental model of the world. A failure to integrate engenders negative views about oneself. I might, for example, be haunted by not lending a hand to a friend yesterday and feel awful about it, having forgotten how often I've been ready to help. Subjects lacking in capacity for integration might not be able to reconcile opposing perspectives into a more nuanced experience of their social worlds. For example, a dependent or borderline PD patient might decide in a particular situation that her partner is not paying her attention and describe him as selfish, whereas only a few minutes earlier, after an affectionate gesture, she found him to be caring.

Understanding others' minds

Thinking about and reflecting on others' mental states is termed "*understanding others' minds*". During interpersonal exchanges we are called to identify and ascribe mental states to others and think, reflect and reason regarding them. In this case too we would single out *emotional and cognitive identification*, that is the ability to ascribe, on the one hand, emotions and, on the other, intentions and thoughts to others, based on their visible behaviour, facial expressions, posture and tone of voice: "That look doesn't convince me. He's hiding something." Understanding others' minds also involves *Relating Variables*, that is the ability to form causal links explaining which cognitive-affective processes lead others to act in particular ways (Semerari et al., 2003). For example, we might realise that the other replies brusquely because he is currently worried about getting sacked and this makes him nervous.

PD patients with difficulties identifying what is passing through the other's mind tend to describe others' behaviour without referring to any thoughts or emotions. They focus on the surface of others' behaviour: "She's got a strange look, doesn't talk and doesn't open up." Sometimes a patient can ascribe emotions to others but in a distorted manner, biased towards a specific affect, at the expense of identifying other internal states; for example, if the other talks loudly, they think he is angry and do not, instead, notice signals indicating, more plausibly, worry. Research into identifying facial expressions in Borderline PD patients demonstrates this tendency to over-attribute to others hostile and rejecting intentions (Barnow et al., 2009; Bertsch et al., 2017).

Difficulties in *Relating Variables* render patients unable to understand what motivates others to act, and prone to providing stereotyped motivations of others' behaviour: "She's jealous because she's made like that. She's a woman."

Much of the difficulty understanding others is schema-dependent. If a patient has a vulnerable self-image, he is very likely to foster some biases leading him to selectively attend to threatening intentions, or to perceive threats where there are none (Salvatore et al., 2012).

Returning to the avoidant student, we saw how he immediately saw in his teacher's ambiguous facial expression that he disapproved of him and intended to fail him. This is a rigid reading of events, supported by a difficulty differentiating, which shows how the patient interprets the other's mind based on his own convictions. He is unable to hypothesise the teacher may have other thoughts, emotions, or intentions.

Decentring is the ability to put oneself in others' shoes, making plausible deductions about their mental states regardless of one's own perspective, manner of assessing and interpreting events, or involvement in the relationship. PD patients, more or less systematically, do not decentre (Dimaggio et al., 2009) and are unlikely to realise that others have thoughts and emotions different from their own under similar circumstances: "If I'd been him, I'd have wanted the ground to swallow me up. I can't understand why he's not ashamed." Subjects not thinking in a decentred way have difficulty understanding they are not always an important feature in the other's mind: "The waitress didn't come immediately to my table. She doesn't like me." However, the most likely hypothesis is that she simply has too much work.

Mastery

The third area in metacognition is *Mastery* (Semerari et al., 2003), which regards skills that enable one to use metacognitive knowledge to make decisions, solve problems and master subjective suffering.

The fundamental prerequisite for mastery skills is being able to perceive problematical mental states or conflictual relationship situations as psychological problems to be solved and to adopt an active attitude as regards their solution. The strategies used by an individual to solve these problematical situations can be organised on three levels of growing complexity (Carcione et al., 2010, 2011).

First level strategies

First level mastery strategies involve implementing behaviour without a significant commitment to practicing reflection. Subjects can, for example, reduce their suffering by directly affecting their physical state with medicines, alcohol, drugs, or physical exercise. Although these strategies render their suffering more tolerable, they do not change their convictions about the ongoing situation to more adaptive alternatives.

This strategy becomes problematic, especially if it is the one patients exclusively resort to: using medicines or drugs to soothe a nameless unease, resorting to compulsive sex to soothe their frustration, or subjecting themselves to physical over-exercise to reduce their stress or increase their self-esteem. When assessing any mastery strategy, we bear in mind not only the quality and complexity of the mentalistic information used, but also the effectiveness of the strategy itself (Carcione et al., 2010). A subject may realise she is feeling "stressed" and know physical exercise calms her, at least in the short term: in this case the strategy, even if operating at a basic level, turns out to be effective.

Strategies involving the body to soothe stress can, therefore, work or not. Using drugs or alcohol is certainly dysfunctional, while taking medicines when appropriate can be beneficial. At the dysfunctional end of such strategies we find people self-harming to soothe stress, binging or starving, extreme physical exercise and compulsive sex. Functional strategies include adequate rest, good lifestyle, adequate physical exercise and relaxation techniques.

Another first level strategy is avoidance, that is, actively avoiding the feared situation and/or reminders of the situation to prevent oneself from experiencing distress. Many patients tend to frequently resort to this type of first level mastery to achieve immediate relief from subjective suffering through strategies that are easy to use. These skills are, therefore, useful to incorporate into strategies for problem-solving, coping and achievement of one's own wishes according to the demands of the ongoing situation. Even if these strategies are simple, they do not become automatic through repetition and learning, but rather consist of behaviours performed voluntarily in order to solve the problem giving rise to subjective suffering.

First level mastery further involves seeking interpersonal coordination. Subjects turn to others for help and support to tackle emotionally challenging situations, like going to the supermarket if they fear crowded places, or visiting a friend in hospital when knowing that the mere idea of doing so makes them despondent. With the other present, subjects are able to confront the feared situations, without questioning in the least the dysfunctional convictions underlying their fear. However, in such cases patients seek help without sensitively considering the other's ability and willingness to provide the help requested: "I feel bad. I need to talk to a friend." A subject might phone a friend at all hours or go for therapy simply because he feels that the company is good for him.

Even though interpersonal coordination is among the simple, first level mastery strategies, many patients have difficulty seeking support, because activated dysfunctional interpersonal schemas make them perceive the other as not available or themselves as not up to asking. When faced with feared responses from the other, such as criticism, abandonment, or oppression, patients distance themselves from relationships, without weighing up whether their choice is appropriate or sounding out the other's mind. In simple terms patients say, "If I find myself in difficulty, I prefer to be alone". To their therapist's question "What do you fear could happen?" they might reply "Better to not disturb others" and not be able to think of anything else to say, not even if the therapist tried to make them focus on a specific person.

For these strategies to be considered metacognitive, subjects need to behave deliberately in a manner they know will enable them to handle their problematic mental states. Let us take the example of a young man who has had an argument with his girlfriend. He might be thinking to use first level strategies to manage his regret and disappointment, by getting very drunk, avoiding places where he might meet her, or asking the first friend he finds to be available to go away with him for the weekend, given that he would not manage a trip on his own. These strategies selected with the simple awareness, based on past experience, that a certain behaviour is able to positively modify problematic states, even if only temporarily.

Second level strategies

Here we switch to ways of problem-solving and regulating distress requiring a greater reflective effort and aiming at independently regulating one's mental set-up. Among these is the ability to strategically activate or inhibit behaviour. The ability to perform self-reflective operations requires that patients perceive and evaluate their abilities, attitudes and tendencies, which can consequently guide their behaviour: "If I'm anxious or feel lonely, I feel an urge to use cocaine. My friends have asked me to go to a disco with them, but I've been feeling vulnerable for some time. Better not to go with them." PD patients have difficulty getting themselves to abstain from actions they know to be harmful, or engage in beneficial behaviour. When they are experiencing stress, they are unlikely to remember that physical exercise will reduce it, and instead stay at home all day, ruminating unproductively. Another second level strategy involves actively redirecting one's attention and concentration previously invested on an intrapsychic or interpersonal problem. For example, ruminating on the idea of being deserted depletes patients' resources to the extent they cannot engage in activities they enjoy yet require effort, or even consider that, if they did take on enjoyable activities, the emotional impact of their problem would diminish.

Strategies at this level allow patients to take a "mindful" approach to inner conflict, as opposed to fighting against or trying to suppress distressing mental states. Moreover, they prevent activation of metacognitive beliefs (Wells, 2005) that either deplete individual resources that could be instead allocated to fulfilling activities, such as "If I think enough about it, I'll realise how to win him back"; or engender negative views of oneself, such as "If I start to think my colleagues will poke fun at me for my intervention, I'll get confused and this will mean I'm weak and not up to it".

Let us consider what the patient who worried after arguing with his girlfriend could do if he used a second level mindful strategy. First, he would recognise that his mind is troubled and could, thus, decide not to continue to feed his worries. He would not attempt to distract himself with other things, but would instead proceed to contemplate his experience, examining his worries as if from a high summit, observing their impact on his body. He would not ruminate on his worries, in an attempt, for example to reassure himself that his girlfriend won't break up with him or to prepare himself for the consequences of the argument, but would rather examine the relationship he has with the worry itself. He would pay watchful attention to his mind and body, be curious about what is taking place inside him, underlying the anxiety and fear that overwhelm him, and patiently wait for his distress to dissipate. And, in fact, as we show later in this chapter and extensively in Chapter 9, abstaining from rumination and other forms of repetitive thought or maladaptive practices, such as thought suppression, is beneficial (Wegner, 2011). An observer position vis-à-vis one's thoughts (Wells, 2005), an awareness of one's emotions, the anchoring of attention on physical sensations and an attitude that facilitates regulation of mental states causing suffering, are also useful in reducing distress (Chambers, Gullone, & Allenb, 2009). We point out that many contemporary psychotherapies, like Wells' Metacognitive Therapy, Mindfulness Based Stress Reduction and Acceptance and Commitment Therapy exploit second level mastery strategies to tackle widely varying manifestations of psychological unease (Chiesa & Malinowski, 2011).

Employing second level strategies requires a good representation of one's inner states and of what one wants to divert attention from; there is no need, instead, for a sophisticated understanding of what others feel and experience. The young man who argued with his girlfriend lacked mastery of second level strategies and could, therefore, think: "She was very angry after our argument. She didn't even want to see me. However I felt the need to talk to her and, after thinking about it for a long time, in the end I called her. She attacked me and was angry and hostile." In this case the patient does not manage to suppress a behaviour he knows is harmful. Later, when they break up again, he manages to divert his attention away from prevailing thoughts about his girlfriend. He is, in fact, cognisant of being able to tell himself "That's enough! Stop thinking about her. Luigi's called. Go and play tennis with him!"

Third level strategies

This set of strategies enables subjects to problem-solve and tackle distress through strong reflective efforts focused on their own and others' mental processes.

Third level strategies require metacognitive processing and complex knowledge of one's own and others' mental processes used for strategic ends. These include:

- The use of a detailed and critical knowledge of one's problematic mental state and functioning in the face of psychological suffering and while engaging in problem-solving, which enables one to address relational problems by changing one's ideas. A patient might, for example, be seized by ideas and emotions stemming from negative interpersonal schemas, such as: "There we are. Now my boss will tell me I'm worthless. Better I correct the document in much greater detail." In the light of her in-session reflections she might get to challenge these thoughts, telling herself: "My usual perfectionistic schema has got reactivated. In truth, my boss clearly told me he trusted me and not to worry even if there are mistakes. I believe I can hand him the document without fear of reproach."

- The use of the right knowledge of others' minds allows for complex, flexible and adaptive forms of mastery in tackling problems of an interpersonal nature. The awareness that the other reacts more favourably to us if we present a problem to him when he is relaxed or we talk to him in a certain way is very beneficial in relationships. A patient handling an argument with a jealous partner is unable to think: "Marco is impulsive, doesn't realise he exaggerates, and gets jealous at every turn. I need to wait until he gets over this, so that we can hold a calm conversation about what happened."

We stress that the forms of mastery that involve revising one's conviction about one's beliefs and using a mature knowledge of the other's mind are among the most difficult to achieve in PD patients.

- A mature acceptance of one's limits in being able to modulate one's own and others' mental states and, thus, influence events. Working through the example of the jealous partner, the patient might feel relieved if she thought: "Marco is very insecure and for this reason he cannot control his jealousy at all. And even if I behave in an exemplary manner and try to make him understand how much I love him, I can't lock myself up at home! However, if I don't falter when faced with his accusations, his jealousy doesn't hurt me. If I then manage to retain my calm and not get angry, he doesn't feel attacked and calms down after a bit. Of course, it is most unfair of him to be so jealous and it certainly irritates me. I'd prefer not to have to face such moments, but I prefer to tolerate this behaviour because, in the end, he's got other qualities I appreciate and we spend some good times together."

This involves a complex set of skills patients achieve with difficulty. For a patient it is a great achievement to manage thinking: "My mother's opinion is important for me, even if I now need it less. I'd be really glad if she were interested in and appreciated what I do. I've tried every way but there's no chance of this ever happening. She's made like that and I've realised I can't change her. She'll always hurt me a bit with her disdainful comments but, never mind, I've learnt to endure that distress and overcome it."

- The ability to put together forecasts about the impact of our actions on ourselves and others. Limited third level mentalistic mastery leaves patients prey to impulsive actions: "She replied with a joke when I asked her to tell me if she loved me. She wanted to show she has me under her thumb and is stronger than me. But now I haven't talked to her for three days. That'll teach her." First, this patient does not use differentiation, which would allow him to doubt his conviction that the other wants to subject and humiliate him. Then he does not seem to grasp that his own punitive behaviour will have a negative impact. An adaptive third level mastery would instead be based on a thorough awareness of the inner states of oneself and the other, which would have enabled the patient to tackle a situation activating relational insecurities thus: "I needed her to tell me she loves me and that evening we were getting along fine . . . so I asked her. Just as always when we talk about feelings, she replied jokingly. This annoyed me, as I got the impression she wanted me under her thumb. It made me angry and I wanted to shut myself away and not talk to her for days. But I know she's made like that; I believe it embarrasses her to declare her feelings. And then it's certain my touchy attitude would have made her angry and turned her away, which is precisely what I didn't want. So I set out to joke too and cuddle her . . . in the end she said it!"

Metacognition and psychopathology

We have briefly described the various metacognitive functions. How are they part of psychopathology? Metacognition is disrupted in seriously ill patients, with PDs or psychoses (Dimaggio & Lysaker, 2015b; Semerari et al., 2003). The malfunctioning of metacognition is associated with levels of functioning and symptom severity (Semerari et al., 2014; Nazzaro et al., 2017). Not all patients, however, display malfunctioning in the same metacognitive functions or of equal severity. For example, when three groups of patients suffering from Borderline PD, schizophrenia and substance abuse were compared (Lysaker et al., 2017), borderline patients displayed better functioning of self-reflectivity and understanding others' minds compared to schizophrenic patients but worse functioning of mastery and decentring compared to those suffering from substance abuse. It is thus important to assess each patient's individual metacognitive difficulty profile and adapt the intervention procedure accordingly (Chapter 4).

Many patients are not good at describing their emotions or thoughts. This is characteristic of avoidant disorder (Moroni, Procacci, Pellecchia, Semerari, Nicolò, Carcione, & Colle, 2016) but can also be found in dependent, narcissistic and obsessive-compulsive disorders, and associated with schizoid traits. Sometimes this is not due to lacking in awareness of one's emotions, as seen in alexithymic patients, but due to high levels of hyperarousal that make it difficult to identify current emotions. In yet other cases we find patients who have always experienced a limited range of emotions of low intensity, and which, for this reason, need to be reactivated to help patients identify them.

Difficulties in differentiating are key in PD psychotherapy. This is an ubiquitous problem in PDs, even if it seems more marked in borderline disorder (Semerari et al., 2015). This malfunctioning strengthens patients' convictions of the validity of their self–other representations stemming from their interpersonal schemas, despite evidence to the contrary. Such patients often do not manage to admit to themselves: "I'd like to be appreciated but fear being criticised because I have the impression I'm worthless." Instead they say: "I'm an idiot and so for sure they'll poke fun at me." They do not say: "I'd like to feel calm and peaceful but tend to fear others will deceive me and take advantage of me, and sometimes I feel like I'm not capable or motivated to react." They do, however, say: "The world is not a safe place. People deceive you and I'm not equipped to protect myself." In this book we shall demonstrate how experiential techniques can stimulate, sometimes strikingly, the ability to differentiate.

Lastly, in the self-reflectivity domain patients can have difficulties integrating. This problem seems to be common to all PDs and typical in particular of borderline disorder (Semerari et al., 2015). It is one of the problems leading to inconsistent behaviour, difficulties remembering benign representations of relationships to contrast with negative ones, or else to building idealised representations of the other where negative aspects are not recalled.

We remind readers that in MIT improving an integration problem is not one of the primary treatment goals (Dimaggio, Montano et al., 2015). When self-reflectivity and differentiation improve, integration also improves, almost automatically. Therapists only need to facilitate this progress at the right moment, with diagrams, functioning charts and reformulations tracing how a patient's way of functioning evolves over the course of his therapy (Salvatore et al., 2016). What we especially aim at is strengthening in patients the complementary ability to realise that in addition to one's negative ideas about oneself and others there are positive and benign ones, to remember these, and allow oneself to be guided by them.

It is important to assess whether the ability to understand one's own or others' mind is disrupted, because its constituent skills are fundamental for the quality of subjects' social life (Rabin et al., 2014). For example, disruptions in understanding others' minds has been found in borderline patients and associated with a worse treatment outcome if present at the beginning (Maillard, Dimaggio, de Roten, Despland, & Kramer, 2017). The most recent literature has demonstrated that Borderline PD patients have difficulty processing information when involved in interpersonal exchanges. They are sensitive to signs of neglect and rejection and do not distinguish situations with a potential for rejection from situations where others have intentions often nothing to do with casting them aside (Brüne, Walden, & Dimaggio, 2016; Domsalla et al., 2014). These difficulties are linked to disruptions of skills which one applies to make inferences about others' intentions, thoughts and emotions (Preißler, Dziobek, Ritter, Heekeren, & Roepke, 2010).

Some research upholds borderline patients to hyper-mentalise during social situations in order to interpret others' mental states, and to over-estimate others' intentions (Domsalla et al., 2014; Franzen et al., 2011; Sharp et al., 2011). In our view, hyper-mentalisation in PDs depends on dominant schemas that lead to interpretations of others' intentions in a schema-congruent manner (Bertsch et al., 2017), combined with limited capacity for differentiation. Some patients, therefore, make quick and arbitrary inferences about what is passing through others' minds. These are often complex and sophisticated, but only consistent with patients' schema-driven expectations, which they are unable to critically examine.

This creates problems. In day-to-day life social interactions are often ambiguous, thus lending themselves to various interpretations. Patients are instead extremely quick to interpret others' behaviour, expressions and conversations in line with their schemas, which leads them to ignore any discrepant, unexpected signals. For example, Borderline PD patients experience relationships through a rigid conviction that the other will dump them or will be hostile (Bertsch et al., 2018; Schilling et al., 2012). An avoidant disorder patient is highly prone to pick up subtle signs of disdain or to imagine them when not present, but has great difficulty understanding if another is sad or worried.

Lastly, reading others' minds requires the ability to disconnect from cognitive egocentrism or the tendency to consider another's actions holding the self as a point of reference (Carcione et al., 2010). We understand problems in decentring as a tendency to consider others' thoughts and emotions should align to our thoughts and emotions and as emerging in reference to ourselves. PD patients often display limited decentring (Dimaggio et al., 2009); in Avoidant PD this malfunctioning, together with difficulties in monitoring, is linked to inhibition and withdrawal features typical of the disorder (Moroni et al., 2016).

Moral rigidity limits understanding of the other's mind: many PD patients insist on saying that others ought to think and feel certain thoughts and emotion in line with ethical standards, and are almost incapable of grasping or accepting that thought flows unfold differently across individuals. This too reveals a difficulty in taking a critical distance from one's own point of view, and disconnecting from one's moralistic perspective, that impedes a flexible and sophisticated reading of the other's mind.

A metacognitive domain of great clinical importance is mastery; analysis of individual cases showed that patients across a wide range of PDs had limited mastery skills (Carcione et al., 2011). Vulnerable narcissism traits were found to be linked to a poor ability to identify complex emotions in others and use emotional knowledge to solve social problems (Vonk, Zeigler-Hill, Ewing, Mercer, & Noserc, 2015). Mastery naturally improves as the quality and quantity of mentalistic information feeding it increase. The richer and more sophisticated one's knowledge of one's own and others' mental states, the more flexible and workable the strategies one can use. From an empirical point of view it has been shown, for example, that a combination of limited awareness of one's emotions and poor mastery predicts the number of dependent, avoidant and obsessive-compulsive traits and moderates the effect of alexithymia on the total number of traits in these same disorders (Lysaker et al., 2014). To put it simply, someone alexithymic tackles problems without adequate metacognitive skills and this leads to the symptoms and relational difficulties manifest in PDs.

Perseverative thought processes, maladaptive behavioural coping and cognitive biases

A fundamental element in maintaining PDs is maladaptive coping strategies, that is the combination of responses – cognitive, emotional, behavioural and motivational – a subject implements, more or less consciously, *in response* to distressing mental states. The goal is to reduce or eliminate subjective suffering. In PDs coping is of central importance so that many among these disorders in fact draw their name from the dominant coping strategy. Narcissism is a search for grandiosity in response to the insidious idea of being worthless. Avoidant disorder draws its name from the tendency to eschew relational situations where others might discover one's faults. Dependent disorder draws its name from the tendency to tie oneself to others to handle one's sense of fear, weakness, vulnerability, and the inability to decide on one's own. Paranoids are so because their main priority is to protect themselves against a core feeling of being vulnerable and exposed to relational threats.

We use the term *coping* (Lazarus & Folkman, 1984) to underline one characteristic of such phenomena, namely that they manifest as responses to distressing mental states. At the same time coping is linked to concepts of *mastery*, described in detail previously, and *emotional self-regulation* (Gross, 2013). Let us review in what ways these concepts are similar or different.

Coping can be conceptualised as a cluster of mastery strategies characterised by minimal or no mentalistic awareness, implemented partially or wholly automatically, and tending to be dysfunctional. Employing a mindful self-regulation strategy in response to distressing thoughts and emotions is among second level mastery strategies. If a subject, in response to the same thoughts and emotions, engages in a repetitive thought strategy or avoidance, we tend to classify it as a dysfunctional coping strategy. By definition, mastery requires a functional metacognitive system. The less the metacognitive functioning, the greater the possibility that a patient will use dysfunctional coping (or emotional self-regulation) strategies rather than adaptive mastery ones to handle distressing, schema-dependent mental states. In simple words, what we name low metacognitive mastery corresponds to maladaptive coping.

The concept of emotional self-regulation, which refers to the combination of processes by which individuals modify the nature of their emotions, regulate their intensity or the way they express them, and change the situation and context where they experience them, refers to a set of distinct, more complex regulatory processes (Gross, 2013).

The two concepts – coping and emotional self-regulation – are the result of strands of research that are separate but very similar in content (Compas et al., 2014). Coping can in fact be considered as any behaviour triggered in response to current or expected states of emotional stress (Eisenberg, Fabes, & Guthrie, 1997). Both covert and overt mechanisms, such as anxious ruminating and reassurance-seeking behaviours respectively, can thus be considered coping strategies. The same strategies, however, can also be considered as different facets of emotional self-regulation capacity. For example, Gross (2013) includes both ruminating and the search for reassurance under the concept of emotion regulation.

Without claiming that the debate is resolved, in this book we consider coping and emotional self-regulation as essentially synonyms and refer to both by the term "coping" (in a broad sense) for reasons of simplicity and readability. Nevertheless, we reserve the option to refer to the differences between the two terms in some cases. We shall frequently use the expression *emotional self-regulation* to indicate strategies used to modulate, more or less consciously, ongoing affective states.

We shall instead speak of coping in the narrow sense, not overlapping with emotional self-regulation, to describe learnt response styles, implemented indiscriminately no matter what the distressing mental state. The link between distressing state and behaviour is in some cases only established through the individual's learning history, with persons having by now automated this protective behaviour that is egosyntonically oriented. Examples of this are a narcissist's grandiose fantasies and an avoidant's tendency towards solitary gratification. Initially they serve as a way to escape feelings of embarrassment, fragility, inferiority and relational awkwardness, but over time patients learn to pursue them as goals in their own right.

Moreover, by using a narrow definition of coping we refer to a set of embodied and pre-reflective responses – for example posture, bodily attitudes and automatic reactions – that patients adopt in distressing situations, but which then tacitly but steadily become part of their way of being in the relational world.

Coping includes, for example, the bodily attitude of Aurelio, 31 years old, suffering from Dependent PD and with a history of trauma. He adopted a limp posture and was always smiling, whatever one talked about, with an extremely conciliatory tone of voice. When his therapist pointed out this non-verbal stance, Aurelio replied he was always like that and it did not depend on the person he had in front of him. The therapist then asked him to try and adopt a contrasting, vigorous and tonic position, and a more decisive tone of voice, and to avoid smiling while he spoke. A few seconds later the therapist asked him what effect he felt from changing his bodily attitude. Aurelio asserted that theoretically it ought to be good for him, because he wanted to show he was stronger in relationships, but in reality he could not do it outside the therapy room because he would have been afraid. When the question was investigated more deeply, it was revealed that this non-verbal attitude had a long history, picked up in violent situations his father subjected him to. Aurelio learnt to be submissive to prevent being attacked, first by his father and then by his peers.

Coping responses are of two types: coping *strategies* and coping *schemas*. Among the former there is a sub-group, cognitive and repetitive ones, which we have not in the past paid attention to, yet which are very important in maintaining PDs and contribute to both maladaptive behaviour and clinical symptoms. We will, therefore, describe them in detail.

Coping strategies: classes and goals

Coping strategies are activated in response to perceived or foreseen distressing mental states and mediate the relationship between these mental states and a wide range of symptoms. PD sufferers use a great variety of dysfunctional coping strategies, more or less voluntarily. The more traditional classification divides coping strategies into behavioural and cognitive. Among the first type we find avoidance, substance abuse, risk taking behaviour, seeking reassurance and interpersonal control. Among cognitive strategies we find worry, rumination, threat monitoring, suppression, distraction, thought avoidance, repression and procrastination.

Another distinction is between *deactivating* and *activating* strategies. *Deactivating* strategies aim at lowering negative emotionality in the short term. They include, only to name a few, distraction, procrastination, avoidance and rituals. Such systems divert attention from distressing representations and produce immediate and temporary emotional relief.

If adopted systematically and for long periods, however, they always turn out to be harmful, since they 1) do not involve the cognitive processing of a problem, and 2) maintain dysfunctional self-perceptions. If, for example, I avoid all anxiety-provoking situations because of a vulnerability schema, I will confirm and strengthen the representation of myself as vulnerable. Moreover, 3) they prevent individuals from practicing decision-making, taking action and problem-solving, thus maintaining adverse life conditions. If a student keeps avoiding university exams and lies to her parents, in the end she will have wasted her time, she will need to deal with a failure of sizeable proportions, feel guilty about the problems she has created, and harbour shame that will worsen her state. Deactivating strategies are particularly harmful for metacognitive monitoring: the more subjects distance themselves from distressing mental states, the more they lose awareness of them, until they have difficulty describing emotions and their antecedents, and understanding that their coping was activated by a distressing emotion (Bilotta, Giacomantonio, Leone, Mancini, & Coriale, 2016). When a clinician asks an Avoidant PD patient "What would happen if you tried to contact those friends you haven't seen for years?", the reply is often, "Oh, nothing, I don't know. It's that I don't feel like it."

Activating strategies also arise with the goal of reducing negative emotionality, but unlike the strategies described here, fail right from the start and increase it. Examples of activating strategies are rumination, which feeds the distress linked to losses, failures or defeats; worry, which fuels the anxiety linked to preoccupations; or threat monitoring, which increases alertness to potentially threatening stimuli.

Activating strategies have various harmful consequences, by contributing to elevations in negative emotionality: they increase anxiety, depression and obsessions and generate confusion as well as a sense of mental overload. When subjects feel overpowered by the distressing emotions that result from coping failures, they often switch to deactivating strategies, which further worsen their condition. For example, ruminating on an anxiety-provoking exam further fuels the anxiety of a student, who only manages to deal with his distress by avoiding the exam.

Interactions among coping strategies

As demonstrated earlier, patients often use various forms of maladaptive coping sequentially. It so happens that behavioural strategies follow cognitive ones. A young man frightened about an exam first implements cognitive strategies, such as ruminating, and then applies behavioural strategies, by not taking the exam. An avoidant PD patient first uses worry to try and control the possibility of being mocked during an appointment and then, as the time for the appointment approaches, switches to behavioural avoidance. The reason for the pattern of this hierarchical relationship is that, in general, cognitive processes precede actions, at least under conditions of low arousal.

In many cases a behavioural strategy, the most typical example being avoidance of schema-provoking situations, can with time become predominant, resulting in a subject avoiding an emotion-provoking situation without contemplating any specific actions beforehand. To immediately demonstrate the clinical impact of such considerations, we point out now that therapists first need to direct their efforts to making a patient aware of the fears underlying her avoidant behaviour by improving her metacognitive monitoring. In Chapter 8 we will demonstrate that early behavioural exposure to previously avoided situations is initially intended to interrupt protective behaviour, so as to let the fears emerge and allow the patient and therapist to become acquainted with them.

To better understand the interconnectedness among various coping strategies, let us look at some examples.

In the second year of his university degree, Claudio, who suffered from covert narcissistic PD, failed an exam for the first time and experienced a breakdown of self-esteem: an old inadequacy schema, underlying a wish to be appreciated, forcefully re-emerged, engendering views of himself as being inadequate and of the other as critical and disdainful. He therefore perceived his coming exams as extremely threatening. Each time he prepared to study a new subject his worry was reactivated, foreseeing that he would feel blocked and fail the exam. These representations caused a significant increase in anxiety, which made it tiresome for him to concentrate on studying. To lessen his anxiety he regularly turned to cognitive avoidance and procrastination: he set about cleaning the house, cooking complicated dishes, repairing the washing machine (which had not been working for several months), or distracting himself with play station. In the end he postponed the exam, to reduce his anxiety. As soon as he had postponed the exam, he looked at himself in the mirror and thought his life was a failure.

Valerio was 26 years old and suffered from Paranoid PD. Every time he found himself exposed to little known social situations, an interpersonal schema was activated, underlying a need for security and views of himself as vulnerable and prey to exploitative and abusive others. This mental image caused him a constant sense of alarm. To manage his fear he engaged in threat monitoring, in order to forestall any hostile intentions or behaviour from others. This caused him to experience significant alarm and naturally exposed him to many false positives, perceiving danger where none existed. Valerio was likely to interpret a gloomy expression as concealing an intention to deceive him. To manage his alarm, he used behavioural strategies, such as testing the other by asking him tricky questions and then carefully analysing the replies in search of signs of deception. He thus had the illusion of controlling others, which temporarily lowered his arousal. The downside was that he did not trust anyone and he repeated this test every time he met someone. The final result was that he led life overwhelmed by sensations of threat and alarm, to the extent that his sleep became disturbed and he also displayed somatic symptoms.

Interpersonal perseverative cognitive coping strategies

We previously mentioned a sub-class of coping strategies significantly contributing to clinical symptoms, to the extent that therapists are required to quickly investigate their presence and apply a treatment model tailored to managing these strategies. These are *activating* cognitive strategies, on which a body of significant experimental and clinical knowledge has been accumulating over the last 20 years, especially in the field of symptom disorders, although they are also very common in PDs. From now on we shall call them Interpersonal Repetitive Thinking (IRT).

IRT has the power to reinforce the interpersonal problems typical of PDs and the associated suffering. Ruminating about the reasons leading to the end of a love affair causes depression, worrying excessively about others' opinions can lead to social anxiety, meticulously scanning distressing interpersonal memories depresses one's mood, and incessantly thinking about how much we desire someone unavailable produces anxiety and sadness and at the same time bolsters relational dependency. The types of IRT we analyse here include rumination, worry, threat monitoring and wishful thinking.

Interpersonal Rumination: Ruminating involves preferentially directing attention and cognitive processes towards one's suffering and the implications of this suffering (Nolen-Hoeksema, Wisco, & Lyubomirsky, 2008). Interpersonal rumination concentrates on negative interpersonal events, their meaning, causes and consequences attributed to past or current relational conditions. Subjects negatively re-evaluate relational episodes that manifest as obsessive thoughts going around in their mind, for example asking themselves, "Why did he behave like that? What did he want from me? Is the fault mine or his? Look how old I am and all I do is collect breakups." Common variants are counter-factual rumination and angry rumination (Denson, 2013), where patients try to modify a distressing memory: "If only I'd done . . .", "If I'd reacted differently . . .".

Interpersonal worry: Worry is a constant preoccupation focused on future situations with an uncertain outcome, which is, however, foreseen to be unpleasant or harmful (Hirsch & Mathews, 2012). Interpersonal worry is a coping strategy common across PDs. Avoidant PD sufferers, for example, ruminate about what others might think of them or how they will be judged, expecting rejection, derision, or indifference. Paranoid PD sufferers anticipate situations where others might deceive, cheat, or mistreat them, resulting in physical tension and anxiety. The distress increases and leads patients to tackle any relational situations putting up a defensive attitude, often by avoiding a feared situation or compulsively seeking reassurance.

Monitoring interpersonal threats: As conceptualised here, this strategy constitutes a defensive response to distressing mental states one experiences or fears experiencing. We had a paranoid patient who watched the shopkeepers at her local market for hours to find out who among them took advantage of their customers by increasing the weight of purchases or charging higher amounts than they should. She did it intentionally, considering it a valid strategy for preventing abuses and misappropriations.

Extensive use of these strategies exposes patients to overestimating danger and over-ascribing hostile intentions to others or interpreting others' actions in a schema-congruent manner, such as: "He wasn't clear because he wants to manipulate me." Naturally metacognitive problems contribute to maintaining maladaptive coping: for example, when patients are lacking in the ability to differentiate, they cannot question the use of the strategy they rely upon in a given situation. Moreover, threat monitoring is a primary, intrinsic aspect of maladaptive interpersonal schemas: schema-consistent predictions, of others being exploitative increases patients' hypervigilance to cues of aggression, deception, or manipulation from people in their environment. Patients pay the utmost attention to what others say and do, and to non-verbal signals. They may, for example, scrutinise where people they interact with look, to detect any exchanged glances of derision.

The difference between this type of monitoring, which constitutes a primary attentional bias, and threat monitoring, the coping strategy we talk about in this section, is that the former is implicit and automatic and the latter is intentional, conscious and driven by precise meta-beliefs.

Interpersonal wishful thinking: The tendency to focus attention retrospectively on a wished-for relational situation. It can take the form of recalling enjoyable moments experienced in real life or imagining gratifying interpersonal situations. Sometimes patients use it in response to negative mental states, for example, thinking back to the best times in a romantic relationship at the moment their partner is leaving them, to lessen the distress caused by separating. At other times, wishful thinking arises in response to positive emotional states, for example, while relaxing or enjoying oneself, to boost the intensity and duration of the pleasant feeling.

In both cases the effect is negative because harbouring OR clinging to the wish: 1) leads to experiencing the current situation of absence with greater suffering, 2) turns even intrinsically positive situations into negative, by bringing the absence and dissatisfaction to the fore. Take, for example, a patient enjoying himself at dinner with friends. He dwells on the thought "How great it would have been to share this evening with my ex" and, as time goes on, his enjoyment of the dinner gets eclipsed, his mind gets invaded by the thought of the other's absence, his mood diverges, and his self-image switches to "I'm a poor loser trying pathetically to enjoy myself in a meaningless situation. It would only be meaningful if I were here with Mara"; 3) produces a longing, leading subjects to act against their own wellbeing, which is typical of dependencies. The following example helps to demonstrate how obsessively maintaining relational wishes and in the least opportune contexts drives one to act counterproductively.

A Dependent PD patient, whose boyfriend recently left her, was visiting Prague with a friend. She was enjoying herself and felt free and independent in a way she had not felt for some time. She could feel this sense of wellbeing and started thinking how exciting it would have been to share this same experience with her ex and soon after started comparing her memories with the present. Although she had considered these thoughts as innocent musings, she rapidly lost contact with what she was experiencing at that moment and found it meaningless. She felt a hint of sadness and no longer drew enjoyment from her trip. While in a state of despair, she texted her ex, seeking comfort in his reply and completely forgetting his controlling manner and mistreatment. He replied to her text and their relationship assumed its former sadomasochistic dynamic.

Patients enlist various processes to apply the strategies listed here: mainly verbal or imagery processes, at a generic or a detailed, analytical level. It is also worth considering the so-called strategies of *gap-filling* (Wells, 2008), that is, scanning memories well in the form of images, frame by frame. It is common in Obsessive-Compulsive Disorder and Post-Traumatic Stress Disorder (Wells, 2008) and we find it in many PDs. In its most common form, patients dwell for a long time on certain episodes, analysing them in detail, and preferentially attend to threat-related information (threat monitoring) while trying to fill in any voids in their memory. In other cases, persons scrutinise chats, emails and so on, while observing and consigning to memory enormous numbers of details that seem unimportant to others, like ellipses, emoticons, or slight contradictions.

This form of perseverative thinking serves many goals. In many cases it aims at unveiling or forestalling threats or revealing the truth. Other patients use it as the regulation strategy of choice, for example, storing an enormous quantity of life episodes for future recall, as benchmarks against which they will evaluate new experiences, to understand if they are doing the right thing or decide which path to take when there are alternative options. Nevertheless, with this meticulous and threat-oriented analysis of interpersonal episodes, they are unable to produce a consistent overall picture containing corrective information that could ease their anxieties, guide them in making different choices and overall engaging in behaviour that is more adaptive. Other persons go back in time, revisiting interpersonal scenes searching for details that can preserve their connection with someone once loved and lost, or deceased. Finally, others scan their memories of events during which they were humiliated or rendered victims of injustice.

As can be seen, gap-filling is a particular way of processing schema-related emotional information that is at the service of other repetitive thought strategies: it can assume the form of threat monitoring, rumination, worrying, or wishful thinking. During and in-between sessions patients alternate between factual descriptions of events, "He got out of the chair, then went to the bar, then greeted a friend with a laugh"; more subjective evaluations of events, such as "He got out of the chair because he wanted to show me he was fed up waiting for me, then he went towards the bar to show me he wasn't looking for me"; or value judgements, such as "He was playing about with his mobile – someone with nothing to do still has to find something to occupy his time. . . . Every so often he looked around – let it never be said that he lets a prey get away. Then he greeted me in a rush – just like all men – and then I smiled as if nothing had happened – in these situations we women are really stupid."

The presence of this type of IRT is confirmed when the following are found in a patient: hypertrophy of memory of certain interpersonal situations with an obsessive focus on details and a strong wish to involve the therapist in this type of analysis, which concentrates cognitive efforts on providing a superfluous description of facts, accompanied by a reluctance to thoroughly investigate their psychological experience and motivations that arose during isolated events.

Schemas and representations of coping

In PD patients' narratives the other's response to the initial wish is disappointing. This activates certain coping schemas. We divide these into two categories: *with wish substitution* and *with wish maintenance*.

Coping schemas with wish substitution

In interpersonal schemas the other's response frequently leads patients to shift into a different motivational system as a coping strategy vis-à-vis the failure of the goal linked to the initial motivational system. Put simply: a patient wishes to be comforted when fragile and the attachment system is activated. She predicts the other will be judgemental and disdainful: "You're whimpering. You're weak." The patient now feels the wish to be cared for has not been gratified and the emerging self-image is that of being worthless and inept. It is possible that the rank system gets activated, underlying a wish to be appreciated, as a result of not having fulfilled her wish to be comforted.

The patient tries to instil a positive opinion of oneself, for example, by behaving well or improving her performance in order to be loved. A positive response indicates that the other appreciates her, for example for excelling in exams. She thus satisfies her wish, associated with social rank, and partly her need for intimacy, associated with attachment, but only conditionally; she assumes "If I'm smart enough, the other will approach me and remain close to me. I just need to hide my vulnerabilities."

In this case the schema linked to rank is a coping schema, helping the patient handle the other's negative response, which denotes the failure in gratifying the initial wish to be cared for. Patients often pursue coping schemas, not recognising that these schemas arose as a result of their wishes being frustrated. They therefore search unendingly for a response that never leaves them truly satisfied. An example will clarify this concept.

Abel was at primary school. He suffered from a depressive episode and Borderline PD, with marked paranoid traits. He was the son of ethnic minority immigrants and was often bullied by a group of peers. He wanted to join his fellow schoolmates' groups and feel included, but over time his prediction that the others would exclude him and humiliate him for the colour of his skin, became ever more consolidated. This is how the self-representation of himself being excluded because he was weak and submissive became progressively established.

Later, at around 17 years old, his temperament led him to lose control in similar situations, reacting aggressively and defiantly. He noticed this was effective in stopping his peers from targeting him to humiliate him. He then started to demonstrate an arrogant self-assurance in situations with the potential to make him feel subjugated. As time went on, Abel formulated a forecast consistent with the coping schema that had now crystallised within him: "If I present myself to be strong and aggressive, others will fear me and I'll feel respected." This is precisely the step taken by Robert De Niro in *The Godfather Part II*!

As an adult Abel seemed very reactive and sometimes overbearing. He tried to adopt a dominant role in relationships but saw himself as weak and felt exhausted by his continuous efforts to defend himself and assert his rank. Although he satisfied his need to belong to the group, he did so only partially and conditionally: people envied and feared him, so they most certainly could not exclude or humiliate him. However, they did not accept him as an equal, for what he was. In the next Box 2.1 we summarise the shift Abel made from the primary to the coping schema.

Here it can be seen how Abel makes a clear shift from one motivational system to another, while losing sight of the primary wish. During sessions he does not find it easy to identify his primary wish of belonging to the group, but dwells on his need to be appreciated and his coping strategy that revolves around making others fear him.

Abel did not manage to enjoy others' company because in his primary schema he foresaw that nobody would be interested in him for what he was and that, if others saw him as he really was, they would find him vulnerable and would be tempted to subjugate OR control him. He detected no signs of inclusion or camaraderie and so immediately concentrated on learning how to present as strong and dominant, so that others respect him.

Wish substitution is at play here: the wish to belong and share in the companionship was substituted by the competitive wish of feeling appreciated and by the primitive fight/flight defence mechanism. This substitution comes with a price however: a group of friends is not the best context for exerting dominance, but perfect for belonging. Subjugating group members may at most provide an ephemeral sensation of strength and power but one feels alone. Little by little his friends ousted OR ostracised Abel from the group.

In therapy people with coping schemas with wish substitution often express their suffering in a confused, contradictory manner, with the distress arising from the failure to satisfy a fundamental wish visible to the clinician but not to the

---

Box 2.1 Example of coping schema with wish substitution:

- *Primary schema*: I wish for inclusion (wish of "Belonging to the Group" domain) but I'm different (core self-representation) ⇨ if I get closer ⇨ the other insults me and excludes me ⇨ I feel inferior and alone, I'm ashamed
- *Coping schema*: I wish to be appreciated (wish in the Rank domain) ⇨ if I look aggressive and authoritarian ⇨ the other fears and admires me ⇨ I feel strong, powerful, superior, respected

patient, who does not realise he is pursuing a wish. He might, for example, seem bored because he feels isolated, but deny any interest in friendships. He might seem depressed or angry about not receiving appreciation, but declare he could not care less about others' respect.

We would note here that therapy for coping schemas with wish substitution aims at helping patients become aware of their primary Wish and encouraging them to reinstate it to its rightful place of priority in the hierarchy among motives. This means patients should be also be encouraged to reconnect with desires they have pushed aside because of the other's negative response and the accompanying distress, as foreseen through the lens of their schemas. In other words, one needs to use a careful formulation presenting evidence to patients that their primary motivation is different to the motivation dictated by the coping schema: for example, their primary motivation is to be autonomous rather than to take responsibility for a suffering other, or to feel supported rather than compete for rank.

A common situation in therapy is the substitution of the wish to explore with the wish for attachment. Patients are driven OR experience a drive to explore but are afraid to do so, so they abandon their wish and desperately seek comfort instead. They often start therapy feeling forsaken but a careful examination of their narrative reveals their initial motive to have been autonomously pursuing their plans. In this example therapy is not intended to repair attachment but to demonstrate that an excessive need for attachment interferes with their exploratory behaviour.

Coping schemas with wish conservation

Coping schemas *with wish conservation* are compensatory schemas substituting a self-image of being weak, asthenic, inadequate, or lonely with antithetical views of the self as strong, confident, appreciated and included. The representation of others consequently changes: from tyrannical, judgemental, contemptuous and abandoning they become accepting, fearful, appreciative and caring. In order to achieve a more positive self-image, patients modify the *if . . . then* procedure, in essence by changing the conditions predicting the Other's negative response.

As can be seen in Box 2.2, the wish remains the same. What is substituted, essentially, is the *if . . . then* strategy. Let us look at the process more closely. Let

---

Box 2.2 Example of coping schema with Wish conservation:

- *Primary schema:* I wish for appreciation (wish) but feel worthless (core self-representation) ⇨ if I display my qualities ⇨ the other will criticise and despise me ⇨ I'm inferior and feel ashamed and despondent
- *Coping schema:* I wish for appreciation (wish) ⇨ if I show I'm brilliant or perfect then ⇨ the other will appreciate me ⇨ I feel energetic, capable, and that I'm worth something

us imagine that the need for appreciation gets activated in a patient. He wants to be appreciated but is driven by a core self-idea of being *of limited worth*. Consequently, if he displays his qualities, he expects the other to criticise him. However, faced with this criticism, he harbours a wish for social rank. Consequently the initial if . . . then procedure, "If I show who I am and what I've done, as comes naturally to me, then . . .", transforms into: "If I correct all my mistakes and try and do something perfect, then perhaps the other will appreciate me."

We recall that, if not treated in psychotherapy, the core self-representation remains substantially unchanged whatever the overlying coping schema. According to predictions congruent to the coping schema, using the previous example, I could think that I would feel worthy if I achieved perfection, however in the background I would continue to see myself as worthless. This insidious sense of self will emerge dramatically when some life event shatters the coping representation. This is the moment when the distressing self-image incorporated in the primary maladaptive schema resurfaces.

We would mention that treating coping schemas with wish conservation means helping patients drop their coping procedures, such as perfectionism in the previous example, and return to using their primary procedures: if I invest the right degree of effort to show what I have achieved, the other might appreciate me. If, for example, a patient driven by attachment engages in an *if . . . then* procedure preventing her from seeking help when needed, foreseeing that the other will deny it, she should be encouraged to openly ask for help, thus defying the predictions of the schema. A therapist should help the person portrayed in the previous example, presenting himself as over-competent, to temper his perfectionism, which he believes is the only way to win others' respect, and to show others different parts of himself, and realise as a result that, notwithstanding everything, he manages to maintain a self-image of being worthy.

We recall that in MIT the main goal is not to change the other's response in real life. If this occurs, it is certainly a beneficial effect we happily welcome. At a certain point in the decision-making process we try, when possible, to get patients to adopt more adaptive behaviour with the hope of improving social relations. But the primary goal is to change the schema! If a patient uses perfectionist strategies while hoping that his real (as opposed to his internalised) hyper-critical father nevertheless appreciates him, his therapy risks becoming distressing. If a woman with affective dependency hopes that, by presenting herself as less compliant, her partner will express his love more openly, she risks being neglected which would confirm her schema. The goal is instead to abandon the coping schema, become aware of their primary wish, and in any case maintain a positive self-image! The benign response we want patients to receive is not the response coming from the other, but first and foremost the response emerging within them.

Coping schemas have various features distinguishing them from primary schemas. First, they are egosyntonic, in the sense that they incorporate less distressing self- and other-representations: dependent patients prefer to view themselves as safe, even if they depend on the support and presence of others to achieve and maintain this image, rather than view themselves as incapable, unstable (?), and at the mercy of events. A narcissistic disorder patient is quick to devalue others if she senses criticism directed towards her; by devaluing the source of the negative judgement, she suffers less.

Finally, patients pursue coping schemas because they enable them to satisfy the wish, that has substituted the primary wish, which is perceived as impossible to achieve. An avoidant patient is more likely to be able to provide care than feel a sense of belonging. In turn, once active, coping schemas produce less distressing mental states: a paranoid's suspicious OR distrustful mental state is certainly unpleasant but nonetheless not as distressing as a state of feeling frightened/vulnerable triggered by the activation of the primary schema. These mental states can also be endorsed as highly desirable and may, thus, not be easily susceptible to change, such as a narcissist's grandiose state or a paranoid's excitement about power, which follow, as we saw in Chapter 1, the activation of the predatory system. Therefore, an MIT therapist carefully avoids directly confronting patients about desirable mental states, because it would jeopardise the therapeutic alliance; the therapist will focus, instead, on helping patients access their primary schemas.

Dysfunctional interpersonal cycles

PD patients contribute to the problems they experience, because of the way they enter real-life relationships. Their actions and expressive behaviour trigger responses in others that confirm the patients' schema-congruent expectations. So-called *interpersonal cycles* thus form and become established (Safran & Muran, 2000).

How is an interpersonal cycle created and maintained? Persons' interaction with relationship partners is driven by their schemas. They might, for example, feel appreciated at a given moment, but expect the other to become judgemental in the future. They then adopt avoidant coping styles: talking quietly, evading glances and concealing information to avoid being fully exposed to judgement. The real other can become irritated at the patient being vague, elusive and secretive. He may think that, if the patient is concealing information, it is because she is incapable and insecure, to which he responds with criticism or irritation. Upon noticing her partner's unfavourable reaction, which may include subtle non-verbal signals, her interpretations of the relationship are no longer schema-dependent, but rather a valid reflection of reality: the other has really become critical. Faced with the other's negative response, the patient increasingly employs the maladaptive coping behaviour, which reinforces the negative reaction of her partner towards her.

A typical example of an interpersonal cycle can be seen in Dependent PD. A patient wants to do something that interests her OR wants to pursue an interest, being driven by the exploratory motivational system. However, she may not be fully aware of her own wish or, as soon as it surfaces in consciousness, she downplays its importance. She in fact fears the other may abandon her if she acts autonomously or criticise her because she did not behave correctly. Because of this she asks submissively for permission or advice, leading the other to adopt a judgemental, controlling, or patronising attitude, in turn reinforcing the patient's sense of incompetence or her fear that she will be abandoned for being unworthy. She now behaves even more passively, which establishes the other's tendency to behave in a controlling and judgemental manner.

Another typical case is a paranoid seeking appreciation from others. He fears being humiliated and attacked. He consequently behaves in a distrusting or aggressive manner, so as to frighten and prevent the presumed aggressor from causing harm. The other will either become fearful of this behaviour or aggressive. These signs are consistent with and reinforce the patient's schema – that the other "really has got something to hide" – or that he has bad intentions: "There you are. I knew he'd attack me. He wanted to humiliate me."

Patients thus shape the conditions that maintain the relational dysfunction, by triggering multiple negative responses from others. There are various ways schemas drive behaviour that maintains interpersonal cycles: 1) Patients select people who tend to reinforce their responses. For example, a subject feeling weak and in need chooses a strong and dominant partner, who will protect her and decide for her, which reinforces her core self-image of being weak and incapable of looking after herself. This choice of partner prevents her from engaging in behaviour at odds with her schema, for example, being confident and strong, capable, active, or curious. 2) As stated previously, on the basis of their predictions, subjects' behaviour triggers precisely the reactions they fear in the other. If someone fears being abandoned and protests angrily at the slightest absence, the other will leave, thus reinforcing feelings of abandonment. 3) Subjects suppress certain feeling states, which do however come to the surface through behaviour and prompt responses consistent with their initial fear. For example, if a subject feels weak, submissive, vulnerable and victimised, he may on a conscious level experience anxiety, but unconsciously experience fear communicated exclusively through non-verbal behaviour. The patient's facial expression, for example, the contraction of the eye muscles and tightening of the lips, will make the other ready to fight, which is what the subject foresaw and feared, confirming the idea he is prey to aggressive others (Safran & Muran, 2000).

We never tire of saying that, even if interpersonal cycles play a significant role in contributing to PD patients' distress, in MIT one should avoid for most of the therapy to centre treatment around them OR to directly disrupt them. We consider premature interventions of this type one of the worst mistakes a therapist can make. We shall demonstrate this more clearly in Chapter 4.

For now it is suffice to remind readers that interpersonal cycles are different from interpersonal schemas. A cycle is a relational process occurring in real-life relationships; a schema is an intrapyschic structure. Naturally they mutually feed into each other: schemas drive the dysfunctional actions generating negative responses and, consequently, cycles. A negative outcome to interpersonal cycles reaffirms in PD patients the beliefs associated with the interpersonal schema.

In MIT schemas are treated first, and only then will the therapist turn their attention to cycles (Dimaggio, Montano et al., 2015). If we prematurely introduced the idea to patients that their actions trigger in others the responses they fear, we would be perceived as judgemental, laying the blame on them: "*So you think I'm the cause of my suffering? So it's me that hurts others?"* To prevent such ruptures in the therapeutic relationship and, consequently, in the decision-making procedure (see Chapter 4) we argue that the cycle is to be examined collaboratively with the patients only after they start differentiating and accessing healthy parts of oneself. The only exception to this rule should be made when a cycle is activated with respect to the therapeutic relationship, in which case the rupture in the therapeutic relationship should be addressed as early as possible.

A new personality disorder maintenance model

Right from our earliest formulations (Dimaggio et al., 2002, 2006, 2007; Dimaggio, Montano et al., 2015) we have tried to provide a PD self-perpetuation model. Over the years we have attempted to refine it and in this chapter we elaborate on the role of maladaptive coping strategies, in particular, repetitive thinking (Ottavi et al., 2016), and the procedural component of schemas.

Let us start with the role of interpersonal schemas. A series of relational motivations get activated in patients: need for attention, recognition of one's worth, exploring the environment inquisitively and autonomously and so on. A schema engenders forecasts of others responding in a frustrated manner: if I seek appreciation, the other will depreciate me; if I seek attention while vulnerable, the other will reject, exploit, criticise me or attempt to dominate over me; if I seek support for to pursue the goals OR plans I have set independently, others will deny me their support, harm me, and abandon me to suffer alone.

Being at the receiving end of such reactions, either in one's imagination or in reality, triggers negative thoughts about oneself and others, as well as distressing emotions. Faced with a tyrannical other, patients are likely to think he is unjust and react angrily. Faced with a neglectful other, patients are likely to think of themselves as non-lovable and become despondent, and so on.

Furthermore, schemas, by nature, increase preferential attention to congruent negative elements in reality (see Chapter 1): if I fear being abandoned, I am very sensitive to cues of indifference or neglect; if I fear criticism, I am highly attuned to cues of threat. Moreover, schemas cause a biased interpretation of reality. If I fear being abandoned, I interpret a look as indifferent, whereas if I fear criticism, I read it as contemptuous. Thus driven by schemas, patients experience the worlds as hostile and dissatisfying, which increases and perpetuates their suffering.

Moreover, schemas reduce the likelihood of engaging in adaptive behaviour. If I fear rejection, I do not seek help. If I fear criticism, I do not take risks by exposing myself. If I fear causing others suffering, I do not pursue my desires when others do not approve of them. As patients' behaviour is dictated by their schemas, they lead their lives driven by negative forecasts and use forms of coping that are toxic *per se*.

But, at the same time, patients do not perform actions aiming at directly achieving their goals. A hypotrophy of action planning skills prevents patients from constructing, updating, or adding detail to cognitive maps that help guide behaviour and provide an enriched, more comprehensive world view, better enabling patients to take on new projects and tackle life's challenges.

A simple example is a young man driven by a maladaptive schema linked to a wish for social rank. He wants to be appreciated, his dominant self-image is that *he is not worth much* and the prevailing response by the other is *despising*. Because of this, as an adolescent he avoids interacting with peers and flirting with girls. At 25 he does not make plans, and lacks in strategies and routine conversational and behavioural skills to form friendships and romantic relationships as well as to overcome the difficulties friendships or romantic relationships present.

The hypotrophy of skills related to planning and entering or maintaining relationships results from coping behaviours, triggered by underlying schemas. These coping strategies provoke others to behave in ways that paradoxically reinforce the maladaptive schemas and interpersonal cycles, as we shall demonstrate shortly.

The procedural component of schemas has a very important role in maintaining distress, especially when coupled with poor metacognition. In fact, patients experience distress in particular relational situations, which they have no control over and without being aware of its causes. A subject may be automatically and unconsciously sensitive to judgements. However, what surfaces in consciousness is only the increase in arousal. He does not know how to say "I'm anxious because I fear being judged and feeling ashamed". The tools he uses for regulating his arousal are thus limited to, for example, compulsive physical exercise, substance abuse, or massive avoidance, which can decrease arousal in the short term. However, he is not aware and, therefore, cannot modify schemas generating and maintaining distress in the long term.

If, instead of criticism linked to the social rank motivation system, patients' distress stemmed from fear of abandonment linked to the attachment system, the mechanisms would be the same. Whatever the motivational system that is activated, the ensuing procedural component encourages affect-dependent ideation. In simple terms: "I fear aggression. I am not aware and I cannot examine critically why I fear aggression, therefore I cannot distance myself from feelings of fear I experience in a relationship." Fear initiates activating string of ideas and fear-consistent scenarios, which in turn maintain a state of hyperarousal. The subsequent rumination-type coping further increases neurovegetative arousal OR excitation.

The role of poor metacognitive monitoring is also fundamental (Dimaggio & Lysaker, 2018). First, this limited ability to read their internal states means patients are less aware of what they think and feel, thus making it more difficult to act in line with their thoughts and affects. At the same time others are less likely to know them for who they really are, leading to interpersonal relationships lacking in true connection and likely to leave patients feeling more lonely, misunderstood and dissatisfied.

People very often implement schema-congruent coping behaviour automatically, unaware of either its cause or its impact on others. For example, paranoids' suspicious attitude often becomes activated without them realising it, so they become alarmed at the distrustful or irritated responses of others that their own attitude has triggered.

Metacognitive difficulties contribute to the maladaptive schemas becoming dominant in many ways. Limited awareness of one's inner world, especially thoughts and emotions, prevents one to become aware of one's own automatisms and controlling them consciously. If, for example, patients do not understand their avoidant behaviour is triggered by their fear of being judged or feeling ashamed, it is impossible for them to question their idea of being worthless and others' degrading or humiliating remarks.

Because of the power of schemas and poor metacognitive monitoring, patients neglect their healthy parts. For short periods they can experience a sense of competence, strength, enthusiasm, lovability and relaxation but they do not notice it, remember it, or store it in long-term memory. If a clinician asks them, they do not know they have these strong and adaptive self-parts and consequently do not let themselves be guided by them in their actions. They felt curiosity, had interests, and experienced love they have forgotten and do not know how to talk about them when their therapist asks them. They consequently lose one opportunity after another to act in line with their own truest wishes.

Even if patients are aware of what they think and feel, not being able to differentiate means they live in an apparently real world, where what they think is perceived as the only truth. The idea of being rejected by a person they fancy is a certain and indisputable fact, preventing them asking for a date, which reinforces their sense of non-lovability or limited worth and maintains underlying tones of hopelessness.

The inability to differentiate, together with the difficulty in making sophisticated and empathic readings of others' facial expressions and behaviour creates a toxic mixture. Patients interpret a moment of distraction in a partner as a sign of abandonment and are convinced of this, without considering that this is just an idea, their own interpretation of a facial expression or behaviour, which may not correspond to the other's real intentions. Driven by the idea the other is abandoning them, patients react with despair or hostility, or perhaps by swinging between these two states, resulting in increased suffering and deterioration of the relationship. When they predict the other's negative response or are convinced that it has really occurred, they experience distressing emotions in relation to these negative ideas. A boss's critical expression makes patients think they have made a mistake and feel ashamed at their stupidity. Such distressing states lead to the activation of coping schemas and dysfunctional coping strategies.

For example, every time narcissists feel they are in need, a primary schema is activated where the other responds by either rejecting or despising them, "You get on my nerves. How weak you are", or constraining and subjugating them. Faced with these responses, the self feels lonely and worthless, or trapped. Patients manage this problem automatically and shift into the rank motivation, trying in turn to subjugate the other or to reacquire freedom from a presumed tyrant. In both cases they do not satisfy the goal driving their behaviour, that is, being cared for, and at the same time the quality of the relationship deteriorates. Furthermore, others react negatively to patients' attitude, which almost always reflects their coping efforts: arrogance and high-handedness is what others most frequently read in a narcissist, and not loneliness or need for support. Anger and malevolence is what others see in a paranoid, and not their insidious fear that overlies their great sense of vulnerability. Timidity and a desire to flee is what others notice in an avoidant patient, and this prevents them from perceiving the latter has abilities, skills, or strengths. And so on.

Coping strategies represent a crucial node in the maintenance of PDs. First, as stated earlier, coping behaviour induces others to respond in ways confirming patients' primary maladaptive schemas: if I avoid situations and people because I fear judgement, others will think me evasive, fearful, and unreliable, confirming my sense of limited worth.

Additionally, coping strategies contribute to maintaining anxiety and depression and reinforce maladaptive primary schemas. For example, ruminating on a suffered offence keeps the negative representation of self as worthless and others as contemptuous and deprecating active in consciousness, salient and emotionally charged. Thinking for a long time about being mistreated victims, or morally superior, or inept and stupid, and faced with ill-intentioned, unworthy, or superior others, strongly imprints within the psyche mental images and intense emotions related to schemas, so that they become established, dominant structures within the mind instead of simple transitory thoughts. Over time, coping strategies and schemas give rise to egosyntonic and wished-for forms of experience and functioning. Examples of this are narcissists' grandiosity or dependent patients' compliant behaviour that offers a sense of being lovable.

At times coping also activates behaviour appreciated socially in specific niches. For example, perfectionism, if not extreme, is appreciated by colleagues and compliant submission gratifies the other, who can reciprocate in terms of politeness. Paranoids' distrust of others fits well in highly competitive organisations where it is useful to forestall adversaries' moves; for spies and mobsters paranoia is certainly considered an excellent quality. Positive social feedback has a price: it sustains the underlying disorder that generates the desirable action.

We now summarise and illustrate the revised PD maintenance model. First, underlying the maintenance there are two elements: maladaptive interpersonal schemas and metacognitive malfunctioning. Additionally, coping strategies, coping schemas and interpersonal cycles further contribute to the maintenance of PDs. Let us attempt to place these domains in some order.

We start with maladaptive interpersonal schemas. Their activation, under real or imagined relational situations, produces forecasts that the other's response will not gratify one's own wish. This causes suffering and produces distressing mental states. The emotions associated with these states generate an affect-dependent ideation, with patients more likely to experience thoughts congruent to these emotions, which then reinforces the original distressing mental states.

Patients try to address these states and tackle the relational situation. They may, for example, feel vulnerable and ashamed, fear judgement, and for these reasons avoid exposing personal information about themselves. They will instead implement particular coping strategies that, in certain situations, can crystallise into recurring coping schemas.

Usually coping strategies and schemas immediately yield the effect of making patients feel in a position of greater ease or control, but indirectly they keep the primary maladaptive schema unmodified (see Figure 2.1). For example, coping based on relational avoidance saves patients from the burden of having to deal with OR saves patients from going through high levels of anxiety or shame, but maintains, indeed reinforces, a representation of the self as weak or inadequate and of the other as overbearing or judgemental: "What a coward I am. I should have shown that guy see I liked him but I couldn't." Moreover, with the use of dysfunctional regulation strategies it is not possible to achieve primary goals or foresee these will be achieved, which generates frustration and psychological distress. For example, if the primary wish is to be appreciated, the use of avoidance – triggered by the forecast of being judged and rejected – prevents access to situations where one could receive real appreciation or achieve goals not linked to the competition system. In the long term patients experience the overwhelming distress of not obtaining what they most desire.

Sometimes with time coping becomes such a pervasive and automatic mechanism as to form a sort of "second skin"; it can become activated even in situations not directly triggering the schema and thus no longer just in response to distressing mental states. For example, relational avoidance can become an egosyntonic and partly wished-for pattern: patients develop a preference for solitary activities irrespective of the prospect of facing a schema-activating situation.

Moreover, coping, especially recursive cognitive/attentional strategies, is responsible for many comorbid symptoms occurring with PD, which in turn sustain negative interpersonal schemas. The chain is as follows: The schema, for example fear of judgement in the social rank/competition system, gets activated. The patient ruminates about the risk of cutting a poor figure. He starts to worry and his anxiety grows. The increase in arousal triggers the affect-dependent ideation further sustaining the state of alert. The patient then realises he is worried and scared. This reinforces his self-image of being weak and incompetent, which maintains the interpersonal schema.

Furthermore, behavioural coping strategies, like avoidance, reactive aggression, perfectionism, compliant submissiveness and so on, on the one hand reduce the chances of satisfying one's wishes and on the other hand activate dysfunctional interpersonal cycles and increase the likelihood of others reacting in a way that confirms one's interpersonal schemas, thus maintaining the process (see Figure 2.2).

Finally, metacognitive dysfunctions render maladaptive self/other representations inflexible and non-differentiated and prevent patients from realising their coping behaviour can be useless or harmful. Moreover, all this provokes problematic behaviour in others that further maintains interpersonal cycles (see Figure 2.3).

A clinical case to help put together the various parts of the jigsaw puzzle is discussed next.

Clara was 31 years old and a bright executive in a public organisation. She suffered from Obsessive-Compulsive PD with passive-aggressive traits. She came for

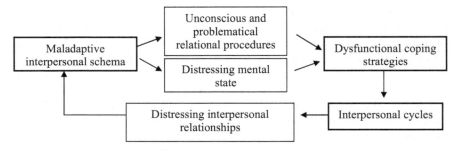

Figure 2.2 Schema, coping and interpersonal cycles

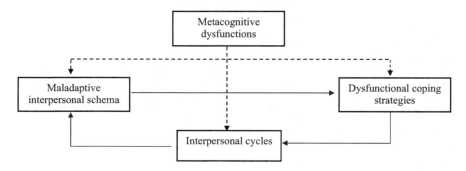

Figure 2.3 Metacognitive dysfunctions and maintenance of disorder

therapy visibly depressed and complaining about not being able to hold an honest discussion with her boyfriend or her mother: every time she wanted to present a plan or an intention she imagined not entirely to the other's liking she experienced a "blockage", preventing her from expressing herself or pursuing her goals. She could not manage, for example, to choose a study course or socially mix with people her mother did not approve of.

She ended up by accepting other peoples' decisions and, without any complaint, enduring others' wishes. This made her feel depressed and worthless. However, she had no idea of the causes of this "blockage". To her therapist's questions her replies were, at most, generic and circular: "It's just that I can't manage, I can't do it." To get what she wanted, Clara had learnt to lie or conceal her intentions. This depressed her even more because it contradicted her moral values: "I'm false." What Clara did pick up and communicate to her therapist was the effect of her schemas and coping strategies, namely avoiding dialogue and what she defined as her "tendency to manipulate". Furthermore, she ruminated on the reason behind this tendency to manipulate, which she considered childish, and directed moral judgements against herself, which increased her depression.

Personality disorder psychopathology 67

What was, instead, almost unknown to Clara was the set of self/other representations becoming activated when she felt the need to assert an autonomous wish. In particular, she did not know which thoughts or emotions caused the "blockage". Her pronounced metacognitive dysfunction, especially regarding monitoring, made it rather difficult for the clinician to pinpoint elements of her subjective experience in Clara's narratives.

The therapist therefore decided to propose the two-chair game. He asked her to imagine that her mother sat on the other chair and to tell her directly she intended to get back together again with her ex-boyfriend, whom her mother did not like. Clara got agitated, fidgety and red in the face. She could not succeed in telling her mother what she wished, just as would happen in reality. However she got inundated by emotions and thoughts, and, by starting out from Clara's bodily experience and exploring what happened in the game, her therapist could thus identify the psychological elements composing her maladaptive interpersonal schema. It sounded like this: Clara wishes to pursue an autonomous goal of her own and seeks support from the other. However, she feels weak and foresees that, if she expresses her intentions outright, the other will not support her and will impose his will, subjugate her OR dominate over her, and make her feel yet more weak and submissive (see Figure 2.4).

Guided by this forecast, Clara experiences intense anxiety every time she activates a wish to assert a need of her own. Worry feeds the anxiety and this causes the "blockage". As her anxiety grows, Clara responds with avoidance. She does not give up her wish, which is positive; however, to accomplish the wish she activates a coping schema *with conservation of the wish*, while modifying the "if . . . then" procedure. Let us see how.

The coping schema is: "I wish to achieve what I like (*this is the healthy wish*). Given that the other will not support me if he really knows what I want, I will convince the other I will do what he wants. That way he will give me his consent and support and will not impose his will on me. I will thus be finally able to do what I like." Acting under the guidance of this schema makes it possible on the one

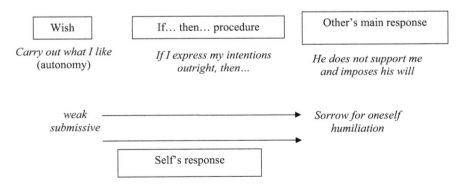

Figure 2.4 Clara's primary schema

hand for Clara to achieve several goals, but on the other reinforces her self-image of being false and, more importantly, makes her feel weak because she realises she has not been capable of tackling a dominant other head-on (Figure 2.5).

Usually, when situations like this occur, responses based on rank get activated: I wish to be autonomous, the other disapproves of and obstructs my plans, and this makes me feel subservient, constrained, oppositional and angry. A coping strategy based on manipulation can thus serve the goal of drawing satisfaction from exerting power: "I outsmarted you and got what I wanted."

Clara, nevertheless, was not aware of any angry feelings towards the other, because she avoided confrontation by holding back or lying. When asked by her therapist to imagine an open confrontation, the same self/other representations emerged as in her primary schema: weak and submissive self, strong and dominant other. Clara thus also had a maladaptive schema, which became activated in rank situations. We do not discuss this schema here because it would complicate the argument.

What is useful to stress is that her sense of weakness, learnt through family dynamics of her mother being dominant and her father absent and invalidating, made her simultaneously unassertive and avoidant of conflict situations where the rank system got activated. She also had an extreme need for support and validation when she experienced an urge for autonomy. It is this that we will elaborate upon through our second case.

Subsequently she employed rumination, another dysfunctional emotional self-regulation strategy, to handle feelings of guilt prompted by the coping schema. Practically, in response to her guilt Clara activated recursive RIT/IRT cycles to try and find the causes of her behaviour, which was contrary to the self-image she aspired to, that of an honest, forthright, open and brave woman. The positive meta-belief leading to ruminative thinking was that understanding the causes of her negative behaviour would have helped her to disengage from it. To summarise,

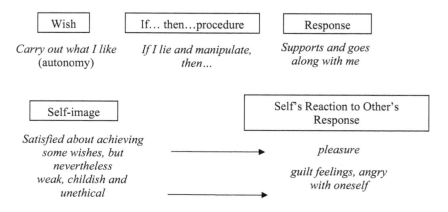

Figure 2.5 Clara's coping schema

Clara's situation followed the same steps as the model described in this chapter and described in Figure 2.6:

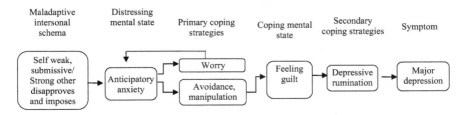

Figure 2.6 Clara: maintenance of symptoms

Clara's problem became more complicated, in that over time some Interpersonal Cycles confirming the schema became gradually more consolidated. Others, especially her mother and her partner, but also colleagues and bosses in the firm where she worked, tended to respond to her coping behaviour in two ways that were distinct but had the same outcome: on one hand they tended to impose their will on Clara, because they saw her as compliant and unassertive, and on the other hand, when they happened to discover Clara's lies, omissions, or manipulations, they got angry and tended to become dominant. This, obviously, seemed to Clara like a resounding confirmation of her maladaptive interpersonal schema.

We have shown that there were various reasons for Clara's suffering. The first directly concerned her schemas: her forecasts based on negative self- and other-representations led her to predict the failure of her exploration/autonomy goal. This is the main reason for suffering in PDs: the forecast that one's wishes will be forever thwarted.

However, do not simply think that MIT is a therapy aiming at hedonism, with patients getting better when they satisfy their wishes. MIT wants to treat patients' representations and schemas, and how they interpret their relational world. So treatment is not about satisfying wishes, but granting them value and legitimacy, together with the *hope* they can be achieved. Life conditions can be favourable or adverse, which depends on life, not psychotherapy. If a patient wishes to feel loved, his therapy is not directed towards helping him find the love of his life, but rather towards consolidating an image of a lovable self that can find another to love. This will be therapeutic, even if in reality at that moment the subject is alone.

Let us return to Clara: she foresaw that, if she acted autonomously, others' reaction would be to obstruct her endeavours. This made her feel frustrated. Another reason for the maintenance, again connected to the potency of her schemas, were her biases in interpreting the other: in her therapist's facial expressions Clara often read nuances of disapproval he did not hold. Furthermore, by virtue of the procedural component of her schemas, right from the start very intense schema-related emotions, especially anxiety, appeared and steered her ideation in a negative direction, which increased her suffering and depleted her attentional and cognitive resources that could be devoted to planning and accomplishing her plans.

Her suffering then got amplified and complicated by secondary coping processes, which, as well as increasing anxiety, made her feel guilt and hopelessness, and in the end depression. Lastly, her negative attitudes caused dissatisfying responses in real others, which added more suffering and contributed to the maintenance of the schema.

In all this Clara could not manage to satisfy her initial wish for autonomy. Certainly, by lying and manipulating Clara was able to partly obtain what she wanted: she obtained conditional autonomy. Nevertheless, she often had to give up on important plans, by going along with others' wishes. For example, she broke up with various boyfriends because her mother did not like them. By telling lies, Clara precluded any possibility of finding someone to support her autonomy.

It is relevant to be open and straightforward when asking for support. Just imagine what would have happened if Christopher Columbus had asked for support from the Spanish monarchs by promising that on his return he would have brought them all the gold in the world. Isabella and Ferdinand would have been unlikely to pay for the voyage.

CHAPTER 3

Use of imagery and bodily techniques in psychotherapy

Therapeutic change and embodied cognition

Changing means experiencing new states in the body and mind. Simply reflecting on one's mental processes in an attempt to acquire new, more functional points of view is often not enough to break up maladaptive thought and relationship patterns reinforced by lifelong use and by now entrenched.

Life leaves traces in one's body and not only one's ideas and the way one conceives social relations. Recurring relational experiences or true and proper traumas shape the way our guts, muscles and senses get organised and arranged in the relationships we live through (Ogden & Fisher, 2015; Porges, 2011; Van der Kolk, 2014). Psychotraumatology has expressed the idea that therapy should work on a bodily level, on the "bottom-up" component. This is based on the fact that dysfunctional relationships during development leave traces in the body. Growing up with threatening reference figures leads, for example, to a chronic hyper-reactiveness towards threats and therapy should help patients deactivate this alarm on a physiological level.

Our approach to embodied cognition refers to cognitive sciences. In recent decades the ideas of William James (1890), Merlau-Ponty (1945/1962), Gibson (1979) and Lakoff and Johnson (1980) that human cognition is embodied (Barsalou, 2008; Pulvermüller, 2013; Wilson, 2002), have regained strength. In the words of Gibson and his '*affordances*' theory, we do not get to know a chair by abstractly analysing its properties, but when we imagine sitting on it comfortably or using it to climb on to change a light bulb. We do not get to know a fruit by analysing its form, colour and smell, but when we hear it saying to us: "Eat me." We get to know the world when we grasp how the objects of which that world is composed are deployable for our goals. Gibson adds "We must perceive in order to move, but we must also move in order to perceive" (1979, p. 223). In fact, there are neurons that get activated both when we observe an object and when we act, so that observing is at the same time preparing action (Buccino et al., 2001). Our interest in the part of change that starts in the body and imagination and extends to the cognitive, semantic meaning reattribution processes arises from these ideas.

The mind does not limit itself to processing information on the basis of past experiences or to reasoning logically. Some questions raised by embodied cognition (Wilson, 2002) are:

1 Cognition is situated, that is we reason while interacting with the outside world and carrying out tasks. Examples of this are driving, cooking and conversing. The mind gets information from the body, which moves while carrying out activities, and processes it with a view to completing tasks successfully.
2 Cognition occurs under time pressure (Brooks, 1991); we reason while interacting with our environment inside a time window where cognitive activity is important.
3 Cognition is used for action; perception and memory are important in that they contribute to the appropriate behaviour for a situation.
4 Abstract cognition is based on the body, an aspect less intuitive and very important for our ends. When we reason without environmental ties, for example when doing a mathematical exercise, or reflect on the meaning of a film, cognition is based on sensorial and motor mechanisms too (Wilson, 2002).

Short-term memory is also partly based on sensory-motor processes. For example, recalling words without sense is more difficult if the muscles that should articulate these same words get blocked. Moreover, when recalling words, the brain areas dedicated to the perception and production of speech get activated. Working memory offloads part of its information in the perceptual and motor control systems (Wilson & Emmorey, 1997).

Similarly episodic memory is embodied (Wilson, 2002), given that it consists substantially of sequences of images where the mind simulates the action of the body interacting with others. Another example is language. In fact, even the passive comprehension of language does not only involve the auditory system but is accompanied by the activation of the sensory-motor areas too (Pulvermüller, 2013). In other words, an activity appearing highly cognitive like understanding phonemes and words is accompanied by the act of simulating their production too.

The mind understands language while the body prepares itself to use it (Schomers & Pulvermüller, 2016). If, for example, we try to name a tool, the left premotor area, typically involved in imagining the grasping of an object with a hand, gets activated, together with an area in the temporal gyrus involved in the production of words indicating that action (Martin, Wiggs, Ungerleider, & Haxby, 1996). If we therefore try to formulate a sentence regarding a particular object, a sort of "motor prototype" focusing on the type of relationship we can establish with that object, for example what type of grip it requires, gets activated in our brain (Borghi & Riggio, 2015). Reasoning and problem-solving skills are partly based on embodied processes too and cognitive schemas include a component anticipating action (Garbarini & Adenzato, 2004), another proof that we get to know the world when we get ready to interact with it.

Experiments have further reinforced the idea that therapy should include interventions working directly on the sensory-motor component: holding light or heavy notepads, solving puzzles, feeling rough or smooth and touching soft or hard objects, influence people's decisions, including social ones, in domains not linked to the exercise itself. An example is when assessing a job candidate while holding a heavy object in one's hand: the candidate seems more suitable. Touching rough objects makes social relations seem more difficult and touching hard ones makes negotiations harder. Judging a candidate after someone has put a hot coffee in one's hand makes one unconsciously better disposed towards him. Similarly, someone judging a criminal in a cold room is less well-disposed than someone doing it in a well-heated one. Moral judgements are also sensitive to physical and emotional sensations: if we assess someone in a dirty room, we will feel disgust and this will make us more severe, without realising it (Bargh, 2017). Sensoriality has a surprising influence on cognitive processes, including in the social interaction domain (Ackerman et al., 2010). Bodily states influence opinion, even with minor stimuli. Schaefer and colleagues (2018) showed that someone having to judge a criminal expressed a harsher opinion if he touched a hard object rather than a soft one. Touching hard objects made the judge "harder" on the criminal!

We do not reflect abstractly on ideas such as hitting the basket or under what conditions we might kiss a girl. The mind and body imagine the necessary actions, plan them and foresee the potential responses (Elsner & Hommel, 2001). We try over and over to hit the basket or approach the girl we fancy and in doing so we learn which strategies are most effective and discard the least effective ones. The body forms ideas about the world while driven by goals and interacting with it. Lastly, the body's relationship with the world influences cognitive processes in the social domain too: we are driven by sensations like hot/cold or dirty/clean when we judge others. Basing psychotherapy on the bottom-up component, from sensoriality to cognition and metacognition, has for these reasons a scientific basis (Gjelsvik, Lovric, & Williams, 2018).

Embodied knowledge includes imagination. Mental images, in the various sensorial modes, for example vision, touch and hearing, are accompanied by the activation of the respective perceptual areas. Imagining in anticipation a movement is linked to a motor preparation of the action imagined (Jeannerod & Decety, 1995; Kosslyn, 1994). For example, imagining rotating a hand in a certain way stimulates an improvement in performance when one really carries out that movement (Berneiser, Jahn, Grothe, & Lotze, 2018). Thanks to this action preparation, the body predicts the consequences of action thanks to simulation. Subsequently, when we actually carry out the action, sensorial feedback adjusts this (Desmurget & Grafton, 2000). The impact of mental imagery on motor processes is highly important: if the link between imagery and corticospinal activation of the premotor areas is poor during development, one can find problems in motor coordination (Hyde et al., 2018).

Very importantly, many areas in the brain include mirror neurons (Rizzolatti, Fadiga, Gallese, & Fogassi, 1996). These neurons serve different purposes: they fire when the person is about to perform an action, but also when he or she observes the same action being performed. This is well-known to neuroscientists and clinicians. Importantly, mirror neurons fire also when an individual imagines herself performing in the first person the same action. This overlap is also present in areas related to emotion experience and understanding: the same group of neurons fire when the person experiences an emotion (e.g. disgust), observes it or imagines experiencing it. Stern (2010) named the way the person performs actions *vital forms*, for example, speaking in a rude vs gentle way. Again, mirror neuron areas serve the different functions of observing, experiencing and imagining oneself adopting a specific vital form (Di Cesare et al., 2018). These data suggest that when changing the way humans imagine acting during social interactions, their behavioural tendencies and the way they position the other in their body and in their mind changes as well.

The impact of imagery on behaviour is not restricted to simple actions. Simulating episodes of future social interactions activates the same networks as amnesic recalling of episodes (Atance & O'Neill, 2001; Szpunar, Spreng, & Schacter, 2014). This is clinically relevant: when we get patients to relive scenes from the past, they are more than remembering those (Schacter et al., 2012). Memory is not an act of precise recollection of facts occurring in a particular way. When recalling, the mind puts back together elements from inner experience – images, sounds, smells and tactile sensations – and combines them in micro- and macro-narratives (Damasio, 1994).

While recalling, the mind is building an emotionally charged scenario. Thanks to the emotional impulse and the connection with premotor and other areas related to action programming and implementation, this scenario has the power in the here and now to prepare for action. For this reason, when we get a patient to process old memories anew, we are helping him to construct true and proper new narratives with the power to influence action. The simulation of episodes from the past also serves the future and the episodes we imagine will occur in the future get formed around pre-existing schemas (Rubin, 2014; Schacter, Benoit, De Brigard, & Szpunar, 2015). If we change the schemas in a patient's past memories we are therefore changing the way she will imagine the future and these new mental images will influence her action.

As an example of the effect of imagery of social situations on behaviour, Gaesser and colleagues (2018) found a prosocial effect in imagining helping another. Persons asked to imagine themselves offering help became more disposed towards offering it in real life and their prosocial behaviour was more marked. It was important for the imagined scene to be clearly located with a precise geographical place and to be vivid.

These data support that when working on patients' imagination, we need to place them as much as possible within a scene defined in space and time. We ensure that their emotions are triggered while recalling a scene from the past or imagining a new way of behaving in relationships. The goal is for them to live the scene vividly, whether they recall it or imagine it, and feel it to be significant here and now (Critchfield, Dobner-Pereira, Panizo, & Drucker, 2019; Ecker, Ticic, & Hulley, 2012). Again: changing the social scenario in a patient's imagination means producing new schemas that prepare her body to act in new ways and are more beneficial and desirable for her.

Emotional and procedural knowledge

Thought processes are accompanied by somatic states which constitute their core. Emotions have a cognitive component and one tied to the activation of physiological arousal. Changes in arousal often precede a change in cognition in the presence of relevant stimuli: if there is a danger in the air, the body reacts before the mind thinks (James, 1890; Le Doux, 2015). This is a form of embodied and implicit cognition. Mind and body together rapidly assess an event, for example, a car approaching fast, as being dangerous. One experiences fear connected to an action tendency, flight, driven by an implicit cognitive evaluation called *appraisal*. Conscious evaluations come later.

Emotions, hedonic tone, cognition and behaviour

Emotions and mood, and the bodily states associated with them, influence cognition and behaviour. Affective neurosciences have demonstrated how emotions are based on a set of circuits arising from subcortical areas and modulated by the limbic system and the upper neocortical layers, which implicitly regulate cognition and behaviour (Panksepp & Biven, 2012).

Examples are ascribing personal importance to an environmental stimulus (Le Doux, 2015) and taking decisions (Damasio, 1994). Some authors have talked of *affect-infusion* processes (Forgas, 2002) and *mood congruent information processing* (Bower, 1981). Someone angry gets seized by increasingly frequent thoughts where the world is hostile and guilty of bringing distress. Someone sad finds pessimistic ideas jumbling together in his mind. Positive emotion psychology adopts similar assumptions. The *broaden-and-build* theory (Fredrickson, 2001) observes that experiencing positive affects widens one's repertoire of ideas and encourages the pursuit of new ways of thinking and acting. In the long term people with higher levels of positive emotions are better at achieving their aims (Lyubomirsky, King, & Diener, 2005). Experiencing positive affects has a physiological impact, by, for example, reducing the effects of fear (Bradley, Codispoti, Cuthbert, & Lang, 2001) and increasing vagal cardiac tone (Kok & Fredrickson, 2010). On the contrary, it is harmful to experience poor levels of positive emotions. In anhedonic individuals low mood is correlated to low motivation (Van Roekel, Heininga, Vrijen, Snippe, & Oldehinkel, 2018). Starting from these assumptions, trying to modify cognition before emotions, the path characteristically taken by Beck's and Ellis' classic cognitive therapies, is only one avenue to therapeutic change (Ogden & Fisher, 2015).

Changing a patient's emotions needs to be worked on so that any new affect experienced produces a consistent modification in ideation (Greenberg, 2002). Modifying an affect, especially the arousal component and its somatic correlates – posture, gestures – therefore fosters cognitive change. Based on this idea an emotional-change-in-therapy model was for example created where patients ideally start treatment by relating experiences they generically name "distress" (Pascual-Leone & Greenberg, 2007). In our terminology this means patients experiencing a negative arousal but, through a lack of metacognitive monitoring, not knowing how to decode it.

The next step is when patients enter into contact with specific emotions, but these are maladaptive, like aggressive anger, anxiety or shame. The therapy in this model leads patients to, in a modulated way, acknowledge and experience more mature emotional states, like assertive anger, primary sadness and solitude, and self-compassion, which until now they avoided (Pascual-Leone, 2018). In this model therapy does not aim at changing the cognitions activating these different affects. It is rather a question of helping patients to acknowledge that they experience them, sustain their experience and at this point discover how their cognitions about themselves change given they are carried into a new affective state (Critchfield et al., 2019; Ecker et al., 2012). Contact with distressing affects is then possible, but now accompanied by benign cognitions, like: "I'm embarrassed but that's normal when you make a mistake in front of your colleagues", "I'm feeling lonely and sad but that's part of me. I can accept it."

Promoting positive affects is fundamental (Carl, Soskin, Kerns, & Barlow, 2013; Ehrenreich, Fairholme, Buzzella, Ellard, & Barlow, 2007). Behavioural and attention allocation techniques are used to encourage the continuation of positive states. "Savouring" consists of dwelling on positive states in past and present experiences and those imagined in the future (Bryant, 2003). "Capitalising" (Langston, 1994) refers to expressive social behaviour, such as sharing or celebrating, which sustain the good mood following positive events (Van Roekel et al., 2018).

What gets delineated therefore is a path of therapeutic change starting with the promotion of positive states and maintaining them in consciousness. We can trigger them in patients by bodily work, attention-shifting or adopting specific behaviours. A therapist can induce them with conversation too, by creating a sense of playful sharing (Dimaggio et al., 2007). When patients experience positive states, it becomes easier to get them to make further positive reflections, tackle tasks with more motivation and plan beneficial activities long term. It is also easier to promote a more detached, superordinate point of view, for observing suffering self-parts. Therapists can, for example, start with a sensorimotor or imagery technique that activates a positive emotion. Once a patient is in it, behavioural experiments are planned, that she will be more motivated to carry out.

What makes our work specific, and we hope unique, is that we explain how to use the techniques, alone and sequentially, on the basis of: 1) a reconstruction of patients' dominant interpersonal schemas; 2) evaluation of their metacognitive skill levels; with a view to 3) working consistently in accordance with a rigorous decision-making procedure that should be applied throughout their therapy.

The procedural component of interpersonal schemas

A schema is not only a set of conscious ideas about oneself and others, but a set of procedures, automatisms, which the body has recorded during development and growing up and which get reactivated in specific conditions (Critchfield et al., 2019; Ecker et al., 2012). A classic example is the triggering of dysfunctional attachment patterns. What happens? A child feels fear. It goes looking immediately for its protective figure for attention. Let us hypothesise that the attachment figure reacts with a mixture of criticism and disinterest. The child is left in a state of negative activation, its fear persists and this is joined by distress connected to being rejected and criticised. On a cognitive level we might say that this is the basis for a representation of the self as not lovable and worthless vis-à-vis an unavailable and severe other.

However, in a development context like this, the child may not develop adequate metacognitive skills for describing so clearly its ideas about self and others. Its body instead maintains traces of the recurrent interactive sequence (Stern, 1985). As an adult the same person might find herself in a state of fear and weakness. Attachment gets activated. Automatisms make her avoid seeking help because the implicit forecast, the habit learnt, is that if the other sees her to be weak, she will reject or criticise her. Her uneasiness, however, manifests itself in non-mentalised forms, like anxiety with unclear causes or somatisations. She seeks help elusively, without supplying any psychological elements to the other. She might ask a friend to have a drink or take drugs together. Alternatively she might try to calm down using physical exercise or ask her doctor to cure what she thinks is a medical condition. In interpersonal relationships she seeks closeness but does not display any vulnerability. She denies needing help while protesting about being neglected.

To summarise, some patients are, or are likely to become, aware of their interpersonal schemas; others are instead driven by relational procedures without being aware of them. In the following example we show that only after mobilising the patient's body did the therapist obtain information with which he could accurately formulate the former's interpersonal schema.

Francesco was a 35-year-old martial arts instructor, with Narcissistic PD. He came for therapy because he was depressed about his girlfriend leaving him. Right from the start, Francesco was puzzled: "Now I feel awful but up to one month ago, before she disclosed her wish to end our relationship, I didn't care that much about her. I despised some things about her and moreover I was very often unfaithful to her without thinking twice about it." Francesco acknowledged he felt sad and melancholy about losing her and angry because he believed himself the victim of a decision by his girlfriend. He was aware of another paradox: he knew that getting back together again with his girlfriend would placate him but was what he wanted. But then why was he so angry? The therapist explored specific narrative episodes to make Francesco capable of describing what he felt and thought immediately before getting angry.

F: "I feel I'm being bullied in these situations".
T: "What do you feel when you're subject to bullying by someone preventing you from getting what you want? Before anger, I mean."
F: "Anger. I don't feel anything else. Anger because they're not allowed. . . . I'm a peaceful type but, if someone acts like a bully, I certainly don't back off."

Francesco switched to his coping reaction and readily recalled situations where he reacted bravely to physical aggression. He was not able, however, to pinpoint the sense of fragility one experiences when undergoing bullying or aggression, which then triggers anger.

The therapist therefore decided to use an "enactment" (Chapter 6), with which to reactivate Francesco's on-the-spot reactions to bullying. The therapist pointed to Francesco's mobile lying on the desk.

T: "Can you imagine that this mobile is of extreme importance to you and you wouldn't do without it not for anything in the world?"
F: "Yes."
T: "Good. Now try to grasp it."

Francesco stretched out his hand towards the desk but the therapist stopped him in a firm manner. Francesco was surprised.

T: "Do it again. Try and pick it up."

Francesco went to take it again and the therapist stopped him. Francesco went red, his neck swelled and he clenched his jaw.

T: "Francesco, I can see your anger. Can you tell me what you felt while I was blocking your hand?"
F: "I felt like an idiot..."
T: "What feeling is that?"
F: "Debased, disgraced, subjugated."
T: "Hmm, subjugated... something like humiliated?"
F: "Yes, humiliated."
T: "So when you undergo some bullying, this triggers a subjugated and humiliated self-image. Only afterwards, does the angry-type protective reaction, making you feel on the contrary strong and combative, start. What does this make you think?"
F: "... I've always felt like that!"

Francesco was struck by this insight. He had arranged his life with the aim of escaping from this feeling of powerlessness. Now he redefined martial arts and other risky behaviours as self-tests, attempts to feel stronger and more protected. He could recall memories where he was small and puny and the others humiliated him. It was now easier to see how his ex's decision to dump him had made him angry. He had interpreted it as bullying, consistent with the competition schema: he had had to give up something to comply with an outside will. He had felt powerless, vulnerable and humiliated, all feelings he was previously unaware of.

Summarising, clinicians can spend a lot of time working on patients' conscious attributions and trying to modify them, but the component connected to fluctuations in arousal, and to implicit, procedural cognition, intrinsically tied to emotions and bodily states, can remain untouched by such interventions.

The body produces ideas about the world while trying to achieve goals, so we aim at changing action patterns. We have two objectives in this respect. The first is exploratory: activating a patient's body so as to render him capable of grasping what type of meanings he attributes when in particular somatic and affective situations. It is a question here of improving self-reflectivity and the links among cognitions, affects and somatic states: "Try and plan yourself a holiday instead of giving up at the start because you feel guilty, and then tell me how you feel." The second is to modify bodily sensations in order to generate a change in core experience. It is a question therefore of changing behaviour, imagined or actual, so as to change idea.

We shall be describing how to act directly on an emotional and somatic level, so that patients make the most of their emotional skills to influence their cognitive processes. With the range of techniques we propose here we do not intend to replace those traditionally used in cognitive therapies and MIT in particular. The aim is to enrich therapists' repertoires by adding tools using mainly the bottom-up change route, so as to have an impact when the conversational component of treatment turns out to be ineffective.

How to work on body and imagination? A list of techniques

We consider here the techniques we use more than others in our clinical work because we attempt to master them and have experience of them. If readers are familiar with other tools, we leave it to them to adapt them to their interventions, although it should be clear that each of the following is to be chosen and applied in accordance with the procedure described in Chapter 4.

1   *Guided imagery and rescripting.* This consists in reliving a problematic or traumatic situation and working through it differently. One can get patients to both relive memories and imagine future situations where they would not know how to conduct themselves. The latter becomes a sort of imagery exposure if it is a question of envisaging how to tackle feared situations, or a true and proper creative exercise if it is a question of inventing ways to relate in wished-for situations.
2   *Drama techniques: two-chair, role playing, enactment.* Rooted in Moreno's psychodrama and Gestalt therapy (Perls, Hefferline, & Goodman, 1951), these have been modified and adopted by various orientations, for example, Schema-Therapy (Arntz & Van Genderen, 2011). Two-chair technique is the tool of choice in Emotion-Focused Therapy (Greenberg, 2002).

    During role-playing, a patient's problematic scene, or one where he could behave innovatively, gets acted out during a session. In individual therapy patient and therapist adopt the two roles (self and significant other). In couple therapy patients can re-enact a difficult moment and then exchange roles. In a group (Chapter 10) it is possible to stage situations involving a larger number of persons. Role-playing is very good at improving theory of the other's mind

80 *Use of imagery and bodily techniques*

and mastery, but we always try to improve self-reflectivity first; in particular we hope for the patients to acknowledge parts of their functioning they was previously unaware of. Two-chair and role-playing overlap substantially. We use two-chair more often for working through past experiences in a new way and giving them new meanings. We use role-playing more frequently for anticipating social situations where patients can try to behave innovatively, often before behavioural exploration in real life.

3   *Bodily work.* We adopt exercises with Gestalt, bioenergetic and sensory-motor origins: *grounding*, breath regulation, physical training, martial arts or yoga so as to increase wellbeing, reduce psychological suffering and improve emotional and behavioural regulation and access positive self-images. Bodily-focused practices help in fostering a metacognitive awareness of the somatic aspects linked to negative self-images, for example, how a certain bodily state indicates that one feels vulnerable. At the change promotion stage, we use them to experience physical states involving strength, energy and so break maladaptive interpersonal patterns.

4   *Exploration and behavioural activation.* At early therapy stages we use even very simple behavioural experiments as a tool for what we call *dynamic assessment* (Chapter 4) with a view to improving patients' comprehension of their cognitive-affective processes if they are unable to identify them solely through self-observation. At the same time behavioural activation and small experiments should improve patients' agency so that they immediately see therapy as a place where they have a causal role in change, instead of depending solely on the skills of the therapist.

The behavioural component is also one of the core aspects in promoting change in many ways. When patients tackle feared situations, try to act in daily life in line with their wishes and to develop their healthy self-parts, and understand what they want and feel entitled to it, they have no fear of acting but do not have the tools.

5   *Mindfulness and attention regulation.* We use mindfulness for various ends, from increasing self-knowledge to fostering the seeds of differentiation, that is, acknowledging one's thoughts are ideas more than facts. Mindfulness strengthens agency: a subject grasps that he is not a victim of his own thoughts but can influence the flow of consciousness. It improves self-regulation too. In addition to the classic mindfulness, we have developed Metacognitive Interpersonal Mindfulness-Based Training (MIMBT; Ottavi et al., 2016, 2019) aimed at fostering differentiation as regards one's maladaptive interpersonal schemas. We also use attention regulation techniques, to deal with intrusive thoughts and images sustaining both symptoms and dysfunctional relationships.

6   MIT-Group. We describe a short-term group protocol, MIT-G (Popolo et al., 2018, 2019), a mixed 16-session psychoeducational-experiential format, where therapists first supply patients with information on the various interpersonal motives driving human behaviour (Chapter 1) and then ask them

to first narrate some problematic relational episodes regarding these systems and then enact them through role-playing.

The objectives of involving imagination and body

Mobilising a patient's imagination and body, in therapy and in daily life, is aimed at generating numerous effects:

1   *Improve metacognitive monitoring.* With patients who have difficulty feeling emotional activation we want to *increase arousal* and lead them to *experience more vivid emotions* and *access affects* they did not perceive before. Simultaneously, if patients are hyper-aroused, they are likely to be confused by what they feel, are overwhelmed by it and are incapable of regulating their behaviour. The goal should therefore be to tone arousal down, so that patients can see their inner states more clearly and achieve the calm necessary for undertaking other therapeutic operations.
2   *Increase agency.* During, for example, an imagery or mindfulness exercise or a behavioural experiment, a patient might find she has the power to modify her mental state, rather than passively responding to environmental stimuli or be overwhelmed by affects.
3   *Differentiate.* That is, discover that one's ideas do not correspond to reality. Before an imagery exercise a patient might think he was incapable of speaking before an audience. After a guided imagery exercise and rescripting or a two-chair game, where he maybe replies firmly to a parent criticising him, he finds he has some difficulty but knows how to express himself. Before a meditation a patient might think she will be gripped forever by anxiety. This indicates poor differentiation – "I believe I'm going to suffer forever and I can't see any alternatives" – and low mastery: "I'm powerless when faced with suffering." After meditation she discovers that the mind has the power to switch to mental states including wellbeing.
4   *Foster access to healthy self-parts.* This is an aspect where the role of the procedures we describe is decisive. Patients with difficulty feeling a sense of effectiveness benefit from contexts where the body is involved: yoga, martial arts, dance, playing an instrument and so on. The sense of effectiveness can increase with two-chair technique or role-playing: a patient might be convinced that she does not know how to reply to her tyrant husband or constrictive mother. As she plays, her fear or guilt begin to be joined by sensations like strength, greater awareness of her goals and willingness to pursue them. The patient might consider herself incapable but during guided imagery she contacts moments where a competent core self-image surfaces and the clinician sustains it.
5   *Increase mastery.* During role-playing, guided imagery and behavioural experiments patients discover new ways to tackle events. Mindfulness and physical exercise bring benefits in those aspects of mastery corresponding to

emotional regulation: at moments of intense activation physical exercise can placate the tension; out-of-control fear of being humiliated can diminish with work on a patient's body where the latter experiences a more positive feeling and realises that when his sense of vulnerability diminishes so does his fear that the other will crush him.

6   *Understanding others' mind.* MIT therapists should strictly not try to improve theory of mind or focus therapy on helping patients to better understand others, if certain preconditions, that is differentiation and access to healthy parts, have not been previously complied with. Only in the therapeutic relationship, using metacommunication, should a therapist encourage patients to consider what the former thinks and feels about them. However, once the preconditions are complied with, we promote a richer, comprehensive and decentred understanding of the others. Role-playing and the two-chair game are particularly useful. In guided imagery patients may notice new aspects in the expressions and behaviour of the others. They discover, for example, that behind another's anger there was fear and behind passivity a sense of powerlessness.

We will describe how to deliver these techniques depending on a patient's functioning level in a specific session. The questions to ask first are: under what conditions should an imagery or bodily technique be applied and with what goals? Before proposing any technique, therapists assess: 1) the state of the therapeutic relationship and the interpersonal schemas active at the moment of the proposal; 2) whatever emotional regulation skills and metacognitive skills a patient possesses at that moment. In the next paragraph we explain if and when to use a technique.

Preconditions for the use of a technique

Involving a patient in a behavioural experiment or asking him to imagine a problematic, and sometimes traumatic, scene or to expose himself to a new situation inevitably activates arousal. Some therapists find this process natural and handle it with a certain ease, but others are frightened. Asking a patient to imagine pain-provoking situations triggers intense emotions in a therapist or a sense of dismay, with sometimes fantasising about catastrophes: "What if the patient becomes dysregulated? Will I be up to handling her reactions? What if, once the exercise is over, he's worse and goes home without any tools for calming down? Will I harm him? Will I trigger too much suffering? Will she drop out?"

We have all asked ourselves these questions. The reply could be to use caution or wait for the right moment. True, but clinicians are more likely to be wrong for doing too little than for doing too much. They do not involve patients in tasks that would be beneficial and for which they would be ready. The real problem to be overcome is usually an excess of prudence. Let us be clear: this paragraph is devoted to the precautions to be used and to how to assess with the utmost precision when and how to propose a technique. But the principle: "one can dare" is at the heart of this book.

The problem is not *when* to apply a technique but "at this moment is it useful, possible and sensible to take such a step?" It can be premature to ask a patient to carry out a behavioural experiment after three years of therapy, just as it can be very profitable to do it ten minutes from the start of his first session. The problem is not time, but checking that preconditions are complied with. If they are, one can proceed and not doing so means delaying the introduction of an effective treatment element. If they are not, it is necessary to wait and hold back the impulse to push a patient towards a wellbeing, whose achievement is premature. Let us now analyse three aspects that we should assess before deciding to adopt a technique.

Therapeutic relationship and active schemas

Proposing any technique whatsoever has an impact on a patient. Emotions get mobilised and the patient sees his therapist in a different light. Understanding what type of light it is proves fundamental before going on; it is a question of quickly assessing what type of schemas get activated in the therapeutic relationship as a result of the proposal. Some of these need to be tackled before starting a particular therapeutic activity. Patients' reactions can cover the entire spectrum of relational patterns, so that we do not discuss them systematically but limit ourselves to supplying a selection of the examples with the greatest clinical importance.

There can be an increase in confidence and hope, and a feeling that therapy can be effective. She can also feel that she herself has control over symptoms and relational problems. Feelings like curiosity, interest, sometimes enjoyment, can appear. Right from the start the patient grasps that the relationship is cooperative and the exploration motive gets activated. A playful and creative atmosphere arises. These are positive prognostic signals.

Frequently, however, the first reaction is anxiety; the technique proposed leads to a greater contact with feared and hitherto avoided, behaviourally and cognitively, aspects of experience. As a result, patients are likely to construct the therapist as pushy or dangerous and to tend to withdraw. Nothing that ought to surprise a therapist or dissuade him from proposing the use of a technique.

Because of possible negative reactions, many therapists are reluctant about introducing the use of imagery and bodily techniques in sessions. We consider this prudent attitude for the most part unmotivated and an obstacle to rapid progress or a successful treatment outcome.

Of course we do not want that psychotherapy makes patients suffer! We carefully and skilfully expose them to a distress they can learn to control and overcome, while moving with hope towards the achievement of goals rendering their lives richer, gratifying and meaningful. A therapist can thus feel authorised to suggest experiments triggering negative arousal.

Caution needs to be exercised during the immediately subsequent step. Once a proposal has been made, therapists pay the utmost attention to the patients' feedback and make as much room as possible for their negative reactions. Let us take the example of interpersonal behavioural experiments. First a list of feared situations is drawn up. The therapist then asks the patient to assess them in terms of the intensity of the fear and to start with the safest one. The therapist explains that success is composed not of a successful exposure, but of attempting and then reflecting on one's reactions to the experience, in order to achieve a richer understanding of one's inner world. At this point the exposure can be planned anew. In the next session outcomes of the experiment are discussed. As a result, the patient will no longer construct the therapist as constrictive or threatening but as his equal, or a benevolent guide, who helps to cross unknown but potentially fertile territories.

Just as we are firm in asking therapists to propose using these techniques, so we are in asserting that they should be ready to give up if a patient does not consider it useful or safe. Insisting would violate one of the basic MIT principles: any action needs to be negotiated and agreed on. If there is no contract or agreement on tasks and goals, therapists cannot move further, no matter how clever their ideas and plans for promoting health appear. If, for example a patient refuses to relive an episode during guided imagery, the therapist should stop and discuss the reasons for this refusal.

The schemas that get triggered when a therapist proposes an imagery or somatic intervention can concern the therapeutic relationship. The patient can construct the therapist proposing a technique consistently with her interpersonal schema: "He's forcing me. He's not interested in what I'm saying. He wants to get me to change because he wants to be rid of me." Moreover, patients asked to perform a behavioural exposure or a somatic exercise could imagine themselves as being inept and incapable vis-à-vis a critical other, even if they see the therapist as benevolent and welcoming.

Frequently, social rank is triggered. Patients see themselves launched towards doing something new, difficult and challenging, and consequently feel ridiculous, incapable and inferior in both their own eyes and the therapist's. At this point, before continuing, the therapist works on repairing the relational rupture (Dimaggio, Montano et al., 2015; Safran & Muran, 2000).

Therapists should focus especially on understanding whether patients are ascribing judgemental or critical intentions or a lack of attention to them. The work on the relationship continues until the patient feels her fears do not correspond to the idea the therapist has of her, that is, that she feels judged but the therapist does not have a negative idea of her. Only at this point is it possible to perform the technique.

In reality it is enough, and more frequent, for a patient to come to doubt: she rationally realises that the therapist is not judging her, but feels judged all the same. At this point it can be useful to momentarily interrupt the work on the technique and ask the patient to recall some associated memories: "So at this moment you feel the need to feel appreciated, but imagine I'm criticising you and consequently you feel like someone worthless in my eyes and it's natural you feel embarrassed. However, you realise that I don't have a negative idea of you, you told me you can see that I'm confident you're up to it. So it's likely that the activation of this fear of judgement, this collapse in your hope of being appreciated, is something you learnt. Can you think of any similar situations?" The moment when the patient recalls memories and finds himself facing core memories again, is when the alliance rupture gets repaired, and it is possible to go back to applying the technique.

Patients often interpret the therapeutic task as a performance to be conducted skilfully, and do not feel up to it. The therapist points out that a schema related to social rank is active. She should then ask the patient to nevertheless attempt the exercise while noticing what affects emerge and with what force the ideas about incapability get activated while carrying it out. This preliminary work is often enough for the patient to accept the exercise.

If the emotions triggered are intense and in the heat of the moment the patient loses his ability to differentiate, that is, at that moment he is not confronting a schema but something that appears real to him, it is opportune to ask again about associated memories. This helps in understanding how much the ghosts of the figures in the patient's history are forcing him to see things only from the perspective of his pathogenic schema.

A patient might realise: "Crikey, I'm looking at myself again with the inflexible eyes of my grandmother when at the weekends she forced me to stay sitting all day in my room doing my homework and reproached me for the slightest mistake." At an advanced stage a therapist can himself recall previous situations where this schema got activated but the patient was capable of tackling it.

The rank motive gets superimposed on the activation of the exploration motive with the idea that the other is obstructing one's autonomy. A patient interprets the therapist's proposal as an order. We would repeat that dominance/submission and autonomy/constriction schemas get activated. Patients see the therapist as an expert who wants to make decisions for them over their heads or someone enamoured of the techniques and manuals to which he gives precedence over them, without being interested in or respecting their point of view. These are schemas likely to get activated with Narcissistic, Paranoid, Passive-aggressive, Avoidant and Obsessive-compulsive PDs.

The therapist should be mindful of the active schemas and show himself ready to give up using the technique. Showing the patient that the technique is not being imposed but proposed, with the choice being made jointly, after a discussion of its rationale and cost/benefits, makes it easier to overcome the rupture. Even if on the spot the patient refuses, the therapist should not resign himself. He should always bear in mind how beneficial the action repertoire he proposes is and how much it will facilitate or accelerate change. There will therefore be a second chance to propose other techniques and again explore the patient's reaction. It goes without saying that, if the work on the relationship rupture is successful, the patient is likely to accept the proposal in that same session.

Respecting a patient's independence does not, however, mean doing without negotiation and especially the idea that a therapy is effective only if there is co-operation in achieving goals. When, in particular, patients with passive-aggressive features repeatedly reject attempts to propose techniques, therapists should adopt a position we term *active impotence* (Dimaggio, Montano et al., 2015) and disclose that at that moment they do not know how to proceed.

Therapists should explain that in therapy there is a means–ends relationship and that without certain activities, for example behavioural exposure, there will be little or no success. It is fundamental for therapists to explain this after modulating their own reactions of frustration, incompetence and judgemental anger. At the same time, therapists should clarify they do not intend forsaking the patient or showing less interest in the job, but simply cannot guarantee improvement. This position is to be maintained patiently and firmly until patients wilfully decide to engage in some extra-session activities or use tools like mindfulness or guided imagery during sessions.

Proposing a technique means attempting to mobilise the exploration system. Activation of this system often involves first shutting down attachment. In simple terms children explore whether it is certain that when they return their attachment figures will be present and ready to welcome then (Bowlby, 1988). When faced with the idea that therapy implies they are active, some patients, especially with Dependent and Borderline PD, fear being forsaken or neglected, with the therapist wanting to rapidly solve the problem and then get rid of them.

These schemas are often a feature of *dismissing* attachment histories: the caregiver responded irritatedly and hurriedly to a child's distress signals and immediately proposed solutions. The child had a sense that the caregiver did not sincerely want to make him feel better: "Daddy wants me to get out of his hair and stop bothering him."

In these cases, persisting with proposing the use of techniques is often a mistake, a sign that the therapist is in a hurry. The therapist should carefully explore which schemas are activated in the relationship and validate them. Patients who felt chronically invalidated when they displayed their suffering hold the healthy wish the therapist listens to their distress and take it seriously, almost without doing anything to solve it. The therapist can interpret this request as a complaint and consider it a problem to be rapidly solved. If, however, the patient's history suggests the therapist maintain a mainly listening and validation stance, the latter should do this but explain the reasons why he will limit himself to taking the distress seriously and accepting it, while not insisting on operations directed towards overcoming it.

Therapists need to continuously re-evaluate this framework and, at a certain point, adopt a position sounding like this:

> I've realised that for you it's important for me to listen to your distress and be close to you. It's what we've been doing together the last few months and here I am, ready to carry on in the coming ones too. However, we need to know that if we keep this way, your suffering won't heal: we are not using the appropriate instruments. We need to decide, together and consciously, and I'll be on your side whatever your choice is. We can avoid taking steps towards change; you'll feel your distress being accepted but the symptoms and problems will stay. Alternatively you can opt for change and getting better, but in this case you'll have to face a bit of distress and overcome some diffidence, so that you

accept some of my suggestions, for example imagery exposure, facing feared situations in-between sessions or doing mindfulness exercises.

If a patient is on the border between attachment and group belonging or caretaking motives – for example looking after parents seen as weak – giving his therapy a more active gait can unleash conflicts of loyalty. The patient, with the therapist's support, envisages carrying out new activities consistent with his wishes connected to autonomous exploration and never put into practice. She considers traveling, enrolling at a university a long way from her birthplace or starting on a music or gym course. At that moment she will think about her significant others' reaction and imagine them rebuking her for her choice and consequently forsaking her or excluding her from the group. She can even picture them suffering. A Dependent PD patient starts fantasising about enrolling at a gym. She gets as far as the reception but is then overcome by images of her partner complaining because he feels neglected, and pouting at her and giving her the cold shoulder. A mixture of sense of guilt for the distress caused and fear of being forsaken throws her into confusion that leads her to forget why she had got as far as the gym entrance.

This patient's reaction would not be a reason for not agreeing on an exploration task with her. Simply state that the aim of this task was to bring to light her maladaptive schemas in all their power, in order to be able to effectively thwart them in the future and not allow them to proliferate in the shadow of her avoidance mechanisms.

The sequence in steps is therefore:

1. Assessment of the state of the relationship and alliance. Are patients constructing the therapist in accordance with their schema? Are there interpersonal cycles active in session? Is there a contractual agreement on goals and tasks? If the reply to these questions is affirmative, one passes on to the following step.
2. Proposal of the technique.
3. Monitoring of both the patient's response to the proposal, and to what happens while carrying out of the technique as regards the therapist. If there are alliance problems, one passes on to the next step.
4. Repairing the rupture and, if necessary, returning to associated memories: "What does what happened with me while you were doing the exercise remind you of?"

Promote emotion regulation

Certain patients can get extremely aroused during sessions. Before applying a technique, arousal needs to be optimally regulated. This can occur through a modulation of the therapeutic relationship. Another strategy is to start with bodily and attention techniques (Chapters 7 and 9) – *grounding* and mindful breathing are examples – until patients recover the ability to look at themselves lucidly and not get overwhelmed by emotion. Therapists should also use the same strategies and techniques, as we shall see in the individual chapters, to regulate arousal with patients getting dysregulated during exercises.

Technique goals as therapy proceeds: progressive improvement of metacognition and access to healthy self-parts

The same technique can be applied with various goals, depending on the different motives, the interpersonal schemas being worked on and the current level of metacognitive skills. A common goal is the activation of the exploration system in the *pretend play* mode. A clinician should propose a technique to try and lead the patient to a stance of curiosity and discovery, with the intention that this mental state take control over distress, anger, shame and so on. Some operations, like role-play, two-chairs and guided imagery, activate the pretend play mode by definition. Here the mind develops relational capacities to the fullest, to the extent that children spending more time doing pretend play display better social adaptation (Lillard et al., 2013). Pretend play is among the mental operations promoting emotional (Jent, Niec, & Baker, 2011) and language (Orr & Geva, 2015) development, cognitive flexibility and creativity (Russ, 2014). It is consequently plausible that reactivating the "as if" mode can put patients' minds in a functioning mode suited to promoting the creation of new perspectives about self and others in a well-regulated atmosphere.

Many schemas ends up shutting down the exploration system. Narcissistic, Dependent, Passive-Aggressive or Avoidant PD patients are driven by the wish to be independent but are faced with the *other* response as *hurt* or *forsaken*, or *critical*, *pessimistic* or *paralysing*. The self's response is to feel obstructed, frustrated, angry and powerless. If patients think the other is suffering, they get gripped by sorrow or guilt and this turns off exploration while it activates caregiving. The same *other* response, for example a resentful and offended closing up, gives patients the idea that, if they persist in their desire for independence, they will lose the other's comforting presence. Feelings of being forsaken, lonely, despondent and frightened about not being up to it, all of them correlated to the activation of attachment, consequently get activated and patients give up. Finally, if patients imagine a critical other, the social rank motive in the defeat and inferiority sub-routine is likely to get activated. Feelings of unworthiness and shame surface, and self-efficacy and self-esteem collapse. This shift undermines exploration too.

In short, the common outcome for the shift towards other motives, generated by problematic responses from the other, is the switching off of the exploration system. Moreover, patients are likely to feel confused about what they are experiencing and to cast doubt on the value of their desires, sometimes no longer realising whether they really had these intentions.

When faced with such problems, a therapist should evoke associated memories to reconstruct how they learnt to inhibit exploration. Once in contact with past memories, therapists can adopt guided imagery with rescripting or drama techniques. This way, patients can manage to overcome feelings of guilt, anxiety or shame while remaking contact with curiosity, enthusiasm and desire to carry out a particular activity.

If patients have difficulty recalling memories – often because their life history has left traces only on a procedural level and not in the form of conscious core memories – or else are against spending time stirring up the past, therapists should try in session to modulate problematic feelings such guilt, anxiety and shame, blocking exploration in the present. Therapists should then try to promote access to healthy parts, either during sessions with bodily work, or by planning behavioural experiments and analysing week after week the narrative episodes occurring around them. This should continue until patients have remade contact with their wish to tackle the world with new tools.

We shall now describe the way the technique goals change as patients' metacognitive abilities to describe mental states, take a critical distance from their schemas and master them, progress. The goals are as follows: 1) improving basic self-reflectivity, activating or modulating arousal; 2) promoting agency; 3) improving differentiation; 4) accessing healthy parts; 5) promoting mastery; 6) improving understanding of the other's mind. Naturally the same experience can affect several variables but we list them separately both to demonstrate in what order a clinician should aim to act, and also to ensure conceptual clarity.

Improving basic self-reflectivity: accessing thoughts and emotions and relation among variables, from dynamic assessment to the course of therapy

The first goal we pursue involving patients in bodily and imagery work is to improve self-reflectivity. In early sessions many patients with PD, eating disorders, Obsessive-Compulsive Disorder and Post-Traumatic Stress Disorder have difficulty describing their inner experiences. A clinician may gather narrative episodes but psychological elements may not surface clearly.

Patients may have difficulty replying to questions such as "What did you feel when your boyfriend was lying on the sofa channel surfing and you were eating one hazelnut after another?", "How did you feel when your mother was checking all the windows to look for burglars?", "What pushed you to drink during your friend's wedding?"

To get the information necessary for case formulation, clinicians can even very early on propose many different types of work. Sometimes, if the therapeutic relationship is good and patients accept the proposal, it is possible to start from the first or very early sessions. We name it *dynamic assessment* (Chapter 4). Therapists for example propose behavioural experiments, practicing simple mindfulness exercises, using guided imagery. The goal of these exercises is to create an action and reflection context facilitating access to inner experience.

We would recall that, according to embodied cognition principles, humans get to know the world by interacting with it, attempting to achieve goals and relating with people and objects. Gaining knowledge on inner states only on the basis of dialogue can thus be insufficient, because the body and mind are more likely to generate ideas and emotions in the natural context for which they are designed: acting. Whatever the exercise proposed during assessment, a patient will have to confront avoidance and automatisms, but while trying to counteract them! This is likely to trigger thoughts and emotions that at this point are available to the therapist and patient for a shared formulation of functioning. The aim of dynamic assessment is not to promote premature change but to create an action context where patients are asked to reflect proactively on what happens inside them in particular contexts and on how they interpret events. We now depict a moment from a dynamic assessment where guided imagery led to important information.

Thorsten was a Norwegian patient, followed by a local MIT therapist, and suffered from apathy and mild depression. He felt there was no momentum in his life, with the days passing monotonously. He worked as a manager in a firm of which he was the owner, but was dissatisfied by his work. He felt sluggish and incapable of reacting, and considered himself immature because he was wasting his time. Comparing himself with other colleagues, he saw them as more satisfied, happy and successful. In comparison he felt small and inferior. He experienced moments of satisfaction only when problem-solving for others, things his clients did not think about on their own. For a few minutes he would feel clever and competent and capable of helping others but this sensation did not last. Thorsten suffered from covert narcissism and had depressive personality traits. The idea of not being in control of one's actions is a typical sign of lack of agency. At the start of his assessment session he did not know how to describe his inner states beyond his feelings of emptiness and apathy and a sense of powerlessness. As a result of the therapist's questions, he recalled that this sense of not being in control was rooted in his relationship with his mother. He talked about how she decided everything for him and there was no room for any disagreement, at the risk of being considered stupid. At the time Thorsten tended to comply with his mother's opinion: thinking about being a musician or pilot, the real desires of his youth, led him to believe he was an idiot.

The therapist decided to explore the inner states preceding Thorsten's self-criticism and consequent paralysis. He asked him to recall an episode where his mother criticised him. Thorsten closed his eyes but had difficulty recalling a detailed episode. However he managed to visualise his mother's face. The therapist asked him: "Can you describe it to me? What can you see?" Thorsten's reply was revealing: "Her face seems kind but her eyes are stiff and her mouth rigid." "What is your mother doing at this moment?" "She's not looking at me." The therapist picked up the importance of the observation: "How do you feel at this moment?" "Sad. As if I didn't count for anything."

As a result of this exercise it was possible to quickly see that Thorsten had two dominant schemas. The first arose from the wish to be appreciated (*rank*) with the idea that the other was better, more powerful (*mother and colleagues*) and critical (*mother*). At the same time attachment was activated with the idea that the other was distant, cold and unavailable. This second schema emerged

Use of imagery and bodily techniques 91

thanks to guided imagery and made it possible to pinpoint the self's response to the other's response, which was of loneliness, despondency and a feeling of being not lovable. Thorsten accepted this exercise gratefully, because it made it possible for him to discover feelings he had not thought about for some time.

We would recall that MIT is not a therapy model with stages. Each session starts by evaluating which interpersonal schemas are active and what current metacognitive skills are, and then by trying to regulate the therapeutic relationship appropriately and stimulating the immediately higher level of metacognition. Given this, if a patient has difficulty identifying thoughts and emotions and establishing links among events, ideas, emotions, behaviour and symptoms, the aim of the various techniques should be to promote self-reflectivity, whether this occurs in the first 10 minutes of the assessment session or after three years of therapy.

To stimulate access to mental states, mindfulness and interoceptive attention exercises are very useful, often in combination with guided imagery and drama techniques. As we showed in Thorsten's example, guided imagery, here of an informal type (Chapter 5), almost systematically generates new information, especially about affects and their causes. Behavioural exposure, both during sessions and between one and another, also has this ability. Exposure operations can be the only ones able to stimulate self-reflectivity where there is a co-occurrence of PD and symptomatic disorders. In such cases the stimulation of metacognition can start with behavioural exposure centred on the symptom.

Saverio was 55 years old and suffered from Obsessive-Compulsive PD. He asked for therapy for panic attacks, which had led him to avoiding using his car. His initial fear was to lose control of it on a viaduct and fall into the void. From then on he avoided roads with bridges, but the avoidance spread as far as stopping him from crossing bridges on foot. During his assessment session he had difficulty describing his emotions and using the term anxiety, which was evident in his nonverbal communication. With difficulty the therapist managed to get him to identify it, but it remained impossible for him to grasp what event or condition was triggering it and what degrees of intensity it reached in various contexts. Saverio clearly felt awkward and closed up when faced with the therapist's questions. The conversation proved to be unproductive. The therapist first explored whether Saverio had difficulty talking with him, given his visible awkwardness, but Saverio said no. The therapist then revealed he had difficulty grasping how Saverio's anxiety worked and proposed a behavioural experiment to understand this better together.

The room where the session took place had two windows filling up the outside wall and in front of them the floor was raised. The therapist suggested him to gradually approach a window and monitor and describe out loud his level of anxiety. Saverio could pinpoint when his anxiety started to rise: near the window he got to 7 on a scale from 1 to 10. He said he would not be capable of getting up on the raised section. The therapist asked him if he felt up to putting just one foot on it while holding onto the frame of the window, which at that moment was open, with one hand. Saverio hesitated but tried and realised that his anxiety had increased to 9. The therapist asked him to stay a bit longer in this position and suggested he do a few simple mindful breathing exercises. His anxiety fell progressively to 6, a level Saverio said he found tolerable.

Right at that moment, without realising it, Saverio got down from the step! The therapist took the opportunity to point out that this was an avoidance mechanism: his anxiety was low but his body nevertheless moved away from the danger. Thanks to this exercise, Saverio's emotional and cognitive monitoring improved and the therapist could tackle panic attacks. After only a few sessions Saverio had already started driving again and after a month he began crossing bridges.

To improve the first levels of self-reflectivity, awareness of thoughts, emotions and event–thought–emotion–behaviour links, is an MIT goal throughout therapy. The ongoing prime objective of the work described in this book is to boost it. With some patients it is a question of promoting basic emotional and cognitive awareness, when, for example, they have difficulty describing what they feel or what thought stirred them towards a particular behaviour.

When metacognition grows, and patients become capable of, for example, saying: "I was angry because as usual my sister left me loads of things to do and couldn't care less", or else "I feel anxious because I've got to hold a lesson with a class and I don't feel sufficiently prepared to be able to face their testing standards", goals become more complex. In such cases clinicians should aim to stimulate access to distressing emotions that are more difficult to pinpoint: guilt or those linked to mourning. At the same time they help patients to see any emotions and thoughts linked to positive self-images. In the autobiographical episodes patients relate, either spontaneously or after being asked by their clinician, elements correlated to pathogenic interpersonal schemas are likely to surface, but there is not what a clinician needs for an adequately precise schema formulation.

Here is an example involving Alessia, suffering from Dependent PD with obsessive-compulsive personality traits. In session 1 she related a memory associated with recent situations where she was criticised, occurring when she was 10 years old.

> "I had to take part in the school play. My mother had given me some money and a little jacket to use for my part. When the play was over I realised someone had stolen it. When my mother turned up I was in despair. I told her everything and she replied that I was an idiot and I deserved it." When the therapist asked her what she felt, Alessia replied: "Angry. I can feel the anger welling up now too. Mummy shouldn't have reacted like that. It wasn't fair."

On the basis of this first version the therapist thought that she was frightened and driven by the attachment motive, and that anger was a protest at being left alone in a difficult situation. However, Alessia displayed signs of restlessness and said she felt confused. There was something she could not manage to say and she started to ruminate: "Perhaps I deserved the punishment. Perhaps I'm wrong to take it out on my mother." The therapist suggested a guided imagery exercise to help Alessia to better distinguish what she felt. Alessia accepted and went back to the school corridors after the play. To the therapist's surprise, she did not talk about her fear about being robbed but about going up to her mummy and being afraid of the latter's judgement: "I'm petrified by what she'll say. I feel my legs trembling." In the guided imagery she asks in tears for help, saying: "Mummy, I didn't mean to do it." Her expression changed, which prompted the therapist to ask her: "What do you feel now towards your mummy?" "I feel sad. I've disappointed her." "Anything else?" "Yes, I'm ashamed because I shouldn't have made a mistake."

As a result of the information acquired during the guided imagery, Alessia's inner world became clearer to the therapist: right from the beginning Alessia was searching for confirmation of her self-worth (rank). She found herself faced with a critical and disparaging other and consequently experienced feelings of dejection and shame, both consistent with the motivational system under way. The despair she reported at the start was anxiety about a feared judgement, and it emerged that her dejection was due to failure and not to being forsaken. At the same time Alessia depicted herself as worthy and deserving approval, and, when faced with her mother's mercilessness she considered her unfair.

Improving differentiation

Patients have difficulty grasping that a significant part of their ideas about themselves, others and interpersonal relationships are the fruit of often automatic interpretations which they are unaware of. Making it possible to see the difference between readings of events and reality is the keystone of therapeutic change. All the techniques described here have an important role in promoting this step.

Many patients, when faced with criticism, consider that observations directed at them have a disdainful tone or are likely to feel threatened. How to help them differentiate? Two-chairs can, for example, get them to grasp that they are capable of replying firmly to a comment they feel unfair, differentiating therefore about their conviction about being inferior and incapable of reacting. They can also feel a greater sense of efficacy, contrary to their belief about being chronically impotent and powerless.

Meditation can be important as regards ideas of not being able to master one's emotions. When faced with intense distress, patients can be convinced they are unable to calm down. Breathing meditation on the one hand calms them and on the other lets them discover that the idea that their emotions are not under their control does not correspond to reality.

Bodily techniques can have a significant impact on taking a critical distance from negative self-images, like, for example, *fragile* or *vulnerable*. We can see them at work in the following example, in a situation where they are interwoven with work on the therapeutic relationship. The change we are going to show can in fact be produced both by work with the body and by the peer position the therapist adopted during the exercise. Let us see.

> Gianni was 26 years old and suffered from Avoidant PD, Generalised Anxiety Disorder and panic attacks. One of situations that triggered panic was gym training. It often happened that Gianni gave a catastrophic interpretation to any signs of tiredness or tachycardia that were the physiological result of his weight exercises. He was convinced they meant he was about to get a heart attack. This drove him to give up training even though he was very keen on it.
> The therapy led Gianni to understand that both the fear of an impending catastrophe (heart attack) and the expectation of a negative social judgement were contributing to activating his attacks. In his view, fainting in front of everyone would have meant the other gym clients pointing him out as being "ill" or "crazy". The therapist helped him to recall memories of his early adolescence where the schema was already present. Gianni wanted to feel accepted by the group but feared he would be rejected on account of the negative opinion others would have of him if they knew him closely. He coped with behavioural avoidance. Over the years the only social activity left was the gym, and even this only through massive avoidance, like staying silent and listening to loud music with his iPod headphones during workouts.
> Grasping that the opinions feared were not necessarily real, but the result of a learnt schema, helped him to question them. As a result, Gianni become more open and less shy at work. Strangely, however, he could not manage to start the gym again. His fear of undergoing a catastrophe was too strong and he could not manage to plan behavioural exposures, no matter how much the therapist made them gradual.
> The therapist hypothesised out loud that on a rational level Gianni was able to question the idea that in the gym he would be criticised, but not while he was actually training. In this situation he experienced such intense and unpleasant physical sensations that they became a somatic trigger for catastrophic thoughts, which deprived him of self-reflection abilities.
> Assisted by the fact that he shared Gianni's love of physical exercise, the therapist suggested they do a short training session together in an adjoining room fitted out as a break room and gym. Gianni welcomed the idea. The therapist asked him to report when he felt the feared sensations. Gianni stopped immediately when he sensed tiredness and a substantial increase in heart rate. The therapist made him feel his own pulse rate and showed him that it too had got faster, as is normal during physical effort. Gianni calmed down and completed the exercise, even if anxiety had not disappeared. At this point the therapist directed his attention towards Gianni's sensations during the recuperation phase – tiredness and breathlessness – pointing out that these were normal. Gianni's anxiety decreased further.

As a result of this, Gianni realised that, when faced with unpleasant sensations that for him indicated weakness, the other, the therapist, instead of being judgemental and scornful, was able to accept and at the same time share them. Gianni thus had the embodied experience of being vulnerable in the company of another felt to be an equal and who accepts kindly.

At this point the therapist attempted to construct some behavioural exercises with Gianni: "Do you think you could try in the gym to reproduce these sensations, that is to experience fatigue, breathlessness and tiredness without closing up, and sharing them with someone?" Gianni accepted this and after two more in-session exposures he started going to the gym regularly again and struck up a friendship with someone his age, with whom he started to train together.

Behavioural exploration has a fundamental role in differentiation because it makes it possible to test how much maladaptive interpersonal schemas are still driving patients' actions or whether, on the contrary, they have acquired a different point of view on the world of relationships. Human beings can simultaneously assess the same event differently: they can at the same time make conscious cognitive assessments in which they are, for example, convinced about not fearing humiliation, but at a procedural level rapidly react in a fight-or-flight mode if they pick up even the slightest signs of a threat to their self-worth or only imagine them.

Of these two dissociated forms of knowledge the one, so to say, truer is that influencing behaviour. To promote change different behaviour from that dictated at a procedural level by a patient's schemas therefore needs to be activated, so as to break the routine. We adopt the *in-session planning-behavioural exposure-reflection* procedure (Dimaggio, Montano et al., 2015; Dimaggio, Salvatore et al., 2015).

Let us imagine that the plan is to expose a patient to a feared social situation. The patient takes note of what she thinks and feels during the exposure and this becomes the subject of the next session. The patient might, for example, fear not being up to passing an evening having a pizza with friends. Every so often during the exposure she feels clumsy but often she enjoys herself and feels welcome, thus managing to take a critical distance from her ideas about being rejected. In the next session she begins, together with her therapist, to revise her schema-dependent convictions, in which she is systematically rejected when exposed to others' opinions.

To stimulate an improvement in differentiation – and, more generally, in metacognition – it is possible to use the different techniques sequentially (Chapter 11). In-session work is the first step. Let us imagine a patient wishing to act independently but fearing that, when he does, the other, for example his girlfriend, will suffer. This leads him to feel guilty and to jettison his plan to be independent and adopt a self-sacrificial behaviour aimed at softening guilt. However, this depresses him; he realises that he is unhappy and thus comes to have doubts about his relationship with his girlfriend: "Do I really love her?"

In greater detail: the patient is convinced his girlfriend will suffer if he starts an art course, which would give them less time together at a moment at which she is feeling down about problems at work. He is also convinced that the origin of her malaise is him and he cannot tolerate the sense of guilt deriving from this.

After asking for associated memories, the therapist can suggest a guided imagery exercise in which the patient goes back to a scene in the past where, at the moments at which he thought about going to university, his mother reacted by showing she felt lonely, depressed and worried about not being up to it on her own. During the imagery exercise the patient is able to make contact with feelings preceding his guilt, like loneliness when he noted that his mother did not accompany him where he was going. Feelings of sadness can re-emerge at the idea of giving up what he wanted to do, which at the time he managed to overcome with anger and by accusing his mother of not supporting him.

The therapist can ask the patient to go back to the scene and express to his mother his primary feelings: enthusiasm about the university course and sadness at the idea she was not there. As a result, the patient's affects switch from guilt and anger to a sadness consistent with both a healthy activation of attachment and a lack of support for exploration. At the same time the pleasure of being in contact with one's own wishes and the energy deriving from it re-emerge.

During the exercise the therapist asks the patient to deflect his attention from his mother's sufferings and focus on his own state of wellbeing and agency. The patient can now differentiate thanks to his access to the healthy self. This is the form of differentiation where a patient passes from: "If I show independence, the other feels bad and it is a fact that I'm guilty of their suffering" to "If I show independence, I think about the other being despondent and I can't follow my own path because I'm guilty of making them suffer. But, on the other hand, when I do what I feel like doing, I'm happy and the other's suffering seems less important to me."

At this point the patient can recall other episodes from which he grasps that his mother was chronically depressed for reasons that had nothing to do with him. On this basis the therapist feels more at ease proposing a behavioural experiment: for example, that the patient tell his girlfriend that for him it is important to do this art course, even if this will involve being away from home one evening a week and at a moment at which she is having to deal with a disappointment at work.

In-session work involves: 1) starting from a recent event; 2) evoking associated memories and helping the patient relive a core problematic episode; 3) getting him to make contact with positive feelings linked to the primary wish, in this case the motivation towards independence/exploration and creativity; 4) attempting imagery rescripting, where one suggests the patient act differently to the past, upholding his independence and approaching the other while valuing his own inner impulses instead of succumbing to guilt; 5) after the imagery exercise, reflecting together on how, contrary to expectations, the patient is not obliged to step in to alleviate the other's suffering and is not in fact responsible for that suffering. Furthermore the patient discovers that, contrary to his fears, he is able to endure guilt; 6) planning at this point behavioural experiments so as to obtain the same results in the here and now in emotionally activating situations. Then, the fear of hurting the other would lead the patient to again interrupt his independent activity and rein back his creative impulses in order to care for another seen as suffering; 7) in the next session reflecting together on what happened when the patient attempted to behave differently. This is aimed at helping him to further put together an idea of himself and the other different from that foreseen by his dysfunctional schema.

The work on differentiation goes on at the same time as that aimed at stimulating access to healthy self-parts, of which we shall now talk in detail.

Accessing healthy parts

Perhaps the most important core characteristic of MIT is concentrating treatment on the stimulation of healthy parts. We work on putting patients in contact with what lies inside of them that is human, universal, vibrant and creative. We aim at helping them to make contact with their primary emotions which they previously avoided or reacted to by using dysfunctional coping strategies. At this point we attempt to evoke more kindly self-representations, where patients accept themselves, consider themselves worthy, competent, lovable and able to act effectively, or see their own limits but address them without being overly demanding. We ask patients to recognise their skills, loves, preferences and tastes, and to act on this basis, by trying to be consistent with what belongs to them, enlivens them and provides them with joy, enthusiasm, involvement and levity.

All these ideas, perceptions and actions are overshadowed by schemas, which lead patients to notice only the negative elements they feature and prevent focusing attention on positive ones. Unfortunately, repetitive thinking keeps a patient in distress and takes away room in the mind for healthy parts. Lastly, patients' maladaptive behaviour, for example avoidance, the blocking of the exploration system and the way they enter interpersonal cycles that disturb their relationships, prevent them from experiencing positive states from which to nourish themselves.

To access healthy parts and ensure they remain in consciousness long enough to stabilise them in long-term memory, cognitive work is often not enough and sometimes completely inadequate. The techniques we describe in this book, on the contrary, stimulate and speed up this access. An example of how this work gets carried out is offered by guided imagery.

Sandro was 40 years old and suffered from Obsessive-Compulsive PD with depressive and passive-aggressive personality traits. He worked as a jeweller, like the rest of his family. He was morally strict with himself and others, and perfectionist. He worked together with his father, whom he described as critical and capable of disapproving of his every action. Sandro related memories where his father, of an irritable temperament, would often rail against his mother. This often happened when Sandro tried to do things his way and made his father unhappy. The response of the latter was to accuse his wife: "You see? Your idiot of a son's made another fine mess." As a result Sandro got the idea that he was the cause of his mother's suffering.

Together with the therapist he recognised that the schemas he had constructed within the family arose from his wish for independence. One aspect of the schemas had the following structure: *If I do things my way, my father criticises me.* The self's response is: *He's right. I'm an idiot. I'm ashamed of what I've done.* At this point Sandro adopted surrender coping mechanisms – *Better to forget about it . . .* – and compliant submission ones *. . . and I'll do as my father says.* This however left the self-part wishing for independence and feeling entitled to pursue it full of anger and frustration.

The second aspect of the schema connected to independence was: *If I do things my way, my father gets angry with my mother and hurts her.* The self's response was: *I'm unworthy and even dangerous, because I hurt my mother; I feel guilty and worried.* Here too coping was to surrender and give up independence.

The therapist got him to understand that he was tired of this way of functioning and that the wish to do things his way was still alive, even if weak. Sandro however knew no other route. He had just gone back to perceiving the emotions he experienced when moved by something giving him pleasure, enjoyment and fun. After several months of therapy he told about a dinner at home where his wife and he had invited 20 people. After work he spent the last two days attending to every detail of the dinner: planning it, shopping and cooking. At the end of the dinner he received a lot of congratulations, but all he managed to say was that he felt the main course had not turned out like he expected, and he ruminated over this while thinking he had ruined the dinner for his friends, who might even criticise him.

However, the therapist picked up a twinkle in Sandro's eyes when he described the preparation of the dinner and how he had selected the ingredients and studied the recipes. At this point she suggested a guided imagery exercise. They chose together to focus on the moment when he was cooking. At the start Sandro seemed worried but then while he was describing what he did it became evident he was enjoying himself and felt on top of the situation. The therapist immediately pointed this out to him and Sandro, surprised, became aware of both these feelings. After the imagery exercise he had a new awareness: he liked cooking and felt up to it.

He had never realised that he cooked for reasons other than simply obtaining approval and that it was the hypertrophy of the competition schema that was obstructing his feelings connected to curiosity, personal inclinations, excitement and competence.

In this case too one can see how, to obtain the same therapeutic goal, access to and reinforcement of healthy parts, it is useful to use several techniques in a sequence. On the basis of what emerged in the imagery exercise, the therapist and Sandro planned that he could enrol in a cooking course. He did this willingly and it was the start of a radical personal change, which led him to decide to work in a branch of the family firm where he was able to no longer have any contact with his father and to regularly carve himself out the time to elaborate on his cooking skills and do various follow-up courses. He is currently considering leaving the firm completely and trying to open a restaurant.

The two-chair game can also be used for the same purpose (Chapter 6). While it is going on access to healthy parts is often successful in a smooth and emotionally intense way. Therapists can suggest patients re-enact dialogues with a character from their narrative with scornful and invalidating aspects. As the dialogue unfolds, the patient, at the therapist's prompting, tries to reply to his critical judge more firmly and assertively. After repeated attempts the patient often accesses feelings of competence, good self-esteem and adaptive anger because he sees the criticism as unjust.

Promoting mastery and further stimulating the development of healthy parts outside sessions

Activating the body and imagination is in itself a mastery precursor, that is, the perception of agency over one's mental state and the awareness that moving in space, changing one's posture and putting oneself for a few seconds in another's shoes influence the flow of emotions and thoughts. We discover we have power over our inner world. With the techniques described here it is possible to improve the ability to master inner experience and plan effective social problem-solving strategies in many different ways.

At a more basic level agency over mental states should be promoted, that is, developing forms, even embryonic ones, of emotional regulation and mindfulness skills. An initial step can easily be carried out during states of emotional dysregulation during sessions.

Mariella was a 39-year-old craftswoman and suffered from Obsessive-Compulsive PD with passive-aggressive personality traits and hypochondria. She started the following session in despair. For several weeks she had been devoting herself to looking after her two daughters because her husband had been abroad for a work assignment. When he returned she asked him to look after their daughters because she needed to finish a new collection for an important trade fair. He refused indignantly. Mariella could not keep calm, was stressed and unable to concentrate on anything, and felt like her life was going south.

The therapist intervened in two different stages. First he reminded her of how, in her relationship with her husband, a schema was active: she needed to be supported in her independence and, when faced with the other's response, that is obstructing and scorning her, she, on the one hand, thought the other was right and therefore got dejected and depressed, and felt paralysed. On the other, she entered a state of angry protest against an unjust and tyrannical other.

In the self's response to the other's response in this schema of Mariella's the experiencing of passivity is key: she was unable to think of carrying out her plans on her own but clung instead to the idea that the other ought to give her support and attention and, while she waited, remained immobile. In this state she also could not regulate emotions, because she did not think she was able to have any influence on herself. Thanks to the therapist's formulation, Mariella realised she was constantly attentive to how the other treated her and could not even concentrate on what she was thinking, feeling or wishing. In this state she started to cry, as she felt in despair and incapable of making any change in her life.

The therapist said: "Right, the first step is to remember that you have the ability to influence your own mind, not let yourself be taken over by discouragement and calm down. We know that this has happened other times and you were able to disentangle yourself." Mariella admitted that this was true and asked the therapist what they could do. The therapist suggested a brief breathing meditation. After five minutes Mariella calmed down and became aware that dysregulated states can be controlled.

All the exercises imitating the way real interpersonal relationships go lend themselves well to improving mastery. Whether one uses two-chairs, guided imagery or role-play in individual, couple or group sessions, it is always possible to imagine and enact more adaptive forms of interpersonal relationships.

First, we ask patients to tell a specific relational episode. Then we ask them to imagine or represent it. At this stage therapists pay the utmost attention to what healthy self-part should be connected with and brought to the centre of action control. Once this is identified, we ask patients to replay the scene while talking and behaving differently and monitoring their state as a consequence of these new actions.

Behavioural experiments are key to this step of change promoting: patients pass from practising new ways of relating as part of in-session pretend play, to practising them in daily life. This makes it possible to break up old procedures and create new ones.

Improving theory of mind

We repeat that in MIT procedures the promotion of theory of mind is a secondary goal, belonging to the more advanced stages of therapy. Before suggesting a patient explore others' minds in an accurate and, if possible, decentred way, she needs to be helped to get to know her own inner world.

Therapists help patients feel their own wishes are worthy and deserve to guide their action. Therapists validate dysfunctional aspects, and in particular help patients at understanding that problematic forms of coping have a sense as they protect from suffering. Albeit dysfunctional – avoiding others or treating them hostilely – it is understandable that patients put them into practice. The key aspect of change is that patients have access to healthy parts and start to differentiate, that is to be able to say to themselves: "I tend to think others have got it in for me, don't respect me and can't stand me, but I believe this depends substantially not so much on their attitude but on my extreme attention to the topic and my quickness to see signs of criticism, rejection and aggressiveness, even if there aren't any."

Only at this point does the MIT therapist shift attention to others' minds, by suggesting patients explore the intentions, thoughts, emotions, reasons for acting and mental processes that lead them to behave in a particular way. Many of the techniques we use stimulate theory of mind and decentring. For reasons of simplicity we describe some role-play where at various stages the patient plays the roles of the two characters present in the scene.

Giulietta was 30 years old and suffered from Narcissistic PD, with passive-aggressive and depressive traits. She had not had a stable romantic relationship for several years and had recently lost her job as a nursery school teacher. She was going through depression, in which feelings linked to a self-image of

Use of imagery and bodily techniques 101

unworthiness were resurfacing. She had achieved differentiation and gained access to benign ideas of herself and others, especially in the rank motive. The therapy was at a stage aiming at strengthening exploration: Giulietta knew she had to live a rich social life and in fact had many female friends. However, because of losing her job, she had had a relapse and the negative schema had got reactivated. She was still able in part to take a critical distance: "My usual thoughts about not being worth anything are back again." However, the schema had power over her behaviour: at moments when she could expose herself to social situations where she might meet a potential partner, she tended to close up because she felt she had nothing to give and felt inferior to others she described as capable and successful.

She told of how a male friend, a young talented artist, whose career was taking off, had invited her to his birthday party. Giulietta had almost decided to not go because she felt inadequate: "He's so cool. He's just been called by a very famous director who wants him as an assistant. He knows loads of important people and has a really interesting life. What could he want with me when I've got nothing to say? I haven't got a boyfriend and I've just been sacked. I'm just not up to going to the party."

The therapist and Giulietta made contact with her wish to go to the party. He asked her if she felt ready to do some role-playing in order to try and breaking the schema, interrupt her avoidant coping and make room for the wish. Giulietta accepted. In the role-play Giulietta was to start off by playing her friend and then return to the role of herself. The therapist's initial goal was to let her get in contact with images where she felt she was worth something. Giulietta described the scene: she was in a pub, by the bar, with the friend and other friends surrounding them. The friend was sitting on a high stool and Giulietta was standing, both of them with their elbows resting on the bar.

Giulietta started by playing her friend. With her in this role the script had some surprising contents:

G: [*in the friend's role*]: "You matter to me. I wanted you to come to the party. You're witty and funny and good at listening. With you I feel comfortable."
T: "Now you're in your friend's shoes, how do you see Giulietta?"
G: "I'm convinced of what I say sitting here. I like her. I'd really like to have her at my party."

The therapist noticed a movement in her face. Giulietta had lowered her gaze.

T: "You are experiencing something else. I noticed that you lowered your gaze."
G: "Hmm, yes [*she thought silently for a few seconds*], like a sort of sadness. I'm sorry she thought about not coming."

The therapist swapped roles with Giulietta now playing herself. He asked her to reply. Giulietta burst into tears and kept crying:

G: "It's really great that he's so keen. I wasn't expecting it."

After her tears of emotion Giulietta continued.

G: "Thanks, you're very kind. What you say surprises but also pleases me. I was also very keen on coming. You're a good person."
T: "How do you feel now when you reply?"
G: "On the one hand, embarrassed. There's a part of me that doesn't believe it, almost. But it's not something very strong. More nuanced."
T: "And what's your dominant feeling?"
G: "I'm happy. I feel almost cool [*she laughs*], a lovely feeling. I'm also glad to be here. I feel welcome and then he's a good guy. It's a pleasure to be in his company."

When thinking about this episode, Giulietta noticed that discovering that in her friend's role she felt sad at the idea that she was not at the party was decisive. It had made her see that his kind words were sincere.

It can be seen that, during the role-playing, adopting the other's perspective made it possible to improve the understanding of him and Giulietta now ascribed new, well-disposed intentions to him. When observing herself from this well-disposed perspective, there was a consolidation of her healthy parts, her positive self-image, important for others, emerged strongly and was decoupled from her real performance, and Giulietta could be appreciated for her human qualities.

Summary

MIT promotes a first form of change: an increase in awareness of one's inner world, that is an improvement in metacognition. This is one of the goals of the formalised procedure, in the part we call *shared formulation of functioning*.

In the part termed *change promoting* we stimulate: an access to healthy parts, a critical distance from one's schemas or differentiation, the enriching of one's action repertoire, a more sophisticated knowledge of the other's mind and, lastly, the construction of a superordinate point of view from which to observe the various self-aspects relating to others and achieve comprehensive panorama. We want patients to acquire a richer, more flexible view of the self in relations, one capable of combining strength and vulnerabilities and to use this knowledge to support social actions they feel to be their own, to the extent that this is realistically possible.

The work on imagery, bodily states and behaviour is a powerful avenue to these goals.

At some moments the techniques enable patients to more carefully observe inner states, distinguish them from each other, name them and live aspects of experience they did not notice before. Other techniques make it possible for patients to grasp that what they think of themselves and others is subjective and that things seen from another angle appear different. Stirring the body and imagination also makes it possible to play on a patient's new, and more sophisticated and flexible, view, in order for him to act differently, in line with his own goals and wishes and overcoming pathological avoidance and coping mechanisms.

Almost all the techniques, as we have seen, make it possible to reach many such goals. As an example, mindfulness has the ability to increase self-awareness, from the most basic aspects of experience to the awareness of being driven by schemas, thanks to the fact that therapists are constantly asking patients to practise it as regularly as possible. Mindfulness again, in our adaptation to PD (Ottavi et al., 2016), makes it possible, once a patient has realised that an interpersonal schema is active and he is ruminating over it, to stop the rumination (Chapter 9).

Guided imagery and drama techniques stimulate both an access to experience and the rewriting of schemas. Once, in in-session pretend play, a patient has relived a distressing scene, she can modulate her distress and then repeat the scene in a search for innovation, by trying, in the suspended "as if" world, to enact different behaviours – verbal and non-verbal.

Behavioural exploration stimulates the improvement of basic aspects of self-reflectivity too, as occurs when clinicians propose a therapy task as follows:

> We do not know what you experience when you feel others are not on your side. Do you feel up to expounding your ideas in our next work session? Not to become an expert and to overcome your problem. We just need you to pay attention to what you think and feel while attempting it. And then pay attention too to how your colleagues react after you've expressed your own opinion. It's not important that you manage to speak, but that you attempt it. And, even if you can't manage, it's still okay. We just want you to try and take note of what thoughts and emotions have passed through your mind and made you freeze.

This same behavioural exploration has, at more advanced stages, the utmost ability to break patterns and lead patients to act in contrast to their schemas and strive, as much as possible, to act consistently with their own wishes and adaptive plans.

Other examples of sequences of techniques can be seen with patients with psychological traumas. Various approaches start with a stabilisation stage, involving bodily work to regulate arousal. Then, as in the case of EMDR, patients reliving their memory in imagination. In the case, on the other hand, of Sensorimotor Therapy therapists first attentively read body signals and then ask patients to adopt a series of postures and specific behaviours with a view to accessing different forms of experience. At, for example, the body monitoring stage a patient may perceive that, when faced with a relational risk, she tends to use immobilisation defence mechanisms. At this point therapists could ask her to adopt postures aiming at attacking, flight or seeking attention, until the patient feels she is no longer passive and has regained control of her traumatic scene.

In the chapters that follow we shall describe the techniques one by one and explain how we regulate the therapeutic relationship when suggesting and carrying out an exercise. In Chapter 11 we shall show how to deliver sequences of techniques. Each chapter will be enriched with clinical examples originating from our clinical and supervision experiences, so as to transport readers inside a session so that they can, in a certain sense, experience at first hand the work we do in order to prepare themselves for putting it into practice with their own patients.

CHAPTER 4

The decision-making procedure and experiential techniques

The step-by-step MIT procedure, manualised in the previous book (Dimaggio, Montano et al., 2015), describes how we carry out each intervention in accordance with the level of metacognitive and narrative skills displayed by a patient at that moment in session. It also explains the rationale that provides rules for when to progress from one intervention to the next.

The procedure consists of two macro-sections: *Shared formulation of functioning* and *change promoting*. During the *formulation* stage clinicians aim to improve patients' narrative and self-reflective skills until they can discover the set of maladaptive interpersonal schemas which shape views of themselves and others, guide construction of meaning assigned to events and, consequently, action. During the second stage, *change promoting*, therapists and patients use the skills they have acquired during the *formulation* stage to consolidate new modes of thinking and feeling that predispose for more adaptive behaviour.

In recent years we have been applying this procedure consistently and we have discovered we can make it more powerful and incisive. We stayed faithful to the principles that have always guided us: patients must first recognise their inner states and then reconstruct schemas. The next step is for them to differentiate, understanding that their ideas do not mirror reality, but are, precisely, ideas, subjective points of view. While patients begin to realise that they perceive the world through their own personal lenses, we help them see that they also hold, deep inside, alternative more benevolent and less pessimistic views of the self and others. They can start, in this way, thinking of themselves as being worthy, as having the potential to be competent and lovable, and believe others to be well-disposed towards supporting them fulfil their wishes. It is of significance that, in this stage, patients discover they have healthy and functioning parts.

Only at this point would we set them on a course to become aware of behaviours that need to be modified for suffering and relational problems to diminish and guide them as they practice modifying this maladaptive behaviour. We revised the procedure, in line with the changes in the psychopathology model (Chapter 1, 2). The idea was to ask patients to adopt, when appropriate at the earliest opportunity following the beginning of treatment, new behaviours and regulation strategies different from their old routines.

We aspire that, in this way, we will draw more information on patients' inner states, those associated with their distress but also those that allow healthy parts of the self and resources the patients did not realise they had to surface. We noticed that the patients responded well to these modifications, so the revision of the procedure underpinning this book arose.

The revised decision-making procedure

The *formulation* stage was, in fact, imbued with operations aiming to introduce change at early sessions: improving metacognition. This gives patients the opportunity to learn how to better describe and communicate their inner world to others, therefore reaching for and accomplishing deeper human connections. We also pointed out (Dimaggio, Montano et al., 2015) that it is possible right from the start to suggest strategies for symptom improvement, albeit limited due to patients' poorly developed metacognitive skills.

The novelty of this approach is that we suggest a number of exercises very early, for example those related to behavioural activation and exploration, with the goal to promote self-awareness more quickly. At the same time, at the *formulation* stage, while patients and therapists are collaboratively trying to understand the formers' schemas, we introduce other techniques for reducing rumination or regulating overwhelming emotions.

For example, we ask patients early on to do physical exercise or listen to music to calm down when their anger towards someone important to them is mounting. These are techniques aimed at promoting improvement in symptoms and affect regulation capacity that we have been using right from the start of treatment. The novelty herein is that early on and as part of regulating the therapeutic relationship to promote and maintain rapport, *we ask patients to practise behaviour that counteracts maladaptive coping*. We shall demonstrate how this is achieved and to what end.

We distinguish these operations from core operations aiming to promote change, because the latter are directed at structural changes that enable patients to take a critical distance from their interpersonal schemas, view their relational world through different eyes and act strategically to satisfy their basic wishes and find their niche in society. This way they recover the sense of a life worth living. We shall see how we immediately ask patients to act differently also to instil an attitude of active resolve against suffering.

Dynamic assessment

The *formulation* stage is enriched by what we term *dynamic assessment*. This consists of activities that aim to assess patients' functioning while observing their responses to the techniques illustrated throughout this book. Dynamic assessment is based on behavioural, imagery, body, or drama exercises, which a clinician would propose not with the purpose of producing a structural personality improvement, but rather in order to engage patients in activities aimed at improving metacognition.

The core element of this approach is encouraging patients to abstain from coping strategies they usually resort to and to devote themselves to their exploration motive.

In collaboration with patients, therapists target any automatic dysfunctional behaviour that arises, driven by maladaptive interpersonal schemas, even if patients do not yet fully realise what they feel and what thoughts and emotions are leading them to act in a certain way.

A therapist should, however, validate patients' coping strategies in attempting these strategies: "Avoiding distress is normal and human. In your shoes I myself would also try to do something to reduce my suffering." After ensuring that patients feel accepted and not judged, therapists could ask them to not enact a maladaptive behaviour, for example, avoidance. They could also ask them to persist and continue to pursue a goal they recognise as their own, even if they hold vague fears of their important relationships being damaged if they did so. Their natural tendency would likely be to freeze:

> You fear that your relationship with your partner would deteriorate if you were more independent, because your partner would not like it. However, you do not know how he would react in reality and how you would feel. You told me that every so often you feel the wish to enrol in a dancing course and we've seen that when you talk about it you liven up and smile. You'd really like it. If I asked you to think about taking a first step to enrolling in this course this week, to get some information about it, would you be willing to try?

Therapists clarify to patients that the aim of these exercises is not to succeed at acting differently, but to attempt to resist and counteract automatisms. The therapist would therefore ask patients to pay attention to thoughts and emotions surfacing at different stages of completing a task: while planning, carrying out and after finishing a task. Likewise, therapists explain early on that not accomplishing a task is not a problem; it is just important to focus on what they experienced when they decided to give up and immediately afterwards, and discuss it in the next session.

Early access to healthy parts

During dynamic assessment we show how to anticipate the *access to healthy parts of the self* operation. Right from the first session, or in any case as soon as practicable, a therapist can explicitly point out when adaptive self-parts surface. These include: 1) more positive self-representations; 2) emergence of adaptive wishes; 3) patients displaying good reflective skills even if they have no control over their problem; 4) hope and confidence in the therapy progressing or the possibilities of being helped; 5) patients knowing how to communicate their suffering clearly and by actively(?) involving the therapist and 6) discovering they have agency over their own mental states.

At this stage, as mentioned earlier, we are not prioritising change, for example, helping healthy parts emerge in place of pathological ones. It is instead intended to complete a shared formulation that includes assessment of a patient's strengths and resources (Padesky & Mooney, 2012).

During this step therapists do not expect patients to recognise positive aspects of the self as integrated within their overall sense of self and consequently change their core self-image from negative to positive. We aim solely at temporarily stimulating patients' awareness they have healthier parts that enable them to perceive themselves under a different light and to function more adaptively. This awareness needs to be experiential.

The patient realises for a moment that she perceives herself as competent, lovable, capable and independent and, for as long as the therapist supports her, she breathes and feeds on this awareness. These early, short moments of health, termed in the psychological narrative tradition as "innovative moments" (Gonçalves et al., 2017) or "sparkling moments" (White & Epston, 1990), are the cornerstones on which to build change. The use of behavioural, imagery and body-focused techniques is a very useful tool for promoting this step.

Techniques and procedures at the various stages

Throughout this book we depict how we adopt any technique irrespective of the intended goals, as we gradually move through the different stages of the decision-making procedure. Some examples include the following: we use simple mindfulness interventions to improve the identification of inner states; while our adaptation of more complex mindfulness interventions regarding interpersonal schemas (chapter 9) help patients regulate schema-related emotions. Guided imagery and drama techniques can first improve monitoring skills and stimulate access to previously overshadowed self-parts, then facilitate differentiation between fantasy and reality and lastly, mastery of problematic interpersonal situations.

In this chapter we do not elaborate on the role that each single technique has in promoting a specific step. We just provide examples of how to apply some of the techniques at each specific step.

Shared formulation of functioning and dynamic assessment

The first shared formulation steps (Figure 4.1) aim at obtaining information that a therapist and patient can use to form an idea of the cognitive-affective processes generating problems and, therefore, which will become the focus treatment. The two first steps are *evoking autobiographical memories*, which involves enabling patients to relate narrative episodes, and *exploring inner states*, including thoughts, emotions, action tendencies and bodily sensations as experienced while the episode was taking place and while they relate it in session.

1a) Evoking autobiographical memories

The first key question to pose in MIT is: "Can you give me an example?" Patients often tend to use metaphors, abstractions and intellectualisations to talk about

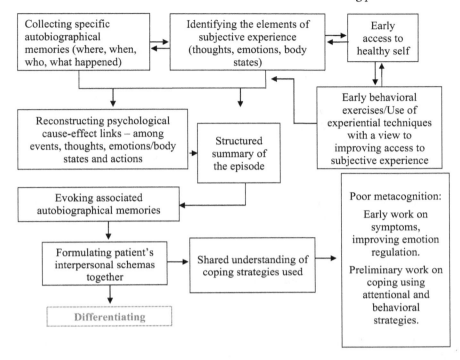

Figure 4.1 Shared formulation of functioning

themselves. Therapists listen to them, validate the parts they understand, and then immediately try to access the narrative dimension. Therapists anchor patients' discourse to specific moments where they interact with others.

Narrative episodes must be defined in terms of space (*where*) and time (*when*), describe the characters on stage (*who*) and what they say, do and feel during the interaction. Therapists ask patients to focus on the details of what happened instead of commenting on the facts and describing what they meant for them.

An impoverished, abstract and intellectualised narrative, requiring further exploration would sound like this: "At home we didn't talk. Perhaps every so often I wanted to say something, but in any case it was pointless and consequently it was better to withdraw. Then again during adolescence, that's normal. They say I was introverted, but what does that mean? I was a boy like lots of others."

MIT therapists do not work on contents expressed like this. They, instead, look for narratives and ask: "Can you describe a situation where it was pointless to talk? Perhaps a time when you withdrew?"

A good story sounds like this:

> I was returning home from school. My mother was waiting for me on her own. My father was away for work and my sister had gone over to a friend's

house. I was nervous and afraid because at school I'd been humiliated by boys from another class. It wasn't violent but they were taking the piss of me for my trousers, maybe my shirt. It was pink. I'd have liked to talk with my mother and ask her not to buy me this kind of clothes any more, that I wanted to choose them myself, that I was old enough now, no longer a nursery school child. But as soon as I got home, my mother noticed I had a strange look on my face, although I don't know what she thought of it. She asked me how my English test had gone. I told her it went well but nothing more than that, and she straight away started saying that it wasn't okay and I wasn't studying enough. I froze and didn't tell her anything else. I believe I ran to my room to shut myself away. I was desperate.

A good narrative is a memory of something happening, not what a patient imagines could have happened. An imagined scene can help a therapist begin to reconstruct the patient's schema structure, but after an initial reconstruction, the therapist needs to ask for memories where the patient recalls having to confront a feared situation.

A patient has difficulties with her boyfriend, goes home for dinner and imagines that, if she told her parents about these difficulties, her parents would accuse her of mixing with the wrong sort of person. This prevents her from talking while her anger mounts at the idea of being misunderstood. Although the schema structure is easily discernible in this example, this is not yet a narrative episode. Therapists should prompt for specific and detailed memories of herself feeling angry at her parents, or at someone else, for criticising her.

We must be careful as certain memories appear to be narrative episodes but in fact are not. Continuing with the previous example, the patient said, "I was at home for dinner. I was sure my parents would criticise me if I told them what had happened and so I didn't open my mouth the whole evening, thinking how awful I'd have felt if I'd spoken. I couldn't stand them."

This memory is located in space and time, and there are clear characters. It certainly also contains some elements leading to an understanding of the patient's schema. In fact, she did not interact with the others but imagined what would happen if she did. It is a memory of a moment of rumination!

The patient was recalling a situation where she acted on the basis of forecasts driven by her schema, and was not talking about relating with others who do and say something to which she reacts. Faced with narrative like these, clinicians still need to search for situations where the patient really confronted the precise reaction she feared or one that prompted her to react in a specific way.

1b) Exploring inner states

Steps 1a and 1b are carried out simultaneously because many patients have difficulty recalling memories and, until they are able to, a therapist tries to extract the contents of their experience from their abstractions. An example is: "It seems to me that, when you talk about the importance of a father's family role, there's a slight note of self-criticism, as if you felt you're not doing enough. Is that possible?" Or else, if we want to highlight emotions: "You tell me there's not room for friendship and the persons you know are self-centred and arrogant. Am I wrong to think you say this with a hint of anger?"

For a more detailed decoding of a patient's inner world there are various routes. One is a detailed analysis of what happens in a narrative episode. Therapists ask patients what they thought and felt as the facts were occurring. Another is to ask what the patient thinks and feels while she is telling the story, because these are the emotions experienced at the here and now.

Dynamic assessment allows to immediately encourage or speed up patients' recollection and sharing of both narrative episodes and richer details of inner experience. Therapists can ask patients to focus on their experiences while engaging in simple behavioural experiments over the following week. The task can be simple: "You told me you're tense and nervous. In the next few days could you try to focus your attention on situations where you felt these states more or less acutely? Pay attention to what you're doing, whom you're interacting with, and where you are. Also try to focus on what's passing through your mind, what you feel and think." The aim is to train patients to use their autobiographical memory and basic self-reflectivity. In this way almost all patients will, session after session, improve their narrative skills and describe their inner states more accurately.

Practically all the techniques we use help to reinforce these aspects. Getting a patient to relive an episode in his imagination or putting him on stage through role-play almost always stimulates access to parts of experience previously gone unnoticed.

Progressing from recalling an episode to reliving it has an enormous impact on the quality of experience. While reliving a memory, patients relinquish their position as a narrator, which in any case creates a certain distance from experience. In fact, progressing from narrating to reliving removes barriers to connecting with one's most basic experiences, in a way that brings patients and therapists closer to areas that, if worked through, hold promise for improvement. We look in detail at these aspects in the next step.

2) *Reconstruction of psychological cause–effect links*

Understanding the cognitive-affective processes driving patients' actions is crucial. Once patients have related a narrative episode and identified inner states, therapists try to comprehend the logical and psychological processes linking the elements of experience to each other. In metacognitive terms it is understood as promoting *relating variables*, that is, understanding event–thought–emotion–behaviour links or, conversely, how a certain affect influences thoughts: anger leads to aggressive thoughts, sadness to depressive ideas, etc. This step is not completely separate from the former: often, when patients are narrating an episode, they begin to explain what prompted their reactions: "I asked him to come and pick me up at the station and he replied that he didn't have time to waste. I went mad and was about to hang up on him."

Developing an awareness of links between external contingencies, inner experience and behaviour is much simpler when patients re-immerse themselves in the heart of an experience during guided imagery or drama techniques. When patients go on stage in the here and now and withdraw from their position as a narrator, it becomes easier for them to focus on their stream of consciousness and discover particularities of experience they had not noticed before. At such moments, therapists pay greater attention than usual to facial expressions and non-verbal communication and continuously carry out contingent marking: "I thought your face darkened just now. Could it be fear?"

With these operations patients can recognise emotions more easily and realise they were triggered by specific actions as performed by others, carried through their cognitive interpretation: "My brother's yelling at my mother. I fear he could hurt her. I'm afraid and feel guilty because I'm not protecting her."

Asking patients to quit the I-narrator position and immerse themselves in an experience as if it were happening in the present is one of the main innovations in this book. Where possible, we want patients to experience what they have just narrated with as few filters as possible, so as to access raw experiences that evoke bodily signals. This would allow a therapist to read patients' non-verbal communication with the utmost clarity and reliability and facilitate patients in connecting with their emotional and sensorial reactions.

3a) Initial access to healthy parts

Early on, while collecting the first narrative episodes and working on regulating the therapeutic relationship, it is crucial to pay attention to patients' healthy parts. The sooner the clinician detects them and brings them into consciousness, the sooner patients recover their confidence and optimism for the prospect of a better future. Of course, this operation is not immediately successful with all patients. Many are overwhelmed by distress and a clinician should restrict himself to validating and accepting this while trying, in collaboration with the patients, to understand what drives their suffering. With the most impaired patients it is difficult to find healthy parts at the start of treatment and so throughout their therapy one needs to aim at constructing them. But with the majority of patients these surface organically.

Healthy parts appear in many different ways: a) patients speak in a manner indicating self-confidence or self-esteem; b) they can connect with their primary wish, even if the outcome of the story is negative. For example, a patient admitting he has a "wish to start a project but there is no support available" reveals a positive, open stance to connecting with and expressing one's exploratory motive. There remains a problematic part, however, in the admission that there is "no support available"; c) some of the characters portrayed during narrative episodes respond favourably, in a caring, supportive manner that signals approval and acceptance; d) sometimes, even if immersed in emotional states triggered by their schemas, patients display a nascent ability to differentiate: "I realise I have this tendency perceiving everything to be bleak, but I can't manage to control it." It is positive that a healthy part of the self is discernible in this case, even if it is only slightly, barely surfacing to awareness; e) healthy parts emerge during the therapeutic relationship. Narrative episodes are dominated by maladaptive schemas, but patients have confidence and hope in the therapy, which means that adaptive relationship schemas exist. Lastly, patients are overwhelmed by suffering but they are still able to effectively convey the meaning of their experience in a way that emotionally involves the therapist.

Clinicians notice right from the start that healthy aspects exist and use them to formulate treatment goals: "There's a part of you hoping for a different destiny. Shall we look for a way to allow this voice to be heard?"; "It is true that you imagine ferocious criticism. But, when you talk about what you like, I can sense you really light up and are willing to explore what opportunities lie ahead."

All the practices we describe in this book can foster access to healthy parts. During guided imagery patients may discover their positive aspects: they might be sorry about the other leaving them, but still feel lovable, whereas until just a few moments before they were overwhelmed by guilt, anger and despair. Short mindfulness exercises help patients become aware that negative emotions can make way for positive affects, even if only for an instant.

3b) Reduction of symptoms and emotional regulation

While trying, collaboratively with patients, to comprehend the role that symptoms serve, therapists offer tools for reducing suffering. They more specifically aim to assess the degree of patients' metacognitive understanding of symptoms and relational problems patients. The patient adopts mastery and management OR emotion regulation strategies consistent with the level of metacognitive skills she possesses (Carcione et al., 2011; Dimaggio, Montano et al., 2015). For example, if a patient only manages to say, "It is more likely to experience an anxiety crisis when I'm under pressure" yet is not able to explain what it means to be "under pressure", therapists give medications or adopt attention shifting strategies.

Techniques involving activation of the body and imagination are useful at this stage. A therapist may, for example, work on a body level (Ogden & Fisher, 2015), by suggesting that they train together, so as to trigger the physical signals a patient interprets as being the onset of a heart attack. Once they are triggered, she can use cognitive re-attribution: "You see? It's only an increase in your heart rate as a result of the physical effort." Mindfulness exercises can also be useful. It is enough for a patient to perceive that what she experiences is nothing more than a demonstration of stress or panic and then to commit to a plan of using mindfulness techniques to succeed in making her worry fade away. Imagery exercises during which patients visualise alternate scenarios to their catastrophic predictions can help them calm down and recover from the grip of panic (Hackmann, Bennett-Levy, & Holmes, 2011).

Moreover (Chapter 9), we use various types of attention reorientation techniques (Wells, 2008) when a patient starts ruminating. The aims are to: a) modulate negative emotions, and b) make patients aware of their positive and negative meta-beliefs and counteract them instead of resorting to repetitive interpersonal thinking. It is, therefore, intended to shift patients' attention from ideas like: "If I think precisely about what led my boyfriend to leave me, perhaps I can convince him to change his mind."

4) Structured summary of events

Once some narrative episodes have been collected and the patient has started to grasp the links connecting events to thoughts, emotional and behavioural aspects of experience, the next step is forming a *structured summary of events*. The elements in the story should be placed in a sequence starting from the wish and core self-images, followed by descriptions of the other's response and the self's reaction, and terminating in the perception that one's goal will remain unfulfilled.

At this stage it is not yet possible to talk about unravelling a person's schema, but rather of analysing one or a few episodes that do not necessarily reflect general modes of functioning. A particular schema can be confirmed only if demonstrated in a variety of different episodes across a range of contexts and, if possible, involving different persons.

The structured summary of events initially develops in therapists' mind, in the form of hypotheses. Once hypotheses can be coherently articulated, therapists will attempt to involve the patient: "Look, let's try and see if I've grasped what you told me." Therapists start to reconstruct the story, while continuously asking the patients if they perceive themselves as reflected in their words. This is a cognitive strategy that benefits from experiential techniques.

Experiential work makes the links among events, thoughts, emotions and behaviour emerge with greater richness and clarity, which provides clinicians with higher quality information. During an experiential practice the patient feels the emotions, and when the therapist refers back to them in the summary, they resonate with the patient.

5) Evoking associated autobiographical memories

Before moving on to the next stage one or more narrative episodes need to be retrieved. The goal is to continue collecting material that can be used to theorise about patients' interpersonal schemas. Multiple episodes are necessary to be analysed in order to confirm the presence of a schema. We say jokingly during our training sessions that, the first key MIT question is "Can you give me an example?", and the second key question is "Can you give me another example?"

The way we evoke associated memories is rigorous, by: a) summarising the narrative episode by reconstructing the experience in a manner that reflects the schema structure. Therapists communicate their formulation in simple language that makes it possible for patients to identify themselves in the reconstructed narrative; and by b) asking if patients remember having experienced something similar in the past.

This is an example:

> So you wanted to act independently, according to your own wishes, but when you saw your partner suffering, you thought you had no right to follow your chosen path and you felt guilty. A part of you, however, rebelled because you considered that it was your right to pursue your plan. Can you recall other episodes from the past where you experienced a situation like this, where you sought your independence yet the other opposed or even obstructed you by communicating that your plans were causing them to suffer? Or situations where, when faced with a suffering other, you felt guilt, anger, frustration, or a mixture of these emotions?

The therapist started from the patient's wish and presented various aspects of the patient's experience which the patient could relate to. It is then up to the patient to direct her mind towards scenes she feels to correspond to this summary. Following this stage, the therapist asks for feedback to further hone her formulation to a version the patient agrees with.

If necessary, and often it should be done by default, therapists validate the patients' experiences: "I can understand why you felt forsaken and angry." Then, once she has ensured that the patient feels welcomed, she goes on to ask for associated memories: "Do any other episodes come to mind where you hoped to be welcomed and the person you were expecting to be supportive or welcoming failed to provide guidance and abandoned you or made you angry?"

Alternatively, if a patient is aware that the feelings and thoughts described in the episode are typical of him or, better still, if he realises that it is a problematic experience he would like to free himself of, the therapist can pose more direct questions: "How did you come to believe that your need or your wish would not be satisfied? Where does this strong sensitivity to signs of being abandoned come from?"

When confronted with such questions, patients very often recall relevant memories, allowing for a shared formulation of schemas. Memories of one's developmental history are welcome, but not indispensable; if patients have difficulty retracing distant memories, therapists look elsewhere!

Even if remote memories do not surface, it is possible to help patients understand their experiences are schema-driven. The therapist will quietly accept it is not always possible to recall the past. MIT is not based on a systematic reconstruction of patients' life stories. Nor is it interested in the origins of a disorder, which often remain unknown. The useful thing is for patients to arrive at understanding that their ways of thinking, feeling and acting are schema-driven and do not necessarily reflect an accurate interpretation of reality. A requirement to achieving this is the collection of narrative episodes with a recurring structure. It is of little importance whether they are recent or distant. Therefore, if patients lack memories from their early years, which are often not effortfully processed for long-term retention, therapists ask them to pay attention to any moments over the next week that resemble, to a lesser or greater extent, the same patterns of maladaptive emotions, thoughts and actions. Therapists ask patients to note down their experience, either mentally, in writing, or through a voice memo, in order to relate this new narrative episode in the next session. Over time, patients manage to perceive that certain intrapsychic and relational functioning experiences constitute repetitive patterns that are schema-driven.

A range of techniques can be very helpful during this stage. While reviewing a recent memory, therapists can use body-focused techniques (Chapter 7) and stimulate an experiential connection with emotional and somatic states, which become the focal point that resonates with the patients the most in the here and now. A therapist uses these somatic states to trigger related memories: "Now you feel this sensation of anxiety and can sense that it is accompanied by a tightening of your stomach. Does some image from the past come to mind? Can you remember yourself experiencing this sensation, your stomach feeling tight?" If a patient describes details of the expressions, tones of voice and gestures of the person he interacted with, the therapist can suggest that he concentrate on these details and ask him if they recall someone in particular.

Enrico was 40 years old and suffered from covert narcissism with depressive personality traits. During guided imagery he was reliving a board meeting, when he presented a report to his colleagues in the data processing firm where he worked. The therapist asked him to describe the faces he noticed. Enrico scanned the situation and then concentrated on the face of one colleague.

T: "What's the face like?"
E: "Impenetrable. Hard, stern, eyes covered by glasses, as if it were a screen."
T: "How do you feel when you see that face?"
E: "Ill. Tense."
T: "Can you help me define this tension? Where do you feel it physically?"
E: "On my shoulders, like a weight."
T: "Like a feeling of disappointment?"
E: "Hmm. . . . Yes, kind of. It's wearing me down. I'm feeling less confident in my report."
T: "Can you tell me anything else about this face?"
E: "It's harsh, cold. I know she won't like anything that I'm saying."
T: "How do you feel now?"
E: "The tension's increased. A bit of anxiety too now."

When the guided imagery was over, the therapist asked Enrico to focus again on the face.

T: "And how's your muscular tension now?"
E: "It comes back as soon as I pay attention to my colleague's face."
T: "What emotion could it be? What might happen? What would you like to do in the presence of that face?"
E: "Get away."
T: "What could your colleague do to you?"
E: "Perhaps . . . anxiety, I'm afraid she would criticise me."

T: "Excellent. Now you're faced with a face that's cold, stern and impenetrable, and you're afraid that some criticism is to be expected. Is this a scene familiar to you? Is there any face from your past that looks at you in the same way?"

Enrico grimaced and the therapist noticed this immediately.

T: "Enrico, your face changed, as if it were twitching with pain. Is that right? Has something come to mind?"
E: "I didn't think we'd get this far. I can see my mother's face. That expression where she pretends everything's going well and you know very well that, whatever you do, she won't like it."

The therapist asked Enrico to describe a situation where he was interacting with his mother while she wore this expression. Lots of memories surfaced. Enrico chose the one when he told her he wanted to enrol in a data processing course instead of law school. This episode helped him reconstruct how his expectation of being obstructed and criticised if he expressed independent drives and desires was rooted in his mother's invalidating and judgemental attitude towards him.

6) Schema reconstruction

Using the psychological knowledge accrued from narrative episodes first related in detail and then relived in-session, for example during a guided imagery exercise, it is possible to collaboratively redefine a schema for patients to recognise as their own. A patient might narrate an initial episode, communicating she desired approval but instead felt criticised, and sharing a relevant memory, drawn from her developmental history, of her mother criticising her and making her feel guilty. Let us imagine that with guided imagery she relives an episode with her mother. Anger surfaces, because she feels the criticism to be unfair, and feelings of solitude are evoked at the realisation of her mother's inability to listen to her and accept her. These thoughts and emotions remain impressed in her memory.

The therapist therefore redefines the schema in a way that resonates with the patient:

> You hold on to your wish to be appreciated, which is normal as it is one of the most powerful engines driving us in adult life. However, it's as if you've learnt that, when you expose yourself to the other's gaze, their reaction will be judgemental, sometimes harsh and disdainful, as in the episode with your mother. At this point you feel a sense of disappointment and defeat, because for a moment you really believe you're worthless. Then you rebel, you feel you deserve appreciation. In the end, you're end up with feelings of solitude, related to the fact that your mother did not accept you for who you were. You still have these sensations, which you experienced so vividly during our imagery game today. You think the hope of being appreciated is remote and that criticism will prevail.

118 *The decision-making procedure*

Patients will feel such a formulation as their own and are more likely to memorise it.

7) Reconstructing dysfunctional coping and self-regulation strategies

In addition to providing a reconstruction of schemas, therapists show to patients that part of their suffering is due to processes preceding, accompanying, or following schema-activating situations.

Such processes may include repetitive thought, such as worry or rumination (Chapter 2). Patients are likely to adopt these strategies while in the midst of interactions activating their schemas. For example, paranoid and avoidant patients will monitor relational threats during their conversations: "How am I to understand if he's going to criticise or cheat me? However, if I behave in a certain way, I can deceive him myself or hide my flaws. But he's attentive and might still find a way to uncover my defences. Let me try to understand what he really means. Maybe he's setting up a trap."

Very often patients activate strategies based on relational avoidance, like a person with Obsessive-Compulsive PD who spent decades avoiding asking his employer for a promotion or a raise he deserved, because he felt morally unworthy. Just as common is the adoption of dysfunctional behavioural coping: alcohol and drug abuse, risky behaviour, workaholism, compulsions/rituals, a persistent search for reassurance, manipulation and so on. The list of coping/self-regulation behavioural strategies is long and therapists should understand in collaboration with patients which strategies are activated in response to schema-related suffering. We help the patients understand how in the long term such strategies amplify the negative emotions they would like to avoid, activate other negative emotions and reduce the likelihood they will fulfil their wishes.

Once the schema has been reconstructed and links between maladaptive strategies and long-term distress have been established, there is often a germ of differentiation, with the patient being able, almost on her own, to admit to herself: "But is it then me that's still trying to come to terms with my mother's views?" This is the first step towards steering away from views of oneself as worthless or of others being unfair to oneself. This awareness is one of the pillars for progressing to the stage of change promoting.

Change promoting

Even if the techniques described here are successful in improving patients' understanding of their own functioning, they deploy their full power when put to the service of change. At the peak of the *shared formulation* stage the therapist and patient have collaboratively reconstructed the latter's main schemas. They now perceive clearly what the patient is driven by and what self-images underlie the activation of a wish: "I wish to be loved. I feel unlovable, even if at some moments I can see that others would give me attention and it would be reasonable to expect it." They now have a definite image of the expected or perceived response by the other: "He's not interested in me, even if I still have a slight hope he could pay attention to me."

Therapist and patient have also reconstructed the self's response to the other's response with much detail: "I think it's normal for her to leave me, because I do not have qualities, and this makes me feel terribly alone." The response may further include the full range of behavioural reactions, more or less dysfunctional forms of mastery over the patient's distressing state: "I withdraw to avoid further distress I am likely to experience when she won't pay me any attention."

The formulation of functioning includes the way in which coping schemas get activated when confronted with the other's response (Chapter 2). "As I can't be loved for what I am, I hope that, by improving my performance, the other will at least appreciate me." This marks the shift to the social rank motive with perfectionist tendencies.

In the renewed decision-making procedure, our formulation includes the initial awareness of healthy parts: a sense of competence, self-worth and of being lovable, curiosity, dynamic drive and interests. Of course, their presence in a patient's mind is limited: he may have accessed these healthy parts in-session, perhaps whilst applying a technique, but negative representations of himself and others may persist in his day-to-day life. This is, therefore, the point at which to move on to promoting change.

At this stage we aim to broaden patients' healthy parts, increase their ability to take a critical distance from maladaptive interpersonal schemas and tolerate suffering, and to interrupt the dysfunctional strategies they use to handle distress, such as rumination to behavioural avoidance. At this stage, patients manage to form a more complex understanding of the other's mind and, eventually, the impact their actions have on others and how these contribute to relational dysfunctions they demonstrate, that is, how they themselves contribute to forming interpersonal cycles. The techniques stimulate change in many ways.

In MIT we establish change operation hierarchies (Dimaggio, Montano et al., 2015). The first goals are: 7a) *to differentiate* and 7b) *to widen experiential connection with heathy parts*. These are separate yet synergistic. On the one hand, acquiring a critical distance from maladaptive schemas requires OR involves assimilating ideas outside one's schemas and accepting one's healthy self-parts. For example, recognising that the view of oneself as *worthless* traces back to one's development history can almost automatically lead to question its truth and, consequently, to becoming open to the idea, at least embryonically, that one is worthy. On the other hand, accessing healthy parts allows one to review maladaptive representations from a different angle.

7a) Differentiating

Promoting critical distance can be done in various ways and the techniques contribute on different levels. It is possible to simulate an initial stage of differentiation using mindfulness and body techniques. Patients may have the idea that they are trapped in a state of suffering they are incapable to escape, and as a result feel hopeless and passive. In this situation they may firmly hold on to ideas such as "I'm weak", "I'm vulnerable", "I'm a failure". Bodily work, from simple breathing practices and body anchoring exercises, or coaching the patients to experience a sense of physical strength, by, for example, clenching their fists or expanding their chest, may help them perceive that as the state of the body changes, then thoughts fly away or negative emotions become less intense and ideas change.

Patients can gradually come to understand they have power over their inner world and realise their views of themselves as being weak or vulnerable can be put aside to make room for alternative views, such as "I'm capable", "I'm strong" or "I'm willing or courageous enough to try". What is more likely to change is the degree of certainty about a conviction: "I still feel vulnerable, but for a few moments I don't consider this to be true." It is even more realistic to expect a change such as: "Ok, during the exercise I felt less fragile, so I remain hopeful. However, the sensation has already come back and at home I won't be up to tackle my usual problems."

A change such as this one is a success, albeit limited. It is important that patients perceive their negative ideas as not corresponding to facts, which they can, therefore, discard and temporarily replace with benign ideas. We have noticed these basic levels of differentiation go hand-in-hand with improvements in mastery: while patients are undergoing micro-changes with respect to their emotions and cognitions, they understand they can influence their inner states and feel better by shifting their attention.

With guided imagery it is possible to increase differentiation. Typically, a patient describes a recent problem. Her therapist reconstructs the episode in a manner that reflects the structure of the underlying maladaptive interpersonal schemas. At this point, the therapist asks the patient to recall any relevant memories. If the patient brings forth a particular memory the therapist can ask him to relive it using guided imagery. By experiencing this relived memory, the patient understands that doubting himself and others in the present is the result of thought processes anchored in past experiences. This helps him change his perspective on the problem.

Ruggero was 40 years old and came from an upper middle class family in a town in Northern Italy where he worked as a civil lawyer. For several months, he had been wanting to change his job and move to the international cooperation field, where he could combine his organisational skills with his humanitarian vocation. He feared, however, not being able to maintain the same standard of living and not being up to meeting the demands of this new job, which would require skills he had never before applied.

His wife supported him, but told him candidly that he could embark on this venture only when he was sure that he would be able to ensure his family – herself and their two children – the same income. His wife was, in turn, a well-established, self-employed professional and did not depend on him financially, as he pointed out. He felt no grudge towards her: he understood her position and felt supported. Nevertheless, at work he felt at times bored and at other times constrained, and he felt embarrassed by the idea of being a fake, pretending to enjoy his work while thinking about a new career. He worried whether it was better to stay in a job he was no longer interested in or take the leap and risk failure. Another element feeding his worry was guilt at the idea of causing problems for his wife and children. He imagined them going through hardship, socially rejected because they were "losers", and becoming depressed. His worries had some ground: his career in the new organisation was not guaranteed, he would have been hired initially on yearly contracts and any financial retribution would depend for the most part on his productivity.

Given Ruggero could see that his wife supported him and that in any case the family would not be left penniless, the therapist hypothesised that Ruggero's worry was caused by fantasies activated by maladaptive interpersonal schemas. He asked Ruggero to focus on episodes from his past where he wanted to act independently, in line with his own inclinations, and instead came across a judgemental another, which made him feel ashamed. He asked him if, alternatively, he could recollect any situations of him acting independently and where others suffered.

Ruggero's expression changed. He said, "I've screwed it up many times". With a mixture of shame and anger he recalled his years at university during which he snorted a huge amount of cocaine. He remembered his mother pretending nothing was going on. Their agreement was that she would not raise any objections provided he would accomplish his mission of becoming an established professional she could flaunt among the town's high society. He studied hard and got top marks, and his mother rewarded him with a high standard of living.

His therapist asked him to explain what it was that he "screwed up". Ruggero was even more embarrassed and lowered his head:

> I was jailed for possession of cocaine, carrying loads of it. I was with my girlfriend and we'd stocked up. There was enough to be convicted for dealing. I could see I was fucked. But then the lawyer was good and managed to convince the judge of the truth: that it was for my personal use and that, as we could afford it, we'd bought a lot. But we had a really nasty experience. It was my fault: I'd acted like a jerk not least to impress my girlfriend – and in fact shortly afterwards she dumped me. The worst moment was when my mother came to visit me in prison: she couldn't care less about me: "You've ruined my reputation. How could you be so stupid?! Now through your fault my life's over. I won't be able to go to the theaters, walk down the main street, go out of the house."

Ruggero's shame and guilt exploded and overwhelmed him. The therapist asked him what he did then when confronted with his mother's reaction. He only recalled wanting to sink out of sight. The therapist suggested reliving the scene with guided imagery, so as to reawaken these feelings, see if other aspects of the experience emerged, and try to modulate these distressing emotions. Ruggero accepted. The therapist noticed first and foremost that healthy parts were missing but conjectured that he could have experienced feelings and ideas about himself different from the negative ones when confronted with his mother's response.

At the start imagery was charged with guilt and shame, but, whilst his mother was directing the accusations at him, the therapist noticed a different feeling surfacing in Ruggero's face. He asked him how he felt and he replied: "Sad." The therapist insisted on working through this feeling and he spoke of a lifelong sense of loneliness: his mother had never cared for him.

R: "She was only interested in making herself pretty. But she couldn't care less about me."
T: "Ruggero, there's a change in your face now, right? What do you feel now?"
R: "Anger."
T: "At the idea that . . . ?"
R: "Come on. I'm in prison, in despair, handcuffed, not knowing what's going to happen to me and the only thing you're worried about is walking up and down the main street?!"

Guided imagery improved the understanding of the narrative structure. Healthy parts that started to counter the negative schema surfaced: the idea of oneself as deserving to be cared for and understood. Sadness was evoked through feelings of loneliness and now filled the room, while guilt and shame vanished. These were good conditions for rescripting.

The therapist asked him to connect with his sadness and to try tell his mother: "You've never cared for me." Ruggero broke into tears and cried for long.

R: "All my life's been like this. She couldn't ever give a fuck about me. I'm still carrying this burden but the problem's hers, holy shit, it's hers!"

At the end of rescripting Ruggero felt tired but at the same time relieved. He felt in connection with his need to be heard and appreciated for what he was, while guilt and shame had disappeared. He also came to realise, he said, that his use of cocaine was connected both to his being neglected and to the all-powerfulness his mother granted him. It should be noted here that post-rescripting reflections indicate progress.

T: "Listen, now we've seen what your current situation reminds you of, and that you feel you didn't deserve being ignored and despised, how do you see your current work problem?"
R: "The decision is still difficult, but no way would my family break up in pieces if I didn't earn very much for a year or two."
T: "Do you feel at fault towards them at this moment?"
R: "No, not now. My wife would never consider me a failure. Sure, there are still practical issues I have discussed with her that I would need to think about, because the choice isn't simple and there are risks. But now I can think about these with a bit more equanimity."

Behavioural exploration is important for differentiating. Usually patients start differentiating in-session but do not manage to do it without the presence of the therapist. Often, and even during sessions, only a short while after differentiating they go back to ruminating and adopting the perspective of their pathogenic schemas: "I realise the idea I'm not worth much is just a personal belief that may not correspond to reality. Sometimes I realise I'm perhaps better than I think. But now, at the idea of going home and talking with my husband, I don't feel well and I'm afaid he'll criticise me if I tell him I want to go to the movies with my friends. Perhaps he's right".

To use behavioural experiments to achieve differentiation we employ the experiential learning cycle: planning/carrying out the experiment/in-session reflection (Dimaggio, Salvatoreet al., 2015; Hackmann et al., 2011; Kolb, 1984). Therapists and patients plan tasks collaboratively, structuring them around what wish patients will try to fulfil and which fears are expected to hold them back. Therapists ask patients to pay attention to their inner experience while carrying out the task and further emphasise that the goal is not to complete a particular behaviour, but the simple intention of trying to do something that schema-driven procedures have prevented them from doing so far. The instruction is simple: "Mind your inner experience while you try to complete the task." In the next session those experiences will be reviewed collaboratively.

Very often patients, on their own or with their therapist's help, become able to distinguish between what they expected, "I won't manage. I won't be capable of doing this. I'll get attacked," and what actually happened, "I felt in control. He reacted well. He was perhaps a bit indifferent, but he didn't criticise me."

7b) Widening experiential connection with heathy parts

Stimulating connection with healthy parts is one of the main reasons, among the many, we have included experiential work in MIT, and all techniques have the potential to promote this goal. While helping patients to take a critical distance from maladaptive interpersonal schemas, behavioural exploration stimulates connection with ideas of effectiveness and independence, a state of curiosity, and feelings of pride, and enjoyment. Patients seek relationships where they can fulfil their wishes: feeling loved or cared for, exploring their environment and looking for novelties, as well as achieving goals in line with their own inclinations.

While interacting with others they often discover their views of self and others are unexpectedly different to what they feared and the images of a judgemental and threatening other fade away. They also connect with self-parts associated with views of oneself as effective, lovable, strong, curious, confident and so on. With the techniques described in this book it becomes easier to stimulate in-session experiential connection with healthy parts. This connection in turn facilitates differentiation: "If I feel to be worth something at this moment, I am more likely to question the idea of being worthless."

As soon as a healthy part emerges, the therapist validates it: "Hang on, at this moment you're describing yourself as competent and I can see you've got a different expression. You seem more confident about your abilities." As a result, patients find it easier to perceive that their core negative ideas about themselves are precisely that: ideas that exist together with other, more benevolent, images.

Experiential work reinforces this way of differentiating. We put a patient in connection with his healthy part using a drama technique, a behavioural experiment and guided imagery. Not only do we point out to him this healthy part of himself, but we also attempt to help him maintain it in his consciousness for as long as possible, by keeping him in connection with the sensorimotor features of this positive experience.

When, a short while later, the patient again becomes prey to his schemas, the therapist finds it easier to point this out: "There you are again, can you see how your mind is quick to go back to thinking negatively about yourself and others?" This way we attempt to facilitate simultaneously the hoped-for access to a healthy part and a consolidation of differentiation: negative ideas do not mirror reality, but are perspectives that are quicker to assert themselves in consciousness, replacing more benevolent views one holds.

Ernesto was 39 years old and was a skilled factory worker. He suffered from Avoidant and Obsessive-Compulsive PD. After a few months of therapy he began to feel effective, competent in his job, and entitled to express his own opinion. However, he reported that these sensations and ideas about himself did not last long and got immediately replaced by negative thoughts, criticising himself for much of what he did.

Through the recollection of memories relevant to these ideas a schema emerged that originated in having experienced his father, who was lost in a world of shame and isolation, ignore his every action, making Ernesto feel he was of limited importance.

Ernesto recalled an episode where he was happy about building a nice sandcastle but his father ignored him, making him feel worthless. The therapist asked him to concentrate on the memory of feeling happy about the sandcastle and Ernesto recalled his sensation of feeling capable, competent and enthusiastic. However, he also described how this sensation was already dissipating, while his memory of his aloof father grew stronger. At this point the therapist first asked him to focus on the somatic sensations associated with his feelings as he built the sandcastle. What emerged were feelings of enjoyment, satisfaction and competence.

At this point the therapist proposed the two-chair game (Chapter 6) and asked him to talk with his father. During the game Ernesto firmly expressed to his father his need to be seen and he repeated with conviction: "I really want you to look at me. It's important for me that you appreciate me. I'm clever; it's a nice sandcastle." Then at the therapist's suggestion he tried to tell him, "I want you to play with me. You never do."

When playing his father, Ernesto initially replied with excuses, but in the end he said it was difficult for him but he would try. Ernesto left the game feeling capable and entitled to ask for attention. His actions had meaning and value. At the same time, he was in touch with a sorrow he was not previously very aware of, evoked by the realisation of his father's character limitations: "It doesn't depend on me. He didn't enjoy anything." As can be seen, in accordance with the decision-making procedure, differentiation sometimes, almost automatically, paves the way for understanding the other in a more sophisticated and decentred way, the subject of the next step.

8) Improving theory of the other's mind and decentring

Once patients can, at least partly, access their healthy parts and differentiate, their ability to understand others grows naturally (Dimaggio, Lysaker, Carcione, Nicolò, & Semerari, 2008). They in fact make less schema-dependent attributions. "If I am vulnerable I am biased to perceive the other as dominating and threatening" (Salvatore et al., 2012). If I realise I am not as vulnerable as I thought and I firmly hold a positive view of myself, the bias will recede and I will be able to see the other with different eyes without any particular metacognitive effort. On the other hand, years of interpreting what goes on around me through distorted lenses renders the interpretation of others' actions less sharp and realistic.

In this case, both guided imagery with rescripting and drama techniques are effective. During guided imagery a clinician should ask patients to very attentively focus and review the details of the other's behaviour. "What was your father's voice like?" "At that point your uncle came to your home to calm your father down. And how did he react? Can you see his face? What's he doing?"

This work often helps patients to discover features of the other they did not know, noticing for the first time, for example, elements of fragility where up until then they only recognised a propensity to dominate. Due to this change in perception they become increasingly aware that others have ways of thinking, feeling and acting that are separate from them. When thinking about her mother's screeching voice, one of our patients said: "It was always like that. She couldn't manage. She shrieked at me, but she did it with everyone. Dad had cheated on her and she felt insecure and she was continuously going over the edge. I realise now that it was weakness."

Drama techniques are particularly good at improving the reading of the other's mind, especially during role changes in the two-chair game and in role-playing. By putting themselves in another's shoes patients can find themselves thinking and experiencing things they would not otherwise be able to imagine. They might, for example, play the role of a scolding parent and experience a feeling of fright and worry for the child (themselves) that they are now observing. Moreover, while in the other's shoes, patients can observe themselves and from this perspective sometimes achieve a double result: understanding the other better and enriching their self-representations.

The reason increasing the understanding of the other is useful is likely related to the human mind's natural projective mechanisms (Dimaggio et al., 2008). The state in which we find ourselves makes us more attentive to certain signals. If we are in a state of vulnerability, for example, we tend to ascribe hostile intentions to others (Salvatore et al., 2012). But as soon as a patient accesses more solid and secure aspects of herself and adopts a more benign attitude, on the one hand, there will be a reduction in her negative attributions vis-à-vis the other and, on the other hand, a state of greater security is likely to stimulate theory of mind (Fonagy et al.,

2002). At this point role-playing makes it possible to exercise skills, now free from the toxic influences deriving from her negative self-representations.

A patient might enact a situation where he felt abandoned by his girlfriend and looked for consolation from a friend, who replied: "She doesn't deserve you." His therapist asks him to change roles and play his girlfriend. From this position he feels compassion for himself and perceives he has a fragility deserving empathic regard, instead of criticism and rejection. This helps him stop behaving with submission and despair, with a view to getting back with his girlfriend, who has repeatedly rejected him.

When we talk of increasing understanding of the other's mind, we are not necessarily referring to a real other. By "*Other*" we instead mean a psychological position, an inner object; we refer to how in accordance with our inner scenario, our schemas, we imagine someone will respond to our wishes. Enriching our understanding of the other means making our repertoire of attributions more flexible. This can, in turn, open our mind to a more sophisticated and realistic idea of others in the real world.

What we first work towards is to help patients develop the ability to read others' behaviour in a less schema-dependent manner. Only afterwards do we promote an attributional style that is three-dimensional, which involves a more precise and careful analysis of non-verbal signals of the other's behaviour. At this point, it is possible to arrive at more realistic expectations, which are context- and person-specific. In this way a patient would progress from interpretations and expectations that correspond to a schematic representation of men as "mistreating" or women as "unpredictable" to decentred interpretations and expectations that are specific to a particular man or woman demonstrating unique features, due to their own unique history.

When patients develop these skills, they are in a position to choose different relationships. They can more easily become aware of themselves construing others in a schema-dependent way. They have developed a series of different "internalised others" (Hermans & Hermans-Konopka, 2010) and can now assess whether they are interested in and attracted by the "real other" as a candidate for an alive, satisfying and warm relationship.

This reading is sometimes the true moment of release from toxic relationships: patients realise that the "real" other has negative features, which are independent to their schemas. In such cases the problem is not a defective theory of mind, as the patients read the other realistically. The problem is that schemas filter reality (Chapter 1), increasing the likelihood that a subject exclusively notices schema-consistent features of reality (Fraley & Shaver, 2000). This is a mechanism also highlighted through research as present in Borderline PD patients, who, when confronted with hostile expressions, tend to approach rather than avoid others (Bertsch et al., 2018). The pathological feature in this example is not so much a patient's interpretation, which is valid, but the tendency to approach the hostile "other". Schemas make us prone to finding certain characteristics interesting and desirable, even if they cause us distress. Having acquired an improved understanding of their schemas, patients are instead able to say: "Yes, that person has certain characteristics that are consistent to my schemas. But now she doesn't attract me anymore."

9) Acknowledging one's own contribution to interpersonal cycles

Interpersonal cycles are among the most toxic PD maintenance factors, with patients' actions being counter-productive and provoking large numbers of negative responses, confirming their most catastrophic forecasts about others (Dimaggio et al., 2007; Safran & Muran, 2000). However, therapists should rigorously abstain from helping patients become aware that they are contributing to others' negative responses, if they have not previously accessed their healthy parts and achieved an acceptable degree of differentiation. One patient had shared with her previous therapist, of a different orientation, how her husband neglected her (they had been separated for a year). In the second session this therapist pointed out to her that her compulsively independent behaviour had contributed to driving away her husband. The patient felt criticised, experienced an intense sensation of guilt, and dropped out.

If the conditions are met, that is, if patients differentiate and have accessed their healthy parts and wishes, they have to understand that having better relationships requires them to change their behaviour. Techniques help in this regard. Behavioural exploration has effects on this domain in a powerful, albeit, indirect way. How is this possible? Once patients become able to act in accordance with individual goals, they find that others position themselves in unexpected ways, different to how they would respond if patients engaged in coping behaviours such as compliant submission, self-sacrifice, perfectionism, or workaholism. At this point they are able to see, by themselves or with minimal help from their therapist, that part of their relational dysfunction is due to not engaging with their healthy parts and to letting others act in ways that then increase their suffering.

One university student felt criticised by her parents. In response she either looked for approval or protested, and both behaviours inevitably ended up causing her parents to criticise her. However, she did understand that the problem was that she was driven by a schema that made her suffer from any criticism directed towards her, including remarks from her friends and boyfriend, and also made her repress any wishes she may have had of behaving independently. Her therapist asked her to try to abstain from coping strategies that involved acts of submission or protesting and instead act in line with her own independent wishes, which the therapist had previously identified and validated in-session. Part of the exercise included paying attention to her parents' reaction to changes in her behaviour, specifically of her making decisions without asking for their authorisation. In her next session she pointed out that her parents became more interested in and curious about what she was doing. She thus realised that as long as she had been acting in a dependent mode, her father and mother had perceived her as infantile, and this kept them in a position of being judgemental and apprehensive.

Drama techniques and imagery rescripting promote the disruption of interpersonal cycles. We recall that the prime goals of these exercises are accessing healthy parts and differentiating. When these have been achieved and consolidated, the same exercises should be used to get patients to behave in a manner that increases their interpersonal competence.

Rescripting, the two-chair game and role-playing, especially in group therapy (Chapter 10), thus become directed at triggering different reactions in real others, with patients trying to adopt assertive ways of behaving in line with their individual wishes, to reduce their diffidence, aggression, arrogance, or compliant submission, and to communicate their vulnerability instead of protesting angrily. During these exercises, therapists get patients to notice how the other reacts and to memorise the types of behaviour appearing most effective and functional. Naturally, after rescripting and drama technique patients need to engage in behavioural experiments where they attempt to maintain these new relational styles.

10) Integrating and constructing a new self-narrative

With a patient's increasing understanding of himself and others a therapist can further enable him to achieve metacognitive integration, by helping him form a view of the self in the world that takes into account the complexity of relationships, the co-existence of points of strength and weakness, and the variation across situations that precede better or worse functioning(Semerari et al., 2003). The patient will see she is driven by multiple, sometimes conflicting, goals. She finally realises how much and in what ways she has changed over the course of her therapy.

At this stage, therefore, we help patients to acquire a consistent self-view and become able to confer meaning to any contradictions by synthesising apparently unrelated features. An important element is to incorporate healthy parts in the patient's identity and self-narrative. We get patients to observe and understand what causes their transitions between healthy and pathological functioning. Through repeated practice they achieve a comprehensive self-view, a picture where positive aspects exist together with suffering which they now accept as part of the human condition, as well as an integral part of their history and personality that can, however, be relieved.

This type of integration is also supported by an interpretation of the therapeutic process, as patients evaluate their progress and how they have changed compared to their starting point. In our previous book (Dimaggio, Montano et al., 2015) we described how for this purpose, the drawing of schemas, diagrams and reformulation letters is of great help, in addition to reconstruction interventions initiated by the therapist. All this work is valid, but the techniques are a precious addition.

A therapist can stimulate embryonic forms of integration already from the earliest sessions by using guided imagery and rescripting or drama techniques, considering in collaboration with patients what causes their shifts between different mental states. These exercises often facilitate patients' connection with healthy parts and a therapist should try to make positive ideas, emotions and sensations last for as long as possible.

Naturally, healthy parts tend to diminish and get replaced by negative mental states, a resurfacing of schemas and rumination. At this point, the therapist makes the following sort of observations, as promptly as possible:

> Wait a moment. Stop. Can you see how quickly you've switched from thinking that it is your right to travel, when you felt OK, to being submerged again by that picture of your father being alone and sad, going back to feeling guilty? Can you see how your mind finds it difficult to maintain a positive state because, almost at the same time when you see yourself as independent and happy, you get overwhelmed by that picture of your dad suffering? At this moment it doesn't matter to us whether it's true or not, that your dad really suffers. The point is that your mind switches on its own from a positive state, of independence, to one of guilt, which cancels out the pleasure of being curious and free to explore.

Interventions of this sort are generally very effective and are useful for achieving integration, which in turn reinforces differentiation: "What I'm thinking is not necessarily true; it's my mind that works like that." Such interventions make it simpler to define the negative scenarios associated to schemas as worrying and to deal with them as such through attentional or mindfulness techniques, as we shall see in Chapters 9 and 11.

Another form of integration is the awareness of having contrasting representations of the self and others (Semerari et al., 2003). With the use of guided imagery and rescripting and drama techniques, patients discover how they shift from negative ideas about the self and others to positive ones. They thus become aware that they swing between different mental states and can identify the internal triggers that regulate these shifts.

Integration interventions in turn foster mastery: in subsequent sessions, when a patient finds himself in the grip of schema-dependent ideas, he can deploy the memory of what happened during the in-session exercises as a lever for exiting this state and re-anchoring himself to benign representations.

Exercises with the body foster integration on a basic level and are of the utmost benefit to a patient. They make a patient see that shifts between states have a somatic trigger and at the same time that it is possible to work through the body. He will form an integrated idea similar with the following: "When I feel criticised, I get overwhelmed by the idea I'm worthless and this makes me feel weak, flaccid, and powerless. However, if I adopt a toned position, such as the one I experienced in-session, these ideas change, at least partly, and I go back to feeling well, capable, in great shape and sometimes ready to tackle difficulties."

11) Promoting relational regulation with advanced mastery strategies

As we saw in point 3b, when patients have limited access to their mental states, a therapist should promote basic forms of *mastery* and use techniques for the treating of symptoms based essentially on the awareness that there is a symptom or problem and something needs to be done about it. These techniques involve, essentially, behavioural or attention regulation strategies.

All the techniques described in this book can promote mastery and reduce suffering: mindfulness and attentional techniques reduce rumination and associated distress. Somatic techniques reduce negative emotional arousal. Drama techniques can then progressively increase the scope to reduce distress, thanks to differentiation: "I can see that my thoughts do not necessarily correspond to reality and I consequently feel better."

Attentional techniques (Chapter 9) aim at significantly reducing symptoms of repetitive thought, by modulating the quantity and quality of the attention afforded to various types of negative thoughts, disrupting the reliance on dysfunctional coping/self-regulation strategies, and teaching patients more adaptive ways of dealing with distress and the representations underlying it.

At the most advanced treatment stages, these same exercises aim to promote more effective forms of interpersonal problem solving. Therapists ask patients to try and solve their relational difficulties by using both what they have understood about themselves – what their wishes, healthy parts and dysfunctional schemas are – and what they have understood in mentalistic terms about others. Patients should now try to use the metacognitive skills acquired to change the course of their relationships in reality, as in the two group programmes we describe in Chapter 10.

Change promotion is summarised in Figure 4.2.

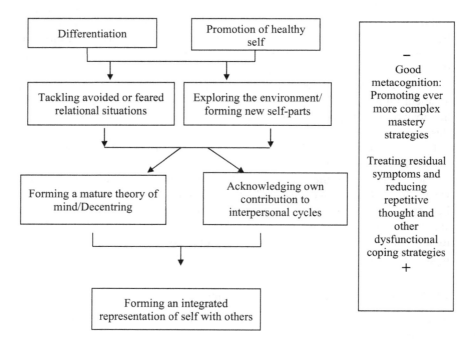

Figure 4.2 Change promoting

The therapeutic relationship and experiential techniques

In MIT, work on the therapeutic relationship is core, ongoing and intensive. Everything we do occurs through the monitoring and regulation of what happens between patient and therapist. The latter should not attempt the smallest step if the relationship is not regulated, except for any initiatives aimed at pinpointing and resolving the rupture. Here we depict how experiential work is applied through the therapeutic relationship.

In this book we suggest many tools for fostering awareness and change at every moment of therapy. This means that MIT therapists are extremely active and look to have tools in their box that can deal with most problems. Being active is beneficial for patients, but only under certain conditions. Which are these?

We note two different therapist approaches. The first is directed towards empathetic understanding and listening and validating patients' distress; the second is oriented towards activating patients, exposing them to situations that are novel, challenging and often a source of anxiety. The first approach is indispensable and one of the core features of the treatment process. With this listening position therapists are often able to facilitate corrective emotional experiences, as a patient who expresses her distress is met by a supportive other, who is present and validates her distress, making her feel understood. Persisting with this approach to relational healing, without at the same time exposing patients to experiences during which they can practice letting go of their coping mechanisms, has a risk: keeping them in a protected and passive situation that does not allow them to independently tackle what they fear and prevents them from constructing new, healthy self-parts.

In the second approach, clinicians should, therefore, ask patients to expose themselves, in sessions by using imagery and drama techniques, and in-between through behavioural experiments. This approach makes it possible to tackle and overcome fears and widen the range of what patients are able to tolerate, giving them a richer social life. The risk here is to expose patients too much, in which case they might feel forced to deal with areas in their life when they do not feel ready or deal with distress when they don't have the necessary skills.

Therapists who prefer the more conservative approach keep patients more protected in an often solid relationship, probably resulting in slower change. Conversely, therapists who prefer the more exploratory approach lead patients into areas with a greater risk of psychological distress; they may be able to effect change faster, yet at the risk of a slight increase in drop-outs. An example is a PTSD efficacy trial comparing Interpersonal Therapy to Prolonged Exposure (Markowitz et al., 2015). Interpersonal Therapy forbade to expose patients to traumatic memories, either *in-vivo* or through imagery techniques, while Prolonged Exposure prescribed both types of exposure. Both stances were effective, but Interpersonal Therapy resulted in fewer drop-outs among patients with comorbid depression. Prolonged Exposure resulted in slightly faster improvements instead.

Of course, the two approaches, empathetic validation and regard offered within the therapeutic relationship on the one hand and use of activating, exposure techniques on the other hand are not mutually exclusive at all! However, it is important therapists know their spontaneous preferences. Some therapists are afraid of causing an increase in arousal and feel guilty if patients suffer because of them. These therapists tend to refrain from exposing patients to challenging situations, which may have provided an opportunity for patients to practice novel, adaptive behaviours in challenging situations.

Other therapists are less able to tolerate patients' distress and therefore take action in order to feel effective and prove that they are good therapists, instead of leaving patients in states of suffering that they themselves cannot tolerate.

A priori neither of the two positions is useful. It is necessary for therapists to first identify and regulate their own tendencies. Then they should ask themselves: on the basis of the case formulation which approach is more appropriate to follow? Is it the validating approach, prioritising the therapeutic relationship, or the exposure approach, mobilising the patient, exposing her to imagery or engaging her in behavioural experiments (Dimaggio, 2019)?

In this book we propose a range of techniques and suggest using them sometimes at the earliest opportunity. These are imagery, drama, sensory-motor and behavioural techniques that increase arousal and promote change with as much speed and incisiveness as possible. This should naturally be the goal of all psychotherapy: curing patients as early as possible and with minimal side effects.

How can this be done while keeping our attention on the relationship and respect for the patient's suffering, with a low risk of relationship ruptures? To start with, we have said that therapists need to know their preferences – expose or not expose? – and regulate them internally.

Another step is to visualise the improvement that would be achieved by using a particular technique. At this point, the clinician suggests an activity to the patient, while explaining that it should help to reduce his distress and enrich his relational life. Patients need to be told that they could experience transitory distressing states. We do this exactly as we would with patients suffering from anxiety disorders. We explain that such a behavioural or imagery exercise can increase negative arousal and at this point one negotiates with patients on the conditions under which they feel they would be able to attempt it.

To forestall negative interpersonal cycles occurring in the therapeutic relationship, it is useful to explain to patients that the therapist has the freedom to suggest various activities or experiments, and they are completely free to say "no" or, if they accept, to report any negative experiences or to interrupt the exercise. Acting on this assumption, which needs, however, to be renegotiated with patients in subsequent sessions, therapists can take more risks, because they know the patient can calmly refuse.

In our experience, these operations are enough for most patients to agree to carry out a wide variety of techniques and experiments. Our stance favours an atmosphere of confidence, hope and cooperation, that instils in patients a sense that they are taking an active part in their own treatment.

The spirit in which a therapist proposes a technique to be applied is fundamental. When we suggest any particular activity, its effectiveness is not our prime goal: we do not hope to solve problems immediately. Every action is aimed first and foremost at generating an atmosphere of curiosity. The spirit is "Let's try and do this, see what happens and watch the patient's reactions, whatever they are". Of course, if we get positive results, we welcome them. If, however, a patient has negative experiences, we first need to modulate them, which results in an increase in metacognition, and this is a success that facilitates the subsequent stages of treatment. If, at a certain point in her therapy, a patient decides to not engage in activities aimed at progress, one needs to change their approach and switch to revising the therapeutic contract, as we show later.

We have explained how to suggest to a patient to be active or try certain techniques, under the safest conditions possible. It is not guaranteed, however, that our best intentions are followed by positive responses. We very carefully monitor the impact of our suggestions. We can risk, to a significant extent, exposing patients to feared situations and getting them actively engaged in behavioural experiments, provided that, after each intervention, we monitor their reaction and make it the focus of our conversation. When we suggest an activity, we should listen to what the patient thinks of our suggestion, how he experiences it and, especially, how he perceives us starting from the point when we suggested the act.

When therapists propose something, patients are likely to quickly perceive them in line with their schemas.

To a therapist suggesting experiential activities patients can ascribe roles like:

- *Judgemental and demanding*: "He's assigned me a task I don't know how to do and so he'll be disappointed in me."
- *Neglectful and uninterested in their suffering*: "He's telling me what to do to reduce my distress because he's fed up with listening to me. He can't understand how profound my suffering is."
- *Domineering and constricting*: "He imposes these activities on me. I'm not free to choose."
- *Violent and aggressive*: "He exposes me to distressing situations that remind me of my suffering and this hurts me."
- *Seductive or eroticised*: "He's getting close to me, to my body. He's hitting on me and I'm attracted."

Therapists should therefore ask patients how they feel about the suggestion they have just heard: "What do you feel when I ask you to go back to that scene where your father attacked your mother?"; "How do you feel about my suggestion that in the coming week you try and resist your impulse to seek to go out with a girl when you feel lonely?" "I asked you, if you get a moment of intense depression, to try nevertheless to get out of bed and do some physical activity. What do you think of me at this moment?" At the same time therapists are attentive to non-verbal signals of relationship rupture, withdrawal or hostility and point them out to the patient with a view to regulating the relationship.

When problems arise in the therapeutic relationship, the therapist needs to shift the focus: no longer making suggestions to the patient to use a particular technique, but repairing the rupture in the relationship. It should be reiterated that this book focuses on how to apply experiential techniques and we have therefore concentrated only on what happens within the therapeutic relationship when we try to apply these techniques. MIT is, however, a model where the work on the therapeutic relationship is ongoing, we just refer the reader to other works (Dimaggio, Montano et al., 2015; Safran & Muran, 2000; Semerari, 2010).

The therapeutic contract

MIT therapists are very active and have a rich toolkit of techniques. Precisely for this reason they are liable to make mistakes. In our experience the most common mistake is pushing patients towards change without first coming up with or updating a therapeutic contract. Patients with PD or histories of trauma can hold schemas of the other as a tyrant they need to resist. Many hold schemas that direct them to becoming dependent on others as a coping mechanism, which they understandably do not want to relinquish. Others come with histories of being abandoned or being ignored and considered weak when they voiced their distress, so that they interpret any attempt to help them improve as a desire to get rid of them.

Assunta, a patient being treated by a female colleague, described her husband as distant, cold, verbally aggressive and contemptuous. She had a girl and a boy, 4 and 2 years old respectively, whom she did not like to look after. She would have liked to separate from her husband but feared she would be doing it only to comply with pressure from her mother, who did not want her daughter to be with a man who was, as she put it, harmful. Her mother tended to impose her own ideas on Assunta and the latter reacted with a mixture of compliant submission, anger at being constrained and paralysis of action.

However, staying with her husband made her unhappy, so that each alternative course of action was, in essence, impracticable. Assunta had a dramatically low sense of agency: she did not act on the basis of what she wished, thought, or planned. With some difficulty, the therapist reconstructed her schemas: her basic wish was to explore independently. If, however, she behaved according to her preferences, she faced a judgemental, disdainful and harsh other. At this point she felt incompetent or alone and gave up with exploration. She also feared physical aggression from another, her husband, whom she perceived as dangerous. At the same time the attachment motivation was activated and she submitted to the other to avoid being abandoned. She returned to the situation that made her feel unhappy, while she wished for independence, which maintained the vicious cycle she was caught in.

Her therapist reconstructed her schemas in collaboration with Assunta but she did not improve. She reacted irritably to any attempts by the therapist to address her problems. The therapist felt angry, powerless and incompetent and her reaction was to try even more to push the patient to change. Her supervisor, one of us, asked her if she had asked the patient what her desired relational state was and especially what therapeutic action she was prepared to take to achieve it. The therapist realised she had not carried out this step. The next session was revealing:

the therapist went back to her supervisor and reported that Assunta had replied, "You see, it's as if I lived in a gilded cage. It's convenient to have my husband's financial support and my mother at hand and I'm not sure if I want to give up this convenience."

This was the reason behind her lack of progress. The therapist was driven by her own need to get the patient to progress, but the latter was oriented towards an egosyntonic maintenance of her dependent coping: she had the vague aim of alleviating her relationship dissatisfaction, but did not know how to achieve this, and neither had she made any plans for achieving it. She preferred the *gilded cage*.

What do MIT therapists do in situations like these?

They renegotiate the contract.

In PD therapies it has become ever clearer how central the contract is, precisely because of the difficulty such patients have in taking initiative to get better (Bender, 2005), for example by giving up dysfunctional coping. Various authors have thus pointed out how important it is to agree on what reciprocal commitments need to be adopted in order to aspire to an effective therapy (Clarkin, Yeomans, & Kernberg, 1999; Links, Mercer, & Novick, 2016; Linehan, 1993; Yeomans, Delaney, & Levy, 2017).

In this, PD therapies are similar to psychotherapy in general. One of the most important ingredients in an effective psychotherapy is the therapeutic alliance, which has three components (Bordin, 1979). Two of them are the patient–therapist *bond* and the *goal*, the agreed objective. Reasonably skilled therapists are usually adequately concerned about these. The goal is already part of the contract: we decide together that the therapy will have this agreed objective.

Therapists often forget the third element, the *task*. They take responsibility for a patient's progress or, without realising it, impose the task on the latter. They envisage the road towards health, decide the patient ought to take it, and insist he go in that direction. This attitude is counter-productive.

Instead, agreeing on reciprocal tasks is the core feature of the therapeutic contract. Once the bond is solid or a rupture has been repaired and the goal is clear, a therapist asks the patient: "What steps do you feel willing to take, in sessions and in daily life, to proceed towards health, towards the goal we agreed on?"

Therapists are authorised to act only after the patient has given them a clear response and said he is ready to take on some concrete commitments. Without an affirmative response, the only work therapists can do is to block, using inner discipline measures, their tendency to push for progress. They can only act when the patient has decided to take on a part of the responsibility for the treatment and to make some steps of his own volition.

For example, a dependent patient might decide she wants to stop behaving submissively. If the decision is a conscious one, she may fail a thousand times but knows she can keep on trying. The perpetrators of domestic violence are treatable, provided they agree immediately with their therapist their intention to give up aggressive behaviour. Patients with obsessive-compulsive and self-sacrificing features can improve, but at a certain point in their therapy need to decide to abstain from hyper-working and pursue relaxing and pleasant activities, while exposing themselves to the inevitable feeling of guilt.

It is not therapists that take such decisions nor can they take it as implicit that the patient will go in that particular direction because it is right, healthy and beneficial. They should ask patients, over and over again, whether they are keeping the goal in mind and whether they are convinced by the fact that only specific activities will lead them in the desired direction. Only after a clear, explicit and sincere "yes" can the therapy progress.

As the therapy evolves, therapists demonstrate more clearly the cause–effect link between in-between-session therapeutic work and reduction of symptoms and problems. During the early stages of a therapy, which may last for many months, a therapist should work on the patient's passivity on a relational level; trying to regulate the relationship and propose solution strategies, although the patient might decide to not adopt them. Therapists accept this attitude but progressively reveal to the patient their feeling of powerlessness and of being excluded from the treatment relationship. It is important for therapists to keep this mentalising attitude, even when the patient tries to ascribe all the responsibility for a lack of progress to them.

This is a delicate relational intervention, where therapists should keep calm and available. In this well-regulated state, they can make an intervention like the following:

> I realise you're suffering and I'm ready to be next to you to support you during sessions to alleviate your distress, to the extent of my ability. At the same time, I can see that you find it impossible, pointless, or too risky to take steps that are required for change to happen. Maybe it seems unfair to you and you feel it's the others that should change and not you. I don't want to push you to do anything. I just witness that in this state I'm not able to promise any further progress. Your therapy will probably just be me supporting you to manage your suffering that may become chronic. If you choose this route, I'll be there for you. In this case, however, the only important thing is that you must not expect therapy to help you change.

Be careful: the therapeutic contract is not something that gets written and signed in blood once and for all at the start of treatment. The point is that throughout therapy, the clinician monitors if there is a contract, an explicit and conscious agreement about set goals and tasks. If the therapist thinks the patient agrees to taking a particular step, but the patient does not take it, the therapist is likely to be mistaken and to not have verified whether an agreement existed.

Precisely because MIT, in the form proposed here, is a very active therapy, each time therapists adopt a technique or think about helping a patient progress to a higher functioning level, they should check whether the latter agrees with these goals, wants to take the necessary steps to change, and accepts the necessary commitments.

After Assunta's therapist regulated her tendency to urge the patient towards change, she asked: "Assunta, very well, I realise that the gilded cage can be comfortable. I understand; I've tried it myself. But, if you don't want to leave it, what can we achieve with therapy? What tools can you give me for me to lead you towards wellbeing?" Assunta was surprised and realised it was up to her to decide about her future. A few months after this intervention she separated from her husband and started to take pleasure in looking after her children. The contract rewriting intervention contributed to reactivating her independence and to her recovering a sense of personal efficacy.

CHAPTER 5

Guided imagery and imagery rescripting

Imagery work has for long been forgotten by empirically supported therapies, being considered ancillary to work on cognition. However, in recent years many therapy models have been concentrating their actions on returning with the mind to core scenes and traumatic memories, visualising liveable future scenarios and getting patients to live them, pass through them and exit them while taking new directions (Blackwell, 2018).

The best example is Post-Traumatic Stress Disorder (PTSD) therapies. In the majority, including Prolonged Exposure (Foa, Hembree, & Rothbaum, 2007), Narrative Exposure Therapy (Elbert, Schauer, & Neuner, 2015), Emotion-Focused (Paivio & Pascual-Leone, 2010) and EMDR (Shapiro, 2012), imagery exposure to traumatic events is core.

In a protected situation patients are asked to recall a traumatic memory, often several times, sometimes with the aim of extinguishing alert reactions, others to change the story. In the behavioural paradigm, prolonged exposure without rescripting (Foa et al., 2007) aims at reducing fear of being overwhelmed by traumatic memories and at discovering one can enter a scene with better emotional mastery skills. In MIT we do not use prolonged exposure without rescripting. We consider it fundamental to work through a relived memory together, aiming at ascribing a different meaning to it and getting the patient to see different endings can be written to dramatic stories (Neimeyer, 2016). A woman overpowered by guilt, shame and fear after sexual abuse may discover that still having these feelings is not necessary, as she can see herself and others in other ways.

In fact the use of imagery rescripting has proved effective in many disorders, such as Social Anxiety, Obsessive-Compulsive, Dismorphophobia or Bulimia (Morina, Lancee, & Arntz, 2017). Reworking and rewriting traumatic memories is also beneficial because it helps a patient to distinguish between the past – "it happened to me then and was awful" – and the present – "Now it's no longer looming over me; I'm safe".

As well as in PTSD therapy, in CBT imagery techniques were used very little for several decades. Only recently have some authors returned to them for treating symptomatic disorders, such as anxiety, depression, obsessions and eating disorders (Hackmann et al., 2011). In the PD field schema therapy has for some time been using guided imagery to get patients to relive dramatic scenes from their past and then promoting rewriting through *limited reparenting* (Arntz & van Genderen, 2011). Reparenting in Schema Therapy requires therapists to adopt the role of a new, healthy parent and try to replace the problematic images of the real relatives in a patient's memories. For example, instead of a punishing parent, in imagery the therapist would embody an accepting one. This is therefore a kind of rescripting with a specific focus.

Padesky and Mooney's work on personality (2012) foresees focusing on a patient's resources and strong points. Therapists should help construct a personal resilience model, using not least imagery, with patients visualising mental scenes where they carry out wished-for activities successfully or satisfyingly and feel competent, or overcome relational problems. Recently Bohus and colleagues (2013) developed a variation on Dialectical Behaviour Therapy (DBT) based on imagery recovery techniques for patients with Borderline PD and histories of childhood sex abuse.

Influenced by this turn, which embraces both the world of cognitive therapy and that of psychotherapy in general, we have systematised guided imagery use in the MIT decision-making procedure. In this book, we do not discuss similarities to or differences from imagery use in the approaches mentioned earlier but limit ourselves to describing our work in as much detail as possible and with graphic examples, while leaving the possibility of making comparisons to any reader interested.

Like every technique described in this book, we are careful to apply it carefully and unceasingly as part of case formulation and decision-making procedures. We use imagery in accordance with the point where a patient is, to promote the immediately subsequent improvement step, and thus work in the therapeutic zone of proximal development (Leiman & Stiles, 2001). Consequently, if metacognitive monitoring needs improving, we adopt imagery techniques to refine and elaborate on case formulation. If a patient starts differentiating and accessing healthy parts, we can use the latter to increase differentiation, making room for new inner relationship patterns and integrating self-aspects with each other.

We begin exposure with therapeutic relationship regulation. Immediately afterwards we concentrate on the intervention we practise most often, guided imagery with rescripting centred on past scenes. After describing how this is done step by step, and supplying various clinical examples, we talk about the problems encountered while it goes on. We then describe using imagery to support positive images and plan wished-for future scenarios and lastly a different type of imagery exercise: not guided and without rescripting.

Regulation of the therapeutic relationship

As shown in Chapter 4, getting patients to relive problematic, often traumatic, memories requires optimal therapeutic relationship regulation before, during and after the experiment. Even asking patients to immerse themselves in memories can produce small relationship ruptures a clinician needs to be ready to handle. Sharing the experiencing of emotionally charged scenes changes the relationship framework, most times for the better but in various cases triggering dramatic feelings. Patients can for the first time feel the clinician to be close and hands-on or get deeply embarrassed about what surfaced without the filter of cognition. Therapists thus know that, every time they suggest and carry out imagery immersion, they need to be ready to work on the therapeutic relationship.

Many clinicians fear getting patients to relive memories in imagery. This fear is mostly baseless. Done with the necessary caution, guided imagery is invaluable and its benefits greatly outweigh the risks. We recall that most post-traumatic disorder therapies foresee exposure to the trauma, *in vivo* or using imagery. Such patients have experienced terrible, tragic or terrifying situations and in reliving the scenes they feel intense and distressing arousal. And yet precisely experiencing these levels of intensity, together with their therapist, is indispensable to the treatment process.

A therapist's fears are about harming the patient or losing control of the session. In reality the biggest problem is the emotional involvement of therapists themselves. Passing from conversing to living often dramatic experiences triggers emotions and memories in therapists similar to the patients'. Reliving a grief scene can lead to recalling one's own losses, reliving abuse can trigger one's own sense of fragility and of having been a victim of someone stronger, and returning to a situation where parents or a boss have obstructed one's growth can trigger an anger never alleviated.

During MIT training, when one of us carries out class sessions with the therapist students becoming patients – they are not simulated sessions but true and proper, intense, engaging and often dramatic ones – what strikes one is the impact on the other students. At the start of the discussion there can be a wall of silence, sometimes embarrassed, sometimes sullen. At this moment, instead of focusing on analysis of the session just finished, the trainer should ask, "What did you feel?" The atmosphere changes, the silence gets broken and the telling of distressing personal memories begins, accompanied by comments like: "I couldn't manage to listen", "If I'd been there, I wouldn't have been up to it", "I totally identified with her. I'd have frozen if I'd been the therapist."

No need to be frightened: this is embodied cognition. The patient's and therapist's bodies are both in the room. While the patient relives the scene, describing it out loud, the therapist's empathic resonance increases and mirror neuron circuits (Rizzolatti & Sinigaglia, 2007) become highly active. When a therapist says, "Let's return there, to your past. Take me with you," he is not using a courtesy formula. The time trip will be made by both, and both their bodies, naturally in different ways, reinhabit the memories emerging.

There is an inevitable emotional impact on therapists and it is therefore important they get ready for it. Whether done through supervision, intervision, personal therapy or mindfulness is not important. It is enough to recall that therapists should, on the one hand, listen to patients and, on the other, allow their own sensations and emotions to surface, and watch and modulate them.

This requires training and self-knowledge. These are certainly laborious operations, but what one gains in exchange is a highly powerful tool. Anyway, guided imagery is likely to lead to intense activation of the therapeutic relationship and ruptures in it are therefore possible, even if at the beginning of the exercise it was solid. Later in this chapter we shall describe how we handle the relationship when problems emerge during imagery work. We anticipate here that, as soon as a therapist sees signs of rupture, he should shift the focus onto repairing them.

What should therapists do after self-regulating and overcoming, on the one hand, their hurry to act and generate change and, on the other, their fear of exposing the patient to suffering, and dysregulating or harming him? There is a principle always guiding any relational action: in the heat of an exercise therapists should assess patients' dominant interpersonal schemas either formally, or, if they do not have all the elements at that moment, intuitively. They should then attempt adopting a position supporting a patient's wish and embodying that of a benevolent other.

If, for example, a patient is driven by independence, therapists should put themselves in a supporter or trainer position. If he is driven by social rank, they should try to boost his self-worth. If he feels forsaken, they should be warm and reassuring. Only the patient's feedback can tell if the set-up adopted by a therapist is right. We do not therefore suggest therapists adopt *a priori* a particular relational position, but one in line with the patient's schemas and with immediate attention to his reaction.

In general, however, we recall that guided imagery and, even more, rescripting are exposure exercises with the effect, intended, of increasing arousal, obstructing distress protection mechanisms and creating new ways of thinking, feeling and acting. If therapists find it easy to adopt a caregiving position, they are less likely to push patients to expose themselves, overcome a certain degree of suffering and renew themselves. Therapists should however act within the window of tolerance, and make patients feel safe and to a certain degree protected, but in our experience this is more likely if the therapist adopts an explorative curiosity position and thus tries to activate the same motivational system in the patient.

If a therapist offers care, the patient may feel protected, but at the same time fragile and weak. If, instead, the former firmly, warmly and persistently pushes him towards an experience hitherto avoided and does not get frightened by the patient's signals of distress, at the end of the exercise the latter will report feeling more solid, strong and capable.

Scenes to be imagined

Traumatic events are probably those most often treated with guided imagery. However, the work we describe here is aimed at using imagery to tackle very different kinds of situation (Blackwell, 2018). In reality, our main target is patients with difficulty accessing inner states and an emotional experience that is over-modulated, suppressed or avoided. In other terms, it involves activating arousal more than calming it, and exploring autobiographical episodes to increase patients' contact with their emotions, get to know them and make them their own.

Scenes we typically suggest patients relive are: memories with themes involving criticism received, being forsaken, solitude, repressed anger, shame, guilt, independence thwarted and inability to carry out action plans. The use of guided imagery, therefore, facilitates access to unrecognised emotions and making them the subject of therapeutic work. Consequently, very many imagery exercises are totally safe and provide the necessary vitality to difficult sessions.

Guided imagery is useful not only for reworking past memories, both recent and remote. Some exercises can concentrate on imagining future, feared or wished-for, scenarios and trying to inhabit them with the mind before action. For example, before carrying out a behavioural task, patients can represent a scene to themselves and try moving within it, interacting with others and reflecting on what happens to them. Such exercises are often the first step towards behavioural exploration in real life. One goal of this work is to desensitise patients, so that real world exposure then causes less anxiety. We take patients to an intermediate zone, imagery simulation, where they gain experience of feared situations, but without the harsh impact of reality and with their therapist accompanying them within a solid relationship. Consequently, they can feel more confident about being able to tackle any difficulties in real exposures.

We shall therefore divide imagery exercises into two macro-categories: 1) working through past memories, imagery being used mainly for this; 2) imagining future scenarios, tackling new situations and anticipatorily exploring the environment.

We focus for various reasons on past memories, as shown in Chapters 3 and 4: a) improving metacognitive monitoring and fostering initial access to healthy parts; b) regulating distressing emotions; c) differentiation and perceiving both that schemas are the result of past experiences and distress does not depend so much on real others as on one's way of representing them. We also help patients to grasp that along, with their negative ideas about the self and others, there are benign and adaptive ones too: they have them inside themselves on an imagery and sensorial level; d) increasing patients' contact with healthy parts and giving them room in consciousness so as to memorise them and combine them in their identity; e) rescripting and imagery involving future scenarios have the goal of stimulating activation of the exploratory system, the reinforcement of healthy parts and planning of more advanced forms of mastery.

Applying guided imagery: processing past memories

Selection of narrative episode

Here we offer some suggestions about choosing narrative episodes to be relived in imagery, not true and proper rules, but anchors for the therapist. To be enacted are preferably 1) narratives featuring limited awareness of mental states present in the episode or emotional inhibition. A sub-type are episodes where poor awareness regards the wish, with the patient incapable of deciding and struggling to grasp which choice would be right; 2) representative episodes, prototypes of patients' maladaptive interpersonal schemas; in which 3) there is sometimes intense psychological distress with true and proper traumatic memories.

Difficulties in metacognitive monitoring can be found in all episode types. The difference is that in episodes of the first type the core difficulty is grasping one's own thoughts and emotions, and the reasons for one's reactions. Patients often realise their inner world is not clear and want to get to know it better, and imagery exercises serve this goal: bypassing the narrator position and remaking contact with the details of the scene in one's autobiographical memory. Here a therapist can explore this inner world more successfully.

In any case the episode is to be chosen together with the patient. The therapist should make a proposal and the patient assess if he finds it interesting, useful or possible to relive it. When faced with a rejection, the therapist should nevertheless feel satisfied and look to politely discover the reasons for it. As in every case where therapists propose an activity the patient rejects, one gains the possibility of accessing the mental states underlying this.

In a certain sense the very proposing of a guided imagery exercise, like that of any technique, is a fruitful form of exposure. The rejection is almost always linked to emotional or relational difficulties. Either the patient fears he cannot regulate the emotions that would surface or does not picture the therapist as being capable of receiving him with non-judgemental interest, or he has both fears.

Patients can also reject because the episode suggested by the therapist is no longer significant then, no longer connected to the problem dominating their mind. After the rejection, therefore, therapists should ask if there are other episodes a patient finds more significant and which could be candidates for reliving.

If patients have limited awareness of their mental states or emotional inhibition, a therapist should first ask for an example of a problematic situation and then try to get it relived with guided imagery. He should explain that it is not clear what wish was driving the patient and what the latter felt and thought in reaction to the other's response. In interpersonal schema terms, in such episodes the wish is not clear: what motivational system drives the patient? Attachment, social rank, affiliation/belonging, exploration?

Patients find it quite easy to describe the actions of another obstructing, criticising or ignoring them, etc. They also manage to report how they behaved vis-à-vis this response: for example, by avoiding contact, fleeing or attacking in turn if feeling criticised or threatened.

Less likely to surface are, instead, thoughts and emotions emerging after the other's response. Among these the most frequent is anger, sometimes not well expressed or termed irritation or annoyance. It is less easy for patients to access emotions preceding anger, like sadness for a loss or solitude, shame and guilt.

To illustrate this, a patient might relate an episode with this structure: "I had to clarify the problem but she didn't answer the phone over and over again. I got annoyed and decided not to call her again." A therapist should instead aim at this type of description: "I felt neglected. I called her because I needed to understand what had driven her to not reply to me and I hoped that in the end she'd accept seeing me. When she kept on not replying, I felt lonely and hurt, as if I didn't count for anything. At this point, gripped by anger, I decided to disappear to get back at her and send her the message she can't treat me like that."

In some cases poor monitoring conceals the wish, with patients unclear about what they would have liked to do or having doubts, often accompanied by ruminations about how they behaved. "What could I have said?" "Did I really want to make that trip?" "Perhaps I was wrong. Perhaps I hurt him with no good reason." Patients are thus disoriented and uncertain about what route to take or unclear about whether what they are doing is wished for and beneficial or compulsive and pathological. The goal of working with these episodes is to help patients perceive their own intentions and goals, in other words their wishes.

Patients often report feeling confused, or guilty and ashamed for what they have experienced, thought or done. This condition is partly similar to the first type of episodes, but here the focus is the dilemma of choice. A patient has a clear point of view on what he wishes, but is less clear about what thoughts and emotions drove him to react by behaving in a certain way as the result of the other's response. It therefore needs to be the therapist who proposes guided imagery to enrich the psychological formulation of the problem and then its working out.

Matteo was an entrepreneur aged 39 suffering from Dependent PD with narcissistic and histrionic traits. We shall describe his history and start of therapy in greater detail in Chapters 6, 8 and 11. Here we concentrate on a situation where he believed he had a compulsive behaviour relapse. The initial focus of his therapy was blocking the forms of coping he compulsively adopted – compliant submission and avoidance – so that he understood his inner states and schemas (see Chapters 6, 8 and 11). Once these were identified, Matteo was able to act in line with his own ideas and maintain a sense of good personal worth. However, he lacked access to his, extra-professional, wished-for goals. The therapist gave him a behavioural exercise: he had to go home and, when the feeling of emptiness preceding his compulsive behaviour got activated, try and do something he wished. Matteo decided to go running. After two weeks he said he had been running every day, but was worried.

M: "I fear I'm in the clutches of dependency again. In the end I get obsessed about everything I do and I reckon I'm doing the same with running too."

The therapist was unable to grasp what mental state was connected to running and therefore decided to do a guided imagery exercise without rescripting, aimed solely at increasing the patient's metacognitive monitoring. He thus asked Matteo to pinpoint an evening, just before sunset, when he went running. Matteo started acting the scene and the therapist got him to describe what he noticed whilst running and what he felt.

M: "I'm going along the lake. There's a wide pavement."
T: "What can you see?"
M: "The sun, almost setting, and the water in the lake."
T: "What effect does it have on you?"
M: "It's nice."
T: "What else do you notice?"

M: "The trees. People walking. A feeling of calm."
T: "Keep on running and tell me what you see."
M: "The sun still. The hills in the background. The rays of the sun about to set."
T: "How do you feel now?"
M: "Good. A feeling of freedom. I feel light, emptied of worries."

When the exercise finished, the therapist pointed out to Matteo he had described a completely positive experience, without a trace of compulsion. Matteo perceived more clearly that, when observing his experience, he was driven by the rank schema, where he interpreted everything he did with the eyes of a critical and invalidating other. The exercise stimulated an increase in metacognitive monitoring, in particular in the healthy parts linked to the exploratory system.

The second type of episode is that where the schema structure is quite clear. There can be various emotions, but still at an acceptable level of regulation. Here the prime goal is to obtain further details about patients' inner experience, and then one should attempt a rescripting so that they interrupt their schemas and act in line with healthy parts. Unlike previous episodes, here the schema is already quite clear at the start and patients already have some idea that these episodes depict schemas and not reality. Imagery is therefore useful for supplying further details to an already well-defined picture and then for rewriting the scene.

In the third type of episode patients experience problematic and intense emotions close to the threshold of tolerance and almost seen as being out of control. Here the aim of imagery is first, emotional regulation (Fassbinder, Schweiger, Martius, Brand-de Wilde, & Arntz, 2016), with the patient not managing to calm down an emotion when he experiences it and feeling a certain, sometimes very intense, degree of activation in sessions too. Here a scene gets typically recalled to overcome traumatic memories. This occurs in various schools such as prolonged exposure (Foa et al., 2007), EMDR (Shapiro, 2012), schema therapy (Boterhoven de Haan, Fassbinder, Hayes, & Lee, 2019) and DBT for patients with sexual traumas (Bohus et al., 2013), just to name a few examples.

Naturally, the classification we have made of episodes is to be understood as a guide for therapists. Many episodes in fact display mixed characteristics.

To select an episode, patients need to be quite clear about *when* it happened, *where* it took place, *who* was present and what *sequence* the action followed. It is acceptable to carry out imagery even when there are memory gaps. Indeed, one guided imagery goal is for details in memories to reemerge and patients should be informed of this.

It is good if a therapist is always ready to be surprised and does not take what contents emerge during guided imagery for granted. In this state of openness he will be readier to perceive, validate and regulate the emotions surfacing during an exercise. For example, a patient might talk about an episode making him angry but then, during the exercise, fear and sense of guilt emerge. Vice versa, when reliving an episode where he says he felt frightened, he may feel intense anger.

It is, instead, useless giving a diagnostic purpose to the exercise if, at the mere suggestion, the patient intensely feels certain fundamental emotions like sadness for a loss, shame or guilt. In such cases the exercise is, in a certain sense, already successful because it has been proposed, and the session can concentrate on working through these emotions. Guided imagery is, therefore, just a first step towards rescripting, which is the true therapeutic goal.

If patients feel over-intense anxiety, a probable sign they are on the threshold of access to traumatic memories, clinicians should carefully weigh up whether to conduct the exercise. They should therefore concentrate on understanding the cognitive-affective processes activating the anxiety and on calming patients. Once a good level of emotional regulation is achieved, they can make the suggestion again. In such cases, if a patient agrees, the exercise can be proposed directly with the purpose of *rescripting* or emotional modulation. The patient returns to the distressing scene and goes through the psychological distress again, while the clinician helps him to master it. In the sections devoted to rescripting and to imagery exposure we shall show how.

When he has both recent and more remote memories and the patient has associated them, the clinician has to decide which to use in imagery. Should he prefer a more remote episode, on the assumption it is a core one and thus more important for the purpose of restructuring the patient's personality?

The reply is: not necessarily. Certainly, if a patient accepts reliving a remote episode this is an excellent indicator and means he is ready for structural change. But it must not be an obligation and the choice of applying guided imagery to a recent episode is not wrong. As always, guidance comes from the affect surfacing. A patient may relate a recent episode and associate with it a piece of family history, but be more emotionally activated by the current problem: the clinician should choose the recent episode. Often, after guided imagery, emotions activating other associations the patient feels yet more important, emerge. It is here, for example, that rescripting can be concentrated.

Carrying out guided imagery

We shall now describe the various stages in imagery: 1) suggestion of an episode, 2) entry using grounding and mindfulness techniques, 3) conducting the experience a first time so that the patient comprehends mental states and increases his ability to feel emotions. Maximum information should be gathered here to obtain a formulation complete and close to the patient's experience of interpersonal schemas, 4) discussion of the experience, 5) repeating the scene for rescripting purposes and finally 6) reflection after rescripting to consolidate what surfaces in memory.

Exceptions to this sequence are possible. In particular, very often it is not necessary to interrupt the exercise after experiencing the scene a first time and getting a clear access to the nuances of inner experience. In fact, if a patient feels his awareness has been enriched, accepts without bewilderment the emotions discovered and maintains an acceptable emotional regulation, even with more intense emotional distress levels, it is possible to continue the exercise by passing directly to rescripting.

Proposal and negotiation

The first step when it seems useful to propose guided imagery to a patient is a structured summary of the episode. Therapists should, therefore, reorganise patients' narratives while bearing in mind the structure of their interpersonal schemas. This is a structured summary of events (Chapter 4). It can even be incomplete, given one of the goals of imagery exercises is to complete and refine patients' understanding of their inner worlds.

Therapists can present summaries with gaps like this:

> I'm still not sure if I've grasped what drove you to ask for your partner's opinion (*lack of definition of the wish*), but in any case, when you saw he was against and rebuked you (*other's response*), you felt a surge of irritation that led you to close up in silence and I'd be curious to grasp what you thought and felt that pushed you to close up (*self's response to other's response where the belief leading to act is not explicit and the emotion is described imprecisely. In this response the behaviour in particular is clear: closure*).

Sometimes guided imagery can be useful even if a patient has only fragmented narratives, little more than flashes, generic and with few references to inner states. The imagery technique can be useful here as in a certain sense it gives shape to a narrative episode. The patient enters a scene that initially has a weak narrative, and then visual details gradually surface, the characters start to move and the mental states appear.

When patients agree to the reorganisation of a narrative and feel it to be their own, but are not clear about all the psychological elements, therapists should explain it is possible and profitable to relive the episode using imagery. Typically, patients are aware of others' reactions, their own behaviour and what the wish was, but have difficulty explaining the cognitive-affective antecedents of their coping actions.

A therapist should therefore explain that the prime aim of the exercise is increasing knowledge of one's inner world. Depending on the goal, the proposal should have a different sound. In the case of metacognitive monitoring problems making it difficult to perceive emotions, thoughts and psychological cause-effect links, it should sound like: "I can see this situation is important for you. I'd like to get a better grasp of what happened inside you when your wife replied huffily. Shall we try and return together to the situation where a wedge got driven between you, so we can both get a clearer idea?"

If patients have doubts about their actions, the proposal can be:

> You aren't convinced you acted for the best. I can see you wanted something for yourself, but it's as if you weren't clear about it, didn't have the right to it, or were almost accusing yourself for behaving like that. Let's return to the situation where you felt you had done something wrong or you weren't convinced about. This will bring us closer to the emotions flowing through you then. With this we'll probably be clearer about what happened to you and can give you greater freedom of choice and action.

The proposal needs to be different if it involves going through traumatic memories or tackling fears. After a structured summary of a traumatic episode, therapists should propose returning to the scene, while explaining the exercise's usefulness and potential benefits. They should calmly and reassuringly explain that returning to a distressing scene is very likely to trigger psychological distress, but with this work it should primarily be possible to see better what in the past is still generating suffering. They should add that this work makes it possible to escape from the suffering using the psychological tools available now.

Therapists should therefore express the proposal with a mixture of caution and full confidence in its usefulness. Negative arousal now almost inevitably increases. It is essential therapists not be frightened by this and not become hyper-protective. We therefore advise an attitude involving gentle insistence, together, however, with careful monitoring of patients' feedback.

We reiterate that avoiding exposing patients to recalling painful scenes can cause distress or fright, which they are in fact unable to master. On the other hand, if a therapist is not convinced a patient can stand an imagery exercise, which is most likely, this deprives him of a powerful technique with proven efficacy. In short, even if a balance between caution, which would induce towards not getting patients to recall traumatic scenes, and confidence, which would lead to encouraging them to relive distressing scenes, is needed, the scales should be tipped towards exposure.

Unless they have a specific training in techniques focused on exposure (e.g. EMDR, schema-therapy or prolonged exposure), therapists, however, tend to not get patients to relive traumatic scenes with imagery. Instead, perhaps with the help of an expert supervisor, they can make the proposal and discover that their patients are perfectly up to bearing the transitory increase in arousal. We recall, moreover, that it is a question of negotiating, which is not possible if therapists do not make the proposal. They should, moreover, inform patients that the latter can interrupt the exercise when they want and agree on signals leading the therapist to stop and return to the present with their eyes open.

It is a question of working by monitoring patients' arousal levels and sense of security at each moment. We recall again that therapists tend to fear exposing their patients and overestimate the risk of dysregulation. They should therefore certainly be cautious and especially never compel patients to undertake imagery exercises. But once they have provided patients all the various ways for calming down and, if necessary, interrupting the exercise, they should try to get them to settle for the time needed at the highest level of arousal tolerable. With this work patients become more confident in their ability to tolerate distressing emotions and rescripting is more incisive.

Patients are, moreover, perfectly able to withdraw from exposure and give explicit signals of rejecting it that therapists need to know how to recognise and accept. We insist: do not be deceived by any increase in anxiety, guilt, despondency or embarrassment. It is totally normal for this to occur when faced with the proposal, and natural for any exposure to feared events according to the teachings of CBT for phobias, obsessions and post-traumatic disorders. With the same sureness with which we suggest patients with panic attacks try getting on a bus, or obsessive patients touch objects they find disgusting and dirty and then not wash, we propose recalling distressing or traumatic memories with imagery. If patients firmly reject it, we should accept this. Similarly, if they emit clear signals of stress and hyper-activation, a therapist can of his own accord take a step backwards and interrupt the exercise, while taking care, immediately before the interruption, to adopt regulation strategies, for example, mindful breathing or grounding, in a calm and validating relational atmosphere. It is important and very useful to explore what happens to patients while dealing with the idea of reliving a distressing memory. In a certain sense the proposal is itself an exposure exercise producing increased knowledge.

In some cases patients seem to maintain their emotional regulation but dissociate. One patient described her father attacking her mother. She was afraid. Her therapist asked her for more details and she replied, apparently calmly, that her father had become a blue stain. Another patient spoke agitatedly about her father's death and said she did not feel up to returning to the scene. Her therapist suggested the signs of hyper-arousal could derive from this avoidance. The patient agreed, calmed down adequately and accepted attempting an imagery exercise. She then relived her father's death, which had upset her in real life, in every detail, without feeling any emotion except a little regret for him. "I'm here but it's as if I wasn't." Her therapist tried everything to get her to face the psychological distress or sense of guilt tormenting her. With no apparent reaction. After the session the patient sent a message to the therapist, to thank him because he had got her to make contact with how much she loved her husband, who was present in the scene and had made her feel supported. She consequently overcame a moment of marital tension.

In general, with these exercises patients often become aware that under certain conditions they temporarily lose control over their inner worlds, something of which they were previously unaware. This helps them to shift their focus from a problem they consider relational to one involving intrapsychical functioning.

In the part devoted to the therapeutic relationship we shall return to the impact the proposal of this technique and all the others has on the relationship with the clinician and how to work on this.

Instructions

Before starting the exercise therapists should supply a few, clear instructions, including visualising a scene, listening to the sounds and voices of those present, noting details and colours and, possibly, reporting any other sensorial elements such as tactile sensations, smells, heat or cold, etc. We would stress patients should narrate their experiences in the first person and the present indicative, for example: "I'm at home and can see . . ." instead of "I was at home and could see . . .".

Therapists should explain it is essential to relive the scene and avoid as much as possible commenting on it. They should therefore forewarn patients that, each time the latter find themselves expressing reflections, they will be interrupted and asked to postpone them until the reworking stage after the episode is finished. Therapists should therefore suggest immediately that patients return to describing what they feel, see and think while in the scene.

If a patient says, "I believe that I didn't feel very sure of myself then because it was a period of general uncertainty and the atmosphere at home was tense", the therapist should interrupt him and tell him, "Okay. Very good reflections we'll find useful shortly. However, now let's return to the scene. How do you feel now your mother told you that? Return and listen to your mother's voice, and pay attention to her face. What's your impression?" If the patient has been correctly prepared, he is less likely to feel invalidated when the therapist asks him to suspend his reflections and return to reliving the scene.

Sometimes, during a narrative episode, especially recent ones, patients recall associated memories. Therapists should take note and show appreciation, but ask patients even in this case to remain in the scene and return to narrating the associated memory only after finishing the imagery immersion.

Preparation for guided imagery

An intermediate step in guided imagery preparation is grounding. In its classic and simplest form grounding – a basic bioenergetics analysis technique (Lowen, 1975) – is achieved with an erect posture, legs slightly open and knees slightly bent. The eyes should be half-closed or closed and mouth slightly open so that the jaw drops and top and bottom teeth not touch. The vertebral column should be correctly aligned so the trunk offloads all its weight on the legs. One should suggest that the patient: 1) pay attention to his legs to perceive the strength and support in them; 2) pay attention to his feet by focusing on their adherence to the floor; 3) feel the support his legs and feet provide to his whole body; 4) imagine his body is a tree, where the legs constitute the trunk and the feet the points from which the roots start; 5) imagine that some long roots start from his feet and penetrate deep into the soil, thus contributing to strengthen yet further the rest of the tree connecting it to everything around it; 6) then direct his consciousness towards any sensations linked to breathing, without modifying its frequency or volume, but letting it become deep and rhythmical, like a wave motion; 7) lastly, imagine living energy flowing through his feet/roots and linked to his breathing: when breathing in, the roots gather energy from the soil and transport it, through the feet and trunk, to the whole body; when breathing out, the whole body yields energy, which, through the roots, gets re-consigned to the environment. The therapist should repeatedly suggest this sense of rootedness and connectedness, and encourage the relaxation/letting go of the body's upper part with the support of the legs/feet.

In an MIT context we use grounding as a general regulation strategy, as we shall see in Chapter 7. In guided imagery in particular we use it to prepare imagery. It has two functions: creating a detachment from reality, by getting patients to focus on their bodies instead of the environment and memories, and stimulating emotional regulation and thus preparing patients for bearing exposures to distressing memories.

If patients are in an adequately regulated state, grounding can, right from the start, be used in abbreviated form, provided care is taken to check that they feel the sense of rootedness. One can ask a patient, sitting, to close his eyes and concentrate his awareness on his body's points of contact with the world: his buttocks with his chair seat, feet with the floor, back with the chair back and hands with his legs, and savour the sense of solidity and firmness this gives. Then one should suggest imagining his feet are the bottom of a tree trunk, which is the starting point of deep roots branching out and connecting it to the room. We ask patients to breathe and notice the air coming in and going out. After a few seconds we ask them to stop thinking about the tree and root images, and keep, if possible, the sensation of solidity and connectedness. At this point one can start guided imagery.

Another exercise capable of furnishing a sense of solidity and rootedness is mountain meditation (Kabat-Zinn, 1990), because of the sense of stability and rootedness it provides. We ask patients to close their eyes and imagine a mountain before them. One should get them to appreciate its solidity, robustness and motionlessness and visualise a series of events occurring near and around it, without it being in the least disturbed: "The seasons, temperature and climate may change but the mountain stays motionless, anchored fast to the soil. Trees fall to the ground, others branch and bud, animals dig out lairs and scrape the soil, but there the mountain stays, imperturbable, like granite. On its slopes, men build houses, make life plans, get born and die, but, while our mountain sees this, it stays calm, solid and firm." We invite patients to visualise their body becoming the mountain, with their head representing the top, their shoulders, arms and sides instead of its ridges and slopes, and their pelvis and legs standing for the bottom of the mountain. Patients ends the exercise breathing consciously for a few minutes while maintaining the image of themselves as a mountain, one that breathes, and appreciating the sensation of strength and stability deriving from this.

This exercise can be carried out fully the first time, to let the patient learn his wished-for mental state procedurally. Henceforward one can quickly recall the same state before the exercise: "Now close your eyes and return to seeing yourself and your body as a sturdy and robust mountain, as we did last time. Pay attention to the body's anchor points and start breathing deeply and harmoniously." After about a minute one should go on by suggesting the patient keep the sensations but let go of the images, and immerse himself in the distressing memory one wants to address in that session: "Now let's go there. Tell me what you see and feel." The imagery exercise has started.

Implementation

Increasing knowledge of mental states and contact with emotional experience

When patients first return to a past scene, the goal is improving self-reflectivity and increasing emotional experience if this has difficulty emerging. Guided imagery is uniquely effective in providing patients with more detailed knowledge of their inner worlds. Think of a sequence where a therapist first listens to a generalised description of a relational pattern.

Mirka, a craftswoman aged 44 was high-functioning and successful at looking after her children after separating from her husband. She had perfectionistic traits and sought therapy only for a sense of "psychological overload" which she could not explain better. She tended to use hyper-efficiency and compulsive independence as coping mechanisms. She was alexithymic and the emotion she expressed mainly was a poorly defined sense of mental tiredness, alternating with satisfaction at her ability to manage everything, affection for friends close to her and anger with her husband, who neglected their children, by now adolescents. Mirka typically started a conversation with: "That idiot husband of mine causes me loads of problems and makes my children suffer", a generalisation that MIT does not accept.

When her therapist asked her for an example, a narrative episode, Mirka pulled out pseudo-episodes, which were in reality situations where she ruminated: "I was on the phone with my son, who had had a problem at school and needed to talk about it with his father. I had to talk to him first, but I already knew that, if I did, he wouldn't understand and wouldn't be available, and that I'd have had to argue with him, and I'm afraid of going out of control." Here there is a little information about her schemas, but not enough.

Her therapist therefore sought out and obtained, clearer and detailed episodes, like:

M: "My daughter Francesca came home Sunday evening. The, old story: you can't rely on my husband."
T: "How did Francesca feel? What did you say to each other? Where were you?"
M: "I went and picked her up at his place. He didn't even answer me on the entry-phone. He got her to answer and she said she was coming down."
T: "How did you feel then?"
M: "Humiliated. He doesn't consider me at all and doesn't even consider his children. He doesn't realise he has to talk with me, even just for their good."
T: "Then what happened?"
M: "I was in the car with Francesca."
T: "How was she?"
M: "Miserable. She told me: Dad's a real idiot."
T: "Oh! Very forthright [*smiles*]. Anything else?"
M: "That was enough for me."
T: "So you thought Francesca. . .?"
M: "Dejected. Sorrowful. But she's right. Her father really is an idiot."

Here Mirka was switching to anger. Her therapist asked her to stop a moment before.

T: "Excuse me, Mirka, I can understand you were really mad at your ex-husband, but return a moment to describing your daughter's face for me."
M: "Ah . . . she was down."

T: "And how do you feel now?"
M: "How should I feel? [*not a protest towards the therapist – Mirka appeared resigned*] It makes me sad. I'd like to do something about it but my ex-husband just doesn't understand."

While she talked about what she felt during the episode, both her sadness related to her failure to look after her daughter effectively and her powerlessness, with her wanting to be helped in her role as mother but feeling she lacked the tools to get her husband moving, emerged more clearly.

This scanning of the narrative episode already brought more information than the initial generalised memory and the subsequent memory where she worried. Primary feelings of sadness and powerlessness, both emotions Mirka does not usually experience, stopping at energy, hyper-activation and anger, are more clear.

Let us, however, see what happened a few months later, when Mirka had improved and was capable of tackling more consciously, with her children, the difficulties they had with their father, without replacing him or attacking him. During the days in question Mirka suffered two bereavements. She came to the session describing herself as sad and borken-hearted, but nothing of this appeared in her non-verbal communication. The therapist asked her for details, in particular about when she went to church for the funeral of the mother of her ex-husband to whom she was close. New details emerge:

M: "It was the church where I first met my ex-husband's new partner. It was at his mother's funeral."
T: "Ah. What can you remember?"
M: "My daughter pointed it out to me. At a certain point she said, "Mum, mum, that's Dad's partner."
T: "Oh God, right then? So your daughter knew her?"
M: "Yes. Can you imagine?"
T: "How did you feel then?"
M: "Humiliated, as if I didn't count for anything. Then she was there and kept on laughing. They had to hold me back from going up to and telling her to get lost. In fact, I was about to do it but I knocked into my brother just as I was about getting up steam. Meanwhile my ex-husband must have understood and, when I looked back again in her direction I saw her going out all breathless."

After the therapist gathered other details, he saw Mirka continued to be in a mainly angry state at the idea of being humiliated and was not giving priority to any distressing experiences. He therefore proposed doing a guided imagery exercise with a diagnostic purpose. What emerged was surprising.

Mirka related the details of the funeral. However, her focus was not on her ex-husband's partner; the scene became intense long before. Mirka described herself listening to the sermon, her grief at the loss of her mother-in-law, to whom she was very close, and especially, with suffering, her children, in front of her, dressed in black and solemn. She could not see them, as their backs were to her, but could touch them. Mirka started to change expression; she was sad and her face winced, displaying intense distress. The therapist asked her to continue with the scene, after asking her if she felt well enough to. Mirka accepted. At a certain point she described her children slipping away from her and throwing themselves in despair on the semi-open coffin weeping and shouting, "Granny! Granny!"

Mirka burst into a torrent of tears and was out of control. He face got deformed by her grief. She was sobbing endlessly and seemed like a child before something towering over it. "My children. I can't do it. Oh God, what do I do?" The therapist was surprised as in the preceding months he had always had to work hard to access her distressing emotions, while here they were bursting forth and Mirka was unable to regulate them. The therapist first validated her, by normalising her experience and talking with a firm and calm voice. The therapeutic relationship was very solid and Mirka relied on the therapist's words.

T: "Mirka, you're now in a really bad state. I can understand. I've never seen you so grief-stricken. I'm close to you and listening. Let's not let ourselves be dominated by this distress."

He now asked her to breathe mindfully, something that only partially calmed her down, and then used grounding while continuing to remain in the same scene. Thanks to this sense of anchoring, Mirka regained control but her emotions remained intense.

T [*maintaining relational presence and a warm voice*]: "What do you feel, Mirka? What makes you feel so heartbroken?"
M: "I'm aloooooone! My children. I'm not up to it. It's too much for me. I'm too weak. I don't know what to do. They're in such a bad way and I've got nobody to support me."

A part of her schema that had never surfaced in full force emerges here: Mirka started her narrative driven by the motivation to provide care, activated when she saw her children suffering. She felt overcome by sadness and wanted to get the distress they felt to disappear, but did not believe it possible. At this point she felt fragile, weak and incapable, and her attachment was getting activated. With her need for attention she saw herself forsaken, with the other absent, which made her despair.

Mirka reconstructed that her parents and brother came up to her and her brother held her hand, but this did not calm her. The representation of the other providing care surfaced, therefore, in the memory, but did not become operative and remained ineffective. Probably, even if the care-giving other is present in the scene, the implicit, procedural representation of the other as neglecting and invalidating, probably embodied by her husband, is dominant.

Once she had self-regulated, Mirka continued to explore the memory and, when concentrating on her daughter pointing out her ex-husband's new partner, felt humiliated: "She's laughing, she's laughing!" The therapist now got her to return to mindful breathing and interrupted the guided imagery.

Features of schemas linked to social rank now emerged. We shall see later where the therapist led the rescripting based on the information available.

It is now clearer how information on patients' inner world gets enriched, and the level of experience increases, while going on from: 1) generalised narratives; 2) the relating of an apparent episode, which however focuses on rumination. This second shift does not always happen: only some patients tell of when, instead of interacting, they are already engaged in fearing the relational consequences without however facing them in that scene. The therapist should however know that he must not consider such episodes good narratives; 3) the relating of a true narrative episode focusing on interaction between characters occurring at the moment of the narrative; 4) episodes relived in guided imagery.

Not always do therapists manage to reach guided imagery and they often stop at the detailed relating of narrative episodes (point 3). This is what occurs most frequently. We want only to point out that, the more we push patients towards first narrating and then the relinquishing of the narrator position, so that they are actors in their relived experience, the more we get first-hand information. We make contact with an emotional activation with which we can grasp cognitive-affective processes with utmost reliability and plasticity.

In the example used we noted that during the imagery there was a transitory moment of dysregulation requiring use of mindfulness (Chapter 9) and grounding (Chapter 7). Both are part of the toolkit with which a therapist can safely activate intense emotions.

In these situations the intersubjective dimension between patient and therapist is important. With his look, tone of voice, posture and ongoing contingent marking a therapist manages to keep the patient's emotional activation high to the point that the latter is able to grasp through echoing him an experience that he is really reliving: "So, now that you're talking about your colleague, you went dark. It almost seems you're ashamed. I can really feel it."

Let us return to describing how to work with imagery. Therapists target questions to enriching the scene with sensorial details: "Where are you? What do you see? Who is there around you? What do you notice? What time of day is it: morning, afternoon, evening?" We ask for a more detailed description of the others in the scene: "Can you see her face? What's the expression? What makes you grasp she's feeling that emotion? What's she doing? Where's she going?"

As the scene gradually unfolds, the questions should focus on how inner experience flows as the relationship evolves: "What do you feel now that you see your sister going away? What are you thinking while your aunt is rebuking you, and how do you feel? Do you like this drawing you're looking at? Do you feel that you'd like to go up to or get away from that group of children?"

We are careful to avoid questions activating abstract/semantic/logical-deductive reasoning or abstract hypotheses on others' mental contents, like: "Why do you behave like that? What would be the right thing to do now? Why does your father address you in that tone?"

Questions to get more detailed descriptions of others are admissible, but always avoiding abstractions. Rather than theory of mind, one needs to promote a situated reading of what others think and feel and what their intentions are. Put simply, this means questions like: "What can you see now in your boyfriend's face? What do you think is passing through his mind now? Concentrate on the tone of voice, how does it seem?" It is, however, fundamental that questions on the other's mind be followed by others on the patient's reaction: "Now that you see him distant, how do you feel? He's gone, how does that affect you?"

At this stage patients are sometimes unable to feel distressing emotions. Therapists can now use the technique involving *repetition of emotionally charged phrases with marking*. They utter clearly and directly, several times, phrases describing the negative self-concept, or any other representation of negative interpersonal relationships: "Nobody loves me", "I deserve to be left alone". Therapists try to give an emotional emphasis to the phrases and underscore their negative nuances. They then asks patients to repeat them aloud, increasing volume, and observe the effects. When the repetition is over, we check emotional reactions and then work on *in vivo* emotion regulation.

Beyond asking what patients feel when recalling a scene, therapists insist on asking what they feel and think now, a subtle distinction, because patients anyway relive a scene as if happening now. But when they change facial expression, posture and tone of voice, they may be more aware of how much thoughts, feelings and bodily states are present right then. We would recall that the exercises are to be conducted generally with eyes closed and patients have less control over the communicational signals they emit, which makes them still more readable for clinicians.

Patients can therefore distinguish between what they feel as if reliving a scene and what they feel now. For example, a patient might say he is afraid while reliving an aggression, while he feels an observer's sadness when he realises what he went through. In reality, asking what patients feel now, during an exercise, is better and more effective than asking what they felt "then", in the past, and we suggest questions in this sense.

We summarise the steps in guided imagery using an example.

Renata was a fitness instructress aged 30. She had Dependent PD and obsessive-compulsive traits. She was perfectionist and self-sacrificing. She sought therapy for a major depressive episode following an argument with one of the gym owners. The management asked her to modify her training programmes and she started to swing between fear of not being up to it and anger because she felt that by doing this she would not comply with a correct training principle. The argument escalated until they reduced her working hours. She found this a failure on her part and an injustice, and started to worry while swinging between the idea she should have behaved differently and been more flexible and another that she had been right to defend her point of view. She additionally felt guilt because earning less could hamper her plan to go and live with her boyfriend and this could make him suffer.

The reconstruction of a recent episode led to the identification of a structure where Renata wished to be independent and had a core idea of a capable self. However, when she tried to act in line with her wish, she had to deal with a stronger, unjust and tyrannical other. At this point she made contact with her weak and vulnerable self-image, which had hitherto been unconscious, and gave up pursuing independence.

If the capable and independent part observes the weak one, it accuses it and feels frustrated: "How can I be so weak? How stupid I am." Via associated memories, Renata recalled moments in her childhood when her father behaved violently and overbearingly, especially with her mother. She related an episode when she was seven, where her father screamed and threatened to hit her mother. Recalling it, Renata was angry. The therapist suggested reliving the scene through imagery. Renata was unsure but then decided of her own free will to tackle the memory.

Entering the scene, Renata focused on her father yelling at her mother. She could see his domineering physique and face distorted by rage. The therapist asked her what she felt when observing him. There was no trace of anger: the patient felt terrorised.

"What makes you afraid?"
"He could attack my mother."
"Look at your mother's face. What can you see?"
"She's afraid."
"And what do you feel when you see that face?"
Renata burst into tears and kept crying for a long time.

The therapist interrupted the exercise and verified in detail the contents emerging in the dialogue following the exercise, which we describe later.

As part of imagery aimed at improving metacognitive monitoring, we add what we call *informal imagery*. Some patients find it difficult to summon up mental states, when their therapist goes looking for a specific narrative episode to help him sound out their inner experience, they do not recall any.

Here one can ask patients not so much to imagine a precise scene, but to construct one from the elements available. The exercise is normally conducted open-eyed and no preparation is needed, given that, because of the prevailing emotional inhibition, arousal is low. Moreover. the patient is likely to have activated forms of coping like suppression and avoidance, so that formal preparation and closed eyes could accentuate these protective mechanisms. Naturally, if patients accept closing their eyes, this is alright. Therapists should therefore suggest patients concentrate on inner space, perhaps while keeping their eyes on a fixed point, to not get distracted. Some anchor points need to be found: the relevant character, the subject and some bodily sensations, albeit only vaguely described. For example, a patient might say she had chronic difficulties with her mother, whom she found critical, but does not know what else to say. The therapist should then ask her to visualise her mother's face, figure, clothing and voice. He should also ask her to place her mother in a time and place, even generically, without having to truly remember something that really happened.

When patients cannot supply further details, clinicians should interrupt the reconstruction and switch to, so to say, shooting the scene. The therapist should therefore ask the patient to imagine her mother, or any imagined character, say or do something. If the imaginary character talks, he should get her to describe the contents and nuances of the character's face, body and tone of voice. If it does not talk, non-verbal aspects suffice. The therapist should explore the patient's reactions to what the character does and says at each moment, to access inner experience precisely when it arises.

Let us now continue and describe the subsequent aspects of the imagery work with Renata, until the rescripting and subsequent reflection stage. We shall alternate the description with other aspects of the work with Mirka. After the expounding of the various imagery application steps, we shall describe three other patients and show case by case how guided imagery with rescripting evolves in line with decisional procedures.

Emotional modulation and reflections: associated memories

After the exercise patients should reopen their eyes and return to the conversation with the therapist. A moment of *debriefing* may be needed, especially if the scene relived has been intense and laden with traumatic memories.

Mirka finished the exercise centred on her mother-in-law's funeral in a state of intense emotional activation. She felt in good hands with the therapist but still had a sense of fragility and weakness, and the presence of her sneering rival disquieted her. The therapist got her to conduct a prolonged grounding until she calmed down and felt steady. The therapist then started the rescripting, in the way we describe later. Here there was no recourse to associated memories, because Mirka was already clear that her tendency to feel weak and powerless vis-à-vis a strong, dominating and humiliating other was one of her schemas, as emerged from the reconstruction of her relationship with her ex-husband and previous romantic relationships. A rescripting aimed at changing the schema could therefore be attempted, starting from the procedural component, given her very intense emotional activation, to bring the patient back in contact with her healthy self-parts.

Generally, after imagery exercises triggering intense emotions, therapists can ask patients to pay attention to sensorial details in the room and describe them, and be attentive to the therapist's bodily states or appearance, until they are anchored again to the here and now.

After some emotion regulation, if required, or directly after the exercise, reflection should start, with the therapist asking for further feedback on how the patient felt the experience to be, after which he can make his own observations. He should dwell on elements that are new when compared with the narrative episode and especially underscore moments where the patient experienced intense emotions, as visible from non-verbal communication. Here schema reformulating becomes pivotal, thanks to the material emerging during the exercise. In fact, thanks to the experience, the elements surfacing typically make it possible to refine the formulation, making it closer to a patient's inner world so she can feel it to be her own.

At this reflection stage the therapist showed Renata her anger was not primary. The upper hand had been taken by her fear of her father's aggressiveness, of which Renata was not at all aware. Together with this, a worry about her mother and a feeling of sorrow at seeing her fragile and submissive emerged. With recent memories and associated core memories available and a shared awareness there are schemas, one can now proceed to promoting change or rescripting.

Rescripting

Giving new shape to patients' stories during imagery is one of the most intense and moving moments in the therapeutic process. It is also one of the most technically difficult and emotionally challenging. Patients are asked to break with longstanding ways of functioning, written in their bodies, and conduct mental acts exposing them to distressing emotions, while driven by a motivation to achieve better health and a right to act independently and of their own free will. A therapist is aware of what he does and senses the importance of it and responsibility for it. Simultaneously he is driven by a taste for discovery, is curious to see where he can get to and glimpses solutions, within reach, to patients' dilemmas and distress. Here there are three load-bearing columns making therapeutic action solid, firmly planted on the ground and secure: the therapist's ability to self-modulate, the formulation of the schema and asking for feedback.

We shall not dwell on the first, except to repeat that during rescripting therapists should be regulated and ready to react unswervingly, robustly and with control of their reactions to whatever emerges.

The formulation of the schema is what renders rescripting possible and beneficial. In fact, at this moment the therapist should steer patients to act in line with their wishes, by interrupting maladaptive coping. If the therapist therefore correctly pinpoints the patient's wish and schema structure, rescripting is likely to be beneficial and fruitful. With a wrong formulation he only gets a resumption of coping and temporary relationship rupture.

Requesting verbal feedback and observing non-verbal markers helps therapists to fine-tune interventions and refine schema formulation. This is all possible, we recall, because rescripting occurs only after conducting a shared schema formulation, and therefore theoretically the therapist knows in advance where he is aiming. In some cases, however, therapists start guided imagery exercises with a diagnostic purpose and then realise there is leeway for rescripting, with the patient responding well to the intervention, the story contents surfacing, mental states clear and emotional arousal increased but well-regulated. Moreover, the therapist has a well-founded idea of what the schema-similar structure underlying the episode is. Naturally, one cannot talk yet of schemas, because the associative work has not been carried out, and so patients do not know they are working on their own ways of ascribing meaning to the world.

In these cases, one can nevertheless attempt rescripting, which is here part of *dynamic assessment* (Chapter 4). It is exactly as if one did a behavioural experiment with diagnostic ends. Therapists do not use rescripting to stimulate differentiation but to block procedural automatisms and see, together with patients, what happens. With this, patients are more likely to realise their problems are in their inner world. When, for example, replying to an invalidating girlfriend, it is easier for a patient to see his difficulty transmitting his own point of view does not depend on his real girlfriend, who is not in the scene in the flesh, but on his own way of reacting. Simultaneously, with this, so to say, direct kind of rescripting, access to healthy parts is quicker. In fact, if a patient, albeit only for an instant, can modify something in his actions or emotions, he discovers he has agency over his inner world and some self-parts are not slaves to his disorder.

Generally, especially with less expert clinicians, we recommend following the canonical procedure: interrupting guided imagery, reflecting together with the patient, fine-tuning the schema and proposing rescripting. However, more expert therapists with a better mastery of MIT and imagery technique can perform the two stages together, in order to work while patients' protective mechanisms are at minimum strength.

In MIT shared formulation comes before change. In such cases attempting rescripting before this joint operation can seem a violation of the model. Actually, the therapist's action involves an early rupture of the procedural part of schemas. The result is, therefore, an increase in metacognition. Patients discovers how they function while trying to change their way of acting in relationships. Naturally, immediately after an early rescripting like the one just described, there should be a detailed reflection stage, so that everything emerging becomes shared and explicit knowledge.

There is a very important technical point: to conduct rescripting a therapist should ask patients to *move* differently in the imagined scene. And consequently act, go away and get close. He should get them to *talk* differently: saying things they find difficult to say and replying like they do not usually manage to.

On the contrary, a therapist should not get patients to *think* differently! As in all experiential practice, in the reality of the exercise change and rescripting need to be from the bottom upwards and the logic-semantic mode needs to be suppressed. Certainly, after the imagery joint reflection is necessary, but during rescripting patients should only try new ways of behaving and their body and voice learn to move differently.

If patients grasp their wish to pursue independence and see the other as critical and scornful, blocking his independence, the therapist can then ask them to continue to act independently, ignoring the other. Or else he should ask them him to assert their own point of view vis-à-vis the other's adverse position.

Again, if the other's reaction is dominating, and the patient has difficulty breaking away, the therapist should ask the patient to introduce another character in a supporter position (Hermans & Hermans-Konopka, 2010). If the patient manages to, he can introduce an adult and benign self-part to support the part needing independence and encouragement. In more difficult cases patients can benefit from the therapist joining the scene and providing support. This is what Schema Therapy terms *limited reparenting* (Arntz & van Genderen, 2011). In MIT it is the last option we choose. It is better for patients to try and bring supporter characters

Guided imagery and imagery rescripting 161

chosen by themselves and which can be themselves or other real life figures, for example, grandparents, friends or benevolent figures from their own histories. Patients thus gain greater agency, feel the therapist is less indispensable for their progress, and have greater confidence in the idea that they are authors of their own progress.

Therapists should in any case lead rescripting like an off-stage voice and suggest to patients the phrases to be pronounced or actions to be performed, while still remembering the schema and which part of the schema they are rewriting.

Renata discovered that behind her reactions of rage there were feelings of fear for herself and her mother. She was not used to considering the fear part of herself and did not know how to handle it. She felt a prey to an overwhelming threat and totally like a girl of seven. Here rescripting in its most usual form is recommended: returning to the scene to write an alternative ending, where the patient manages to tackle the problematic relationship while feeling more competent, strong or effective.

After grounding in abbreviated form, the therapist took her back to the dinner table with her parents. Renata chose to remain a child, to not use her adult part, and felt it was right to reply to them like when she was 7. Her aim was feeling entitled and capable of asking her father to not frighten her.

Returning to the scene Renata's arousal increased again and she was frightened. The therapist suggested breathing deeply. He noticed she tended to lower her head and asked her to hold it up. The simple gesture of exposing her chest more made her more frightened. The therapist noticed this and encouraged her again to maintain the scene where her father yelled at her mother. She asked Renata if she was managing to remain in the situation and, albeit hesitatingly, she answered yes. The therapist now asked her to tell her father to stop attacking her mother.

R: "Daddy, don't attack Mummy."
T: "How do you feel?"
R: "I'm a bit frightened."
T: "Try saying it again."
R: "Don't yell at Mummy. Stop it."
T: "Up with your chin again if you can. Now try telling him, 'If you attack Mummy, I feel bad.'"
R [*with a feeble voice*]: "If you hurt Mummy, I don't like it. You mustn't do that."
T: "Say it again with a firmer, more powerful voice. Breathe deeply and expand your chest."
R: "Don't do that. Don't yell. I don't like it."

The therapist encouraged her and validated her expressing herself assertively.

T: "How do you feel?"
R: "Confident."

Then she unexpectedly froze and immediately broke into tears.

T: "Do you not feel up to continuing? What's happening to you?"
R: "I can't do it."
T: "What are you feeling right now?"
R: "Daddy."
T: "Yes? What can you see?"
R: "He's got an ugly look."
T: "Threatening?"
R: "No. Surprised."
T: "Surprised? How?"
R: "He didn't expect it. But . . ." [*Renata cries again*].
T: "How are you now?"
R: "I feel guilty. I've made him feel ashamed. Who knows how bad he feels now I've spoken to him like that."

The therapist agreed with Renata that the exercise finish here. On reopening her eyes Renata was dumbfounded; she did not know she had these feelings. In the next section we shall look at the joint reflection following rescripting.

Post-rescripting reflections

The step following rescripting depends largely on what emerges during the exercise. The therapist should typically start by asking for feedback on the experience. The conversation can have various ends: 1) validation of the experience surfacing and consolidation of contents in long-term memory; 2) identification of healthy parts; 3) identification of remaining problems but with an increase in differentiation. In practice therapists help patients to perceive their problem has an inner nature rather than depending on others; 4) renegotiation of the therapeutic contract: establishing new goals and tasks.

If new features of the patient's inner world emerge, and self-reflectivity improves, the therapist summarises them and underscores their importance. Thanks, often, to rescripting, patients' understanding of their schemas gets enriched with the healthy, functioning parts. Patients discover they have resources and features of their inner world not crushed by their pathogenic representations and the therapist should ensure he emphasises this, so that the healthy features are more likely to stay in long-term memory and not get lost when imagery finishes.

A post-rescripting renegotiation of a schema might sound like:

> You were convinced pursuing your own wish would have been impossible because the other would have criticised and crushed you. At this point you were beginning to not believe in your own ideas, were getting convinced you were worthless, and were seizing up. Now we have seen that you're able to make contact with what you like doing and feel, at least for some moments, you can do it, your idea makes sense and pursuing it makes you feel good.

As per MIT procedure, access to healthy parts and differentiation proceed synergically. In the experience patients make contact with their ability to escape from the schemas, express their fears, seek reassurance and obtain it, protect themselves from attack and pursue their own ideas. This contact alone helps to refute, at least partially, schema-dependent beliefs. Simultaneously it helps make patients aware their suffering and problems are internal and do not necessarily depend on others' behaviour and intentions.

Patients switch from: "I've no freedom of movement because my mother blocks me" to "When my mother takes fright or criticises me, inside me there's a growing feeling of fear and paralysis I don't know how to counter". The focus of treatment now becomes the mental state, which is malleable, and not hoping for different behaviour from the other by acting differently. The patient recovers agency over his inner world.

Naturally, rescripting, even if successful, does not cure pathology on its own and does not change schemas permanently, by replacing pathogenic ones with more benign and adaptive ideas. What patients anyway gain is power over themselves. A typical reaction to successful rescripting is: "I've grasped I can act and behave differently, but when I leave here I don't know what to do." This too is progress, because it facilitates formulating the therapeutic contract anew and establish agreed goals.

The end of rescripting thus coincides with a renegotiation of the contract, goals and tasks. For example, patients differentiate cognitively but realise that under the pressure of intense emotions they lose the ability to distinguish between negative imagination – "I'm incompetent and the other criticises me" and more benign or realistic alternatives – "I'm convinced I'm incompetent but it's not necessarily so and, even if not everything I do turns out perfectly, I can still be appreciated". In the presence of this enriched representation of functioning a therapist can suggest operations regulating the patient's inner world ranging from mindfulness, leading to letting negative thoughts flow but without allowing them any power, to attention regulation strategies (Wells, 2005; Chapter 9).

After rescripting the contract frequently foresees the planning of behavioural experiments (Chapter 8). This involves either finding situations in the coming days which patients might find themselves tackling, or actively creating situations resembling those experienced in rescripting where patients are driven by the same wishes and face the same problems. The experiential learning principle (Kolb, 1984) thus gets applied: patients try to act in line with their plans, as during rescripting, and then report the experience in the next session in order to reflect upon it.

After guided imagery with rescripting Renata and the therapist reviewed the formulation of functioning. She now grasped that, when she asserted her need for security, she found herself facing an unexpectedly vulnerable other and feared hurting him. The vulnerable other was embodied by both her mother and father. Towards both Renata had feelings of sorrow and guilt, linked to an inverted attachment: she took care of them for fear of losing them and finding herself alone. Renata thus understood better both why she was so easily prey to guilt feelings towards her boyfriend – she recalled seeing him alone and unprotected in situations where he was fragile – and because the reduction in working hours after the argument had been so distressing.

In fact, she knew she had done something in a convinced and consistent manner, but realised that behind her anger at the injustice undergone there was guilt. She linked this feeling to that towards her father during rescripting: "If I assert my plans, I'll hurt those close to me." She now remembered various memories where she acted in a self-sacrificing way to avoid making the other suffer. With this understanding her guilt feelings could be considered the core element in her future treatment.

The therapist concluded the session by planning behavioural experiments: he asked Renata to monitor her guilt feelings and, when they arose, try to continue acting in line with her goals without resorting to self-sacrificing behaviour.

Guided imagery with rescripting: two cases

What now follows is a description of two clinical histories, Dean and Alma, to show how guided imagery with rescripting evolves with each step it attempts to achieve.

Dean

Dean was in therapy with an Australian colleague. He was 50 and worked as a financial consultant in Brisbane. He suffered from depression and covert narcissism, together with Obsessive-Compulsive PD traits. He sought therapy because he felt paralysed in his work, describing himself as immobilised and a professional failure. He was apathetic; nothing stirred him. He was perfectionist and tended to procrastinate, on the one hand because nothing prompted him to act and, on the other, because he felt competent and capable of doing things at the last moment. Simultaneously he realised this attitude was not very fruitful and did not help in running his business. He appraised himself against his own perfectionist standards, harshly criticising himself and thus exacerbating his feeling of failure. When talking about how he came to do his current work, he told how his choices had been influenced by his mother, who in his second session he described as being fearful, controlling, demanding and hyper-critical.

"She had total control of my life. There was no way you could disagree. She'd decided I would become a doctor and told everyone in front of me: he's going to be a doctor. When I didn't manage to finish my university course, she wouldn't let me hear the last of it. Then I enrolled in Economics, which in her opinion was the route to odd jobs." In his third session a new element emerged.

D: "My mother was worse than I told you about the other time."
T: "How do you mean?"
D: "She suffered from Paranoid Schizophrenia. She got diagnosed for it later; we didn't know then."

T: "What was happening at home? What age are we talking about?"
D: "I was about 10. I couldn't sleep at night."
T: "What did your mum do?"
D: "She stayed awake all night. She was convinced burglars could break in and so she went around from one window to the next to check."
T: "And you?"
D: "I was under my bedclothes, with my eyes open wide, not moving, frozen. If I'd moved a single muscle, she'd have noticed."
T: "What did you feel?"
D: "Fear. I looked out of the window and every leaf stirring froze me even more."

His therapist asked him to relive the episode using imagery, as he wanted to explore these feelings of paralysis with him, and Dean accepted willingly.

During the scene Dean experienced fear very intensely. He listened to sounds coming from the house and heard the steps of his mother opening and closing doors. For him they indicated danger. He pulled up his bedsheet, covered his head and became motionless: "I can't do anything. I have to avoid giving signs of life. If the burglars looked in through the window, they might notice I'm here and come in and kidnap me."

The therapist asked him to look at the window and observe what he could see outside. Dean was even more frightened. He could see the leaves stirring and the shadows, and was afraid someone was there, ready to come in.

At this point the therapist interrupted the exercise and asked Dean to breathe mindfully. Leaving the scene, the therapist satisfied himself that Dean had gone back to a good regulation and this was the case. Dean felt the therapist had guided him well and sensed him close throughout the experience. The reflection stage could thus start.

The first thing emerging was that Dean now grasped his paralysis at work was linked to the paralysis in the relived episode, something he had not managed to understand with just the memory. Here, therefore, as well as increasing monitoring, the imagery exercise made it possible to recall memories and link them to the current problem.

Dean could see how strong the feelings of fear and powerlessness he had during his infancy were and how they were amplified by his mother's paranoid behaviour. The therapist suggested returning to the scene, and after explaining what it was, asked him if he wanted to attempt *imagery rescripting*. The declared goal was to try to calm down Dean the child and overcome the paralysis.

They agreed on introducing Dean the adult to the scene and the latter, at the therapist's suggestion, sat on the bed next to Dean the child and cuddled him. Initially Dean the child continued to be afraid. Dean the adult suggested he get up but the child refused. Dean the adult told him there was nothing outside, that they could go and look together and that he could hold his hand.

Dean the child accepted, understood that Dean the adult was not afraid of the people outside and overcame his hesitation. Dean the adult took him by the hand and they got close to the windows: "You see? Nobody there" and Dean the child returned to bed reassured. At the end of the rescripting Dean felt more relaxed and effective. In particular, a sense of deep feeling for himself when he was little surfaced and he was very happy with this emotion, which smashed the wall of apathy that had been suffocating him for some time. He could now see more clearly where his feelings of passivity and being switched off came from. He was not yet capable of unblocking himself but was confident that the therapeutic work could help him.

The post-rescripting reflecting proved fruitful. Dean saw that, in the light not least of other recent narrative episodes, his dominant schemas were two. The first was linked to his wish for approval (social rank), which met a critical and invalidating other. The self's response was submission, with a consequent block of independent action and reduction of agency.

The second schema was linked to the activation of attachment, with Dean starting from a fragile and fearful self and asking for attention from another (his mother) fearful in turn. In response, he felt weak, terrorised and at the mercy of dark forces, and froze. Again, the outcome was the blocking of independence and the exploratory system. Dean thus grasped that his tendency to be passive, switched-off and abulic, to be on autopilot as he said, had historical roots.

They therefore planned self-observation exercises for between sessions to pinpoint when he became defeatist, switched off or procrastinated. The idea was that in such situations he could recall what he had found out in-session and try to maintain his independent actions, while putting aside any thoughts or emotions that would block him. Dean had already had mindfulness experiences and therefore agreed with the therapist on doing 15-minute meditation sessions when he could feel sensations emerging during guided imagery surfacing, so that they did not grow until they dominated him.

Alma

Alma was a sports psychologist aged 28 and suffered from Dependent PD. She sought therapy because she was suffering on account of a relationship with a man she described as being "distant". She told him she wanted to understand what their relationship consisted of, given that for two years "we've been splitting and getting back together". She asked him what his intentions were while they were having a coffee and he replied that he wanted to be together. She was happy. However, in the following days the man disappeared. She told the therapist she was getting over it, but in reality she displayed signs of negative arousal: getting agitated and a tense facial expression. The therapist pointed this out and she realised it was true she did not know what to call the emotion. The therapist pointed out that something was showing in her face. Alma concentrated on her inner state and, albeit with some difficulty, grasped she was sad. Then she immediately closed up: "It's not a problem. I'm used to dealing with it alone."

The therapist asked where she had learnt to solve her problems alone, even when down and needing comforting. Alma perceived it was something that over her life she had made her way of doing things: the idea was that, if she caused problems for her parents, she would harm them, and she felt guilty. This conditioned current choices: "I left home two years ago to continue my study programme and to not let them see when I have problems with my studies."

The therapist tried to draw out situations where she felt alone, before she activated her compulsive self-care coping mechanism and before she was governed by her sense of guilt at the idea that, if she asked something for herself, she harmed the other. Alma could see her boyfriend's permanent indecisiveness led her to swing between displeasure and justifying him because she feared it was her who was wrong in asking him for more. "Perhaps he rejects me because I'm too forward and don't leave him enough room for manoeuvre."

She focused together with the therapist on the moments immediately after her asking her boyfriend to define their relationship. It was a scene occurring a few days earlier: Alma was without him but with some female friends in a sort of discotheque where everybody listened to the same music, but through headphones.

During imagery Alma returned to a moment at which she looked at some chat messages from the sports group of which she was a member with her boyfriend. She sent a message joking and wishing goodnight to everybody. She expected her boyfriend to wish her goodnight privately before going to bed. Using imagery the therapist asked her to concentrate on the exact moment when she looked at the screen with the chat while waiting for her boyfriend's reply. Alma realised she was sad and anxious. Her anxiety was situated in her chest. She cried when she contacted her sadness. The therapist pointed this out and observed aloud, trying to echo Alma's thoughts: "He's leaving me alone. I feel really sad." When the exercise finished, Alma relaxed and smiled, and told the therapist she felt better because the latter had been able to notice her sadness and validate it.

As shown, guided imagery for diagnostic purposes does not need, especially at the start of therapy, to concentrate on core scenes. In fact, emotions are often more likely to surface in recent scenes, especially those patients want to tackle and solve in therapy. However, with the emerging of emotions and an understanding of relationship nuances it becomes easier to move towards associated memories. A patient now feels emotionally that the current problem is an echo, the repetition of a historically learnt emotional pattern.

The therapist asked Alma for associations regarding moments of loneliness. She remembered her parents were always working, even up to 10 in the evening, but she was alright at home and found company in her brother. She had difficulty recalling situations where she felt alone. The therapist then asked her about when she had seen her parents worried, to try to understand the origins of the schema where she harmed dear ones. Alma recalled a recent episode: there had been a fire at work and her mother was extremely worried. With this picture of her mother Alma felt guilty and powerless. The therapist validated her and asked her if she considered these feelings problematical but Alma asserted they were entirely normal.

The inverted caregiving coping was egosyntonic for her and could not, therefore, be made the subject of change. The therapist then went back, with polite insistence, to asking her if she remembered past experiences where she felt alone. With difficulty Alma remembered brief moments when, aged 9, they took her to a summer camp with her brother. There a brief moment, where she felt lonely and wanted to go home, surfaced. "Not back to Mum and Dad," Alma stressed, "but home." The rescripting concentrated on this episode.

Alma first perceived that not being able to expect attention went back to her childhood. She realised that she had, as a reaction, developed a compulsive self-sufficiency coping mechanism. She reformulated with the therapist that, because of this, when she wanted to be loved she immediately foresaw the other being distant and a part of her took it for granted that this was normal, the other was by nature unavailable and she did not have the right to ask.

Alma went back to the camp, to the time in the evening when she felt alone and would have liked her parents to come and get her. She telephoned, but her mother replied she would not come. Alma froze and felt that it was not possible to rebut this, her mother was right and she should stay there like all normal children and not cause problems. The therapist pointed out how strict her opinion about herself was then and that it was wrong to treat a lonely child like that. Alma started crying again. Initially she was able to hold the tears back but then, when the therapist insisted crying was fine, she let herself go.

T: "How do you feel now?"
A: "Weak."
T: "How do you mean 'weak'?"
A: "Wrong."
T: "Well, the opinion about the little Alma has returned. Shall we try and combat it?"
A: "It's difficult."
T: "Do you feel up to trying?"
A: "Ok."
T: "Well then, Alma, try repeating out loud: 'I feel weak. It's normal, I'm a child.'"

Alma tried but blushed and froze. The therapist asked her what she felt, but she did not know how to reply.

T: "Could you feel ashamed?"
A: "I don't know, perhaps. It's that I feel ridiculous, a child complaining. What was so difficult about staying at the camp?"

The therapist insisted she not succumb to the critical opinion and try and resist it. He asked her to stay on the phone and tell her mum she could not do it. Alma was in difficulty; she said her mother was too hard and one could not move her. The therapist then suggested introducing the adult herself to the session to help the little Alma. The idea seemed doable to her and this is what they did.

T: "Now you're an adult. Can you see the little Alma?"
A: "Yes"
T: "How does she seem to you?"
A: "Despairing, alone. I feel sorry for her; she shouldn't be there."
T: "Go up to her. Try saying something to her."

A: "You feel lonely but now I'm here."
T: "Very good. How do you find her?"
A: "She's looking at me, staring."
T: "What effect does she have on you?"
A: "Affection. I'd like to hug her."
T: "Do it."

Alma imagined hugging the child and said she had a feeling of warmth.

T: "What feeling does the child's body give you?"
A: "She's relaxing, letting herself go, like a flow of warmth between us."
T: "Is it still important to talk with Mum?"
A: "Are you asking me or the child?"
T: "Reply from the point of view you feel more yours at this moment."
A: "The child would like to say it's not right that Mum behaves like that."
T: "Then let's try and tell Mum that. Hold her hand."
A: [*while her adult self makes the gesture of taking her hand*]: "Mummy, I'm weak. I'm a child and it's right that I'm not up to it and you have to come and get me."

At this point she felt anxious: "I feel stupid."

T: "Hold the child's hand tight. Tell her to stand up with her back straight, and to talk out loud."
A [*addressing her child self*]: "Don't be stupid. You're right. Say out loud what you think."
T: "How do you feel?"
A: "Better! Stronger. Less silly."
T: "Try again."
A: "Mummy, you shouldn't have left me here. I need you."
T: "What effect does this have on you now?"
A: "As if I was lighter."
T: "Where do you feel this?"
A: "Here [*indicating her shoulders*], as if I'd got a weight off me. And I feel stronger. The contact with my adult self holding my hand is nice."

During the reflections that followed Alma grasped that this behaviour was typical of her; in situations of need she was incapable of consistently and calmly asking for attention. She swung instead between paralysis, angry protest and shame at the request just made angrily. She added that finding out she could help herself was a surprise. She said that with her child eyes she felt admiration for the adult herself, saw that part of her to be capable, solid and reliable, and was now letting herself slide inside these pleasant sensations.

In the next sessions Alma tried to ask her boyfriend for attention and availability, and this time, faced with his indecisiveness, she managed, even if painfully, to detach herself. She realised that it was as if she stayed tied to the scene where she hoped her mother would come back to get her, but asking for comfort was pointless because it would have been met with rejection, and breaking off from the telephone impossible. Now she felt she needed someone to figure in her life more constantly, but needed first to let the sense of being lovable and able to be cared for grow within her.

Problems activated by imagery and managing them

Suggesting the reliving of an often distressing scene can provoke various negative reactions: fear of losing control of emotions and being submerged by despondency or anxiety without any chance of a solution, sense of constriction or violation of one's privacy by the therapist. Often these fears are poorly expressed and take the form of instinctive and non-mentalised reactions: "I'm not up to it", "I don't feel like it", "I can't do it", "I prefer not".

Here the therapist should discard suggesting the exercise immediately and politely explore the reasons for the rejection: "It's not a problem if you don't accept. It's not experience and frequently it can be seen as a disturbance or a worry. What effect did my suggestion have? Understanding what leads you to reject gives us some important information." If patients have difficulty putting together a reply and accessing the contents accounting for the rejection, the request is likely to have caused a rupture in the alliance or occurred while a rupture, which the therapist was not aware of, was under way. The focus therefore shifts to repairing the rupture.

During imagery patients can experience intense and sometimes extremely powerful emotions. This alone is not a problem as it is one of the goals. However, if a patient feels an emotion becoming overpowering it is indispensable that the therapist take note and pay attention to any previously agreed stress signals. If the patient is too overwhelmed by the emotion to remember to ask that the exercise be interrupted, the therapist should pay attention to any signs of intense suffering or loss of emotional control and ask the patient if he feels up to continuing or prefers to break off for a moment and continue later or stop altogether. We recall that it is important to help patients to see they are capable of reliving distressing episodes. Consequently, before interrupting, a therapist should try to calm the patient with breathing exercises, grounding techniques and encouragement, empathy and support for exploration: "I realise it's very difficult to relive this scene and experience these emotions. Are you still up to it or do you prefer a break? It was going well: you're very good at opening up, telling about yourself and showing me these features of your history (or of your inner world)." A therapist can ask patients to note whether they feel reassured by his presence and to pay attention to it: "Does thinking I'm here with you help you? I'm close to you and have emotionally entered the story with you."

When a patient gives clear signs of wanting to interrupt, one should stop and, after exiting the imagery, reflect about what drove him to this. Under these conditions the patient is likely to be able to describe the cognitions and affects in the episode, which until shortly before he could not perceive or define.

Sometimes during guided imagery patients dissociate, usually only slightly. The therapist is likely to feel frightened or guilty for what happens, to consider he has made a mistake, not handled the episode correctly or gone too far. The iatrogenic aspect cannot be excluded, but if a patient dissociates it is generally not of concern and the therapist is not responsible. Imagery is in fact a sort of dissociative experience induced under controlled conditions.

Moreover, many patients have dissociated aspects of their experience in the past and putting them in contact again with episodes that their consciousness has not integrated can reactivate their dissociative defence mechanism. It is impossible to foresee for sure who will dissociate, when and to what extent; the important thing is to be ready to handle it. We repeat: these are usually small-sized phenomena and from this point of view inducing them in-session is positive because they make clinicians aware of a part of a psychopathology they have not seen previously. Once the experience is over, the clinician should point out the start of the dissociative episode to the patient and tie it to the relational context in which it developed.

Patients thus become more aware of the contexts where the mind becomes vulnerable and understand better still the impact certain relational contexts, both real and especially internalised, have on them.

Ivana was 70 years old and suffered from generalised anxiety disorder and panic attacks. An idea of being inadequate, not up to situations, leading her to fear humiliation in public, emerged rapidly during therapy.

She told of a situation where she had in fact felt humiliated. It was the day of the end of year play, in the theatre of her school, a church one, with all the families present. She was there with her adoptive parents. At the start of the episode she was cheerful and happy about her father being there as he was usually busy with his work. Ivana recalled a nun showed a drawing done by another child. She liked it a lot and even now remembered its lively colours. The nun promised it as a present to anyone who could name the seven kings of Rome. The therapist suggested reliving the episode using guided imagery.

Returning to the scene, Ivana relived when she raised her hand, sure she knew the reply. She felt a mixture of anxiety and enthusiasm and, especially, wanted the drawing. Her father stopped her, by putting his hand on her arm and saying, "Forget it". In spite of being invalidated, Ivana did not become less motivated and her wish to have the drawing was strong. She went up on the stage and assuredly listed the kings. The nun pointed out she had forgotten the first one. Ivana repeated the list, once again omitting Romulus. The nun told her she had not, unfortunately, won the drawing. The therapist asked her what she felt then. "Bewilderment", replied Ivana, "a feeling there was a weight on my chest . . . in the pit of my stomach . . . a sort of anxiety . . . as if something somewhere was crying". The therapist echoed her:

T: "As if something somewhere was crying."
I: "As if I was crying."
T: "So you feel sad too?"

I: "Yes, but on the other hand I can sense that this . . . is staying here. . . . It's not that it's spreading to other parts."
T: "You're crying inside yourself."
I: "Yes."

Ivana came down from the stage. Now she could feel all eyes on her and the other parents' pitiful expressions. At the therapist's suggestion, she lingered over a woman's face: "It was as if she thought 'poor little thing.'" Ivana now felt beaten and the feeling got stronger when she went back to her seat and her father greeted her with an: "I told you so" and her mother looked gravely straight ahead as if Ivana had never got up. The therapist asked her what she felt.

I: "I made him cut a poor figure."
T: "What do you feel, the poor show you put on or guilt?"
I: "Shame and then guilt. . . . I say to myself 'but look, how could you think of that?'"
T: "So you're also thinking 'How could I have dared expose myself like that?'"
I: "Yes, I could have stayed still."
T: "Where do you feel these guilt and shame sensations?"
I: "I feel a bit light-headed, my mouth very dry, like needing to drink a bit . . . because for me water is a cure-all. It helps me in all my panic attacks. . . . I feel like an empty shell."
T: "An empty shell . . . as if you'd lost your energy . . . strength . . . your body's letting itself go."
I: "It's a strange sensation. . . . It's as if I felt there was only the shell."
T: "Only the shell . . . and so the sensation of having disappeared, of being almost insubstantial. . . . Now we've lost the convinced, wilful part we saw at the start of the scene."
I: "Yes, now I'm tending just to not let anyone see that I feel really hurt."

The therapist now suggested Ivana attempt rescripting. He helped her to focus again on her desire for the drawing and the pleasant sensations she felt on seeing it. He asked her to say, with a firm and ever more stentorian tone of voice: "I want that drawing. I like it." Ivana realised she scarcely felt the right to say "I want"; it came more naturally to say "I should like".

As they continued the rescripting, the therapist suggested the little Ivana address her father and ask him to be confident in her. Ivana hesitated; she could not imagine how her father would react. The therapist asked her to visualise her father's face while asking him to be confident in her. Her father was serious, but not threatening. The therapist suggested she ask him again to be confident in her. Ivana managed this time with more conviction.

Ivana added, "If you stay calm, I've got the reply and I can get that drawing."

At this point the exercise was over. Ivana felt grounded and had overcome the sense of defeat, fear of judgement and unworthiness. After the exercise Ivana reflected that she would always have liked her father to be proud of her, but this had never happened and being aware of this made her sad.

Finally, when the therapist asked her for feedback on the experience, Ivana was pleasantly surprised because she manged to feel what until then she had only written in her poems, that is the pleasant sensation of feeling her body empty: "I knew I was there, but at the same time I couldn't feel myself" and added "You feel your body like a shell and so you aren't there . . . you're air, a spirit".

Note that Ivana returned in her mind to the guided imagery situation where she was heavily exposed to feelings of guilt and shame, while experiencing physical sensations similar to panic attacks. The sensations were of emptiness and lack of energy. She now reread it as a pleasant sensation, showing she had dissociated the distressing part of the experience.

Ivana's dissociative experience was not serious and the guided imagery exercise was useful in diagnosing it *in vivo*. Anyway, the episode described was a good example of how, when recalling distressing memories, patients can lose the intactness of their awareness. It is not usually a question of an iatrogenic effect, but of the possibility of observing, during sessions, dissociative phenomena that patients possess in daily life but have not displayed to their therapist. Therapists now generally ask patients to watch when the phenomenon reoccurs and, especially, what the relational antecedents of the dissociation are.

Overall, as Young and colleagues point out (2003), imagery with traumatic memories is to be handled with greater caution than other types of imagery, for example when trying to overcome avoidances. With traumatic memories greater attention needs to be paid to signs of explicit rejection by a patient before starting imagery immersion or prolonging it. With avoidances it is correct to insist more on tolerating distressing emotions.

When a patient's arousal increases and he has difficulty regulating it, but does not display explicit signs of wanting to interrupt the experience, a therapist can intervene to help him regulate his affects. He can ask the patient to regulate his emotions by focusing on his breathing or practising mindfulness as necessary, until he sees his emotions as something not frightening or uncontrollable and the threatening images are no longer looming and have a real quality (Hackmann et al., 2011). Another very useful practice is to stop the scene and work on the patient's bodily state, asking him to adopt a more energetic posture, squeezing his hands against each other, clenching his fists or pressing with his feet on the floor. Very often this produces a change in bodily state making it possible for patients to feel strong enough to continue the exercise.

Therapists can interrupt the exercise and get patients to anchor themselves to their environment: the therapist, lights or furnishings, until emotions are regulated.

Whatever the problem, it is fundamental to reason about the state of the therapeutic relationship. The therapist should ask the patient what effect experiencing distress caused by the imagery experiment he suggested has: did he feel coerced? Ill-treated? Forced? Not understood? Or did he interpret his difficulties in carrying out the exercise as a sign of inadequacy, seriousness of his illness, incapability, cowardice, weakness or excessive fragility? Here the therapist should ask the patient how he feels he is seen by the former considering these negative ideas about himself: does he imagine the therapist is disappointed, displeased, angry or judging him? Once the therapist and patient have grasped the relational set-up created as a result of the imagery, it is possible to pass on to repairing the relationship (Dimaggio, Montano et al., 2015).

Guided imagery for tackling future scenarios

At the change promotion stage a decisive role is played by behavioural activation and engaging in gratifying activities compatible with a subject's goals and values (Hayes et al., 2011). In MIT the contract with the patient foresees the latter attempting, as soon as possible and ever more intensively, to actively seek wellbeing and envisage desirable life paths.

As ever, it is a question of negotiating within the therapeutic relationship: the patient is free to not manage, to stay blocked and paralysed, and to adopt protective coping. He knows that the therapist will continuously place him before the option of actively choosing wellbeing with the awareness that evolution and change depend partially on good in-session work and partially on behaviour activation between one session and another.

The underlying idea is it is not enough to know what is not right and interrupt pathogenic behaviour. It is necessary to move actively towards what is good for the patient, and there are often obstacles to the patient embarking on this satisfying existential path.

Here too imagery and the body help. Patients may imagine a concrete situation to tackle, think of a desired behaviour and perform it in their mental scenario, or feel a sense of self that they aim at "wearing" while interacting with others. This naturally does not ensure they then manage to really act this way, but it helps in preparing themselves to tackle the situation with a certain knowledge of what could happen and starting out from a sense of activity, conviction, ability and competence.

The benefits from anticipating future scenarios with imagery are various. First a patient creates for himself a cognitive/affective map of the territory he is going to explore. Without beating about the bush, he can build a realistic, possible future scenario, including some difficulties that could in fact arise together with the benefits he could draw from this new action. At the same time he can imagine more benign or "realistic" and reasonable finales when before he saw catastrophes or ill-defined dangers.

Another benefit consists in triggering an "embodied" awareness in the patient of the authentic wish pushing him towards this future event. If he imagines facing an exam, the wish he has to remember is either getting good marks or advancing in his studies towards a life path chosen independently. If the patient starts to take measures to prevent his parents suffering because of bad marks, or to protect himself from potentially looking foolish, he is driven by coping and this harms him. Attention to coping – for example: "How can I avoid hurting my folks?" – blocks

Guided imagery and imagery rescripting 175

out the primary wish, from which the patient distances himself. Restoring the original motivation is a fundamental step towards acting with determination and purpose in the world.

Furthermore, with anticipatory imagery one can focus on beneficial mental states rather than feared ones, and this reinforces motivation and increases the sense of agency. When we move towards a desired goal we certainly need a realistic map of what we are going to face, but we also need to trigger and almost look forward to the desired state.

To expose oneself with determination to an exam, one needs to clearly visualise the scenes where one is proud, satisfied or happy at passing it, feeling self-esteem and envisaging the deserved leisure time afterwards. To decide on tackling a journey towards a distant destination we let ourselves be filled with the sensation of wellbeing, energy and freedom we will feel on arriving, instead of letting ourselves be blocked by thoughts of hardships, long queues and tiredness.

If we want to court someone who interests us, we can certainly think about how best to introduce ourselves to make a good impression; this is normal and natural. But it is especially important to remember what we like, what attracts us or makes us curious about this person. This is a motivational impulse better than being appreciated and avoiding a rejection or cutting a poor figure.

To tackle future scenarios using imagery, we build a sort of internal laboratory together with the patient. The core consists in getting patients to "wear" the mental state they seek. If it surfaces in past memories, we start from here. Otherwise we stick to when a patient experiences it in-session, either of his own free will or as a result of therapeutic work aimed at making healthy parts emerge. One should then help the patient to build the image of his desired future around this state.

Once patients have slipped into the future scenario, they should be asked to perform some body movements aimed at "gripping" the mental state sought for and obtained, to involve the body in the action of wishing for and "inhabiting" this desirable condition.

The steps are as follows:

1 Clearly identifying the wish and the behaviour one wants to adopt to achieve it; acknowledging the underlying negative self-representations and dysfunctional forms of coping used hitherto
2 Recovering a benevolent core self-image on the basis of narrative episodes collected
3 Starting imagery work: promoting regulation and entering the scene
4 Making patients enter an "internal laboratory" where they can imagine tackling their target problem or reaching their wished-for state, while continuing to keep contact with their healthy self-representation
5 Asking patients to move physically towards this image, making the wished-for state felt bodily, letting them savour the state of their self and then terminating the exercise

Imagery focused on possible futures can concentrate on tackling seemingly problematic relational situations in a new way: like, for example, managing a conflict situation assertively and without slipping into the complementary attack-flight pattern. Nevertheless, the technique can also be employed for behaviour connected to merely imagined relationships, when the schema is active in the mind: planning starting writing an article without letting oneself be blocked by anxiety at the idea of a critical opinion, or passing an evening at home even if one feels alone, without drinking too much.

Loredana was 28 years old and suffered from Narcissistic PD with Obsessive-Compulsive PD traits. In her romantic relationships the trigger activating her schema, attachment-based, is seeing the other as reluctant and indecisive: she interprets this as lack of interest and this activates both a feeling of being forsaken and a shift to a coping schema linked to rank.

On the one hand, she interprets limited interest as a sign of poor lovability, which evokes the core self-image of "unworthy". A healthy image of being worth something surfaces and can be seen when she gets angry about another's behaviour: "He shouldn't have treated me like that. I'm worth much more." The dominant other's response is both to "dump" and "criticise and despise" her. Loredana takes this response to be true, agrees with it and therefore despises herself. Also linked to the activation of attachment there is the idea of a self vulnerable vis-à-vis a "cheating" other. This again causes the shift to rank: "I'm stupid. I let myself be cheated", "I should have realised before how it was going to end". However, she also feels anger and contempt towards another she sees as "cowardly, with no balls" and "dishonest".

When she has to face the other's passive and distant response, she resorts to coping behaviours: she becomes contemptuous, domineering or rejecting. This activates an interpersonal cycle where her partner becomes stuck.

Loredana started going out with a man of her own age, Giorgio, who proved very affectionate and understanding, but was still engaged in a previous, long-term relationship. He asserted it was on its last legs but he needed a little time to take a step that would turn his life upside down, making him change his residence and feel guilty towards his old partner.

This situation powerfully activated Loredana's interpersonal schema: although she noted the strong attraction he showed her and his efforts to move towards closing the previous relationship, Loredana got very often struck by distressing emotions when he was not totally available, for example on public holidays, at weekends or simply when she wanted to contact him and he could not reply because he was with the partner with whom he still lived.

Her emotional suffering was not so much linked to her urgent need for Giorgio to be there, as to her not feeling important enough to push him into quickly finishing his old relationship. Cognitively Loredana was aware he needed time, but under the pressure of her distressing emotions she lost a decentred point of view and yielded to behaviour driven by her schema.

Loredana then understood the schema and started to differentiate. She managed to control her aggressive and deprecating responses better and this triggered

Guided imagery and imagery rescripting 177

her negative interpersonal cycle less often. Giorgio passed ever more time with her and told his partner he no longer loved her, but her distress did not diminish. Let us see how the therapist constructed an imagery exercise involving anticipating a future scenario. First, he foreshadowed the work to do, anchoring it in the schema.

T: "Usually when you feel the other to be distant we have seen you become gloomy and nervous, start on a fight with Giorgio and send him text messages you already know he can't comply with fully. And then whatever reply he sends makes you angry and contemptuous. If he complies with your requests and rushes over to you, it leaves a nasty taste in your mouth because "it wasn't a willing choice. I had to ask him for it. He's got no balls. He's not up to taking decisions on his own." Now, instead, in our internal laboratory let's imagine a different Loredana, tackling non-competitively the delicate moment where she wants Giorgio and he can't be totally there. A Loredana we already know because she has revealed herself in other contexts, who functions well, is recognised and appreciated without having to get angry or fight, but lets things happen."

Let us see how the patient responds and the exercise evolves.

L: "There's a part of me that doesn't want to let him off even once."
T: "What does this part of the self want?"
L: "It fears that if it doesn't get riled, Giorgio won't pull his socks up and will just sit down and carry on as before, staying with his partner."
T: "And what will this make you feel?"
L: "As always: an idiot, not worth anything, not good enough."
T: "Has there been any occasion where you've felt calmer and have been able to handle a situation without worries, that is without fear of feeling under-valued?"
L: "Yes, in my work [*she is a trainer*]. Since I've been coming to therapy I've managed to feel ok. When some trainee poses a loaded or irreverent question, something that before would have made me go off, now I handle it differently. I welcome it. I connect with it smoothly and things go better."
T: "Do you have a self-image that replies like this to the student's loaded question?"
L: "Yes, I see myself smiling, calm, relaxed, confident."
T: "Ok. I suggest some imagery work. OK?"
L: "Ok . . . I'm a bit anxious, but ok."
T: "Close your eyes. . . . Imagine a staircase before you going downwards. The steps are all coloured and lit. Go down them. When you get to the end of the staircase, you see before you an open door from which a reassuring light is coming out. Go in. Inside there's an inner room, your mental laboratory, a safe place where you can experience new things, new forms of relationship. Imagine it the size you want and furnish it as you like, to make it comfortable. Can you?"
L: "Yes. I'm in front of a big window overlooking a garden."
T: "Good. Now, in front of that window retrieve the image of yourself calm and smiling in uncomfortable or tense situations. Can you?"

L: "Yes."
T: "Ok. Now imagine that the reason for the tension is wanting to speak to Giorgio but, as he is with his partner, you foresee him not calling you back, but sending a simple text message and with a little delay. Imagine yourself calm and confident. Now pick up your mobile to write to Giorgio. How do you see yourself? What do you write to him?"
L: [*crying*]: "I can't. I don't want to. If I do it he'll take advantage of it."
T: "Good. We know this part that controls and defends itself. Now let's try to not defend ourselves, here in the room giving onto the garden. Try and write something with the calm attitude we've made contact with."
L: "Yes, I can."
T: "How do you see yourself?"
L: "Calm, tender. I'm writing to him that I love him and miss him, but I'm not asking him anything to put him in difficulty."
T: "Ok. Now try and get up, still with your eyes closed. Imagine that this calm and tender Loredana is there, before you. Now take a step forward and take possession of this image. Put it on."
L: [*very tense, sobbing*] "I can't. I'm not up to it. I'm disgusted with myself.... But why do I act like this?"
T: "Let's leave aside the questions for now. Let's stay in the scene. We've seen this mechanism many times. Come on, go and pick up the Loredana you like, that works [*Loredana, calmer, takes a step forward*]. How do you feel?"
L: "Better. Calmer. Without fear."
T: "Good, Loredana, stay for a bit with these sensations.... Now leave the room, return up the stairs, breathing with each step, up to the surface. Then open your eyes."

Loredana appeared relieved and relaxed. The therapist suggested trying to recall the scene in the room with the view of the garden in the coming days, to recall more easily her wished-for self state. He asked her to do it especially when she knew her dysfunctional schema would get activated powerfully. Loredana was going to be on a mission doing training and knew that in such situations she felt the wish Giorgio was there more intensely, precisely when he was not available.

On Saturday evening, after work, Loredana was in her hotel. She felt lonely and wanted to speak to Giorgio. She could not, because at that moment he was with his partner. Her schema got activated and her emotions resurfaced. She recognised and was waiting for it; it was expected. The awareness that it was the schema being activated, and not necessarily real abandonment, already helped her to alleviate her punch in the gut feeling.

She sat on the bed, breathed in and recalled the figure tried out during therapy: smiling, calm, relaxed, confident. She could see herself a bit detached from Giorgio, but not angrily; she simply felt there was this unpleasant thing and it could happen, but that was not about her really being unlovable or the other being weak or dishonest. Loredana did not achieve this using conscious reasoning, nor was she consoling herself with self-injunctions: she was looking at the picture of herself smiling, calm, relaxed and confident she made contact with starting with the in-session exercise. She realised she felt a slight detachment and feeling of kindness towards herself. She thus managed to successfully handle an evening, which in other situations would have produced much more suffering and triggered coping behaviour harming the relationship.

CHAPTER 6

Drama techniques
Two-chairs, role-play and enactment

Interpersonal schemas are rooted in the body (Stern, 1985) so that changing them requires not only changing cognitions but also breaking bodily rooted habits in the form of motor schemas. Creating new action patterns, including the motor component, may be more powerful than cognitive restructuring.

With *drama techniques*, as we define the different practices included in this chapter, we stage problematic scenes and rewrite their dialogues. Episodes are thus re-enacted and not just recalled, and the body is involved in their rewriting. Patients can adopt different perspectives and see the world, physically, from different angles. For example, a patient with Avoidant PD is driven by the social rank motive and expects criticism. If he faces actual negative judgement, he sides with it, so that his self-as-unworthy image is confirmed. He consequently feels ashamed, lowering his gaze and voice, and his legs are feeble. These are aspects of the schema. If a therapist asked him to respond differently, by raising his head, looking the other in her eyes, speaking with a steady voice and tensing his muscles, he would experience a different sense of self when facing a critical other. This is the type of sensorimotor change we are referring to.

The drama techniques, mostly inspired by Jakob Moreno and Fritz Perls (Moreno & Moreno, 1975/2012; Perls et al., 1951) we most often use are: *two-chairs*, *role-play* and *enactments*. These are living a new golden age, thanks to Emotion-Focused Therapy (EFT; Greenberg, 2002), Schema Therapy (Arntz & van Genderen, 2011) and Sensorimotor Therapy (Ogden & Fisher, 2015). Two-chairs and role-play are similar, though in the former the patient plays different characters, while in role-play and enactments therapists become actors.

EFT, in particular as applied to PD (Pos & Greenberg, 2012; Pos, 2014), has influenced the way we use two-chairs, but our adaptation is closely connected to the decision-making procedure (Chapter 4). Unlike Schema-Therapy, very rarely in MIT do therapists directly confront the other. We prefer patients to confront problematic others, with a therapist's support and guidance, and often ask them to enact a dialogue between self-parts (Centonze, Inchausti, MacBeth, & Dimaggio, 2020).

Two-chairs consists in bringing self-parts into a dialogue, for example a part seeking relaxation confronting an inflexible moralist. Sometimes the other's role is that of a character from a patient's life narrative: father, mother, partner, etc. At others, a part of the patient gets highlighted, named and enacted in a chair.

A second chair gets placed in front of the patient's, so the latter does not look at the therapist, who is in a certain sense off-stage. In one chair the patient typically embodies a vulnerable and aggrieved self-part encountering invalidating responses from the other. In the other chair, as we said, the patient either plays the invalidating other or embodies a self-part responding negatively to the patient's wish, for example, a critical part or one obstructing autonomy. The patient passes from one chair to the other while interpreting the two roles. In all the dialogue, as we shall see in the rest of the chapter, the therapist guides and accompanies the patient, while always remembering what the schema he is trying to change is and what the metacognitive skills to be reinforced at that moment are.

Role-play arises naturally from a narrative episode. The therapist selects a piece of a scene where the focus is a dual relationship and asks the patient to stage it. It usually starts with patients in the role of themselves and therapists embodying the other. If role-play is conducted in a group (Chapter 10), the group members play the others and the scene can include more than two characters.

The scene is then repeated with role-reversal. Sometimes, if a patient has difficulty describing the other's inner world, she can start with the latter's role. By observing what the patient says and does it is thus simpler to get information on this character and the patient can then return to playing herself. The therapist monitors any fluctuations in the patient's inner world while passing from one role to the other. This typically ends up with the patient trying to respond in a new way, consistent with his underlying wish, and forsaking his usual coping mechanisms. He is thus able to see the scene from several perspectives and look at himself, in a certain sense, from outside. Often, by playing the other, she adopts a position towards the self different from her schema. Becoming the other while the game lasts can also stimulate theory of mind, with patients discovering, for example, that in the other's shoes they do not feel critical but worried or overburdened.

Unlike the two previous techniques, based on staging dialogues and narrative episodes, *enactment* consists of enacting true and proper relational actions and can occur in pre-established forms. The therapist is an actor and creates conditions reproducing schema-similar situations in the room, by, for example, physically turning his back to patients or immobilising them.

Overall, indications about drama techniques and their goals are similar to guided imagery with rescripting. The reader can therefore refer to Chapter 5 for why, how and with what goals to use a technique and how to select an episode. We briefly summarise them here and offer some suggestions about choosing between guided imagery and drama techniques. We then describe how to perform them.

Drama technique goals

Gestalt therapy (Perls et al., 1951) created the two-chairs technique to promote a deeper level of experiencing and to foster self-awareness. Drawing on this tradition, Greenberg and colleagues (2002; Pascual-Leone & Greenberg, 2007; Pos & Greenberg, 2012) operationalised and empirically supported it in EFT for different disorders (Paivio & Pascual-Leone, 2010; Pos, 2014). The idea was to re-establish contact among self-parts that had lost the ability to communicate and formed instead relations of dominance and hostility, and stimulate new forms of relationship among these parts. In EFT patients are traditionally asked to start a dialogue from a critical position in one chair and then to switch chairs and reply from the self-part experiencing shame, humiliation and other negative emotions vis-à-vis the disdainful criticism.

We use two-chairs, role-play and enactment with the following aims, which refer to different steps in the procedure:

1 *Improving access to one's inner world* and *intensifying affective experience*. During the various enacted episodes patients' arousal increases and they access emotions and cognitions linked to the episodes. What patients think and feel now may be similar to the original experience. But it is not fundamental for experience during the game and that at the time to be the same. It is a question of reactivating memories and memories are construction, rather than recalling, actions. Accordingly, what counts especially is what patients think and feel here and now, because they thus perceive the schema-driven way they make meaning out of a specific type of interpersonal relationship.

   Apart from being aware of what they think and feel, patients also need to experience adequate levels of emotional activation. Drama techniques are invaluable for this and clinicians can use them to increase arousal if this is too low and a patient is switched off, empty, emotionally flat, or avoids distressing emotions.

2 *Recovery of agency over inner world*: When patients attempt rewriting by, for example, replying to critical voices during two-chairs, they realise they have the ability to react to negative characters from their inner worlds and, in the same way, to regulate their emotions during the dialogue. They, in fact, realise that when they reply differently to a deserting, obstructing, dominating, accusing, suffering and blaming other, they know how to modulate their psychological distress and thus have power over their suffering, an agency they were unaware of.

3 *Starting to differentiate*: When patients become aware they have difficulties during drama techniques quitting their schema-dependent relational mechanisms, they realise their problems do not so much depend on real people as concern their own inner functioning. This is particularly clear in enactment and when, during two-chairs, patients play self-parts. The very structure of these activities cuts the real other out of a scene and puts patients in contact with features of their inner world. Patients know they are reacting to an artificial gesture by their therapist or talking with a neglecting self-part. When they realise they have distressing reactions and negative ideas, they are likely to grasp that these are their embedded ways of reacting. This is the most basic form of differentiation, that is, realising one has a way of functioning and one's ideas are subjective.

   If, for example, a patient tries to reply to a critical parent and cannot manage, she realises that the problem lies not in the real criticism, given that the parent is only impersonated but in her *unworthy* core self-image, by now internalised and believed true.

4 *Fostering differentiation, adopting new points of view and accessing healthy parts*: When therapists adopt drama techniques with the very purpose of change, patients realise they can embody different parts on their inner theatre and that, with changes in perspective and the role played, their way of seeing and feeling relationships changes too. At the same time, they acquire a critical distance and the ability to give a voice to healthy self-parts.

5 *Integration*: This is the final outcome of drama techniques (Greenberg, 2002). During the reflections following the exercise, patients acquire a more complete and consistent view of their self and representations of it with the other. They are aware they have fragile parts together with their healthy, competent and strong ones, and realise their representations of the other can have various nuances and change depending on how they are approached. At the same time, they realise their mental state evolves in line with any new actions they undertake.

Differences between drama techniques and guided imagery

The user instructions for drama techniques largely overlap with those for guided imagery with rescripting, so that generally therapists can employ the technique they master more confidently. Drama techniques can be more reassuring because patients maintain eye contact and this increases the feeling of control. The therapist may propose reliving an episode in imagination and the patient may refuse because he fears the experience to be too intense or disquieting if he has to handle it without looking at the therapist. He may fear being flooded by emotions. This indicates that his need for relational security is high and he requires feeling his therapist present and comforting him. The therapist may instead suggest choosing a piece from the episode and staging a dialogue between two characters using a drama technique. Patients thus nevertheless tackle their problem but in a context they feel safer in. The therapist therefore first ensures that patients feel understood and welcome, but then gently and gradually directs their attention and gaze towards the character they are confronting, thus leaving the therapist himself in the background.

Guided imagery has the advantage of being able to stage complex scenes, with several characters. This makes it possible for patients to reverberate with many and various features of what is being staged and face the impact caused by dyadic, triadic and group interactions. They can thus learn what happens to them when multiple schemas come into play by, for example, realising that the distressing element in a scene is linked to how one's father treats one's sister, or from feeling excluded from a relationship between one's partner and another person and so on.

In imagery patients may notice non-human elements in scenes, which may evoke contents: walls, furnishings, features in the surrounding nature. They can, moreover, use memories in multiple sensory ways: sounds ("What tone does that voice have?"), smells, colours ("What clothes is this person wearing?"), touch elements. Drama techniques do not have this ability and patients consequently concentrate necessarily on the relationship with a single character in a narrative and a specific schema.

To sum up: compared with drama techniques, imagery makes it possible to get more sophisticated information about schemas or relationships, but is more likely to worry patients. Drama techniques instead focus on just a few elements in an episode, but can turn out more reassuring and controllable. They also, in particular role-play and enactment, mobilise the whole body and are not limited to activating pre-motor schemas, as occurs in guided imagery with rescripting. Involving various muscular-skeletal areas can put patients in contact with features in their experience, and in their way of being on stage and reacting, which they could not discover in imagery.

One can sense that drama techniques stimulate theory of mind and decentring when patients change roles. This is true, but the primary goal is to encourage self-reflectivity. When patients switch characters, they see themselves primarily from another perspective and acquire a different way of looking at themselves.

There is a change in not so much the reading of the other's mind as the role in the schema patients ascribe to the other. In simple terms, when a patient takes the place of a critical father and from there discovers himself benevolent towards himself, he is not more accurately interpreting his father, whose real thoughts remain unknown. He is instead embodying a benevolent other, as the healthy part of the schema.

However, drama techniques can make patients capable of widening their range of ideas, emotions and intentions ascribed to the other and in a more subtle, realistic and decentred way. To explain, in one case a patient might adopt a critical father's role and think: "Here I get affection towards myself." This is a schema change. In the second case the patient thinks: "Here I feel worried. I believe my father had lots of problems at that time and, even if he was fond of me, he reacted like that for fear of not being able to support us financially. And so, even if he did it badly, it's as if he wanted to galvanise us into having success in order to not have the same problems he had had." This is an increase in theory of mind and decentring.

If episodes have aggressive or violent contents, one negotiates whether to use a technique and which. In some cases, patients consider exposure in imagery safer because they would be frightened to re-enact a scene in their therapist's consulting room. Re-enacting role-play where the therapist plays a violent character can frighten patients, which leads Schema-Therapy, for example, to prefer the use of guided imagery in such difficult situations (Arntz & van Genderen, 2011). In certain cases, patients can prefer two-chairs and role-play because with their eyes open they keep control and are not afraid of being overwhelmed by negative feelings.

In yet other cases, enactment can be a very strong way of exposing patients to feared relational situations, provided they accept it. A typical example is when patients include their therapist in their pathogenic schema but maintain a minimum level of differentiation, as in the following example.

Piera had Dependent PD and dissociative symptoms. She told about her ex-boyfriend, who was emotionally and physically violent, and suffered from flashbacks and intrusive thoughts, which included a sort of residual attraction. Piera was well aware that in reality she would not in any way contact him. All this was underpinned by a history of domestic violence: her father beat her and her mother took her husband's side. The therapy was going very well and in a short while Piera was able to overcome her intrusive thoughts about her ex-boyfriend.

However, fight-flight activation signals persisted, both in the therapeutic relationship and that with her current partner. Piera described him as understanding, calm and loving, but simultaneously she was sometimes scared, without any real reason. During certain arguments at home, for which she considered herself responsible, Piera asked him to leave because she needed physical space and freedom. Her boyfriend then felt dumped and, in distress, sought explanations. "At such times," said Piera, "he puts himself between me, sat on the bed, and the door. He blocks my way out. Just thinking about it scares me."

In addition, at various other times Piera said she was afraid of the therapist to the extent of having micro-dissociations during sessions, where she saw the therapist change size, becoming very little, the size of a smurf, or a giant four metres high.

When Piera dissociated, the therapist stayed still, curious and not explicitly caring. Piera reacted well to this attitude and said seeing the therapist curious calmed her down, because she did not see him worried and simultaneously realised he did not see her as fragile or in real danger. While Piera told about the last episode where she had felt afraid of her current boyfriend and felt literally put in a corner, the therapist noticed she seemed scared, had difficulty speaking, dilated her pupils and stared.

T: "What do you feel towards me, Piera?"
P: "I'm afraid."
T: "Oh yes? What frightens you?"
P: "You're a man. I don't know. That's enough, I reckon."
T: "How do you see me right now? Am I changing size, becoming bigger or smaller?"
P: "You've become bigger, even if not a lot."
T: "Am I threatening at this precise moment?"
P: "Um. . . . No, not so much. I mean, I'm a bit afraid, alright, but fundamentally I'm pretty calm. I mean I'm sure you wouldn't do anything to me."

Piera's schema was active in the transference: she was afraid the therapist would physically attack her but simultaneously was soundly aware he would never hurt her. Piera knew she was in good hands and from this position observed her own scaredness without being overwhelmed by it.

These are perfect conditions for attempting an enactment, involving the therapist in a simulation of the problematical relationship. The therapist first explained to Piera what he proposed doing:

T: "Well now, Piera, if you think you can bear it, I'll get up and place myself between you and the door. I'll stay there and you can tell me how you feel. Then we'll assess together if I can get closer and how far. What do you think about it?"
P: "I feel quite calm, OK, let's try."

The technique had two goals: strengthening differentiation, that is, making the patient experience *in vivo* that she was afraid of the threat but no real danger was around, and training agency over the feared mental state, by getting Piera to realise she had the ability to calm down even after being gripped by fear and an onset of dissociation. We shall shortly show, in the section about conducting the techniques, how the enactment went.

Imagery and drama techniques can be used sequentially. The technique sequences are the subject of Chapter 11. Here we limit ourselves to pointing out the specific interaction between these two techniques.

Initially, for example, guided imagery is used to evoke emotionally highly intense episodes from the past and then attempt rescripting them. In subsequent sessions patients relate recent episodes, linked to the same schema. A therapist can then start from these narratives and build new forms of dialogue among self-parts in two-chairs, or simulate the performing of new and more adaptive behaviour with role-play.

An example is a patient using guided imagery to relive an episode linked to family relations during development and attempting imagery rescripting successfully. She manages to respond differently and comes out of this with an interpretation beginning to be different, where she reacquires agency, control and sureness. In subsequent sessions, when tackling relatives in the present, she is able to communicate differently with them in two-chairs or role-play.

How to set the stage

Here we offer some suggestions, rather than true and proper rules, for deciding which scene to enact and for anchoring a therapist's action. As always, the starting point is an as clear and detailed narrative episode as possible. There are various options for choosing it: 1) reviewing the most important ones and deciding together with the patient; 2) homing in on the most distressing one; 3) compiling a scale with the patient, who chooses the least intense or the one with the most tolerable contents.

Once an episode has been chosen, therapists and patients pinpoint the characters to put on stage. One can opt for two possibilities and invite patients to interact with: 1) a character from their inner theatre, their imaginary landscape (Hermans & Dimaggio, 2004); 2) a protagonist in their episodes. For example, if a patient talks about her critical and severe mother, she can be asked how much she agrees with the disdainful point of view of herself. If she agrees with the criticism, one can propose two-chairs, involving the *self-as-criticised*, and the *disdainful self*. We recall that, when describing a schema we talk of "other", we are not talking about a real person but a figure from the patient's inner theatre, a position in a narrative.

If we, therefore, say a patient wants appreciation and, if she expresses her qualities, the other criticises her, by "other" we do not intend a physical person. We do not talk of a true father, mother, partner or boss, but of a tendency to ascribe a certain way of responding to one's wishes.

The other's position can easily be embodied by patients themselves. We see this typically in concepts that include the word: self. For example, *Self-esteem* means a patient wants to be appreciated and watches himself from an internalised position appreciating the self. "I esteem myself" means, in schema terms: "I wish to be appreciated. If I myself watch what I am doing, I find it effective."

Self-criticism means patients embodying a critical other and adopting a derogatory attitude towards themselves. When playing tennis and making a poor shot, we say to ourselves, "You were awful". It means we wished to be appreciated, watched our performance and judged it in a spiteful other's shoes. Promoting a dialogue between self-parts means acting on the interpersonal schema.

If, instead, patients say they disagree with the criticism or, in general, the other's negative response, two-chairs has first and foremost the goal of improving monitoring. Patients are likely to have core self-ideas of which they are unaware. What happens to them when faced with the other? In what way does a response by the other, they say they do not agree on, make them suffer? Why on earth, when faced with lack of support, do they lose agency and automatically resort to problematic forms of coping?

We have seen that in the EFT tradition two-chairs is typically used to interrupt *criticism/victim of criticism* dialogue patterns and this is perhaps its main use (Pos & Greenberg, 2012; Pos, 2014). We can, however, stage various other relationship patterns, for example, when patients are driven by the exploration motive but face a suffering and blaming other. In two-chairs or role-play the therapist proposes they assert their independence and respond differently to the suffering other, without succumbing to the guilt feelings linked to the activation of inverted attachment.

Carrying out drama techniques

We now describe the various steps involved in two-chairs, role-play and enactment:

1 *Selecting the pattern on which to interact*. While patient and therapist agree on what scene to stage, the therapist summarises the pathogenic dialogue in line with the interpersonal schema: "So, when you were discussing with the colleague who reprimanded you, you would have liked to be appreciated but when faced with the reprimand you felt like a silly child, were embarrassed and couldn't manage to reply except to justify yourself. Is that so?"

2   *Preparing the scene.* In two-chairs the therapist sets up, so to say, the stage. It is important there be a break between the therapeutic conversation and the play-acting. The therapist should make use of the spaces and furnishings of his consulting room. Typically, if a patient is sat in an armchair, he is asked to move it and turn it round so it is in front of another armchair or chair. It is important for the two chairs to be arranged so that the patient does not meet the therapist's eye and can concentrate on the dialogue between the characters.

Once the scene is set up, the therapist invites the patient to describe the two characters, what they normally think and feel, their appearance, the posture they adopt, with what tone of voice they speak and what they say to each other.

If the game is between inner parts, it is important to name the characters (Konopka, Hermans & Gonçalves, 2018). Unlike Schema Therapy, which tends to use theory-laden language – "vulnerable child, healthy adult" – in MIT we invite patients themselves to name their self-parts.

We believe patients in this way have maximum agency over the staging and, especially, learn to as specifically as possible see which self-aspects come into play at particular moments. Giving names to characters then helps in seeing when they appear between one session and the next: "Yesterday it was the Critical Judge who started talking"; "I replied as if I was the Court Jester"; "At such moments the Naive Little Girl comes out", "I'm trying again to be Super-Mum".

Regarding role-play and enactment, the therapist describes in detail what she and the patient are going to do and where to place themselves. An idea about what type of emotions could surface, at least the most likely ones based on previous experiences, can be useful. If a patient is susceptible to fear or guilt feelings, the therapist should warn her that these could resurface and in this case they will not let themselves be surprised and will find the time and tools to calm and regulate them, while, if they are too intense, the game will stop.

With Piera's therapy, for example, the therapist began by saying:

> Now I'll stand between you and the door. This way I'll recreate the situation where your partner was standing between you, sat on the bed in the corner, and the door, thus blocking your way out. In that episode you were swinging between fear, a sense of constriction and anger towards your partner. You may experience some or even all these emotions. You could of course feel other emotions and we'll take them into consideration. When we've grasped how you feel and ascertained you're able to tolerate these emotions, I'll ask your permission to take some steps towards you. With each step I'll ask you how you feel and what you think. Most of all, you can ask me to back off or interrupt the game if the feeling of threat becomes intolerable.

Carrying out of action

Drama techniques are in two stages: 1) during the first the aim is to improve cognitive-affective monitoring, including the initial identifying of healthy parts.

To do this, on the one hand patients' arousal needs to be increased if they are hypo-activated or inhibited and, on the other, they need to be calmed if they are dysregulated to the point of not being clear about what they feel or whether they are overwhelmed by it; 2) rewriting of the dialogue among the parts, differentiation and access to healthy parts.

Increase in monitoring/regulating emotions

During this first stage, if patients are over-regulated, the goal is to improve access to inner experiences and increase the intensity of emotional expression. On the contrary, for patients with moments of dysregulation, the first aim is good regulation and then one can start the game to dig more into inner experience. With patients with emotional hypo-activation, it is important therapists not adopt a caring attitude or aim at soothing suffering! Patients need to remain in contact with this distress, which they are in fact discovering now. It is good for therapists to adopt a curious and exploratory attitude, aimed at stimulating patients' rescripting skills. Therapists therefore confidently and energetically support the expressing of distressing feelings and patients' ability to rewrite the stories revolving around them. Of course, if patients give signs of wanting to feel the therapist closer, the latter should readily adopt a caring stance.

At this first stage interventions aim at understanding the cognitive and affective features linked to patients' self- and other-representations. If, in two-chairs, patients already possess a certain contact with suffering, the dialogue begins with patients in the part of the, for example, unworthy or unlovable self. They might give voice to a situation where, because of her flaws, she was afraid she was not a good mother and then sit in the critical judge's chair.

If, however, at other times patients' arousal is low or they have difficulty describing what they feel, we ask them to first give voice to the character embodying the other's negative, for example, neglecting or contemptuous, response, because the feelings linked to this part, for example, contempt, are more likely to emerge.

When patients are in a problematic other's chair, a therapist asks, as always, what they think and feel when playing the other and how much they themselves believe in the things they say from the other's position and addressed to the suffering self-part. Often, when patients play the other, it is very clear what they think of themselves. When embodying, for example, a critical other, they address themselves harshly and bitingly: "You're an idiot. You're worthless." This part of the game has an important function, that is, it gets differentiation to start and this then continues with rescripting, as we show later.

At this point patients begin to grasp how much they identify themselves in the other's response and how much the problem involves not so much what a partner, parent, friend or colleague think, but the fact that *they agree with this negative perspective*. They start to grasp that they are not contending with a real negative response, but with their own schema, where their wishes are in the hands of a self-part that stops them being achieved: "I want to be appreciated. I do something and discover I'm incompetent, which means I'm worthless."

At this stage even if we have obtained a beneficial effect in terms of a temporary increase in differentiation, we stay concentrated on increasing monitoring of the inner world.

After patients play the other, the therapist asks them to return to their own chair and embody, for example, their unworthy and suffering part. Emotional arousal is likely to be strong and the schema active now, and this is the best situation for beginning to respond in new ways and break the pattern. Usually at the start patients succumb to the problematical other and respond by feeling weak, inferior, humiliated, subjugated, powerless, passive, needy or fragile. All the negative emotions, from sadness to anger, guilt to shame and anxiety to frustration, tend to emerge and take over patients.

If patients are not yet emotionally connected with their problems, almost always something happens when they try to respond to the other. They discover they are unable to reply, because they are blocked by emotions and affects that can typically be fear, anxiety, shame, guilt and powerlessness.

During this first stage, therapists first of all encourage the expressing of every nuance of distressing thoughts or emotions. The initial access to healthy parts now becomes fundamental. If a therapist notices elements of experience diverging from the schema, innovative features involving, for example, protest or creativity, she insists that patients express them out loud. While still trying to maintain an exploratory curiosity attitude, therapists continuously seek feedback about what patients think and feel at a particular moment and constantly track cognitions and emotions and link them to expressive markers (Greenberg, 2002; Ogden & Fisher, 2015). Typical interventions are: "How do you feel now? What are you experiencing? Did I notice you lowering your gaze? What's happening inside you at this moment? Your expression has become more morose. Could you be downhearted or worried? From the posture you've adopted I have the impression that it's as if you felt defeated, right?"

As regards the communicational aspect, therapists encourage the verbalisation of feelings. We often ask patients to give full voice to any negative ideas, both in the problematical other's chair and in the suffering self's one. For example, if a patient says he has made a mistake, the therapist can ask: "Say it out loud: I'm worthless. I've really screwed up," until the negative emotion fully emerges (in Chapter 5 we use the same strategy during guided imagery).

When patients have difficulty handling emotional distress, the therapist adopts regulation tools:

1. Asking patients to breathe mindfully and getting them to pay attention to a breathing becoming as much regular as possible, with deep breathing out periods
2. Using grounding, by, for example, getting patients to concentrate on their feet, strongly rooted in the ground
3. Encouraging and validating, by stressing it is normal to feel distressing emotions and pointing out to patients they are managing to control this: "Say 'its normal for me to feel this emotion. I can wait for it to pass'"

4   Using sensorimotor type regulation (Chapter 7) as well as breathing and grounding. For example, if patients adopt a limp posture, with dropping shoulders, lowered gaze, head bowed and arms dangling down their sides, a therapist encourages them to become more toned by pulling up their shoulders, raising their chin, tightening their fists and pressing one against the other. Once the emotion is regulated, the therapist switches to investigating patients' thoughts and cognitions about themselves until they manage to access a more solid self-image like: "Now I feel better, stronger. I think I'm worth something"
5   Asking patients to consider that the therapeutic relationship is good: "Think about me being here. How do you see me? Do you now sense I'm on your side? Are you aware I'm confident you can endure this emotion and not succumb?"

Rescripting, differentiation, strengthening of healthy parts

After increasing both metacognitive monitoring and the level of experience, patients are more aware of what thoughts and emotions make them suffer in specific relational situations. Simultaneously their clinician highlighted their healthy parts. It is now time for the dialogue to counteract the schema. We repeat: even when we work on changing schemas, our prime goal is to simply stop them functioning automatically and collect any thoughts and emotions emerging. The first result we obtain is an improvement of metacognitive monitoring, which a therapist should be happy about!

Patients are now aware of what happens to them when they fight their schema. They discover that the persisting of a problematical dialogue pattern does not depend on the real other but on the way they represent him to themselves. Finding that, while they try to reply in a different way their voice gets blocked, their body goes rigid and their energy diminishes, helps them in this. They now understand that: "It's me who has difficulty getting out of this situation." Naturally this awareness is unstable and only present in the here and now of a session. Work needs to be repeated and the drama rescripting should be followed by repeated behavioural exposures for differentiation to become stable.

Once negative thoughts and emotions have surfaced and patients are aware that their rescripting difficulties depend only on their being stuck in a problematical relational pattern, the dialogue in two-chairs and role-play aims at personality change.

As in guided imagery, the key to drama rescripting in MIT is anchoring it to the formulation of the schema. A therapist has to forecast where to lead patients. Naturally, he knows he can make mistakes; the important thing here is the patient's feedback.

There are two solutions available:

1   Aiming at reactivating the primary wish, hidden by coping. Take, for example, a patient driven by the wish to explore sexual feelings or the need to belong to a group. With such wishes the patient portrays the other as critical, neglecting

or suffering, which activates rank, attachment or inverted caregiving. In their dialogue the therapist therefore aims at getting the patient back in contact with the original motive, by asking the latter to say things like: "Mummy, I'd like to go out with my friends. I don't want to stay at home because you're complaining about a headache"; "I like what I'm doing. I don't care about your opinion."

If, for example, when describing a date, this patient becomes prey to fantasies about being criticised and rejected, she can be asked to focus on features of the other person that she likes and which attract her, thus stimulating the reactivation of exploratory curiosity and sexuality and deactivating social rank. The therapist therefore asks her to say out loud: "I like this person. He excites my curiosity. I feel attracted" in order to let her contact the correlated emotions and physical sensations. Inevitably the ideas of being worth little resurface and the therapist politely asks the patient to let them flow and concentrate again on the wish.

2   The therapist keeps a patient in the same motivational system, but encourages him to recover his positive self-image, by replying differently to the problematical other. For example, if he feels abandoned, he can be encouraged to say: "I deserve your attention. It's not fair that you neglect me." If he is suffering because of criticism received, he can say, "I behaved correctly. I deserve appreciation. You can say what you like but I know I'm worth something."

Let us see how her therapist used enactment to tackle Piera's fears of aggression and trigger different responses. The therapist got up. He was about two metres from Piera, who immediately reacted.

P: "Oh God, now I already feel tension is mounting. A hot flush. You look very tall."
T: "Okay, Piera, so has your fear got activated? Are you afraid I might attack you?"
P: "No, not really, but my fear was nevertheless that."
T: "How are things now?"
P: "Still tense but a bit calmer. It's bearable."

Up to now the therapist was creating the conditions for an activation of arousal linked to the plot where Piera sought care but faced a violent and unpredictable other. The therapist chose to metacommunicate about the therapeutic relationship to regulate Piera's emotions and suggested she verbalise her fears and assess whether the therapist's mind was a threatening place or freely explorable. Proceeding like this also has the advantage of giving patients agency over the relationship, which is completely lacking in histories of violence and abuse. This first part of the drama technique thus already worked as a corrective emotional experience.

The therapist increased the level of exposure, while still giving the patient full control.

T: "Now I'm going to make a step towards you. Do you allow me?"
P: "Yes. That is, wait a moment. Oh God, what stress.... Anyway, yes, I can endure it."

Drama techniques 193

T [*The therapist takes a step. Now he is about one and a half metres away*]: "How do you feel now?"
P: "Like before. Not calm, but I can manage it. To be sure, how did you get this idea?" [*laughs*].
T: "Yes, terrible! [*laughs*]. I'm happy you are smiling. It means there's stress but you can bear it. Can I take another step?"
P: "Wait a moment."
T: "How do you feel?"
P: "The fear has grown a bit."
T: "Where do you feel it?"
P: "In my chest."
T: "Can you try and breathe deeply?"

Piera took some long and regular breaths and calmed down.

T: "Better now?"
P: "Yes."
T: "Excellent, Piera. Can you see you manage to calm down on your own?"
P: "It's true. It's not easy but I manage to."
T: "Will you allow me to take another little step? Bear in mind that in any case during all this exercise I'll never get too close to you. At most I'll get to one metre from you but not less" [*drawing with his arm an imaginary line he will not cross*].
P: "Well, I don't know if I could bear more than that. Yes, you can take another step."

The therapist went on. Now he was near the imaginary boundary he had just drawn.

T: "How is it now?"
P: "My anxiety's risen. I can feel my heart beating. I feel really hot. It's like I'm trembling."
T: "How do I look?"
P: "A giant. You're four metres tall."
T: "Do you feel ill? Are you afraid?"
P: "My heart's beating. Oh God, how agitated. I'm trembling too."
T: "Piera, if you want, I'll back off immediately."
P: "No!"

Piera's reaction, sudden and surprising, is of fright. Now she is afraid that, if she asks the therapist to back off, he will get offended and desert her. A trace of sadness appeared in her, which Piera acknowledged. The therapist did not reassure her or tell her: "Take it easy. I won't do anything to you or abandon you." He simply showed he was relaxed and calm through his tone of voice and posture and then asked Piera to explore his own mental state. This way Piera could decide on her own if he was harbouring threatening intentions, a sign of residual activation of the schema, or he had benevolent intentions.

T: "Well, Piera, now is a difficult moment, but you're managing to speak about it. If at this moment you asked me to back off, you'd fear I'd abandon you. However, if you leave me here, you're afraid I could hurt you. How do you see me mainly at this moment?"
P: "No, you're calm. You wouldn't harm me."
T: "And could I be offended if you asked me to back off?"
P: "No, alright, it's not possible. It's exactly the same as happened to me with Livio [*the ex who beat her*]. That's why I wasn't protecting myself; I feared being abandoned."
T: "Excellent observation, Piera. Now let's stick with us. Do you think you're able to calmly ask me to back off if you feel the need?"
P: "I reckon I don't need to. It's going better."

In the session extract described, the therapist staged the patient's feared situation in the therapeutic relationship. This belongs to what we shall later on call *free enactments*. It reactivated pathogenic schemas linked to attachment. If Piera felt vulnerable, she felt the need for attention but feared the other would attack her. If, in response, she protected herself, she feared wounding the other, who would consequently go away, leaving her alone, in a state of intolerable vulnerability, which reactivated attachment.

The therapist exposed her, which let her experience fear of being both attacked and abandoned. He gave the possibility of exploring the therapist's own mind, until she accessed the idea he did not in reality want to either attack or abandon her. She now calmed down. In the reflections that followed Piera realised how powerful her schemas were and began behavioural experiments to interact differently with her partner. Some months later the couple had a baby daughter.

Reflecting in order to consolidate in memory what has emerged

This stage is identical to guided imagery post-rescripting, so we summarise only the main elements: 1) validating patients' ability to engage emotionally difficult work. At the core is 2) highlighting every innovative element emerging. The therapist shows patients their healthy parts and points out that they feel better when they let themselves be guided by primary wishes, instead of succumbing to the problematical other or adopting dysfunctional coping; 3) identifying any residual problems and differentiating. The therapist summarises the schema and reinforces the idea that it is an internal structure rather than a description of reality. She points out to patients how they swing between situations in their experience where they succumb to their schemas and others where they exit them. She underscores how the patient is now aware of how this depends on the functioning of her own mind rather than on reality and that she can act upon her own mind;

4) reformulating the therapeutic contract, as in post-guided imagery and rescripting: redefining the aims and what tasks are useful for pursuing them. Mostly, it is about preparing behavioural experiments for consolidating change and widening the range of relational experiences (Chapter 8).

We shall now illustrate some clinical cases where it can be seen how we use two-chairs and role-play both to improve monitoring and increase differentiation, and rewrite schemas by reviving healthy self-parts.

Role-play: Elisa's case and promotion of decentring and third level relational mastery

In some cases, role-play makes it possible to promote understanding of the other's mind. In MIT we are strict, concentrating on encouraging a more sophisticated, flexible and, in a certain sense, realistic reading of the other only if patients are aware of their schemas, differentiate with a certain constancy and are in contact with their healthy parts (Chapter 4). When these conditions are met, seeing the other differently consolidates the steps achieved hitherto. For example, patients grasp even better that the other reacts in certain ways for his own reasons and not because he views them negatively.

This decentred awareness facilitates real interactions: patients enter relationships free from the pressure of negative expectations, have less need to resort to coping and grasp others' intentions and vulnerabilities better. This makes their communications smoother; patients grasp it is pointless being stubborn to try to evoke a reaction that will not be forthcoming, simply because the others are different from their expectations. These are sophisticated relational mastery forms (Carcione et al., 2011) and role-play and drama techniques can stimulate them.

Elisa was a 30-year-old pop singer and singing teacher. She had Borderline PD with marked dependent traits. She sought therapy because she was in a relationship with a tyrannical, aggressive and cocaine-using man. She herself used cocaine every so often, especially when other musicians she sang with used it at parties. In the earliest sessions Elisa realised she could not manage to leave her partner because she had always been dependent in relationships, starting with her father. She described him as anxious, critical and hyper-protective, not least because her mother died prematurely when she was six. She told about how difficult it was to have authentic communications with him or for her to rely on him as she had always aimed at "not getting him worried".

Elisa had never told him about certain adolescent problems, even if he had shown himself interested in her and her present and past concerns. Once her father had asked her something, but she rambled and then cut it short. "It was a lost opportunity", she commented. The therapist asked her to role-play the episode. Elisa started by playing herself, and the therapist, a woman, her father.

E: "When I was a girl [*hesitates*] . . . I felt lonely. I couldn't manage to tell you, but I've often felt the need to talk to you."

The therapist listened in silence, consistently with the script. Then she asked her how she felt. Elisa managed with difficulty to recognise a hint of sadness. The therapist suggested they switch roles, mainly to stimulate the identifying of Elisa's inner state. The idea was that, by observing herself from her father's viewpoint, Elisa might notice different nuances in her experience.

Elisa was initially worried while playing her father. Then a feeling of affection for his daughter emerged.

T: "Try and voice this emotion."
E (*father*): "Tell me how you are."
T: "Tell her: 'I'm keen to listen to you.'"
E: (*father*): "I'm keen to listen to you."
T: "How do you feel?"
E: (*father*): "Sorry for her."
T: "Well, let's switch roles then. Be yourself again."
E (*in the role of herself again*): "Dad, I need to tell you something [*hesitates*]. There was a nasty situation when I was 16."
T: (*father*): "Do you want to tell me about it?"
E [*bursting into tears for a long time*]: "I was in with the wrong crowd. I was taking cocaine. I didn't know what to do."
T: (*father*): "You've never told me that."
E: "You were unavailable, too anxious. You just weren't up to it."

The therapist asked Elisa how she felt and her sense of loneliness surfaced clearly, together with hints of hope and strength. She grasped it was the time to speak, that it was right to do so. She was worried about her father but this blocked her only up to a certain point. The therapist asked her to invert the roles again so that Elisa spoke as her father.

E: (*father*): "Try to understand, Elisa, I've always feared not being a good father to you and your sister. I was afraid about not managing to bring you up well. This is why I was always telling you off or checking on you. I called you continuously."
T: "How do you feel now in Dad's shoes?"
E: (*father*): "Sorry."
T: "Do you feel you want to keep listening to your daughter?"
E: (*father*): "Yes, I'm ready."

Elisa returned to playing herself. She told her father about an abortion she had at 19. She started crying again and felt that expressing her sadness was beneficial. She no longer needed to protect her father, whom she stopped seeing as fragile. Now she saw him worried but firm and simultaneously no longer judgemental. The role-play significantly changed her options for expressing her vulnerabilities and problems and the representation of the other, now capable of listening, was also modified.

These were the conditions for a behavioural experiment, that is, trying to speak with her father. The outcome was surprising. Elisa told him about using drugs in the past, without mentioning that at that moment she was still using them occasionally, and the abortion. He was overwhelmed by very intense emotions and could not manage to speak. After a few days he gave her some letters he wrote after her mother's death and where he revealed that she had committed suicide when Elisa was 6 and her sister 4. He had never been able to talk about it, as he feared the negative impact on their growing up, and only Elisa's asking to be listened to gave him the motivation and strength to hand them over. Elisa read them and, in high summer, passed two weeks shut in her bedroom crying. Thinking about her mother suffering made her sad but she was especially overcome by the idea that her mother, by preferring to die rather than looking after Elisa, did not love her. After extended therapeutic interventions she was able to remake contact with the idea of being lovable. A year after this episode she left her abusive partner and stopped using cocaine.

Two-chairs: Matteo's case

Matteo was the businessman with Dependent PD and narcissistic and histrionic traits described in Chapter 5 and to whom we will return in Chapters 9 and 11. Two-chairs was used several times during his therapy, especially for strengthening differentiation and acquiring agency over his mental states. After four sessions Matteo recognised his actions were driven by the *self-as unworthy* core idea and this was linked to the relationship with his disdainful father. Because his father had health problems, Matteo took over the running of the family firm but they still had daily work contacts.

M: "The problem is my father. He's always made me feel an arsehole. He's obsessed about people cheating him and, if I've got a work problem, he immediately tells me that they've screwed me because it's me that's incapable ... at the end of the day I'm on alert because first of all they cheat me and then, if it happens, I have to feel an arsehole too because I haven't been careful enough and I had it coming to me."

The therapist proposed enacting an episode where Matteo had been criticised recently. They chose one where his father accused him of giving way to an employee's improper request. The game started with Matteo playing himself.

T: "Okay, Matteo, your father's here before you. Talk to him."
M [*hesitating, embarrassed*]: "Look, Giovanni said he arrived late because of the traffic. He didn't even consider that he wouldn't be paid for that time. I made him understand that it wasn't acceptable."
T: "How do you feel, Matteo?"
M: "An arsehole. That I always let myself be cheated and I'm weak."
T: "Well, Matteo, now you're seeing yourself through your father's eyes, I think. Do you want to try taking his place?"

Matteo agreed and sat in his father's chair.

T: "Now speak like your father spoke to you."
M: "It's difficult sitting here."
T: "How do you feel?"
M: "Um . . . maybe worried?"
T: "How do you mean?"
M: "That my son's not up to it."
T: "Great. Try speaking from this position."
M: "Okay, I'll try [*pausing and concentrating*]. As usual, you've let yourself get screwed. I can't trust you. You let everybody walk all over you. You're so stupid that you don't learn and they quite rightly screw you."
T: "How do you feel now, Matteo?"
M: "I am becoming upset."
T: "Feeling you're your father?"
M: "No, for what he says."
T: "Ah good. Then take your place again."

Matteo changed chairs again.

T: "How do you feel now? You've just heard what your father told you. You're an idiot. You've allowed yourself to get screwed."
M [*with a nod of his head and shrugging his shoulders meaning 'obviously'*]: "Stupid."
T: "Stupid and . . .?"
M: "He's right to some extent, that I'm worthless."
T: "What emotion is it?"

Matteo had already worked on these scenes and recognised that this time too he was feeling guilty, as if he had not done his duty.

T: "Where do you feel this guilt feeling in your body?"
M: "On my shoulders, like a weight, something on me that's knocking me down."
T: "How much do you feel this sense of being worthless?"
M: "In part I'm quite riled. I'm fed up with hearing the same things."
T: "And where do you feel this anger?"
M: "In my hands. I need to move them. I can feel they're agitated."
T: "Very good, Matteo. So focus on your hands. What thoughts are passing through your mind?"
M: "That it's not fair him talking like that."
T: "Can you still feel the weight on your back?"
M: "Yes, still yes. As if it was crushing me, even if a bit less."
T: "Pull yourself up then, Matteo. Keep an erect posture. Straighten your neck and push your chest out. Think that you're dispelling the weight."

Matteo breathed deeply and changed his posture. His face was more relaxed.

T: "How's it going?"
M: "Better. The weight has almost gone away."
T: "Excellent, Matteo. So now try and reply to your father."
M: "You've got to stop criticising me. I realised on my own that I shouldn't let him off scot free."
T: "How do you feel?"
M: "Riled. I can't bear him any longer."
T: "Try telling him: 'I want to work on my own.'"
M: "I want to work on my own."
T: "How do you feel?"
M: "Convinced. That it's the right thing."
T: "Repeat that to your father."
M: "I want to work on my own. Do things my way. I can handle the employees. I don't have to justify myself to you anymore. It's my job."
T: "Very good. How are you now?"
M: "Freed!"

Thanks to the role-play Matteo managed to see that, when faced with his father's criticism, he swung between a sense of weakness, "heaviness" and limited worth, and the idea he had been criticised unfairly and blocked in behaving independently. During the reflection following the role-play Matteo realised he had the power to exit his state of submission and, if he drew on this sense of energy and rebellion, could stop depending on his father's opinion. We point out that relations with the employees had been the subject of other sessions and Matteo knew he gave in out of fear of being abandoned, which was at the core of his schemas, and had therefore already agreed on trying to do some experiments to act more consistently with his ideas while blocking submissive compliance.

Some months later Matteo realised many of his problems connected to guilt feelings were not linked to his father alone: "My mother is much more important than I thought." He related that she had always been suffering and mournful and now he understood that she had an eating disorder.

M: "My mother got to weigh 40 kilos! Then she complained she wasn't up to it, that we gave her problems [*him and his father*] and didn't respect her."

The therapist asked him for an episode where he faced his suffering or critical mother. A recent scene surfaced:

M: "It's happened a thousand times. As soon as I put on a few kilos, she starts to get a fixation: 'You eat too much. You're fat. This isn't okay.'"

He felt angry, but kept silent because he feared hurting his mother.

T: "How do you fear hurting her? What would you like to tell her?"
M: "If you've got a fixation about your weight, it's not my problem!"

The therapist used two-chairs. Matteo started in his critical mother's chair, given his mother had deprecated him when he went to see her.

M (*mother*): "Look what a belly you've got. You must have put on at least 5 kilos. I can't look at you. When are you going to go on a diet?"
T: "How do you feel in Mum's chair?"
M: "Awful. It almost disgusts me to see this belly."
T: "Ok, now go to Matteo's chair. Reply to mum."
M (*himself*): "Always the same! Is that all you think about?"

Matteo stopped. He became sombre. The therapist investigated this change and it immediately emerged guilt had taken over.

M: "I make her feel ill. She's weak."
T: "Well, Matteo, it means you're keen on your mum. But now that you feel guilty, try and continue nevertheless. What do you want to tell mum?"
M: "I come to see you because I'm happy to but you make me stop wanting to."
T: "How are you now?"
M: "Still guilty."
T: "Sure. It's not easy replying to mum. Try then to tell yourself: 'I'm OK like this, even with these 5 kilos.'"
M: "I'm OK like this. I don't want to listen to you."
T: "How do you feel?"
M: "Look, strange. As if until now I'd been thinking about my belly and it made me uneasy, as if it was too big. Now I couldn't care less."
T: "Perfect! Still feeling guilty?"
M: "No. Not at all."
T: "This is the time to reply to mum. What do you tell her?"
M: "Stop these fixations about weight. You've already ruined your own life. Don't ruin mine too."

After this role-play there was a decisive change in Matteo's self-sacrificing tendencies. Note that, thanks to breaking the pattern where he submitted to criticism to avoid making the other suffer and feel guilty, Matteo acquired a more detached view of his mother, noting her weaknesses without feeling responsible for them. Simultaneously he became better at curbing the guilt feelings stopping him from complying with his needs when others had a bullying or disrespectful stance towards him. He then accused a person who was swindling him and did not renew the contracts of employees with a poor work performance.

Guilt obviously undermined autonomy: Matteo gave up pursuing his own goals to not make the other suffer. After several months of therapy, the relationship with his father changed radically. Matteo first rewrote the schema regarding personal worth, by accessing the idea that the self was worth something and, thanks to this, stopped his father criticising him again. His father's attitude consequently changed and on the few occasions he attempted to be disdainful, Matteo did not take any notice.

However, his parents were separated and his father felt lonely. He thus turned up repeatedly at Matteo's house and stayed there for several days. Once, Matteo was travelling for work and when he got back, the house was devastated. Matteo in fact had two Jack Russell dogs, that he kept in a compound, because if let out they killed the other farmyard animals he had. He had given his father instructions to keep them in the compound but his father did not comply. The dogs had killed the hens and run into the house, which had become, in Matteo's words: "A Quentin Tarantino film: blood, feathers and shit."

Matteo protested and got angry: "I asked you to do one thing and you didn't do it." Matteo defended his right to decide autonomously, in this case about how to deal with the dogs. However, one month later his father took up residence again at his house. Matteo told the therapist he did not know what to do. The therapist asked him what his wish was, if Matteo liked having his father home. Matteo replied "No". He was blocked by guilt feelings: he saw his father alone, tired and sick. The idea of telling him to return to his own home made him think he was mean.

The therapist anchored Matteo to the wish to have his own space and to manage his home his way. Matteo remade contact with these sensations but the guilt still remained. The therapist reminded him it was schema-dependent, but he had been able to overcome the feeling when facing his mother. Matteo remembered he was able to not let guilt guide him and accepted replying in two-chairs to his suffering and intruding father. Matteo started in the "self" chair. Guilt immediately increased at the idea of telling his father to leave. The therapist suggested not minding about the guilt and focusing on his wish for autonomy.

T: "Try telling your father you want to be at home alone."
M: "Dad, I'm happy to see you but I'm taking you home later."
T: "How do you feel now?"
M: "A bit guilty but less than before. I'm sorry for him."
T: "Try making an appointment with your father, for example, "I'll take you home but we'll meet again when. . . . How does that sound to you?"
M: "Better."
T: "Let's try. Talk to your father."
M: "Listen Dad, I'm happy to see you but I've got things to do and need to be at home alone. Next week I'll come and pick you up and we can go to that fair in Ravenna we talked about."
T: "How do you feel?"
M: "Better, a little guilty but it's tolerable."
T: "Now take your father's place. He's just heard his son doesn't want him in his home."

Matteo changed chairs.

T: "Talk from your Dad's chair. What does he say?"
M: "Alright."

Matteo does not add anything else.

T: "How do you feel in that position?"

Matteo's reply from his father's chair is unexpected.

M: "It's normal. Okay like that. Everything in its right place."

Thanks to the role-play Matteo stopped ascribing the suffering role to the other when faced with him behaving autonomously. We recall that what was at stake was not the ability to grasp what his father thought and felt, but to interrupt schema-dependent type attributions to the other. That same evening Matteo spoke with his father and took him back home, without his father protesting. Matteo related that they were both happy at the idea of taking the journey together.

Case-specific and codified enactments

In enactments, therapists reproduce the schema triggers so as to access the widest range possible of emotions experienced. With over-controlled patients the goal is to make arousal increase so that they realise their problematical behaviour is a form of coping, a dysfunctional regulation of emotions they did not know they felt. With patients featuring emotion dysregulation, enactments aim at facilitating access to distressing emotions involving vulnerability, such as shame or sadness, instead of sticking to reactive ones like anger (Pascual-Leone, 2018).

Free, case-specific enactments

The therapist first identifies the type of coping patients adopt, and then counteract it. The principle is behavioural exposure, with the difference that therapists actively participate in the scene. Usually, therapists either embody the feared negative response of the other or act out first what the patients fear.

Flora was a 42-year-old office worker with Dependent and Avoidant PD, panic attacks and social phobia. In therapy her problem of increasing her circle of social relations, something she desired, was being tackled. She got blocked by her shame about her physical appearance and was unable to plan behavioural exposures. The therapist asked her what body part embarrassed her particularly and she focused on her feet. The therapist suggested she take her shoes off in sessions, but Flora could not. He then decided to himself enact the feared situation.

T: "If I remove my shoes so I'm in my socks, which could have holes in them, will you do the same?"
F [*smile*]: "Let's see. Anyway, you start."

The therapist removed his shoes. For the record, his socks did not have holes. Flora was amused.

T: "What do you think?"
F: "Nothing wrong. It's fun."
T: "Do you feel up to doing it?"
F: "Ok."

Flora removed her shoes. To increase exposure to shame, the therapist suggested that the rest of the session they both stay shoeless squatting on the chairs, with their feet on the cushions. Flora accepted and at the end of the session was very relaxed.

In other cases, therapists embody the problematical other, sometimes unexpectedly, with the aim of disorienting a patient. Naturally they provide all the necessary explanations immediately after the experiment. For example, with an avoidant patient stating she does not want to be boring but not managing to say what the emotions correlated are and not relating narrative episodes, therapists suddenly get distracted, reading their notes, looking out the window or adopting a disinterested and apathetic look, until they notice nonverbal signals. They then ask what the patient thinks and feels. Only after accessing the contents of experience do they explain the exercise.

Codified enactments

Collision

A patient is asked to move freely about the room and the therapist does the same. A few seconds later the therapist collides shoulder to shoulder with the patient. The game now stops and one finds out what the patient feels and thinks, and what self-image she endorses. Therapists have to ask questions in the heat of the moment, so that patients do not have time to detach from the emotion.

Binding grip

This can be very useful for getting mental states linked to the frustration of the exploratory motive to emerge. It consists in blocking a patient, by, for example, clasping his wrists or wrapping him in a rather tight hug, and asking him to move.

Within certain limits the therapist should resist any attempts by the patient to break free. The game stops when the patient names the emotion.

David, a 50-year-old military officer had Obsessive-Compulsive PD with passive-aggressive traits. He had been undergoing therapy for about six months for a depression arising after being shifted to an office following assignments abroad that had made him feel alive and active. Now he felt restricted by rules, working hours and his superiors controlling him. Anger was the emotion he was most likely to report. Regarding his depression he described especially apathy and anhedonia. When he perceived limitations to his autonomy, in whatever context, he immediately adopted avoidant behaviour, but was entirely unaware why. He just said, "It annoys me. Better to get out of the situation," a form of coping causing big problems in intimate relationships and in his work. David compulsively sought a way out of any situation he considered coercive. For example, if he found a queue of cars, he would immediately try an alternative, even much longer and more complicated, route, just to avoid being blocked in the traffic.

David was aware he was vulnerable to constriction and had realised that always avoiding could have harmful consequences, given that he had had to struggle with both his superiors' criticisms and losing job opportunities, and his wife's dissatisfaction. However, he did not know why the flight mechanism got activated.

The therapist suggested the binding hug technique and David accepted. The therapist wrapped his arms around him and asked him to move. As soon as he felt the grip, David started to frenetically thrash about. After a few seconds the therapist freed him from the hold, after noticing a state of anxiety David verbalised clearly. This time David understood his distressing primary state much better, which he had only sensed in his narratives, that is, anxiety and a sense of constriction rather than anger. Furthermore, in the thick of this primary emotion, he very quickly managed to access associated memories that had not previously emerged.

Feeling constricted reminded him of memories where he had to give up having fun with other children and stay at home doing homework. He could see them running and hear them laughing but he could not do this, because he had to comply with his parents' demands, not imposed forcefully but expressed clearly in words, to be a "big boy" and not waste time on foolery, because they needed him. He considered his parents weak and this made him feel lifeless. Now every tie made him feel dejected at the idea of losing the possibility of feeling alive again.

Turning one's back

The main aim is to trigger vulnerability towards being abandoned and feeling the other distant. It gets used with patients who, when faced with a neglecting other, react with coping states like anger, contemptuous indifference or detachment, and do not perceive distressing primary states.

PROCEDURE

The therapist stands before the patient and ask her to talk about any recent difficulties or problems making her agitated or anything she is keen on communicating at that moment. After a few seconds, the therapist turns her back, goes off or starts doing something else, like putting the room straight, writing in her diary or looking at her mobile. The exercise then stops and the patient is asked what she feels on seeing the therapist is ignoring her.

Overall, free and codified enactments turn out to be very powerful in activating emotions and the cognitions associated with them. To perform them, therapists need a very precise negotiation, with an explanation of what they are going to do and warning that the reactions could be intense. With free enactments, therapists sometimes surprise patients with their actions and it is one of the very few situations where we intervene without prior bargaining. We do it when we have very carefully assessed the state of the therapeutic relationship and are almost totally certain the patient can endure our action directed at activating the schema in the therapeutic relationship. In any case, a careful rereading of the therapeutic relationship is needed after enactment and the job of repairing any micro-fractures in the alliance inevitably brings out precious information.

CHAPTER 7

Body interventions

MIT uses body interventions to stimulate awareness of psychological functioning and enrich the mental landscape. This is an approach consistent with therapeutic practices involving the body (Eckberg, 2000; Lowen, 1975; Reich, 1933/1980). More recently sensory-motor psychotherapy (Ogden & Fisher, 2015) has shown how many physical habits – gut feelings, postures, habitual voluntary gestures and facial expressions – constitute the somatic correlates of relational schemas internalised through repetitive experiences. The body records the traces of how we related to important figures during our history (Van der Kolk, 2014). One might imagine a patient who from an early age displayed to his caregivers a need for attention with a submissive attitude and received a welcoming response. When, on the contrary, he acted autonomously and assertively, the reply he received was criticism and discouraging messages. As an adult, this patient has a slightly "collapsed" posture and a downward and hesitant gaze, in that from early childhood this type of bodily attitude was implicitly linked to a lower likelihood of receiving rebukes, compared to a more assertive and "proud" bodily attitude.

The opposite example is a patient who has stored in her body – for example, as an empty feeling in her stomach – what happened when she proved not up to the effort of studying and her parents disapproved. This patient acquires an erect posture, jutting chin and straight back, as a bodily response with the functions of both forestalling rejection and warding off physical sensations and distressing emotions correlated to rejection.

To sum up, the body stores the memory of repetitive intersubjective experiences. Unlike the sensory-motor approach and attachment theorists, in MIT we consider that these experiences regard all motives. A patient seeing his vital impulses towards exploration obstructed by his mother's voice shrieking "No, be still!" learnt reflexively to surrender himself on the sofa, where he could be visually controlled by his mother. This bodily response becomes automatic and gets transformed into a consolidated schema, for example, the tendency to feel and display listlessness and tiredness when in life a patient has an inkling of a wish or project. This patient is not unlikely to lose agency, with the exploration motivation getting turned off.

Interpersonal schemas rooted in the body become part of one's identity and contribute to regulating posture, expressive behaviour and how the body interacts with objects and others totally automatically and unconsciously.

An avoidant patient's indecisive handshake, lowered gaze and stooping shoulders point to how much he pre-reflexively expects a humiliating opinion in response to his wish for appreciation. The lack of metacognitive awareness in these automatic, somatic processes makes schemas difficult to modify. The patient can say: "I feel down, dejected and listless, and I can't cope" instead of: "I expect others to reject me and this makes me sad and I can't see how to get their interest." It is difficult to modify something a patient is not aware of. But even when patient and therapist manage to access the psychological meaning of these somatic experiences, combatting schemas is laborious, because bodily, procedural automatisms are powerful.

In addition to how interpersonal relationships leave physical traces (Van der Kolk, 2014), we would recall that bodily sensations have the power to influence cognitive processes and our decisions in the social domain (Bargh, 2017). From all this it emerges that a body contains traces of interpersonal relationship styles. These traces consist in characteristic gut, sensory-motor, postural and expressive patterns that influence cognition without subjects being aware of them. Altering the bodily layout therefore produces cognitive change.

These are the main reasons why MIT complements procedures aimed at acquiring self-reflective awareness of schemas with body interventions directed at changing the *somatic*, *procedural* and *implicit* component of interpersonal schemas. These are interventions aimed at stimulating emotional regulation, increasing awareness of schemas and why we ascribe particular meanings to interpersonal relationships, and promoting change by facilitating access to healthy parts.

The body techniques used most frequently come from: sensory-motor therapy (Ogden & Fisher, 2015), Reichian and bionergetic therapies (Lowen, 1975; Reich, 1933), like *grounding* and *integrated mindfulness*, martial arts, like *chi kung, tai chi chuan* and *jiu jitsu* and *yoga*. We would specify that clinicians use any body interventions they have in their repertoire, without tying themselves down to those listed.

In this chapter we describe how MIT uses body interventions during three different steps in the decision-making procedure: 1) the *handling of symptoms* and *emotional regulation*; 2) *joint formulation of functioning* and *dynamic assessment*; 3) *change promotion*. At each step the different techniques can be combined with those described in previous chapters. For example, we combine grounding exercises with mindfulness techniques to regulate arousal or encourage perception of inner states; at another stage the same exercises, combined with guided imagery or role-playing, are useful for taking a distance from emotions activated by interpersonal schemas.

We use simple breathing techniques to help patients reduce arousal during a guided imagery and rescripting intervention. In fact, during guided imagery they often experience an increase in arousal. If very intense and difficult to tolerate, work on breathing and on the body in general helps to regulate emotions and prepare patients for the rescripting stage.

There is now a concise description of the techniques and immediately afterwards details on how MIT uses them as part of the decision-making procedure

(Chapter 4), based on the three goals described here. For the sake of brevity we do not depict how each single technique can be used for each of the goals in the decision-making procedure. We focus on the various goals and supply examples of how some of the techniques are useful for pursuing them, alone or together with other imagery, mediation and experiential interventions.

Body techniques

Grounding

In Chapter 5 there is a detailed description of *grounding* (Lowen, 1975), and how we use it in MIT. Here we recall the main features. We ask patients to adopt an erect posture, with their feet parallel and separated by a distance corresponding to the width of their shoulders and their knees slightly bent. Their eyes can be half-closed or closed, with their jaw muscles relaxed. We ask them to pay attention to their legs and feet, so as to perceive the strength and support they offer the body. We ask them to imagine the body as a tree, where their legs constitute the trunk and their feet the points from which the roots spread out and penetrate deeply into the ground. We lastly ask them to imagine a flow of vital energy passing through the feet/roots and linked to the rhythm of their breath: when breathing in, the roots collect energy from the ground and transport it, through the feet and trunk, to the whole body; when breathing out, the whole body yields energy, which, through the roots, gets redelivered to the environment. Therapists should repeatedly suggest this feeling of rootedness and connection, and encourage the relaxation of the upper part of the body and its yielding to the support of the legs/feet (see Figure 7.1).

The sensory-motor approach shows how *grounding* very often produces a sense of balance, solid rootedness and proprioceptive awareness of the body in space, stimulating the regulation of arousal in both patients with hyper-arousal or hypo-arousal, and in those swinging between the two extremes (Ogden & Fisher, 2015).

Relationally integrated mindfulness

Relationally Integrated Mindfulness (Ogden & Fisher, 2015) starts with *tracking*: during sessions a therapist should pay utmost attention to patients' mimical expressions, posture and ways of breathing, suggest they apply *mindful* attention, free of judgements and endorsing, to these, and help them to ascribe psychological meaning to them.

For example, an unexpected "collapse" or stiffening in posture or a sudden quickening of breathing provide important information about the emotions experienced by patients while talking. These physical elements linked to current experience usually take place below the awareness threshold. The first part of a therapist's intervention aims at diverting patients' attention from the flow of narrative and conversation towards a mindful awareness of bodily experience.

Body interventions 209

Figure 7.1 Grounding

Simple statements verbalising current bodily experience sound like: "While talking to me about your father it seems your body's about to flop", or "It seems your breath's getting faster now you're describing what happened at work". After using *tracking* to focus on the part of bodily experience to be explored and labelling it, a therapist helps patients to understand its meaning, by encouraging metacognitive monitoring, with questions like: "While telling me that it's as if your spine wasn't holding you up any more, what do you think and feel?"

Chi kung

Chi kung is a founding element in Chinese medicine and traditional health principles. It consists essentially in a number of postures linked to deep diaphragmatic breathing. In one of the simpler ones (Figure 7.2) subjects stand, with their feet parallel and at a distance from each other corresponding to the width of their shoulders, their legs slightly bent, their shoulders relaxed, their tongue resting on their palate, their eyes half-closed and their arms stretched out at shoulder height and slightly bent at the elbows, as if to hold a ball of a size such that the fingers would be about 20 centimetres away from each other.

With practice this achieves alignment among the various joints and, similarly to *grounding*, lets subjects feel a sense of the body being rooted to the ground.

Figure 7.2 A *chi kung* posture

Subjects maintain this position and concentrate on the flow of their breathing. The deep, diaphragmatic breathing practiced in *chi kung* is from the stomach. When breathing in, the stomach and pubococcygeus (used to interrupt the flow of urine and contract the anus) muscles contract, while we achieve the lowering of the diaphragm by expanding the solar plexus muscles. When breathing out, the stomach and pubococcygeus muscles relax. In this type of exercise, the breathing out is longer than the breathing in and can last until a subject manages to reduce his breathing to only three or four times per minute. Diaphragmatic breathing can influence one's psychological state by modulating one's neuro-vegetative disposition (Lee, Kim, & Moon, 2003; Zheng et al., 2014). By boosting the inhibition exercised by the myelinated component of the vagus nerve on the sympathetic nervous system, this breathing reduces one's heart rate and physiological arousal (Porges, 2011). It can also slow one's thinking and boost attention to the present moment (Chapell, 1994; Lu & Kuo, 2003). A subject thus experiences a state of environmental security (Porges, 2017 and the anxiety-provoking and/or perseverative thoughts usually connected to negative neuro-vegetative activation diminish.

Hatha yoga

One of the fundamental exercises in Hatha yoga involves the postures – the *āsana* – connected with breathing control. One important *asana* is the *warrior pose*, where subjects breathe out and widen their legs until their feet are about one metre apart (Figure 7.3), raise their arms, straight up and parallel to each other, above their heads, stretch their fingers towards the ceiling and relax their shoulders, turn their left foot 45–60 degrees to the right and their right foot 90 degrees to the left, and line up the right heel with the left one. Subjects breathe out and turn their chest to the right, with their pelvis facing straight ahead, lower their left heel until it touches the ground while keeping their leg straight, stretch their tailbone towards the floor, as if there was a thread pulling the last vertebra of the spine towards the ground, and slightly bend the upper part of the back backwards. They breathe out and bend their right knees by about 90 degrees, positioning them above their right ankles, so that their calf is vertical.

Subjects should feel an impulse coming from their heels and running through their legs, stomach, chest and as far as their arms. They then put the palms of their hands together and point and stretch their fingers upwards. The head is to be kept still, looking forward.

The final position should be kept for a minimum of 20 seconds and then repeated using the other side. With time subjects learn to keep it up for longer, by balancing effort and relaxation and easing their breathing. This produces a physical sense of vigour and wellbeing thanks to the muscle toning, and, psychologically, a sensation of effectiveness and mastery of tiredness.

Body exercises deriving from martial arts

One of us has studied martial arts like *jiu jitsu* and *tai chi chuan* and how some of their principles can be combined with psychotherapy. *Jiu jitsu* is a *martial art*,

212 *Body interventions*

Figure 7.3 Yoga, warrior pose

a form of personal defence and a combat sport. *Tai chi chuan*, like *chi kung*, is not only a martial discipline, but also an essential element in Chinese medicine. Even therapists not wishing to practice them systematically can find therapeutically useful body exercises in disciplines like these. For example, a typical *tai chi chuan* technique involves combining a violent diaphragmatic breathing out with punching at a purpose-made soft punching-ball. This technique can help patients to reduce the dysregulated arousal obstructing exploration or impeding rescripting during guided imagery.

This same technique, making patients experience a sense of strength and effectiveness, can be useful for combatting a perception of the self as *weak, fragile* and schema-driven. For this purpose it can also be useful to get patients to experience this sense of strength and vigour while practicing a simple *jiu jitsu* hold.

In our experience it is not rare for some strongly symptomatic patients or ones with limited self-reflectivity, little susceptible to traditional therapeutic exploration, to instead be open to body exercises derived from these disciplines, making it possible for their therapists to access psychological contents through experience. A seriously alexithymic patient, incapable of accessing emotionally significant episodic memories and verbalising his emotions, might, for example, during the *tai chi chuan* "fist" exercise, show uncertainty and appear tense, and on the basis of this *in vivo* experience his therapist helps him to access a sensation of ineffectiveness and an *inadequate* self-image. By repeatedly practising the same exercise, the patient, encouraged by his therapist, is able to access a capable and vigorous healthy self-part.

It happens that other, inhibited-coerced, patients, especially adolescents and young adults, show interest and a natural propensity for the systematic practising of these disciplines. A therapist with the right skills can use this for therapeutic purposes, or work with a martial arts instructor. The practising of *sparring* in *jiu jitsu* is particularly useful for this purpose, as we shall see in a clinical example in this chapter: it is a sort of ground wrestling carried out in a fluid and relaxed way. *Sparring* reproduces the features of playing as reinterpreted by Polyvagal Theory (Porges, 2017). It lends itself, therefore, to a sort of mobilisation activating the defence system, but in a "simulated" mode, in the "as if" world (Lillard et al., 2013). Subjects launch themselves in a sort of wrestling but know that the other, in his "adversary" role, does not really intend to harm them. The interaction takes place in an atmosphere of security, making it easy for subjects to mutually regulate their neurovegetative states towards calm. In the context of technically oriented wrestling, the two participants thus feel those sensations of pleasure and belonging normally experienced in situations involving social attunement and social involvement.

On this basis, the sensation of powerlessness produced by being pinned down on the ground by an adversary in a dominant position, which beginners often experience in wrestling, placing them in contact with their sense of vulnerability, ineffectiveness or inadequacy, occurs in a sporting context where the other is seen simultaneously as a source of security and support. Gradually a subject learns through somatic experience that these negative sensations are not incompatible with a sthenic position vigorously and strategically tackling one's fear and concerns about defeat and failure.

Now we have illustrated some of the body techniques we use, we shall show how they get incorporated in the decision-making procedure.

Body interventions to stimulate mastery of symptoms and dysregulated states

PD patients often come to therapy with pervasive symptoms and/or emotional regulation problems. This is linked to the seriousness of their PD rather than to any specific PD (Dimaggio, Carcione et al., 2013; Dimaggio, Popolo et al., 2017). Regulation problems can be coupled with both hyper-arousal and activation of the threat defence system and hypo-arousal, somatic switching-off and devitalisation (Ogden & Fisher, 2015). Symptoms and dysregulation obstruct the exploring of narrative episodes required for completing the *joint formulation of functioning* through interpersonal schema reconstruction.

The request for help in these cases primarily includes an as rapid as possible attenuation of symptoms and suffering. Therapists therefore try to provide strategies both consistent with a patient's request and helpful in removing obstructions to exploring schemas.

A patient with strong symptoms or hyper- or hypo-arousal needs first of all to profit from the regulatory function of the therapeutic relationship, as well as from support from drugs, if necessary. A therapist's work takes place both during sessions and outside them, by telephone or messages, with emotional sharing and validation interventions to soothe any out-of-control emotions (Livesley et al., 2016). On this basis he proposes the regulation strategy most suited to patients' metacognitive levels (Carcione et al., 2011; Dimaggio, Montano et al., 2015; Semerari et al., 2003) and in tune with their preferences.

A therapist possesses a range of interventions and assesses on a case by case basis which to use, and whether to use a combination of body, imagery and cognitive techniques. For example, with very agitated patients managing only to say, "Doctor, I'm ill. Help me!" distraction strategies could prove unfruitful because their high arousal would stop them focusing on other stimuli.

A therapist therefore asks such patients to carry out a *chi kung* technique to calm down through postural rooting and diaphragmatic breathing. Once calmer, the therapist uses mindfulness to help them to identify their negative thoughts and let them flow.

With another patient, not dysregulated but anxious about having a heart attack, a therapist can use physical exercise, for example, a number of push-ups, to get him to feel the physical sensations he fears (e.g. tachycardia or breathlessness). He then shows how they represent a normal physiological response to effort and, now he has exposed the patient to the sensations feared, gets him to reattribute them cognitively.

Among the techniques described earlier, *grounding* and *chi kung* are also useful for controlling impulsiveness. They can also be effective with patients whose dysregulated negative arousal is accompanied by dissociation tendencies. In this case, body techniques are useful for interrupting dissociative states and remaking contact with reality. Lastly, they can prove effective in "reawaking" devitalised patients, by making them aware again of their body.

In the following example we show how the therapist used *grounding* to promote mastery of the dysregulated emotions and symptoms obstructing detailed exploration of schemas. Before portraying the case we repeat that MIT does not uphold that symptoms depend solely on maladaptive interpersonal schemas! Schemas contribute to symptoms and their persistence, but there are also proximal factors like catastrophic beliefs, repetitive thought processes such as ruminating

(Chapter 2; Wells, 2005), behavioural avoidances and so on. The work we describe is, therefore, on the one hand performed prior to exploring schemas, and on the other, aims directly at combating a symptom *per se*.

Clara

Clara was a 20-year-old student, eldest child of a couple of university lecturers, and suffered from Obsessive Compulsive PD. In her first session she told how she had always had a shy character, with little interest in making friends, as she had always "given priority to school". After finishing high school with excellent marks, she enrolled at the Medical Faculty in her town, in line with her parents' wishes. A few weeks into the course she was gripped by ruminations, doubting whether she was up to understanding the lectures or becoming a doctor. Once she happened to see a doctor in a white gown on the TV, and this triggered her ruminating about becoming a good doctor. The ruminating ended up lasting all day; it stopped her studying or going to her lectures and led her to shut herself up at home. This gave her strong guilt feelings, which reinforced her ruminating.

In the isolation of her room derealisation phenomena began to manifest themselves. She was gripped by the sensation that the world around her was "strange" and was terrorised by the possibility of going crazy. This led her parents to call a psychotherapist. From her earliest sessions Clara made heartfelt pleas for help in making her thoughts and sensations of extraneousness vis-à-vis reality less insistent; she was not capable of relating narrative episodes situating these phenomena in a relational context. It was therefore impossible to aim at reconstructing her interpersonal schemas.

The intensity of her obsessions and dissociation and the resulting negative emotions needed to be reduced. The therapist first, in a normalising and validating manner, explained how her intrusive thoughts and derealisation worked and showed her that they represented an exaggerated version of phenomena anyone could experience, so that they did not indicate impending madness. This psychoeducational intervention was repeated several times, including by phone between one session and the next.

When Clara had calmed down, the therapist started *grounding*, to be used in derealisation cases, for her to remake sensorial contact with reality and her body and quench the agitation deriving from this derealisation. She accepted willingly. She learnt to master the technique in-session and then practised it between sessions. Consequently, after a month she mastered any instances of derealisation well. Based on this the therapist tackled the perseverative thought forms, that had previously contributed to triggering her derealisation, with the attentional techniques described in Chapter 10, and managed to significantly reduce her intrusive thoughts.

The therapist could now explore specific narrative episodes and grasp that her symptoms got exacerbated by the activation of a schema where, starting from a wish for independence, she expected another who, instead of supporting her, criticised her. This led to a self-response where Clara switched to the competition motivation and adopted perfectionistic coping. However, even when improving her performance the other's image remained critical. This put Clara in contact with a powerless, ineffective and frozen core self-image.

Francesco's case

Francesco was 31 and suffered from illness anxiety disorder and Avoidant PD, with paranoid and depressive traits. He was the only child of a wealthy family of shopkeepers and he was a manager in the firm. He sought therapy because of anxiety attacks he had had for several months. Francesco had a limited self-reflective capacity and did not relate narrative episodes except when concentrated on his symptom, which did not make it possible to understand his schema structure. Moreover, he refused any drug treatment being too worried by the side effects. The therapist grasped how much Francesco's negative arousal and pervasiveness of his symptom needed to be reduced first.

First, after analysing a set of acute anxiety episodes, he explained mechanisms underlying symptoms with a diagram on a blackboard. He showed Francesco how his symptom was fed by his exaggerated attention to body signals to which he assigned a catastrophic interpretation, because of the triggering of his cognitive attentional syndrome consisting of monitoring threats and worry (Wells, 2005). For example, a mental image – for example, a memory of his uncle in a hospital bed – could make him worry about ending up in the same situation; this worry in turn triggered body signals like an increase in heart rate. His focusing on this sensation ended up making the subject of his worry real: he was soon going to be on his death bed, in hospital, for a heart attack. This provoked an increase in his tachycardia and breathlessness, which constituted in turn a confirmation that he was having a heart attack. Francesco could identify himself in this reconstruction and seemed relieved. The therapist then taught him the *chi kung* posture and diaphragmatic breathing, devoting part of the next sessions to the joint practice of this exercise. Francesco quickly felt how the centring of his body in space and the spontaneous slowing of his breathing rate caused by *chi kung* modulated the body signals previously frightening him, for example, his heart rate frequency and "heart pounding feeling". Based on this body experience, the therapist helped him to differentiate between his catastrophic mental representation, with these signals indicating impending death, and reality, that is, anxiety.

Outside sessions Francesco gradually learnt how to use *chi kung* when his anxiety increased. In such instances he felt stronger and then started diaphragmatic breathing. This lessened his symptom and let the therapist explore his inner experience. In the following section we describe the next part of his therapy.

Body work during joint formulation of functioning

Many PD patients are poor at relating their inner experience. A clinician has great difficulty collecting narrative episodes or even extracting fragments of stories. In any case psychological experience does not surface clearly. Patients often do not reply to questions like: "What did you feel while watching your wife talking with your friend?", "What drove you to refuse that dinner invitation?"

Other patients have a different difficulty: they remember facts, but are emotionally distant from them, do not link emotions and physical states to the memories and recall the past in an abstract, generalised and intellectualised manner. Furthermore, many have difficulty reconstructing psychological cause–effect links. In their stories emotions seem to arise without reason; questions like "When did you start feeling so sad?" receive replies like "I don't know. I often happen to wake up like this and it goes on for hours."

Lastly, many patients do not link present suffering to moments from the past. To questions like "Can you recall other instances in your life when you felt this sense of worthlessness?" the replies are, for example, "I don't know", "It's never happened to me before".

Body interventions, often interwoven with imagery, drama, meditational and behavioural techniques, can help in overcoming such problems. More specifically, in the context of the joint formulation of functioning, they facilitate: 1) early access to healthy parts, 2) recalling and exploration of narrative episodes, 3) self-reflective awareness of previously inaccessible inner states, 4) recalling of associated autobiographical memories.

Early access to healthy parts

With a *grounding* exercise, and the sensation of being rooted to the soil and solidity, patients calm down and their therapist helps them to focus on a healthy part able to perceive a sense of effectiveness in their managing to calm down and looking after themselves. Again in early therapy stages, body techniques, possibly used together with mindfulness, help discover that negative emotions, even if only for an instant, flow away and leave room for positive affects. Patients thus access embodied self-images like "sturdy", "calm" and "capable" and this prepares them for differentiating vis-à-vis schema-correlated negative images.

For example, when at the end of his first month of therapy, Francesco was more in control of anxiety thanks to *chi kung* exercise, his therapist switched the focus to the goal of stimulating contact with a healthy part present in the background. While, at the end of the session, Francesco was conducting a *chi kung* exercise, the therapist suggested he focus on the emerging self-image. Francesco realised he felt "stronger" than the previous frightened and fragile Francesco, a passive victim of anxiety, and "more intelligent" because he was capable of better grasping his body's signals.

Clara's therapist also emphasised that she had managed to master her derealisation situations and anchor herself to the sensation of rootedness acquired in the exercise. He pointed out to her that, thanks to an ability acquired with training and dedication, she had managed to deal effectively with a vulnerable self-part. Clara agreed and was satisfied with herself. When, after several more sessions, the therapist proposed the following reconstruction of her schema – self wishing for independence, other not supporting but criticising, so that self, notwithstanding its perfectionistic coping, remains powerless and ineffective – Clara fully recognised herself in it. She now realised that her sense of rootedness experienced during *grounding* and that of effectiveness when successfully tackling her derealisation with body techniques were very much in contrast with her ineffective and powerless self-image. This gave her confidence and motivated her to undertake other steps towards change.

Recalling and exploration of narrative episodes, self-reflectivity, reconstruction of associated memories

Interpersonal schemas do *not* only manifest themselves through thoughts, convictions and behaviour, but also constant body habits: neuro-vegetative activation profiles, muscular spasms, movements, facial expressions and postures. With this presupposition, body interventions, often together with imagery techniques, aim at helping patients with limited self-reflectivity and incapable of recalling emotionally significant episodes, to increase their awareness of the interoceptive, muscular-skeleton and expressive signals they usually process unconsciously, thus being able to reflect on their personal meaning. In other words, a therapist helps patients to trace back from body signals to schemas.

In the following example one can see how, thanks to *relationally integrated mindfulness* combined with an exploration-aimed imagery technique, the therapist stimulated both the recalling of an emotionally significant episode, the self-reflective awareness of inner states and the reconstruction of psychological cause-effect links, and the emergence of associated memories.

Mario

Mario, a university student of 24, suffered from Obsessive Compulsive PD. His family had prominent job positions and had always expected him to perform very well at school. Mario did excellently in his high school final exams and was very keen on university. After his first exams, passed with top marks, his performance went downhill because of a romantic disappointment. He asked for therapy for a severe depression, combined with ruminating about the idea of being irremediably "behind with his exams". The ruminating was stopping him from studying effectively and increasing his depression.

In his first sessions Mario used an articulate and refined terminology. He replied with intellectualisations to attempts by the therapist to evoke narrative episodes. The therapist had the unpleasant sensation of being reduced to the role of a passive spectator of Mario's intellectual qualities. Moreover, Mario appeared emotionally detached and kept an extremely rigid and "composed" posture.

The therapist internally checked his irritation at Mario's apparent disinterest in dialogue and imagined how strong Mario's difficulties in both describing his emotions and establishing true contact with another person were. Using *tracking* of Mario's body signals, the therapist therefore noticed the unnatural and affected rigidity of his posture, and his tendency to breathe often and not deeply.

He decided to point out these elements of his body experience to Mario to try and shift his mindful attention to them and then grasp their psychological meaning.

T: "Sorry if I interrupt you, Mario. I was listening carefully to your account of how you feel afflicted by your difficulty in getting back to studying effectively and, believe me, I can feel your worry in its entirety. But I was also very struck by several details . . . the posture you've kept on that armchair since we started talking and your breathing rate. I'll explain myself better. Your posture expresses the utmost personal dignity, but – I must confess to you – I imagined keeping such an erect and immobile position for so long and . . . felt fatigue and muscle pain. I also imagined breathing like you . . . this way (*the therapist imitated a series of light breathing actions with his chest held rather high*) and I had the sensation of a breathing never managing to go as far as it could . . . satisfactorily. . . . What do you think? Do you also notice these things?"

M [*curious*]: "Well, in fact . . . you are spot on. Now I think about it, I do it often without realising it."

T: "I see. . . . Can I then suggest a very brief exercise? [*Mario, curious, nodded*] Could you, this time intentionally, keep that position and way of breathing? In fact, if you can, could you try and accentuate them a bit?"

M: "Okay." [*Mario conducted the exercise*]

T: "Now, while sitting with such an erect and rigid posture and breathing like that, I'd ask you to make the effort to simply experience the physical sensation deriving from it, without judging it." [*After a few seconds Mario blushed deeply*]

T: "Mario, I see you're blushing. Can you tell me what you feel and what images are surfacing in your head? You're free to tell me everything that comes to mind."

M: "Hmm, in fact I can feel that same sensation . . . that really horrible sensation I had when I was in front of my lecturers . . . having to do an exam."

With this exercise the therapist helped Mario to grasp he had seen him as a critical judge, in front of whom he needed to "sit up straight" and speak articulately and impeccably to not be considered stupid, and that his wish to be helped and understood by the therapist clashed with his expectation of mortifying criticism.

The therapist validated Mario telling him he could understand his automatic need to adopt this posture and way of speaking to forestall the perceived danger of humiliating criticism. Then in passing he told Mario he did not feel critical towards him at all, but suggested in particular he explore his own mind: "In your opinion, what do I think of Mario at this moment?" Mario recognised, with conviction, that he did not find the therapist critical at all, but on the other hand still kept a very "composed" posture, as if on a physical level he still had his fear of imminent criticism.

The therapist then proposed a mindfulness exercise to help him make greater emotional contact with his suffering part, with a non-judgemental attitude. He furthermore told Mario that the exercise could be interrupted at any moment if it proved in any way unpleasant.

T: "Could you close your eyes and breathe deeply? [*Mario did this*]. . . . Now, when you feel up to it, switch your attention to your 'stupid' self-image. . . . In your mind there's just 'Mario's an idiot. Mario thinks, 'I'm an idiot.' (*The therapist slowly repeated this last sentence three times. Mario seemed very concentrated and nodded slightly, with a frowning expression and furrowed brow*). Now please describe to me what you feel physically, your sensations at this moment."
M [*with a sad voice and expression*]: "I feel stupid. I'm ashamed."
T: "I can understand, Mario, and I'm sorry. But I'd ask you to keep this sensation a little longer and try to tell me where in your body you feel this sensation of shame and this stupid self-image."

Mario made a slow gesture with an open palm, drawing a circle around his stomach.

T: "Try and imagine who's in front of you while you feel this sensation in your stomach."
M [*after a long pause*]: "My father."
T: "OK, you're in front of your father. Take three deep breaths, more even if you like, and keep your eyes closed (*Mario nods and does this*). Try and tell me what happens in this scene where your father is in front of you, while you feel stupid and ashamed."
M: "I've just told him I got top marks in an exam. I'd really like him to smile and congratulate me. But he looks at me with a disgusted expression because I'm just one of many, mediocre students behind with their exams."

Thanks to this experience, Mario accessed a group of associated memories about his relationship with his father, and a general schema where over the course of his life his wishes for attachment and appreciation had received only criticism and aloof requests for exceptional results. Mario had learnt to combat the resulting feelings of inadequacy and non-lovability with perfectionism.

To give an example of how a body intervention can be used in support of an exploration-aimed imagery technique, making it possible to overcome an obstacle to carrying out the latter, we shall now go back to Francesco's case to see how it subsequently evolved.

Interweaving of body and imagery interventions: Francesco's case

Francesco was able to manage his anxiety, making it possible to explore significant interpersonal episodes in order to understand his schemas. The therapist focused on his professional context, where Francesco complained of a generalised "malaise", and asked for an example. Francesco remembered various difficult moments in the office, especially during breaks when he had a coffee from an automatic vending machine, where he met some of his colleagues.

The therapist then suggested the patient concentrate on a specific scene and conduct an imagery exercise with it to analyse it in detail. Francesco accepted. The therapist first took all the preparatory steps (Chapter 5) and then began the exercise.

T: "OK, go back to the vending machine scene and describe it to me."
F: "At the machine were Alfonso and Roberto, two younger colleagues. They smile at me and greet me." [*suddenly Francesco blushed deeply and his face got twisted into a distressful grimace*]
T: "Francesco, is all OK? Your expression's changed . . ."
F: "Do you mind if we stop? I'm sorry."
T: [*calmly and reassuringly*] "Certainly, no problem. Open your eyes too. (*Francesco opened his eyes*). Do you feel up to describing for me what you felt?"
F [*long pause*]; "I think a lot of shame and anxiety when imagining that scene . . . describing it."

The therapist validated Francesco and suggested that for a few minutes they perform together the *chi kung* exercise he had learnt previously to watch together any effect it had on these negative sensations. After a few minutes practising *chi kung*, Francesco's face relaxed. The therapist then asked him to watch how his anxiety and shame changed and Francesco replied smilingly that with the exercise they had diminished. The therapist pointed out yet again that Francesco had managed to endure a situation of suffering thanks to a strategy he had by now mastered. He therefore suggested they could use this sense of greater solidity to continue with the imagery exercise.

Francesco accepted and grasped that in the episode he had feared that, notwithstanding their signs of cordiality, his colleagues considered him "a spoilt brat", who had got a managerial job through nepotism. This made it possible to access a series of associated memories, where his wish for acceptance and belonging was linked to expectations of rejection, criticism and humiliation.

Body interventions in change promoting

Therapy change promotion hinges on improving schema-reality differentiation skills, acquiring a critical distance from schemas and contact with healthy self-parts. As regards differentiation, it is a question here of the type where patients pass from: "This idea of myself and others is true" to "At certain moments I see myself and others this way and I believe it but, now I'm experiencing different sensations, I've got different ideas about myself and others". Very often patients are capable of carrying out reasoning like this when the joint formulation of functioning and representation of the dialogue with their therapist have become consolidated in their minds. Especially in the safe environment of therapy sessions, differentiation can be significant. This does not stop schemas getting reactivated in outside situations. We have pointed out that this is a normal and foreseeable phenomenon.

How do we tackle the problem? In line with the embodied cognition principle, we ensure that it is especially patients' bodies that acquire experiences of the self and the world that revolutionise their schemas, and then suggest they observe what their bodies experience. Guided imagery and rescripting, drama techniques and mindfulness lend themselves to this goal as they put the body in the heart of a scene, powerfully trigger the schema's distressing physical and emotional correlates and make it possible for patients to modulate them.

The body techniques described here can strengthen these interventions. They encourage a sense of strength and mastery, which can be useful when excessive negative arousal obstructs schema rescripting exercises. Bodily experience, combined with the imagery and experiential techniques described in the previous chapters, increases agency when compared to the suffering states connected with a schema, fosters differentiation and strengthens healthy parts.

Encouraging schema-reality differentiation and strengthening healthy parts

We now hope to get patients to discover that their expectations about themselves and the world do not correspond to reality. Body techniques are useful for this, both alone and combined with imagery, drama, mindfulness and behavioural exposure techniques. Out-of-control fear of criticism can diminish with work on the body where patients experience strength and discover that, when their feeling of inferiority diminishes, so does their fear about the other crushing them. Simultaneously, patients are helped to experience physical states of strength, energy and effectiveness, completely new for them. We ask patients to observe that, when their body responds well, ideas and emotions veer towards the positive.

Not only the techniques suggested by us but even the most elementary bodily experience suited to this goal can prove useful. In the foreground there is the body as a vehicle of sensations informing patients of a new, positive self-perception, free of their schemas. If, for example, a patient tells her therapist that, with the help of therapy, she has started to play tennis and feels particularly strong and effective when she hits a topspin forehand, in contrast with an inadequate schema-driven self-perception, the therapist intervenes to reinforce this positive perception and recommends the patient to refine ever more her *mindful* attention towards the bodily experience of the "forehand" during tennis practice.

In the following example we show a therapist combining a body intervention with guided imagery and rescripting, with a view to stimulating differentiation and reinforcing a healthy part.

Franca

Franca was a 47-year-old housewife suffering from Dependent PD with obsessive and depressive traits. She came to therapy for anxiety, depression and panic attacks. These symptoms stopped her from enjoying things she was previously keen on and restricted her independence. For several months she had not gone out of the home except with other family members, for fear of panic attacks. She was obsessed by the worry that her only daughter, nine years old, could get ill. When ruminating, she thought of herself as an inadequate mother and a danger for the other: "I must close the bathroom window; otherwise she'll catch cold and this'll make her ill. If this happened, she could die and it would be my fault."

Her therapy first helped Franca to grasp her anxiety mechanisms and master the associated intense negative arousal. Medications reduced her anxiety and depression. As a result, it was possible to explore some interpersonal episodes with a view to accessing her schema.

In one episode she related she lay down on the sofa to rest after a hard day's housework. As soon as he got home, her husband said, derisively: "There you are, your favourite activity." Franca related that she had felt very angry and shut herself up in the bathroom to cry. The therapist helped her to observe that in this episode she wished for a sign of affection from the other and instead felt she received contempt, and to recall various episodes where, as a child, she had not felt loved by her father, a figure she admired very much but at the same time distant and aloof. Franca grasped that her wish for love clashed with a representation of an aloof and humiliating other; her unlovable self-image had unconsciously led her during her life to seek to get love from male figures by complying with their wishes, and to avoid humiliating criticism because of her excessive fear of mistakes and ruminating about how to forestall it.

Franca then grasped that anxiety, linked to her ruminative worry about harming her daughter, were fed by her fear of receiving contemptuous criticism from her husband. Thanks to this awareness, Franca managed ever more, in the next stage of her therapy, to cognitively differentiate this schema from reality. This encouraged her to explore situations where she could find affection and wellbeing. For example, Franca had always been a keen reader and wanted to share her impressions. For a long time she had not opened a book because she thought she had lost the desire to. Actually, what was blocking her was her fear of being derided by her husband and subtracting time from her domestic and maternal commitments. With the therapist's encouragement, and thanks to what she was discovering about herself, Franca grasped that her desire to read was still alive, joined a reading circle, where she met kindred souls, with whom she made some significant friendships, and overcame her fear of being humiliated.

Nevertheless, she complained about always feeling inferior and the loser in her relationships with significant male figures: her husband, father and elder brother. To stimulate differentiation the therapist then combined a body technique with guided imagery and rescripting.

He first taught her the *warrior yoga position*, by practising it with her in-session and recommending she train at it for a few minutes every day. Then, in a subsequent session, he got Franca to stand in front of him and, after some deep breathing with her eyes closed, he asked her to imagine she was face-to-face with her husband telling her contemptuously: "There you are, your favourite activity."

Franca made contact with her sensations linked to this scene – sense of vulnerability and being the loser – which she felt as a hole in the pit of her stomach. The therapist then asked her to open her eyes and adopt, together with him, the warrior position. Encouraged by the therapist conducting the technique together with her, Franca kept the position for a couple of minutes. The therapist then asked her to close her eyes again and describe how her body felt. Franca described a sensation of muscular tone, strength and solidity. The therapist proposed returning with guided imagery to her husband addressing expressions she saw as contemptuous at her, and suggested making her reply stem from this sensation of strength and solidity. Franca assumed a calm but firm expression and said: "When you speak to me like that, I feel mistreated and humiliated by you. Maybe it's not your intention but be more careful how you speak to me."

Based on this experience, which was repeated other times in the subsequent sessions, Franca soon managed to be more spontaneous, firm and assertive with her husband and father. A few months later she started couple therapy with the former.

Stimulating active exploration of the world; exercising understanding of the other's mind

Once they have identified positive, healthy and working self-aspects and valorised them in sessions, therapist and patient try to promote the latter's ability to remain in positive states and experience them during daily life. It is a question, in other words, of activating the exploration system and promoting the experimenting of new behaviour with a view to enriching the patient's repertoire of relational procedures and schemas or ascribing meaning to events.

Let us imagine a seriously avoidant, isolated and anhedonic patient who, with the help of therapy, has grasped his schema based on expecting humiliation and now expresses the wish to go out for a pizza with his friends. His therapist shows this patient how much this wish is the expression of a vital and new part that contradicts his schema and gets him to dwell over the associated physical sensations, emotions and thoughts. He then encourages the patient to achieve his wish in the real world and accompanies him in this gradual exposure.

The body exercises described at the start of this chapter can assist in healthy, vital and vigorous parts, that counter schemas, emerging. Once they have mastered these techniques, patients can use them independently to change mental states at difficult moments, promote wellbeing and maintain it.

We recall that body techniques, often combined with imagery and meditational interventions, can help patients to take healthy and vital parts out of sessions through exposure. For example, a patient managing with the two-chair technique or role-play to adopt an assertive position vis-à-vis her internalised, tyrannical and constrictive father, but very fearful of exposing herself in the same way outside sessions, can gain from a *chi kung* or *yoga grounding* technique the required feeling of sureness and strength to complete the exposure successfully in real life.

That is, patients can use the body techniques learnt in sessions to pluck up courage and overcome avoidances and pathological coping mechanisms through exposure, and thus leave the *comfort zone*, while of course respecting the window of tolerance. Healthy parts can thus sprout outside sessions. Lastly, when patients display a particular propensity in this sense or a specific desire, we also, at an intermediate-advanced stage, propose group martial arts, which, in requiring a certain degree of social exposure, put patients in a condition to improve their understanding of the other's mind.

Alfredo

Alfredo was a 19-year-old student suffering from serious Avoidant PD with paranoid traits. At the start of his therapy he displayed marked depression and social withdrawal. His depression had somatic correlates: he felt he had a rigid and awkward "wooden body" and was embarrassed by it, even if, objectively, he did not display any physical or function defects. In his life he had always wished to play sports but from an early age a sense of physical and psychological inadequacy surfaced. It gradually grew until it exploded during the first year of high school. Because of his social avoidance, culminating in truancy, his school performance collapsed and for two consecutive years he did not pass his end-of-year exams.

Alfredo displayed a moderate self-reflectivity. Already in his first session it was possible to pinpoint that he tended to play truant because, each time he saw a group of his fellow students chattering with each other in class, he felt embarrassed at the idea he might be mocked. However, he could not manage to differentiate reality from his schema-driven perception. His reading of the other's mind was also dysfunctional and mainly self-centred. For example, Alfredo often had the feeling in class that certain fellow students were laughing at him, while trying not to let him see it. Such problems seemed to arise in the therapeutic relationship too and here it was possible to access his fear of criticism in action. Alfredo seemed very wary, closed and diffident when conversing with the therapist. He replied to questions in a concise and essential, even if very polite, way. In spite of the patient's formal correctness, the therapist felt constantly scrutinised by his enquiring gaze, as if he had to be continuously careful to weigh his words to not offend or hurt him.

The therapist controlled his own stress and built up a joking and open atmosphere in the session, confiding some details of his personal life. For example, when talking of Alfredo's unexpressed wish to play sports, the conversation veered towards perception of the body and the therapist shared his love for martial arts with Alfredo, telling him their primary goal was precisely improving bodily self-perception, and that he was also a *jiu jitsu* teacher. The patient confessed he knew about this side of the therapist's life, as he had read it on the internet, and was very curious, as he had always wished to do martial arts.

This transition made the session atmosphere more relaxed. Alfredo became gradually more spontaneous and shortly afterwards managed to relate a set of episodes going back to primary school, where his teacher rebuked him sarcastically and mocked him in front of everyone, by often underlining Alfredo's awkwardness or calling him a "clumsy oaf", which made all the class burst into laughter. Alfredo had never had the courage to tell this to his parents, figures described as looking after him well enough but simple and humble, for fear of repercussions from the teacher. In *shared formulation of functioning* the therapist helped Alfredo to grasp that his wish for acceptance, belonging and appreciation, which had, understandably, been taking shape in him from when he was small and continued to healthily manifest itself in his life, for example with his fellow students, was linked to his expecting humiliation and "sarcastic criticism".

Early on Alfredo had consequently developed a hyper-sensibility to judgements and humiliation and a hyper-vigilance towards potential signals of disapproval or mocking by others, a tendency towards distressing social avoidance, an exaggerated attention towards himself, and a hyper-monitoring of his movements and is body. To avoid behaving like a "clumsy oaf" he had become rigid and restrained, including in his facial expressions. Alfredo identified himself entirely in this formulation and showed himself grateful to the therapist.

Alfredo's mood gradually improved, his social isolation and truancy diminished significantly, even if not entirely. After about one year, Alfredo announced to the therapist he was in love. It was the girl in question who took the first step. It still occurred that, if a situation triggered a perception of himself as inadequate and "a clumsy oaf", a marked diffidence and excessive attention to his body, manifesting itself as an unnatural physical rigidity, got reactivated.

Alfredo told about a bowling match with his girlfriend and her friends, where he kept silent and on the sidelines, thinking incessantly, "They're all better than me ... better looking, more intelligent, more laid-back ... she could have chosen one of them, and she'll probably do it soon." At that moment he again felt his body was "wooden" and got every shot wrong, which made his team lose three times.

The therapist therefore proposed an individual *jiu jitsu* lesson with him. If he liked the experience, he could continue with one lesson per week. Later he could assess whether to enrol in a group course conducted by the therapist. Alfredo accepted enthusiastically. During the first lesson he incessantly got the feeling of being wooden.

As soon as the therapist finished explaining a technique, Alfredo would immediately say: "I'm not up to it." But when he tried the movements, he managed to do them quite well. The therapist jokingly underlined this inconsistency; immediately after explaining a movement, he told Alfredo: "Now you try, even if we both know very well you won't manage." It was then, in *sparring* especially, that Alfredo's body displayed an innate skill, together with a new ability to free himself from the rigidity in which his schema had always reined in his limbs. After wrestling the therapist explored with Alfredo the emotional states he had experienced and the latter realised he had first felt angry at his inability to surprise the therapist, who was able to counter his attacks while staying completely relaxed. Then, as the *sparring* gradually proceeded, Alfredo began to enjoy himself and feel a sense of freedom and mastery of his body he had not known. He realised, moreover, that the therapist was not simply "working" with him but was enjoying himself too. Lastly, he felt satisfied at feeling exhausted when the wrestling finished.

After four individual lessons Alfredo enrolled in the group course. The final stage of his psychotherapy occurred when he was starting his martial arts. After only three months he was in every way a good, tough *jiu jitsu* wrestler. Whilst practising and combating some more expert group members, his feelings of being wooden and inadequate, and his expecting to be mocked resurfaced in his consciousness but were rapidly worked out and regulated, not least thanks to signals of group spirit and kindness from his training companions. Very soon Alfredo challenged his schema outside the *jiu jitsu* classes too. For example, at school, where he built a solid sense of belonging with his fellow students.

His body's somatic memory, the automatic recalling of the feeling of strength, flexibility and fluidity experienced while wrestling, and his internalised sense of brotherhood with his training companions, were forming a new self-perception.

CHAPTER **8**

Behavioural exploration and activation

When trying to change behaviour it is possible to better understand schemas, because the obstacles to new actions surface. With behavioural exercises the body, acting differently, becomes a powerful long-term tool for interrupting the procedural component of schemas. We use behavioural exercises for five reasons: to 1) better understand patients' inner worlds; 2) interrupt bodily-rooted, schema-related procedures; 3) expand healthy self-parts; 4) foster differentiation; 5) increase agency. One effect of asking patients to do behavioural exercises between sessions is its good impact on the therapeutic alliance, as we shall describe.

Finding the cognitive-affective antecedents of problematic behaviour helps in identifying maladaptive schemas. A patient might have a theory about his functioning, but if his clinician explores what the former thinks and feels immediately before activating problematic coping, like avoidance, he can get a more accurate and a close-to-experience formulation of functioning.

Intercepting problematic behaviour and stopping patients automatically performing it thus helps in improving metacognitive monitoring. If, in early sessions, the level of subjective distress is tolerable, emotional regulation acceptable and the therapeutic alliance good, we ask patients to try and stop automatic coping for a short period of their choice and see what happens.

If the coping is perfectionism, a therapist asks: "You work almost without limit but we can't see well what you fear and avoid. What would happen if you clocked off earlier? Next week could you try and go home earlier, even just 5 minutes, than the usual 8 o'clock? It's not important to succeed but just to try. And pay attention to what goes through your mind at that moment."

Similarly, if the coping is self-sacrificing a therapist asks:

> You're likely to give up an evening for yourself, because you feel it's a good mother's and wife's duty. But you can't tell me what would happen if you went out. We can't grasp what your fears for your husband and children are. Next week could you either try and wait a bit before turning down an invitation or even leave yourself room to plan going out? You don't have to do it really, just imagine it and possibly try and do it. And observe the thoughts, emotions and physical reactions you experience then.

Our goal is not as such to dismantle coping, but to obstruct protective automatisms to access the nuances of inner worlds. As we showed earlier (Chapter 2), coping provides short-term protection from psychological distress, but reduces metacognition. Getting patients to expose themselves to feared situations makes negative arousal increase, painful emotions safely emerge and monitoring grow (Dimaggio & Lysaker 2015a, 2015b; Gordon-King et al., 2018b).

Furthermore, people need to feed on healthy actions. Cognitive change alone does not ensure wellbeing if a patient's body is motionless and he does not act in accordance with passions, desires and preferences. Between one session and the next it is indispensable for patients to act in line with the new view of the world emerging during therapy. They thus strengthen their healthy features and practise adaptive relational strategies with which they can realise their wishes are valid and that there is hope they can be fulfilled. Patients also learn how to regulate the pain they experience when they foresee their wishes being unmet at the moment, so as to persist with adaptive actions. To summarise: behavioural activation 1) increases negative arousal and thus facilitates knowledge of negative emotions and the factors triggering them, and 2) increases contact with healthy parts.

Moreover, behavioural experiments support differentiation. If patients acquire a new perspective but continue to avoid feared situations, react aggressively if scared or pursue perfectionist standards, it means they have not really changed their minds, given that schemas continue to dictate action. Therapists thus need to continuously suggest such patients pinpoint their negative schema-dependent predictions and maladaptive coping, and adopt more adaptive behaviour. Lastly, MIT includes a behavioural component for improving agency. This is linked to the therapeutic relationship and contract, and to patients' attitudes towards therapy. Among the core PD problems is a lack of *agency*, action produced independently and goal-directed (American Psychiatric Association, 2013). PD patients are likely to be passive, see themselves dominated and controlled by others (*alien self* in Bateman and Fonagy's terms, 2004). Lack of agency/independence is at the root of passive-aggressive, dependent or paranoid-type schemas.

Patients think their lives will only improve if others stop blocking, humiliating, attacking or tyrannising them. They consequently adopt attitudes involving passive resistance, dependence, diffidence or protest. All these features tend to take over the therapeutic relationship and obstruct alliance formation. Patients ascribing an *omnipotent healer*, *tyrant* or *critical judge* position to their therapist are not active in therapy.

Therapists are likely to react with anxiety, doubts about their abilities, guilt or frustration. Their own coping mechanism is a tendency to be hyper-active, proposing one task after another and trying to convince the patient they have hope or pushing him towards premature change. None of this works and the friction between therapist activism and patient passivity increases.

Such problems require self-regulation from therapists, who should first become aware of their tendencies towards activism, caregiving and pressure to change. They need instead to accept their momentary feeling of powerlessness. Once therapists avoid contributing to creating and maintaining toxic interpersonal cycles in sessions (Dimaggio et al., 2007; Mitchell, 2000; Safran & Muran, 2000), the therapeutic contract needs to be explicitly worked on. At this moment we introduce the concept of *necessary activity*.

The intervention sounds like: "Look, I realise you don't find the solutions I've proposed hitherto for solving your problems useful or feasible. But I don't have many other cards to play; I don't very well know what else to offer you. We need you to choose something leading to wellbeing between one session and the next; otherwise it's very likely I can only accompany you in your suffering, soothe you during sessions and wipe the sweat from your brow, but I won't be capable of truly leading you towards change and wellbeing." In most cases, such interventions are effective, with patients choosing to behave differently in everyday life. They anyway reduce alliance strains.

More generally, starting from the earliest sessions, therapists explain that it is useful for patients to *try and do something* between sessions and that without this active contribution, their ability to promote change is limited. The capacity of negative schemas, especially those linked to rank and passive/aggressiveness, to undermine the therapeutic relationship is thus much reduced.

Another typical situation where therapists can intervene by proposing behavioural exercises to reactivate patients and avoid therapeutic interpersonal cycles is: a patient understands she is driven by schemas but has no power over them or protests with the therapist, saying that, in spite of understanding, this changes nothing and her relational suffering and dissatisfaction persist. We ironically define this as the *withering question*: "I've grasped I tend to function like this. So what?" This question may arise from reasons other than problems in the therapy relationship. Patients have a sincere inability to plan actions directed at change. They would like to try and break problematic patterns. At this point therapists try to suggest actions aimed at combating the automatisms for the sake of exploration. Patients thus enter the experiential learning cycle (Kolb, 1984).

Overall, behavioural interventions often manage to: 1) increase metacognitive monitoring as part of dynamic assessment, promote agency/independence and deal in advance with psychological symptoms; 2) reduce symptoms in advance using behavioural activation; 3) consolidate differentiation; 4) promote actions consistent with wishes and inclinations in order to boost the exercising of healthy self-features, increase the prominence of positive schemas and enrich relational life.

Behavioural interventions

Over the years, awareness has mounted that behavioural work is an effective psychotherapy ingredient, common, for example, to third wave therapies. For some symptoms such as OCD or panic attacks, behavioral work is among the first treatment options (Meyer, 1966). Of particular importance in the PD field is behavioural activation. This arose as a treatment for depression (Lewinsohn, 1974) and there is solid proof of its effectiveness. It is fundamental in PDs given that patients lack agency (Bender, Morey, & Skodol, 2011; American Psychiatric

Association, 2013; Dimaggio, Salvatore et al., 2015; Links, 2015), do not initiate adaptive actions driven from within, and tend towards behavioural inhibition and avoidance (Dimaggio, Salvatore et al., 2015). There is a growing tendency to consider behavioural activation an indispensable part of PD in many therapy orientations (Linehan, 1993; Shahar & Govrin, 2017; Yeomans et al., 2017). In PD behavioural activation aims at constructing representations of self as effective and endowed with agency (Levy & Scala, 2015). As Yeomans and colleagues point out (2017), behavioural activation supplies precious material on which to reflect in the next session. This is material that, without engagement in the world and action, would not be available for joint reflection.

We distinguish *behavioural activation* (Lewinsohn, 1974), with the aim of combating depressive symptoms by keeping a patient active and avoiding the creation of vicious circles reinforcing negative ideation and favouring the possibility of obtaining positive environmental reinforcements, from *behavioural exploration*, the tendency to move around the world driven by curiosity, with the intention of gaining new perspectives on the self and others instead of staying confined by forecasts consistent with schemas.

Overall, behavioural exercises have two goals: 1) to start from healthy wishes and suggest patients act in line with these, and 2) to interrupt maladaptive coping. The exercise in this second case involves asking patients to focus on moments where their actions are driven by protective behaviour and to interrupt them – naturally always remembering the importance of carrying out adaptive behaviour.

In practice the two targets converge: while attempting to carry out wished-for actions, the obstacle patients meet is dysfunctional coping – like, for example, avoidance, perfectionism or self-sacrificing, which they should try to interrupt. However, while trying to interrupt dysfunctional coping, they are more likely to make contact with their desires and try to pursue them.

The structure of behavioural activities in MIT is consistent with Kolb's experiential learning cycle (1984): planning, performing, reflection. The stages (Dimaggio, Montanto et al., 2015) are: 1) planning new forms of behaviour while formulating forecasts about what type of experience patients will have when acting innovatively and about the social consequences of their new actions; 2) behavioural exposure/exploration, that is, adopting new behaviour driven by thoughts and emotions favouring wellbeing, adaptation and widening of social relations; 3) ongoing in-session reflection about new experiences until they are combined in the self system.

We now describe how behavioural exercises evolve as therapy goals change.

Dynamic assessment, improvement of metacognitive monitoring/promotion of agency and autonomy

Right from the earliest sessions a behavioural component can be included in the therapeutic contract. We ask patients to try something they do not usually do. We insist that this is an operation forming part of *shared formulation of functioning* and the key word here is "shared". The goal is to achieve a more accurate view of the cognitive-affective processes underlying interpersonal relationships. We now describe point by point the key elements in behavioural exercises aiming at increasing monitoring.

Rooting behavioural exercises in an intuitive understanding of schemas

To propose a behavioural exercise, therapists need to have already constructed inside themselves a hypothesis, albeit incomplete, about what the dominant interpersonal schema is, and be aware that the exercise will serve to corroborate, enrich or refute this hypothesis, thus achieving a more accurate formulation.

Selecting target behaviours

Based on the schema formulation just described, albeit intuitive and incomplete, we propose as target behaviour for patients either 1) undertaking wished-for actions patients have hitherto waived, or 2) interrupting a coping behaviour.

Negotiating goals and objectives

When proposing an exercise, we clarify that the patient is not obliged to do it and we shall in no way criticise her. What is important is that she devotes even a small amount of time each week to trying to behave differently, no matter whether she manages or not. The useful part is paying attention to one's mental processes when trying to undertake the exercise.

The two next parts describe the extra-session experiential exercises, no matter with what goal and at what point in the decision-making procedure they are performed.

Self-observation

As almost the sole task that is necessary, therapists ask patients to pay a conscious and deliberate attention to their stream of consciousness when attempting an exercise. Therapists ask them to take note of what they think, experience and feel when trying to adopt new behaviours. Patients should especially try to note both any positive states – effectiveness, freedom, relief, enjoyment, self-confidence and competence – and the surfacing of negative thoughts and emotions hampering the execution of actions.

Joint reflection in following sessions

Whatever the outcome of these actions and whether the patient manages to enact new behaviour or not, the important part is creating an atmosphere of joint, inquisitive and non-judgemental reflection in the next session. Therapists should be ready to validate any patient action, as long as they intended to try and do something, no matter what the outcome. If patients did not try, therapists focus on their thoughts and emotions before giving up. This is in any case precious material where interpersonal schemas surface with their utmost power and pervasiveness. Joint reflection is useful for planning the next actions. Every moment of post-behavioural experiment reflection leads to a modification in joint formulation of functioning.

Matteo's example shows how to use behavioural experiments during dynamic assessment and how they produce improvements in metacognitive monitoring and an increase in agency and sense of effectiveness. In the following example one can see the entire sequence listed earlier: *Rooting behavioural exercises in an intuitive understanding of schemas; selecting a target behaviour; negotiating form, goals and objectives; observation between sessions; joint reflection in the following sessions.*

Matteo, described in Chapters 5 and 6, had his own business, which he had run for several years with his father and now alone. Matteo resorted to seductive behaviour, seeking superficial and thrilling relationships, both sexual ones and friendships, apparently only as forms of gratification. It soon emerged this was a form of coping vis-à-vis a fragile sense of self. Matteo asked for treatment because of his relational dependency. He started the first session looking constantly into the void, with a lost look, full of anguish. He had a sort of relationship with Veronica, mother of a baby girl, who rejected him, ignoring his calls and insulting him if he asked to see her while simultaneously considering him her partner. Matteo passed his days waiting for a signal from Veronica: checking WhatsApp and Facebook, writing her loving messages and not receiving a reply. He ruminated for hours, until he got exhausted, about why Veronica acted like this and hoped she would change her attitude and start loving him again. These are forms of repetitive thinking, especially desire thinking – "If only she'd contact me, I'd be OK" – and rumination – "What could I have done wrong to make her go away? Or else it's her that's made like that, but then what are her intentions?"

Behaviourally, he sought attention compliantly and submissively, hoping to ingratiate himself with Veronica and thus bring her back. The result was an increase in obsessive rumination and a true and proper depressive state. His work efficiency fell; Matteo could not manage to devote himself to the firm and began to have financial and personnel management problems.

Matteo's monitoring was poor and completely focused on fruitless attempts to understand Veronica's mind, with the result that he no longer knew how he felt and why he sought her so agonisingly. He only managed to say he loved her and did not want to lose her. We underscore that in such cases interventions to stimulate the reading of the other's mind are forbidden in MIT! Therapists should not ask patients to mentalise, forming a more complete or, say, "realistic" idea of the other's mind, because the sole result would be to increase rumination. As Matteo's monitoring was poor, the goal of behavioural experiments, right from the first session, was to increase it.

The therapist: 1) gained an intuitive understanding of the schema features; 2) thus chose a potential target behaviour; 3) negotiated the performing of the exercise with the patient:

> Well, Matteo, you're suffering a lot, I can see it. Your affair with Veronica almost steals your soul and you pass your days thinking about it. We know it hurts you, but you can't manage to stop thinking about it. However it's difficult to grasp what's happening to you to lead you to feel this affair's so necessary. It's not clear to me what leads you, at a specific moment in the day, to think about Veronica, interrupting what you're doing, and drives you to phone her or send a message, asking for a confrontation or a date. We know you do it driven by what you described as "stress", but not much else. To help you we need to know Matteo better. So, could we, in the coming week, note the situations where you realise you've got an impulse to phone, text her or check Veronica's social media posts? You could then try, purely experimentally, to not do it. Resist as long as you can, even a few seconds or minutes. The important thing is to try. You don't need to succeed; we're just interested in you paying attention to what goes through your mind when you try and resist the urge to contact Veronica. Even if you don't manage to try this, it's enough if you tell me what stopped you in terms of thoughts and emotions.

Matteo accepted the idea willingly; it seemed difficult but even just thinking about it he felt for a few moments a sense of effectiveness and hope. He started the next session full again of distress, despair and rumination. He incessantly asked himself for the reason behind Veronica's ambiguous, contemptuous and rejecting behaviour; he thought he was worthless but simultaneously rebelled against the idea. When the therapist asked him to speak specifically about when he tried to perform the exercise involving abstaining from contacting Veronica, his expression changed: he opened his eyes, hitherto concentrated on empty space and his worries, wide and became alert.

M: "It went OK! I tried not to call her . . . last Thursday, the day after our session."
T: "How was it?"
M: "Easy."
T: "And how did you feel?"
M: "I can hardly believe it: at that moment fine, strong. For a little while I couldn't care less about her. Who the fuck are you, behaving like a bitch?!"
T: "Seems excellent."
M: "Sure, even if it didn't last! After a bit I felt awful and texted her. Naturally, she didn't reply. I felt an idiot after contacting her."
T: "It's inevitable, even the mere fact that you resisted the impulse for a few minutes and felt able and strong is excellent. Thinking back to that situation, how do you feel now?"
M: "Good, in fact. I'm satisfied with myself."

T: "Matteo, try and return with your mind to the moment at which you resisted the impulse. Were you aware of what drove you to seek Veronica?"
M [*thinking about it for a while*]: "I felt shit. Useless, but not just with her. A general feeling of, I don't know, not being up to it. Something almost physical, even now I feel it, like a restlessness in my legs."
T: "Can you see what's making you restless? What are your thoughts now?"
M: "Look, after Veronica didn't reply for some time, I phoned a girl who was flirting with me and went out with her. I couldn't stand the stress."

Compulsive seduction now started. Matteo regularly dated a woman he did not like, but who was like a nurse to him and several women for a one night stand. Matteo's behaviours were a mixture of affective and sexual dependency, but their reasons were unclear.

The therapist asked him to abstain from compulsively seeking sex. Laughing, Matteo realised that the exercise made sense and wanted to try. It had been a long time since he allowed himself an evening at home and he realised he wanted it, even if he was scared about not knowing what to do once alone.

The therapist repeated that the goal was not staying alone at home but trying to resist the impulse to telephone a woman to spend the evening together and to grasp what happened to him before that call. The therapist now began to locate Matteo's behaviour more precisely in an interpersonal schema, that is, the dysfunctional handling of a self-response to a still unclear other-response. A state of loneliness and inability surfaced, suggesting the activation of wishes for attachment, independence and rank. The only thing certainly surfacing was his dysfunctional coping. As with the rest of the schema there were only clues about the underlying motives, and elements hinting that the core self images were: *lonely, incompetent* and *paralysed*. The therapy goal was now to explore Matteo's inner experience, making it possible to better understand the elements in the schema.

Matteo performed the task. What emerged was surprising and provided much more information about the schema. What we describe now will clarify for the reader why in MIT we forbid therapists to make reconstructions based on their own theories or generalised autobiographical narratives. The reason is that, once raw subjective experience in the flow of consciousness prior to dysfunctional coping is accessed, patients' functioning often appears profoundly different from what therapists hypothesised.

Matteo narrated that after the previous session he had tried that very evening to abstain. Towards 6 p.m. he considered calling a girlfriend he knew would be available. He resisted and then noted that first he could only perceive a state of psychomotor agitation. Then he noted a wish to stay alone, but not knowing what to do, how to spend time. He was driven by the autonomy motive and lacked plans and structures for organising behaviour, which he realised was a trait he had. After walking around his flat aimlessly he realised the wish to call the girlfriend was disappearing. Distress linked to his work was instead increasing. Matteo now told how he realised he had come home worried because some workers in his firm were misbehaving. He was afraid to confront them for fear of losing them, but simultaneously not reacting made him feel submissive and inept. Then Matteo, in a way that surprised the therapist, added:

"The problem's my father. He's always made me feel an arsehole. He's obsessed about people cheating him. If I've got a difficulty at work, he tells me they put me in that position because I'm incompetent. . . . I'm on alert because they cheat me and, if it happens, I have to again feel an arsehole because I've brought it on myself."

With the analysis of a series of narrative episodes, Matteo and the therapist were able to describe psychological cause/effect links and then the schema: Matteo wished to be autonomous and effective, and to perform his work his way. He represented the other as mainly ill-willed and strong, cheating and subjugating him. He then shifted to attachment, considering himself vulnerable and incompetent, and feeling scared. With the activation of attachment, he described the other (his father) as unable to soothe and comfort him and a strict and angry judge. This answer turned attachment off and triggered a shift to social rank, where Matteo saw himself as unlovable because he was unworthy.

At this moment he started to compulsively seek women. It was a form of coping to regulate his sense of being forsaken and unworthy. Cognitive avoidance was present too. Summarising: Matteo wanted to be independent. The other cheated him and he felt gloomy and an idiot for letting himself be cheated. As he felt weak, his need for care also got activated, supported by an unlovable self-image. Then he fell into a state of emptiness and paralysis. To handle both his distress at feeling unworthy and unlovable, and the state of emptiness, he compulsively sought either care or sex. Succeeding in seducing led to a temporary increase in self-esteem and an excited state that swept emptiness away. Once the woman he had seduced was no longer there, Matteo fell back into the original negative state. We shall see in Chapter 11 what happens when he instead sees a woman as a caregiver.

Thanks to behavioural exposure – the task of abstaining from coping – monitoring significantly increased. The therapist asked for associated memories, which Matteo immediately provided: the main character was his critical, disparaging and contemptuous father, who had always humiliated him and called him incompetent, in private and in public. Matteo blushed out of shame and simultaneously felt angry, because of his self-part that felt his father's criticisms to be unjust.

Thanks therefore to behavioural exposure, it was possible to formulate together his functioning, something impossible thitherto. We summarise it in the following diagram (Figure 8.1)

As can be seen, Matteo's functioning turned out to be quite complex and, especially, unpredictable compared to what could be hypothesised at the start. His sexual dependency was mainly coping for regulating distressing emotions linked to the incompetent, unworthy and neglected self. The overarching motive was autonomy, which, however, met a threatening and deceitful other. Matteo's reaction to this threat was fright, which activated attachment. The other did not provide care but humiliated him and this generated a shift to social rank, which again met a contemptuous other, his father. Matteo now enacted rapid cognitive avoidance and

Behavioural exploration and activation 237

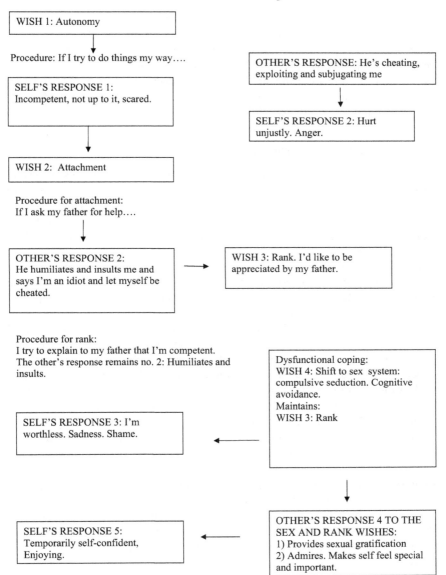

Figure 8.1 Matteo's maladaptive interpersonal schemas

activated sexuality both as a form of gratifying arousal, so as to change his mental state, and access a compensatory narcissistic gratification.

At the same time as sexuality aimed at, on the one hand, avoiding thoughts and, on the other, restoring a competent self-image, sometimes, when faced with the other's criticisms, attachment got activated again, something we shall describe in Chapter 11.

Based on this formulation, it was possible to agree on some short-term therapeutic goals: continuing to reduce coping, devoting more time to the autonomy motive and trying to access a sense of competence and personal worth without resorting to the admiring gaze of the women he landed. Matteo made very rapid progress in all these areas and after two sessions decided to break off his relationship with Veronica, whom he no longer contacted. His ability to work efficiently and feel a good self-worth also bloomed quickly.

Early symptom work through behavioural activation

Behavioural activation was conceived in the 1970s to deal with lack of positive experiences in depression (Dimidjian et al., 2006; Lewinsohn, 1974). The idea was to get patients to find satisfying, pleasing and relaxing activities and devote time to them. Now it is used to get patients to be proactive and problem-solving (Kanter, Puspitasari, Santos, & Nagy, 2012) and act in line with their values (Hayes, Strosahl, & Wilson, 2011).

Getting patients to activate themselves and practise pleasing activities, consistent with their interests, is not only useful with depression but also chronic pain (Kim, Crouch, & Olatunji, 2017), anxiety disorders (Boswell, Iles, Gallagher, & Farchione, 2017), post-traumatic disorders (Cloitre, Garvert, & Weiss, 2017), eating disorders (Tchanturia, Doris, Mountford, & Fleming, 2015) and psychosis (Hasson-Ohayon, Arnon-Ribenfeld, Hamm, & Lysaker, 2017). How does it work? First, it facilitates a shift from mental states involving suffering to others involving effectiveness, pleasure and relaxation, and this is a relief in itself. Second, because of the time spent in beneficial activities, it leaves less room for attention to chronic pain and anxious, depressive or post-traumatic ruminations (Boswell et al., 2017; Cloitre et al., 2017; Kim et al., 2017).

In PDs passivity and a lack of goal-directed actions increase interpersonal rumination about unworthiness, being forsaken, resentment, despair, powerlessness, fear of criticism and so on. A passive attitude, concentrating on avoidance and inhibition, is lethal for therapy in general. Patients transmit intense distress to therapists, but do not provide footholds for reducing them.

Early focus on behavioural activation combats passivity and from the start takes the therapy into the therapeutic contract area: "I can help you but we need to agree together what I can do during sessions and what you're willing to do between sessions."

We continuously recall that this is not an assigning of tasks a patient has to do. It is grasping that therapeutic progress is born from activity. Magic beliefs about therapeutic improvement or a therapist's all-powerful ability to cure without the patient needing to make an effort thus get prevented or scaled back from the start. Patients know immediately that without a contribution from them the therapy has limited to no usefulness.

Naturally, early behavioural activation is carried out in stages too: *Selecting the target behaviour; negotiating the exercise, procedures, goals and objectives; observation between sessions; joint reflection in subsequent sessions.* Here the target behaviour is not chosen on the basis of an intuitive understanding of the schema. The goal here is simpler: combatting symptoms and unease. The behaviour should therefore be chosen based on patients' preferences and what they consider it possible to do. A therapist should not be ambitious; what counts is grasping the patient's action intentions. Whatever activity, even the slightest, is suitable for this aim. Patients are to be validated even for just trying.

Cinzia was 29 and suffered from Obsessive-Compulsive and Dependent PD, with covert narcissistic traits. She was currently not working but in the past had had some important international cooperation jobs. She would have liked to study medicine or psychology, but an unplanned pregnancy had stifled these projects and she was seized by depression, hypochondria and generalised anxiety. She had a history of restrictive anorexia, with the urge to be thin, otherwise she felt a failure. Her psychological symptoms were accompanied and partly triggered by physical symptoms such as muscular pains, fasciculations and paroxysmal pain. Cinzia however admitted that she was suggestible: if someone mentioned a symptom, the next morning she had it. The combination of fasciculations and muscle pain led her to get numerous neurological check-ups. Top specialists ran all types of scans and tests and reported something like a demyelination in certain areas but tended to exclude multiple sclerosis. Cinzia got exhausted with these tests but could not manage to abstain from them. Her relationship with her husband was problematical: she saw him as invalidating, critical and distant. Because of both this and her idea that her body was ugly and diseased, her sexual desire had disappeared and she had not had sex for several months. She was driven by an inflexible sense of duty preventing her from allowing herself anything relaxing. Critical perfectionism and ambition often go hand in hand: Cinzia aimed for high professional goals but was never satisfied enough.

She agreed with the therapist that her therapy would at the start be limited to reducing her anxiety and hypochondriac worries, understanding the psychological nature of her physical symptoms better and reducing depression. The therapist hypothesised that, in accordance with models where hypochondria is supported by perseverative thinking, continuous monitoring of bodily signals was harmful to her. More long-term goals agreed upon involved personality, that is, tackling her weak and incompetent self-idea and grasping the reasons for her dissatisfaction with her relationship and her susceptibility to feeling misunderstood by her husband and relatives.

During the earliest sessions, therapist and patient managed to formulate part of the schema together. Her dominant wish was autonomy/exploration but she saw the other as constraining, obstructing her independence and imposing his point of view, which led her to shift to rank and adopt the submission subroutine. For example, she did not want to get pregnant, because her priority was work, but let her husband force her.

Under the activation of attachment, she thought "I fear I'm ill. I'd like to be understood and comforted" and displayed a wish to be understood, but the other ignored her. The other could be embodied by her husband – "He doesn't understand me" – or mother – "I need assistance when I'm with my child but she's never available".

The self's response to the neglecting other is first linked to the weak core self-image: "I'm alone. I'm not up to it. I feel I'm in a dark cave. I could be preyed on by animals."

Cinzia felt abandoned and shifted to social rank. The other ignored her and she thought she deserved it because she was a silly little woman and was sad about this. If, when faced with a neglecting and critical other, an underlying image of self as lovable and deserving assistance instead surfaced, she thought the other was treating her unfairly and got angry.

If she realised the other was spiteful, she adopted perfectionism to cope with her failure to fulfil the social rank motive: "If I'm perfect, the other will appreciate me." This was what underlay her ambitions. Unfortunately, she still pictured the other as critical and so endlessly raised the bar or gave up, feeling exhausted and powerless.

As regards attachment, Cinzia also imagined a violent, fragile and unreliable other – built in her father's mould. This led her to on the one hand feel scared when she felt fragile, and on the other block attachment and shift to inverted caregiving, driven by feelings of pity and guilt.

Cinzia often experienced emptiness, linked to poor agency and inhibition of exploration. In her words: "I'm at home alone. I'd like to do something but can't think of anything. I can't manage to grasp what I'd like. I only sense emptiness, I feel like shit and get stuck with this feeling." Here, in seeing herself empty, she adopts a critical, contemptuous stance towards the self and shifts again to rank. Caregiving is a coping to overcome it: "When I help someone in the street, it makes me feel happy and fulfilled."

The therapy focused immediately on reducing anxiety and rumination, especially via an explanation of cognitive attentional syndrome and detached mindfulness techniques (Wells, 2005). Patient and therapist then pinpointed that symptoms appeared especially after a whole day at home attending to her son. Cinzia felt physically tired and started to pay attention to muscular sensations. This activated a generalised attention to body signals and threat monitoring got triggered: "Could this sensation be a sign of multiple sclerosis?" Cinzia was also taken over by an ugly, diseased and weak self-image. Her body became a source of pain and disgust and she got blocked. With the therapist she agreed on a behavioural activation task: starting playing sports again, running first at home on the treadmill and then in the park. Cinzia immediately grasped that it was a good idea.

The behavioural activation task had a relational significance. We recall that, as pointed out by Control-Mastery Theory (Gazzillo et al., 2019; Weiss, 1993), patients have expectations, both conscious and preconscious, about how their therapist will position herself regarding their interpersonal schemas. If a therapist behaves in ways reinforcing the problematic other's position, she does not pass the test, and the patient does not improve and does not get involved in behavioural tasks. If a therapist adopts a position supporting a positive self-image and a healthy, adaptive wish, she passes the test, the alliance improves and the patient is more likely to engage in therapeutic tasks. Cinzia realised that her therapist supported her independence, rather than inhibiting it, like the figures she had been used to during her history.

Behavioural activation was successful. Health anxiety and general anxiety diminished. While running, Cinzia contacted an active and free self-image. She linked these ideas to images of greenery while she ran and to a perception of strong muscular tone. Furthermore, in seeing her body as a source of wellbeing, she returned to feeling sexual desire and had sex with her husband after a long period of abstinence.

Let us now see how behavioural exercises are used to stimulate change, that is, improve or stabilise differentiation, of which patients are already capable during sessions, and build healthy parts.

Consolidating differentiation

The use of behavioural experiments for consolidating differentiation is located at a very precise point in the decision-making procedure (Figure 8.2).

Let us consider patients achieving an acceptable degree of differentiation during sessions, thanks, for example, to work on associated memories, with which they grasp how the ways they ascribe meanings to relationships depend on their personal history. Very often they achieve an initial differentiation through guided imagery or drama techniques. They realise they are driven by schemas conditioning their way of thinking and feeling regarding relationships. On the other hand, they know it will be difficult to transport this critical distance skill between one session and the next. This is the moment for planning behavioural experiments to strengthen differentiation, via repeated attempts to perform behaviour at odds with schemas and consistent with healthy parts – an aspect we shall see in the following paragraph – followed by in-session reflection about the results of the experiments.

Planning this type of experiment is quite simple, given that a certain level of differentiation has already been reached: patients know what their problem is, have a preliminary critical distance and know they will not keep it if they do not exercise it.

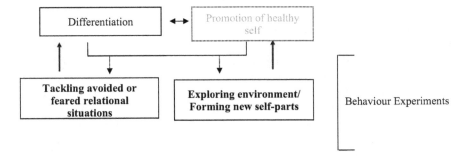

Figure 8.2 Behavioural experiments and differentiation

After three months of therapy Matteo was aware of his schema. He realised he often acted submissively for fear of being forsaken, which had negative consequences, for example, not asking his employees to make up hours lost through arriving late and not enforcing debts. Matteo realised that such behaviours were dictated by his attachment schema, where, if he sought help, he felt weak and exposed to the other's threats, so that he gave up and complied. Simultaneously, if he behaved independently and stood up for his rights, he imagined another resentfully forsaking him and here too he gave up carrying out his autonomous plans. While relating these things, he swung between a sense of strength, at the idea of having the right to carry out his own plans, and fear, trembling as he spoke of the consequences. He knew his trembling depended on the schema but he experienced it all the same.

He and the therapist then planned an exercise. They identified two situations where either a customer was visibly trying to swindle him or some worker had a threatening or arrogant attitude. They agreed Matteo would try to contact the customer and note down every hesitation he had. Or he could deal with the worker by enforcing his rights and speaking firmly, without backing away. Matteo left the session with a feeling of confidence and competence. In the next session he told about talking directly with the police about an attempted fraud and their reply was to not yield to the man's requests because they knew him well. He thus felt supported and did not surrender anything that was his by right.

He then spoke several times with the worker and reminded him he had already given him what he was due and there was nothing to threaten or complain about. Matteo was proud of himself for the results obtained. During the in-session reflection, he reported having lots of hesitations, linked to an intense activation of his fear of being attacked, not so much for its consequences as for fear of being subjugated and rejected.

He now for the first time narrated an episode when he was 25: a man he believed to be a friend and who had become a constant dinner guest at home, swindled him and Matteo was involved in a judicial inquiry of which he could not grasp the causes. He remembered the judges' inquisitorial manner, his feeling stupid and his deep shame on reading the criticisms of the detective who interrogated him. Matteo discovered he was only one of the many people swindled and involved through no fault of theirs in the enquiries. At the time, Matteo asked for support from his father, who insulted him for letting himself be cheated.

The outcomes of the behavioural exposure exercises were therefore that Matteo: 1) became more aware his fears of criticism and being forsaken were schema-dependent; 2) could behave independently or adopt a dominant rank position, without the other becoming aggressive and taking revenge. As repeatedly pointed out, promoting differentiation should occur simultaneously with access to healthy parts. While Matteo increased the critical distance from his schema-dependent ideas about relationships, he accessed the option of activating the independence/exploration and rank motives and felt a sense of energy, determination and self-confidence, all self-states he until shortly before experienced ephemerally only when he successfully seduced a woman.

Promoting healthy parts and pursuing wishes

Patients with disorders like depression, PD, eating disorders or sexual dysfunctions suffer from many forms of inhibition of living a worthwhile life and are anhedonic (Dimaggio Montano et al., 2015). They have difficulty perceiving their wishes or letting themselves be guided by them until acting in line with them enriches their lives. They remain stuck, which prevents them from drawing positive reinforcement from wished-for and enjoyable activities.

A well-balanced personality includes positive self-images, based on situations where we catch ourselves in the act of doing things we feel our own and consistent with our preferences and skills. We need to observe ourselves playing, building things, making plans and putting them into effect. MIT has always been guided by the idea that therapy is not only dismantling an illness but especially building psychological health (Dimaggio et al., 2007). Here we describe how to do it.

Already during the early therapy stages we help patients to identify healthy parts using imagery or drama work, or early behavioural activation. Positive ideation needs to find room in consciousness so that it colours ideation. This is in accordance with positive emotion psychology (Fredrickson, 2001).

Performing adaptive behaviour between one session and the next is among the main factors underlying long-term therapeutic change. Once differentiation is consolidated during sessions and also appears intermittently between sessions, therapists should therefore, from a certain point onwards, gently maintain a focus on acting in line with what patients have learnt about their functioning.

Annamaria was 52 and had been doing individual MIT for two years and group-based MIT for one year. In the past, she had suffered from dissociative amnesia after breaking up with a partner. She woke up from the amnesia after a month and believed it was 20 years before. After a few months she recovered her memories. Her therapists reconstructed that it was as if she had returned to a few months before her father's death. Her developmental history was dramatic: her mother did not want to look after her for her first 14 years and she grew up with a nanny, by whom she felt loved and whom she loved. At 14 her mother abruptly fired the nanny as she wanted to take control. Annamaria's core feelings were that she was worthless and she hated her mother, towards whom she had frequent outbursts of anger. After her father's death, her mother kept switching partners and put the family fortune at risk. Annamaria had to ally with her sister to tackle their problems, sometimes unsuccessfully.

She functioned very well at work. She had low self-esteem, but her perfectionism and sense of duty, consistent with some Obsessive-Compulsive PD traits, had socially adaptive aspects. Moreover, her need to please others, her boss and colleagues, had good prosocial side effects.

Her dependency on the other's love and validation led her, however, to live bigamously for more than 10 years, simultaneously cultivating two relationships, almost two families, in two different towns. Recently she had also acquired a lover, by whom she felt sexually exploited and abused. To cope with her perception of being abused she used a mixture of compliant submission – accepting sexual encounters – angry protest and rumination, whose contents focused sometimes on her lovability – "Why do these things happen to me? What's wrong about me? What do I do to not get myself loved?" – and sometimes on rank – imagining taking a stand with her lover, not submitting and replying to him aggressively. Annamaria asked her lover for a real relationship. He said brusquely that he would never leave his wife. This rejection sent her into a serious major depression lasting several months together with a regression in her functioning and metacognitive skills. She felt weak, inept and completely incapable of planning anything, and lost her critical distance from her schema-driven negative ideas. She could not imagine a future with any purpose. She was dissatisfied with her long-term partner; they no longer had sex and she felt constricted, chronically invalidated and not respected by him. But simultaneously she could not plan actions arising from her own wishes.

The therapists at first insisted Annamaria activate herself behaviourally, solely to counteract her severe depression. They asked her to get up in the morning, take a walk and look after herself and the home, even if she did not see any reason for it. Even without grasping the sense of these tasks but given she had no hope or life plan, Annamaria accepted, not least because of the very solid alliance she had with the therapists and the support from her group. After a few months, not least because she recovered her valued and adaptive representations of the self with other, Annamaria improved and her depression diminished.

She finally understood that her dependent features, that is passiveness, submission, compliancy, angry rumination – leading to protest – and desire thinking, needed treatment. As regards her angry protesting, the therapists insisted this was not an assertive behaviour but a continuous asking the other for an authorisation to exist and act independently, pointless because the only important authorisation is internal. Rumination did not last long, because she quickly replaced it with desire thinking. She passed quickly from "He's behaved badly with me and makes me angry, and I need to tell him: he has to respect me" to "If only he behaved like when we're together. I can recall that lovely time we met and making love with him is so captivating. Why doesn't he grasp that being together could be like this?" Naturally, these forms of repetitive thinking deprived her yet more of agency and reinforced both Dependent PD and depression.

Annamaria had now partly acquired and partly recovered a consistent and integrated self-view and grasped the usefulness of working on these features. She then managed to break off the relationship with her lover, even if not the one with her long-term partner: she felt she was not able to make it on her own. The therapists negotiated with her that she continues, with wider goals, some of the exercises started during her behavioural activation. Once Annamaria started to go out and to look after herself, the therapists asked her to consider what she might like to do alone. She had thought of going to the gym or taking dance lessons. She went several times to the gym but turned around before getting to the reception.

She finally decided, with her face lighting up and a show of energy and enthusiasm, she would like to learn tango. She enrolled in a course and immediately reported a sense of effectiveness and wellbeing. A competent and solid self-image surfaced. She realised this was not enough, because she still tended towards relational dependency. She said she was tired of him and felt constricted, but, thanks to the therapists, realised she did not adopt independent behaviour because of both her fear of loneliness, linked to her still dominant incompetent, inept and disjointed self-image, and her guilt feelings, connected to inverted caregiving.

She imagined that, if she acted independently, her partner would be left on his own and suffer, and guilt inhibited exploration (Gazzillo et al., 2019). Rank too was an outstanding obstacle: when proposing to her partner things she liked, to do either together or on her own, he sometimes protested critically and contemptuously and sometimes passive-aggressively, by missing or forgetting appointments. As with her mother, Annamaria reacted by alternating angry protest – which naturally did not help her to behave independently – and switching off.

The therapists insisted Annamaria would not make any more progress with just in-session reflections, because much of her behaviour continued to be schema-driven. She accepted these comments and planned and performed new behaviours. In her relationship she started to assert her needs: having dinner later, eating things her partner did not like, furnishing their home to her taste and getting a dog. Despite her partner's protests, this time Annamaria persisted with her chosen behaviour and drew from it a feeling of strength, satisfaction and pride.

Lastly, she realised she loved travelling and that she had been stopping herself because he partner did not share this love at all. To the therapists' surprise and joy she planned and carried out first a trip to California and then another to a Greek island with some female friends. Returning from both, with an enthusiasm infecting the other patients in her group, she related her experiences, the places visited, people met and sense of novelty she breathed in these new places.

Supported by the therapists, Annamaria continued to focus on behavioural exercises, which gradually strengthened differentiation, especially when her problematic schemas got activated. Simultaneously, she enriched herself with healthy schemas, built around the exploration motivation, where she saw herself an agent, inquisitive and competent. Furthermore, when rank got activated, a solid and capable self-image, deserving appreciation, emerged. She started working again with energy and conviction, and forcefully asked for a job transfer from where she was, where she did not do anything interesting and her skills did not get exploited. In her new office she got appreciated by her colleagues and bosses and in the end won a promotion to a job with more responsibility.

At advanced stages of a successful MIT, it is typical for patients to 1) differentiate consistently during sessions and be aware of what triggers situations where schemas again take the upper hand and 2) identify healthy parts and feed on them, even if sometimes, often due to stressful life events, these are obscured by the resurfacing of schema-driven core images of the self and other.

At these therapy stages most of the remaining work, directed at preserving and building on results, gets done outside sessions. Between one session and the next, patients adopt behaviours consistent with their healthy parts and reduce coping behaviours. When ideation remains negative even in the presence of beneficial life choices, patients could adopt practices like meditating on schemas (Chapter 9) to get this ideation to slip to the outskirts of their consciousness. Alternatively they should work on their body (Chapter 7) in a bottom-up way, by, for example, adopting a different posture, which modifies emotions (Greenberg, 2002), with ideas consequently becoming consistent with the new emerging affects (Chapter 11).

CHAPTER **9**

Techniques for restructuring attention and treating cognitive coping strategies

Patients may be clearly aware of their schemas and how they interpret relational events, the life circumstances leading them to develop a distress-causing self-image. Now they need to be helped to modify how their minds process information, with direct action on their attention to distressing mental states. This attention is crucial in both promoting psychological wellbeing (Wolkin, 2015) and maintaining disorders (Wells & Matthews, 1994). A worried attention, concentrating on suffering and directed at eliminating it, leads to adopting dysfunctional emotional self-regulation strategies, like worry, rumination or thought suppression. An aware and accepting attention, anchored to the present moment facilitates, vice-versa, optimal emotional regulation (Wadlinger & Isaacowitz, 2011). Research shows that disciplining attention makes it possible to deactivate nodes in the brain default mode network – involved in mind-wandering – in various types of perseverative thought and reinforce areas to which self-monitoring and cognitive control are delegated (Brewer et al., 2011; Taylor et al., 2013). Paying attention to body internal signals, the body's position in a room and sounds reduces stress and improves awareness and emotional regulation (Craig, 2015; Knowles, Foden, El-Deredy, & Wells, 2016; Schulz & Vogele, 2015; Shafir, 2016).

For these reasons in both shared formulation of functioning and change promotion we adopt specific procedures for abandoning those dysfunctional coping strategies based on Interpersonal Repetitive Thinking (IRT) with a decisive role in producing symptoms and relational problems (Chapter 2).

The techniques we describe have three distinct goals; 1) *assessing coping styles*, a part of the shared formulation of functioning; 2) if patients have difficulty experiencing the distressing states which we shall then treat with attentional techniques, one needs to trigger them with the somatic and action tendency component attached; we therefore describe *how to induce* such states; 3) when patients activate coping, we regulate their mental processes with *attention remodulation* techniques.

We discuss four techniques in detail: 1) *splitting attentional space*; 2) *dynamic attentional regulation* for ruminating; 3) *mindfulness* and 4) *Metacognitive Interpersonal Mindfulness-Based Training* (Ottavi et al., 2016, 2019). The last is a codified and manualised group intervention, of which we describe the interpersonal and schema awareness applications. We explain how we use each technique at each step in the decision-making procedure.

Assessment of coping strategies

Reconstruction through narrative episodes

To understand how patients resort to IRT and its harmfulness, narrative episodes can be analysed in detail. Therapists help patients to pinpoint the wish driving them, together with the self- and other-representations surfacing. Simultaneously, while exploring the self's reaction to the other's response, they investigate two sets of phenomena: 1) the immediate emotional and behavioural reactions linked to activation of the negative self-image; 2) coping/emotional self-regulation responses.

Bruno had Avoidant PD and found himself at an unavoidable office birthday party. As soon as his colleagues arrived, he felt anxious because of the activation of his schema foreseeing an unlovable self and a critical and distant other. Bruno saw immediately that behavioural avoidance was impossible; his anxiety surged. As a coping strategy Bruno now activated relational *threat monitoring* (Chapter 2): he watched his colleagues interacting and assessed, consistent with his schema, they were uninterested in him because they saw him as clumsy. Anxiety stabilised at a high level, while embarrassment increased with physiological correlates like sweating, blushing and muscle stiffness.

After the party Bruno *ruminated* about his social inadequacy and the indifference of the others, interested only in those who were part of the same "club". He then engaged in foreseeing similar potential scenes in the future, for example he was already *worried* about an elderly colleague's retirement party. He sought escape routes (*avoidance*) like taking sick leave. To deal with anxiety, shame and depression associated with the memories of the event and his forecasts regarding similar events, and to help getting to sleep, which was impeded by his incessant ruminating, Bruno resorted to hashish and alcohol abuse, thus adopting *behavioural coping strategies*, corresponding to low mastery skills.

Once having identified coping, the therapist followed a typical Metacognitive Therapy (Wells, 2005) procedure, first aimed at making the patient aware of the consequences of adopting this type of IRT, with questions like: "After ruminating for hours about the feared situation X how did you feel? Better or worse? Did you find any solution for the problem worrying you?"

Once patients have recognised IRT is not a solution and increases suffering, one can focus on their positive metacognitive beliefs, that is, those responsible for the adoption of a certain IRT. One can ask, for example, "What is the purpose of your ruminating over what happened?", "What use is it to you?" Attention is then drawn to the negative metacognitive beliefs because of which patients believe they cannot control IRT ("If you wanted to, could you stop ruminating?") or consider it dangerous ("What do you believe would happen if you kept on ruminating?").

Lastly, other coping strategies, both cognitive – like avoidance, thought suppression or distraction – and behavioural – like reassurance-seeking, perfectionism, alcohol and drug use, workaholism – are considered. Clinicians help patients to establish the relationship between all these forms of response and the schema-correlated primary mental state and explain the link between the maladaptive schema and coping. Diagrams may facilitate this operation.

Noticing the appearance of repetitive thinking during sessions

It often happens that patients stop to negatively evaluate and assess their distressing experiences and, while they do this, the therapist notices their mental state veering towards the negative: they are ruminating right in front of her! The therapist should not now dwell on the rumination contents as much as the process itself and therefore point out to patients that they are at that moment feeding suffering. She asks them if this is their usual way of relating to a distressing experience.

Now, when patients are aware that, on recalling a distressing episode, they tend to engage in a long set of evaluations leading to a worsening of their mood, the therapist elicits positive and negative meta-beliefs supporting maladaptive coping strategies.

When envisioning a feared situation, patients use expressions like: "And if it then happens that...?", becoming gradually ever more tense. In these cases, a therapist concentrates on the ruminating process patients implement "live" and points out to them that their minds are organised around the forecasting of negative, albeit improbable, possibilities and this invariably leads to powerlessness and an increase in anticipatory anxiety.

Some patients regularly reply to their therapist's normalisation and validation with a: "Yes, but...". Sometimes a rupture in the therapeutic alliance of the competitive, confrontation type (Safran & Muran, 2000) is underway. Sometimes, instead, the response depends on rumination. For example, a patient seeks evidence absolving him from feeling responsible or wrong – his core self-representations – but at every therapist's formulation, tends to become the "devil's advocate", challenging the therapist's every observation. The patient is not competing with the therapist; he is just seeking a full and reassuring, albeit impossible, absolution. The therapist suggests he explore the consequences of this attitude: "By saying, 'Yes, but...' did you notice an increase or reduction in your guilt (or anxiety...)? Does this mechanism get activated only in relational situations or when you're alone too? What's your purpose in implementing this mechanism that then proves to be harmful? Could you avoid this 'Yes, but...' reasoning, if you wanted to?"

Induction

Any self-regulation technique can be applied successfully provided that one manages in-session to trigger sufficiently intense schema-correlated mental states. In the simplest cases it suffices to recall a specific memory where patients experienced schema-related suffering. Sometimes, however, the memory emerging does not include affect experience. Patients often subtly dissociate, that is by accessing distressing images but without feeling unpleasant emotions. We then need to activate the emotions in-session. We describe a few techniques, without claiming they are a comprehensive list.

Direct induction techniques

A therapist tries to trigger the maladaptive interpersonal schema and get hot somatic-affective states to spring forth together with distressing self-images. Several preconditions are necessary. First of all, being clear about where in the decision-making procedure (Chapter 4) to move. We may be in the basic steps and only want to reduce ruminating in general, or at the point where interpersonal schemas have been formulated and agreed on and we want to reduce IRT. It is then necessary for the therapeutic alliance to be solid and the patient in agreement. The rationale of what is going to be done needs to be explained and curiosity stimulated. These are not techniques based on surprise or shock. Therapists start by saying something like: "You often happen to feel bad and, when this occurs, you get overwhelmed by waves of emotions, that you end up handling in a way that amplifies your suffering. Now, I'd like to together try and regulate emotions here, so you can get experience of how one can respond to distressing affects. In order to do so, we need to trigger them. Do you feel up to letting yourself be invaded a bit by the emotions you know, so to say 'experimentally', in order to look together for a remedy you can then use in daily life?" The therapist now explains point by point what he is going to do and asks the patient to report any emotions and when they surface.

a) Repetition of emotionally charged words

The procedure consists in repeating several times a word or sentence representing patients' negative opinion of themselves and asking them to note the effect on them. This is used with patients tending to judge themselves severely and ruminate when their schema-related negative self-image gets activated.

Mariella was 32 and had Narcissistic PD with perfectionist features. She had been receiving therapy for one year and her schema was clear to her: she wished to be loved but felt she was worth little; if she let herself go in a romantic relationship, sooner or later the other left her or disappointed her. In both cases she saw herself as a "silly little woman" who let herself be "cheated" by everyone, making her feel humiliated. To cope, she shifted to disdain and interpersonal control. Furthermore, albeit less than in the past, she ruminated by asking herself if her partner was right for her or not and whether she should leave him. By now Mariella could grasp her core emotion: a sense of humiliation linked to a "without balls" self-image. The therapist suggested looking together for a way to regulate her distressing mental state, to be applied outside sessions.

To do this the humiliation needed to be triggered in-session. The therapist proposed the task of repeating emotionally charged words, by choosing those Mariella frequently used: "You're a silly little woman", "You're worthless", "You've no guts". He repeated these words haphazardly until Mariella was overwhelmed by humiliation. She was sure this was not what the therapist thought and recognised it was her own idea. The next step has been regulating her mental state with mindful methods, which we depict later.

b) Viewing emotionally charged images

The procedure consists in suggesting they look for affectively charged images: photographs, telephone messages, or pictures or texts from social media. The important element is looked at or read with patients until they experience emotions consistent with the scene. This is used with patients with strong emotional reactions to specific interpersonal situations.

Angela was 35 and had Borderline PD. Her romantic relationships got worn out by her jealousy, that made her overcontrolling and angry, driving partners away. She ends up with the confirmation she is unlovable and unworthy, vis-à-vis another rejecting her and preferring a more attractive rival. Angela grasped the schema, but could not access alternative self-images when angry or jealous. She asked the therapist to help her to modulate problematic feelings and behaviors because she feared destroying her current relationship too, with a partner she describes as keen on her but exhausted by her jealousy.

The therapist suggested Angela view a picture of her rival. She chose the latter's Facebook profile, which she often looked at to see whether there had been any contacts between her and her partner. The photo portrayed her rival by the sea, smiling. Angela stared at it, as requested by the therapist, for about a minute. While she looked at the picture, her tears gushed: she felt she was uglier and sure to be discarded. She felt sad and then immediately anxious and angry imagining her rival in her partner's company. She felt these emotions in her throat and heart.

The induction was successful and they switched to regulation. After validating Angela, the therapist asked her to stick with suffering, to not dispel it, and to not shift to judgements about her rival, her partner or herself. He asked her to stay in contact with the feeling of unlovability and simultaneously led her to regulate her emotions by using the "splitting attentional space" technique, which we shall describe shortly.

After the exercise, the therapist used the material emerging to strengthen differentiation: Angela grasped that this "unlovable-self" idea said nothing about her as she really was, and was rooted into her history marked by abuse and humiliations from both parents. Her rival now became unimportant to her because she had taken on a more positive self-image. She realised that, when jealous, she was driven by the old sense of worthlessness and grasped her therapy goal was to overcome this idea and not to control her partner.

Attentional techniques and repetitive thinking: shared formulation of functioning and initial mastery

Therapists guide patients to grasp early on the link between coping and suffering, before even understanding they are driven by schemas. Interventions with this aim sound like:

> From the initial information gathered we can see that in certain situations featuring X and Y you feel an intense suffering, like a punch in the gut. However,

we also know that this is not all there is to the suffering. You: "take your work home with you", by ruminating about what happened, foreseeing what might happen and so on. This aspect of your suffering gradually becomes a problem in its own right: your mind remains focused for a long time on the distressing event, reliving it and foreseeing it, producing an increase in negative emotions, until it produces the symptoms which prompted you to seek help.

Patients generally do not have difficulty grasping that they will tend to feel some distress but will be able to not focus totally on it.

During dynamic assessment in the very earliest sessions, therapists can try and regulate emotions with the techniques we describe later. There are various advantages. Patients readily understand that the therapist: 1) is working for their wellbeing; 2) is engaged together with them in stimulating positive or less harmful mental states and 3) is getting them to be active in the therapeutic process. All this has important consequences for the therapeutic alliance.

Early use of attention regulation manoeuvres makes it possible to counteract negative meta-beliefs about the uncontrollability of repetitive thinking (Wells, 2008). Sometimes already in the first session, if the clinician has conducted a rigorous assessment and managed to elicit some well-structured narrative episodes, patients are capable of grasping that part of their suffering stems from repetitive thinking. Well, it often happens now that they express the conviction that it is not within their power to decide whether to worry. That is, they have a *negative metabelief* about the uncontrollability of their thought (Wells, 2008). The most direct and effective way now to modify this meta-belief consists in testing, with them, if it corresponds to the truth or not.

The therapist proposes an experiment: "You say you can't stop yourself ruminating about episode X, that it's not you deciding what to think when the memory appears. Ok, let's see if that's really the case. I'd like you to close your eyes and try to retrieve the memory of the episode."

She then continues by applying a simplified version of the attentional space splitting technique we describe later: she asks the patient to select a scene representative of episode X that activates her repetitive thought and contemplate it until some negative emotion appears. She then asks her to divide her attentional space into two, with half of her attention engaged in contemplating the distressing scene, while, simultaneously, the other half is used to listen to noises in the surrounding environment, either inside and/or outside the consulting room. After a few seconds the therapist asks for feedback about the intensity of the negative emotion. In almost all cases patients report a decrease in and sometimes a disappearance of the negative emotion.

After receiving the feedback, the therapist asks the patient to let go of the image and listen attentively to noises around. She then asks again for feedback and, if the patient has relinquished the image, finishes the exercise which, in this shortened form, lasts less than three minutes.

If patients are quick to retrieve the negative memory and start to ruminate during the time devoted to listening to sounds, then the therapist asks them to divide their attentional space into three: retrieving the distressing image, listening to sounds and simultaneously paying a part of their attention to bodily sensations, for example in the hands or feet, or from breathing. She suggests they maintain this three-part attention until maintaining the distressing image becomes difficult. They now let go of it and remain focused on the two sensory sources remaining.

In the debriefing the therapist shows patients they are capable of letting go of distressing images, contrary to what they thought. They learn by experience they have power over their minds and repetitive thinking. In a few rare cases patients may reasonably object that it was not them who defeated their tendency to ruminate, since their attention was in reality steered by the therapist. The latter can suggest they repeat the exercise alone: she leaves the room or does not intervene for the three minutes of the exercise. This variant is very often successful.

The results after the first attempt are naturally unstable! In the following days and weeks patients continue to use IRT. What they have achieved is discover they have agency over their mental processes, which is a fundamental ingredient of overall change. Patients then try and regularly practise the exercise to achieve the reduction of emotional suffering desired.

Attention remodulation techniques

The exercises described henceforth can be applied both during dynamic assessment and throughout the joint formulating of functioning, and during change promotion. In the first case it is a question of working on symptoms when metacognition is poor. An improvement in the therapeutic alliance is also achieved because patients discover the active, exploratory and co-operative nature of MIT.

The use of attention modulation and mindfulness at the *change promoting* stage, when the awareness of schemas is by now developed and one is working on boosting differentiation, is instead aimed at reducing symptoms and replacing dysfunctional coping with more mature forms of mastery. It aims particularly at reducing any residual resorting to IRT that patients enact even when they are aware that schemas do not necessarily tell the truth about them and the others. Such patients continue to suffer because of the combined role of ruminating and the procedural component of schemas, which activates painful bodily states from which they have a hard time freeing themselves.

In this section we concentrate on attention regulation techniques. Maladaptive interpersonal schemas have the power to focus patients' attention (Chapter 1). When they have constructed new views of the self and others, their attention gets naturally directed towards more varied or pleasant features of the world and they are ready for healthier relationships and planning their future. Nevertheless, their attention still automatically shifts towards problems and during change promoting patients need to be helped to control it. This treatment step helps in preventing relapses.

What are these techniques about? Their purpose is helping patients how to deal mindfully with what hurts them instead of judging it and engaging in dysfunctional problem solving. Simultaneously we show them how to gradually pay a certain amount of attention to their bodies or sensory stimulation, to deprive the emotion of fuel until it dissipates. This is part of *acceptance* (Hayes et al., 2011), that is, not avoiding negative emotions and experiencing them without judgement, and of *mindfulness* (Kabat-Zinn, 1990, 2003; Bishop et al., 2004). Patients are guided to watchfully and curiously focus on what causes distress and to try to incorporate any unpleasant sensations in a wider sensory awareness of the body and environmental stimulation. By doing so, distressing thoughts and emotions appear and disappear in the stream of consciousness. This "refined" regulation of attention belongs to secondlevel mastery strategies (Chapter 2; Carcione et al., 2010).

Attentional space splitting technique for rumination

To conduct this technique it is important to select images from memories with a high schema-correlated emotional content. This way, if patients tend to ruminate, they do it immediately. The scene/frame selected should accurately represent the distressing features of the event remembered and elicit significant suffering. The main actor in the image selected can be the patient, the other or both.

Stefano was 37 and had Obsessive-Compulsive PD. He chose a scene where he got reprimanded at work for finishing a job late. He could see his desk with piles of papers waiting to be dealt with. He saw the manager approaching him with the stern face of someone about to pronounce a guilty verdict. He saw the manager's eyes homing in on him and felt fear and shame.

Marisa, 60, with Dependent PD, selected a scene from 15 years earlier that still caused her distress: she was at home in the living room and talking on the phone with her partner. Speaking from Germany, he told her he had another woman and would not be returning. Marisa could clearly see the furnishings and the sunlight at sunset arriving from the windows. She saw herself and the dress she wore that evening. She felt a distinct, sharp pain; her throat felt tight and her heart pounded.

This procedure can be applied to any type of IRT. What changes is the scene to be selected. With rumination, patients should be asked to retrieve their schema-correlated autobiographical memory with the highest emotional intensity. With worry, we suggest patients imagine their most feared situation, like for example seeing their partner having intimacy with another person or public humiliation. We now describe the steps in detail.

Focusing on the frame with the highest emotional intensity

We ask patients to close their eyes, access the painful scene and concentrate on the emotionally charged image. We introduce the exercise like this: "Now we'll assess if it's possible for you to have that distressing thought in your head without being completely overwhelmed by it. I would ask you to of your own accord recall the memory and we'll try to be alert and aware, and avoid either chasing it away it or ruminating on it. Close your eyes and select the frame representing best the overall memory and with the greatest emotional intensity."

Techniques for restructuring attention 255

The therapist ensures that the patient has managed to focus on the scene and then asks him to maintain the image in his field of consciousness for a bit and notify him when an emotion appears. When this occurs, the therapist asks him to specify in which area of his body the emotion is situated.

Soft anchoring to senses and first splitting of attentional space

Patients are asked to let their hands drop by the sides of their bodies and pay attention to any sensations emerging, without losing sight of the painful image. Obviously, any other sensory source can be chosen too. The hands are generally easy to feel, particularly sensations of heat or tingling in the fingers. Patients have to *simultaneously* remember the two stimuli, the painful scene and their hands. After a few seconds they are asked what they notice. In the majority of cases patients feel a reduction in the negative emotion and report having difficulties sustaining the image. The therapist asks them to not let go of the painful scene and, if their bodily sensations tend to seize the major share of attentional space, urges them to recall it. This serves to reinforce their ability to remember painful scenes but paying them a limited amount of attention. Therapists note this is a reasonable goal, rather than hoping to be free of suffering, which is difficult and would correspond to avoiding the distress.

Further splitting of attentional space

The therapist now asks patients to subdivide their attentional space into three parts, by introducing a new source of stimulus, usually auditory, like noises coming from outside the consulting room. The therapist again asks that the three sources be kept *simultaneously* in patients' attentional space, while telling them it will be more challenging. It is useful to suggest shifting attention quickly from one stimulus to another: *painful frame*, *hands* and *sounds*, and then try to catch all three simultaneously, even for a short moment, and then go back to passing from one to another. After about 20 seconds the therapist asks patients if they are doing the task successfully and how they feel. If the alliance is good, patients usually complete the task and discover they have difficulty maintaining the source-of-suffering image. Negative emotions become less intense or disappear.

Letting go of the image

At this point we ask patients to mind only tactile and auditory stimuli and ignore the image for a couple of minutes, during which the therapist stays silent. Patients are warned that, if their distressing memory returns, they must not shut it out but only devote as much attention as possible to the other stimuli.

Conclusion and reflection

The therapist helps patients to realise that if they do not feed the distressing image with rumination and pay attention to sources such as their bodies and sensory stimuli, the image previously making them suffer becomes less important. Afterwards, once they have distanced themselves from the memory, they can see from different, and often more benevolent, perspectives. These complex, nuanced and mentalistically rich reflections are part of third level mastery strategies (Chapter 2; Carcione et al., 2010).

Dynamic attentional regulation technique for ruminating

This task has the aim of reducing negative meta-beliefs about the uncontrollability of ruminating and, consequently, increasing agency over one's mental states. Moreover, we teach patients an effective and independent way of regulating mental states.

Unlike the attention splitting procedure described earlier, this does not require focusing on a static image, but intervenes precisely when patients are plunged into verbal ruminating. This change is necessary, in that patients with worry often do not arrive at foreseeing catastrophic scenarios in detail but simply fear them. Worry is usually an anxious repeating of things expressed verbally with few mental images (Borkovec et al., 1983). To simplify, we could say that worry is the repeating of sentences starting every time with terms like "Oh my God, and if. . .?". *Interpersonal* worry regards being criticised, being humiliated in public, getting rejected, being cheated, etc.

In sessions we show patients how to modulate worry after intentionally activating it, in four steps:

1   Activation of ruminating. We ask patients to talk about their worries and then to assess the emotion intensity they progressively feel on a scale from 0 to 100.
2   Ruminating *alternating* with sensory awareness. When patients reach level 50, we ask them to let go of their thoughts and concentrate on outside and bodily stimuli selected previously, like those originating from noises, hands, feet, etc. We ask them to signal when they feel worry is fading away or when the somatic sensation linked to the emotion has decreased to a level lower than 10.
3   Ruminating *combined* with sensory awareness. Patients are asked to ruminate afresh, but this time with the indication "While you ruminate, I'd like you to keep a part of your attention fixed on the sensations coming from your hands. I'd like you to do both things – ruminating and concentrating on your hands – simultaneously, even if at the start it can seem a bit strange." After a while the therapist checks the emotionality level reached.
4   Conclusion and discussion of the experience. Here, therapists make patients note that they are able to reduce rumination.

Fausto was a bright anthropologist of 40 with Obsessive-Compulsive PD and Generalised Anxiety Disorder. With therapy he learnt he was driven by a maladaptive schema activated by a wish for social inclusion, with a painful different/imperfect and unlovable self-image, and the other portrayed as fit/handsome/rejecting.

Fausto knew he ruminated in order to regulate emotions but this boosted worries. He started by, for example, thinking about the work he had to do at the library to write an article. He then began worrying about not enduring the lack of human contact, saw himself as weak and felt anxious. Given his fragile health he feared being infected by diseases. Meta-worries got activated (Wells, 2005): he worried about spending too much time over these fears and going mad. He feared others would consider him crazy and dangerous and reject him. He was now terrified and desperately sought reassurance from doctors, friends and relatives. In the end he got depressed at again appearing to be incapable of self-regulation. He was very clear about the negative effects of ruminating, nevertheless, ruminating exploded under stress.

During relapses Fausto started sessions trying to convince the therapist his worries are reasonable. The therapist interrupted him and pointed out he was ruminating and asked if he realised this. Fausto grasped this easily, but could not stop. The therapist then asked if he wanted to try and interrupt it and Fausto accepted.

T: "Fausto, I'd like now for you to try and ruminate, as you usually do. However, I'd ask you, while you do it, to note here the level reached progressively by your negative emotions, without distinguishing among anxiety, sadness, despair, etc. [*hands him a sheet of paper with lines numbered in tens*]. Allow me to interrupt you when your emotions reach 50. Okay?"
F: "Okay [*starts ruminating*]. In fact, it's not difficult, because things are going better. But I'm not right. I often think I'm obsessed and depressed, that I'm insane. That I can't go on holiday with others because I'm not normal. There, I've got to 30."
T: "Keep on . . ."
F: "No, it's that I get thinking that I'm dangerous, that I can't get along with others. Everyone else looks normal to me, even the lunatics in the asylums seem more normal than me . . ." [*marks 40*]
T: "Go on."
F: "I also think I perhaps ought to be put away too. That I'll never have a normal life . . ." [*marks 50*]
T: "Okay, Fausto, now let go of these worries as much as you can and pay attention to outside sounds and your hands. Let your hands dangle from your chair so as to clearly feel the sensations coming from them. . . . Can you manage? [*Fausto nods*]. Good, keep on with that until you feel your head lighter or the unpleasant physical sensations drop down. Tell me when that happens.

After about one minute Fausto states he had no negative physical sensations and felt his head clear.

T: "Now, while you talk about what worries, I'd like you to bring part of your attention on the sensations coming from your hands. Do the two things simultaneously – ruminating and concentrating on your hands – even if it seems strange. No need to note your emotional level. I'll ask you it every so often."

F: "Okay [*starts ruminating*]. I often think the work I do is useless, because I'll never be able to finish my research due to my obsessions. Instead the others manage and live normally. Sure, no one would like to spend time with me knowing I am obsessed. Even my parents don't know everything. Otherwise they'd despair . . ."

After about two minutes the therapist asked Fausto at what level his emotionality was.

F: "No, it's hasn't risen much."
T: "Okay, proceed."

After another two minutes with similar questions and answers the exercise was done:

T: "You see Fausto, it occurs you can quickly enter and exit your worry, and anyway, when you happen to really have your mind crammed with worries, you can limit their emotional impact very much, simply by paying a share of your attention to a sensory stimulus."
F: "Yes, in fact, when I ruminate I've got my mind 100% focused on my problems, and I try and get out of this by thinking more. It doesn't come automatically to me to limit the attention I give to my worries and shift it to concrete things. It's like you say: it's as if I was at the cinema watching a horror film that fills me with fear, but tried to handle the fear by hoping that the scenes become benign. Instead, in such situations I ought to decide to leave the cinema and see the world and listen to its sounds. Otherwise I'm always inside my head, where at the end of the day the film never changes."

Mindfulness

The interventions described earlier require a generic, mindful-type attention from patients. We shall now describe two types of mindfulness based interventions: 1) using mindfulness in individual sessions; 2) Metacognitive Interpersonal Mindfulness-Based Training (MIMBT) (Ottavi et al., 2016, 2019), an independent MIT programme we usually apply when patients are already familiar with their maladaptive interpersonal schema and are involved in change promoting operations.

Mindfulness in MIT

Mindfulness is a common, usually temporary, mental state: we experience it by intentionally paying attention to sensory sources and reaching an awareness of the slightest and ordinary sensations coming from it, like a slight tingling if we concentrate on our feet. The purpose of mindfulness practice is to make the ability to consciously concentrate on the world more solid and stable. To train this skill, we use mindfulness meditations, exercises where we get patients to pay attention to various sensory sources and/or mental objects, and observe them without judging them or holding them back.

How does cultivating conscious attention anchored to the body facilitate the therapy path and help to reduce suffering? The goals for which we use mindfulness vary depending on where patient and therapist are in the decision-making procedure (Chapter 4).

The first goal is to improve *metacognitive monitoring*. Paying attention to one's own inner world, thoughts, emotions and bodily states, without judging them and while observing their spontaneous transformation, helps to identify them. Therapists ask patients: "How do you feel while remembering these episodes?", "What passed through your mind a second ago?". They then ask patients to keep paying this type of attention to their inner world in daily life, particularly in the here and now of interactions evoking schema-related suffering. But to learn to do it alone, patients need to practise, and this is the point of doing mindfulness exercises and then repeating them as homework.

The second goal is to *catalyse the processes stimulating differentiation*, that is, the awareness that suffering depends especially on one's view of the world. Mindfulness helps in grasping that thoughts, emotions and sensations are mental events and not correct interpretations of reality (Teasdale, 1999). The same criticism or abandonment does not produce the very same emotional response in everyone; some get just grazed, while others are deeply wounded.

The third goal is to *reduce resorting to dysfunctional coping strategies* and replace them with more adaptive ones, based on reorienting attention, acceptance and self-compassion (Gilbert, 2005). For example, awareness meditation helps in replacing immediate reactions to distressing mental states, linked to patients' schemas with a mental and behavioural non-reactivity, an openness to unpleasant emotions and an attitude of self-benevolence.

Mindfulness in imagery exercises: induction and exiting

Using mindfulness before applying imagery and bodily techniques can strengthen their effect. The majority of imagery and sensory experience induction techniques are based on anchoring to awareness of sensory sources. This stage has the primary goal of marking a change of pace compared to the conversational approach, which occupies the majority of therapy session time. If therapists evaluate that self-regulation is needed before exercises, they may devote four or five minutes to induction.

The steps to induction are:

1 Promoting awareness of the current state of one's organism. Closing one's eyes and remaining silent for a few seconds, possibly with the indication that one take note of the activity in one's mind at that moment and general state of one's body.
2 Promoting awareness of posture. Paying attention to the body's points of contact with the floor and chair, facilitating the sensation of the body's gravity.

Then paying attention to the alignment of the spine to promote a comfortable and erect posture, providing a sense of energy and solidity.
3 Promoting awareness of breathing. Paying attention to the physical sensations linked to breathing, letting patients choose the body part where these sensations are most marked.

After these steps patients generally experience a decrease in arousal, enough to facilitate the surfacing of memories and images and make it possible to immerse oneself in the experience. From now on, therefore, the soil is ready for imagery or bodily techniques.

The conclusion of experiential exercises requires letting go of the images and remaining with the bodily sensations. The latter can be pleasant – as in the case of immersion in an exercise on healthy parts – or unpleasant – as in the case of recalling distressing memories. The end of the exercise gets preceded anyway by a return to a state of mindfulness focused on breathing.

A few conscious breaths suffice if the emotional state displayed by patients is positive or neutral. Wider space will need to be devoted to mindfulness in cases where the experience has left distressing traces. In the concluding stage, therapists remind patients to postpone reflecting over the experience until the exercise is completed.

Mindfulness for in-session emotional regulation

If patients come to sessions agitated or, due to the memories emerging, get emotionally dysregulated, the first operation to carry out is working via the therapeutic relationship. The therapist makes his warm, watchful and validating presence felt, follows patients' suffering step by step and makes them confident that they can together alleviate it. Later, however, it is necessary to use other technical tools to regulate patients' inner states and promote metacognition, which tends to worsen when arousal mounts (Semerari et al., 2003). Mindfulness improves regulation for various reasons. First, it leads one to open up to suffering, unlike relaxation exercises, which patients in reality adopt with the more or less conscious aim of avoiding psychological distress. Second, it does not require concentrating on a task, which is very challenging for patients who are agitated, but only exploring the mental state just as it is. We do not ask patients to ignore any tensions and concentrate on something, but to be aware of all the tensions in their bodies at that moment and observe any changes therein. Being in contact for a certain time with suffering, in the double position of experiencing and observing psychological distress, reduces arousal.

In the paragraph devoted to the attentional space splitting technique we saw how it is possible to combine awareness of sensory stimuli to images loaded with intense affects and let the latter get weaker and then disappear from the consciousness. It is important to sensitise patients right from the start to awareness, including short meditation exercises. With meditation therapists need to remind patients to take note of the thoughts and affects overlapping with or replacing sensory sensations, and to mind them, name them and observe the power of attraction they have on the mind, and then leave them in the background and try to reconnect to the sensory stimuli.

When applying mindfulness in individual sessions, a therapist asks for feedback. For example, after suggesting patients pay attention to sensations coming from their feet, she asks: "Are you managing?", "Can you feel something?" The aim is not to get a detailed description of their mental state – something reserved for the inquiry stage – but simply to monitor how the exercise goes and make patients feel the therapist's presence.

Accordingly, the therapist looks for minimalist replies like: "Yes", "No" or "I'm trying but am not sure." If patients embark on more complex reasoning, like: "No, but the fact is I've never had a good relationship with my body, because . . .", the therapist tactfully interrupts and asks them to leave comments until afterwards and remain in touch with the sensations.

For patients with limited agency over their mental states, this help is absolutely necessary and, as the exercise gradually moves forward, the therapist reduces the number of questions and leaves them ever longer in contact with their inner experience, postponing the exploration of what occurred during the meditation until inquiry.

Mindfulness for extra-session emotional regulation

Mindfulness needs to be practised in daily life for its benefits to manifest themselves. Therapists teach various exercises to perform, so that patients can choose the meditations they feel most congenial among, for example: breathing meditation, walking meditation, those involving seeing and those with a mix of sensory focuses.

What it is indispensable to teach is body scanning, because, beyond being therapeutic in itself, it helps induction before imagery and drama techniques and reinforces patients' ability to anchor attention to the body and senses. It consists in systematically and progressively paying attention to every body part, from the feet to the head or vice-versa. Patients pay attention to all body segments, sub-divided into sub-units: for example, the scanning of an arm is split into several stages, with attention resting on the fingers, then shifting to the palm, then the back of the hand, wrist, forearm, elbow, upper arm and shoulder. In its complete form it lasts 20 to 45 minutes, but, with patients who have already learnt it, a "condensed" version can suffice. For example, instead of dwelling on each point in a foot, attention is paid to the foot in its entirety. Like this a body scan lasts about three minutes and helps in understanding which body parts distressing emotions and thoughts are connected to. It is a manageable form; patients can practise it at home, in the office or on the metro.

We advise patients to practise mindfulness frequently outside sessions, even for only a few moments. They can try and interrupt the flow of thoughts and focus for some seconds on sensory elements, by, for example, paying conscious attention to breathing, for three breaths, during work breaks, before devoting themselves to something else. They can use their mobile alarm, which, by vibrating, reminds them to stop for about 10 seconds, just enough time to interrupt the flow of thoughts and pay conscious attention to sounds or the scenery.

Help for performing longer exercises in daily life can come from audio recordings: for this purpose the therapist suggests patients record the meditation instructions with their mobiles, to be able to listen to them again at any moment.

For PD patients *informal mindfulness exercises* to be performed in relational contexts are very useful. For example, becoming aware of one's posture and noting the mental state, *while* engaged in listening to a person or even in the midst of a conversation. These awareness situations *during* interpersonal transactions help patients to be aware of what is happening inside them and what impulses drive them: receiving more attention, withdrawing from a relationship, protesting and so on. When they happen to find themselves in schema-activating contexts, they can seek a mindful state in the here and now of the interaction with a view to regulating their affectivity "online".

Enrico was 29, with covert narcissism, and sought therapy following a major depressive episode arising one month earlier. He was team leader in an office and the hub of all relationships. He felt satisfied and gratified and his work became the main focus of his life, even to the detriment of a long-term romantic relationship, which ended one year after he started this job. Things changed when a new employee, Stefano, got hired. Although his position was junior to Enrico's, he quickly became the centre of attention, everyone sought him because he was available, likable and smart. Enrico felt envious.

Office became hell for him: when he saw his colleagues laughing at Stefano's jokes, Enrico saw himself excluded and his self-esteem collapsed. He realised he was changing his postural stance and expression and this became a new problem, because he feared that, seeing him dejected, his colleagues would imagine he was insecure, touchy and of little interest, and would exclude him. Consequently, when he felt envy or shame, he started to ruminate, ending up developing depression and considered changing his job.

Arriving at the change promotion stage, the therapist proposed Enrico engage – during the week – in pinpointing any activation of his maladaptive interpersonal schema – "I wish for appreciation but, if I'm not the smartest, the others will ignore and exclude me, making me feel worthless" – on a timely basis and recording the event in a notebook. The following week Enrico conducted the task perseveringly and also succeeded in differentiating, but his schema-correlated suffering stayed high. He therefore asked the therapist what ploy to use in torrid situations, when he got that "punch in the guts" activating, even if only for a short while, his rumination. Enrico had already performed various mindfulness exercises in sessions and practised them with discipline at home too – which had made it possible for him to reduce his rumination and exit from depression. The therapist then proposed he become aware of his breathing *during* interactions with his colleagues, and simultaneously check his inner state, while naming any emotions surfacing. With this exercise he was able to attenuate the "punch in the guts": as soon as he saw Stefano drawing relational success, Enrico, rather than avoiding and leaving the room, adopted an attitude of conscious openness to the inner echoes the scene caused him.

All this made it possible for Enrico to regulate his mental state in the here and now of an interaction, while accepting a temporary self-esteem decrease, avoiding activating maladaptive coping strategies, observing what happened to him without judging it, letting the distressing mental state slowly recede. From then on the schema-activating experience at work became gradually less explosive and the "punch in the guts" less intense and lasting.

Being present to ourselves during an interaction inevitably leads us to be halfway out of a relational exchange; we are partly actors and partly audience. This is an advantage in therapy and a fundamental help for change. Paying attention to the self deflects it from the other and gives patients a centring on themselves during relational exchanges. Limiting relational involvement in some situations is a very low price to pay for reducing suffering!

Metacognitive interpersonal mindfulness-based training

Over the years we have developed group interventions with the aim of accelerating certain change processes and/or tackling specific problems like IRT or social skills (e.g. Ottavi, D'Alia et al., 2014; Ottavi, Pasinetti et al., 2014, Inchausti, García-Poveda, Ballesteros-Prados, Ortuño-Sierra, Sánchez-Reales, Prado-Abril, Aldaz-Armendáriz, Mole, Dimaggio, Ottavi, & Fonseca-Pedrero, 2018). Metacognitive Interpersonal Mindfulness-Based Training (MIMBT; Ottavi, D'Alia et al., 2014) is one of these. It can be used as a stand-alone treatment, but here we describe it as a module that can be added to individual therapy. We thus use it with patients aware of their schemas and working to promote change, but still adopting IRT in schema-correlated distressing mental states.

In a pilot study (Ottavi et al., 2019) all 27 patients completed MIMBT and displayed a very high level of participation (96% of sessions). MIMBT significantly reduced use of metacognitive beliefs supporting ruminating and improved depression, awareness and regulation of emotions.

MIMBT: protocol

MIMBT lasts nine sessions on a weekly basis, plus one individual one. It gets performed by two MIT therapists who are also mindfulness instructors. The number of participants varies between six and 12. The participants are preferably PD sufferers, especially with prevailing over-control. The protocol structure is modelled on Mindfulness-Based Stress Reduction (MBSR; Kabat-Zinn, 1990; Figure 9.1) and is subdivided into four parts (Figure 9.2).

In the first session mindfulness is presented with explanations and short *rapid commutation* exercises which aim at getting patients to understand experientially how to switch from a type of attention focused on their inner dialogue or mind-wandering (Killingsworth & Gilbert, 2010), to one of watchful awareness. To achieve this switch, therapists get patients to pay attention to body parts, like

Session	Focus	Contents
Session 1	Introduction	Presentation of the training. Rapid commutation exercises.
Sessions 2–4	Body	Body scan; meditation on breathing and sounds; walking meditation; mindful yoga.
Sessions 5–6	Thoughts/emotions	Meditation on flow of consciousness; meditation on positive and negative thoughts and emotions.
Sessions 7–9	Interpersonal schemas	Meditation on distressing interpersonal experiences; interpersonal awareness meditation; meditation on the interpersonal schema: basic, with rescripting and self-compassion.

Figure 9.1 MIMBT structure

feet or hands, or to ambient noises. They thus get the latter to feel how easy it is to switch rapidly, even dozens of times, from one type of attention to another, thus reinforcing their agency over their mental states. Still within the first session, imagery exercises help patients becoming observers of their minds.

The second part – sessions 2–4 – is aimed at learning the basics of mindfulness meditation. The sessions concentrate on anchoring to the body and sensory experience. The meditations, of a gradually increasing length, have as their focus sensations regarding kinesthesia of posture, the whole body (body scan) and certain bodily functions (breathing, seeing, hearing, walking). The instructions formulated by an operator follow the typical structure of meditations described in mindfulness manuals (Kabat-Zinn, 1990; Segal, Williams, & Teasdale, 2002), so that we are not going to repeat them here. At this stage patients learn to use the body as an emotional self-regulation tool.

The third part, sessions 5–6, focuses on observing the mind. The core of these sessions is meditations on thought flow, positive thoughts/emotions and negative ones. In this case too the structure of the meditations is shared with other mindfulness-based approaches. The start is again anchoring to the body involving paying attention to posture and breathing. Patients are then asked to pose as observers of any thought or emotions emerging, without judging or criticising them and without becoming involved with them. They only have to take note of what passes through their minds: thoughts, emotions, desires, aversions, etc., and the bodily states correlated to them.

In these sessions we help patients to identify repetitive thought strategies they use most to handle distressing mental states and learn to defuse them with anchoring to the body, disidentification with the contents of thought and non-judgemental observation of their thought flow.

The fourth stage covers sessions 7–9 and focuses on interpersonal themes. The core is constituted by *interpersonal meditations* and *meditations on interpersonal schemas*. We describe this part in detail because it is the one most specific to MIT.

Interpersonal meditations are conducted in pairs and aim at increasing awareness of what being-with-the-other evokes. Patients pay attention to thoughts, emotions and bodily states springing from the presence of the other in the exercise. For example, in one of these paired meditations with eyes shut each focuses on the breathing he feels in his abdomen. At the sound of cymbals both open their eyes and direct them towards their partner's abdomen, watching her breathing and trying to attune to it. When the cymbals sound again, both raise their gaze to look in their partner's eyes, without communicating anything but just to note the sensation of being with the other. The link to breathing is maintained in the background while the majority of attention is directed at the other's eyes. To modulate the intensity of the experience, one can shift one's gaze towards one's partner's abdomen or even close one's eyes until one is not ready to look at the other's eyes again. When the cymbals sound again, both close their eyes and stay in the company of the reverberations of the experience. Afterwards the meditation gets wound up and experiences are shared in the group.

In another interpersonal meditation, after induction – awareness of posture and breathing – at the sound of the cymbals one of the pair has to talk about one emotionally marked autobiographical episode. While speaking, she should simultaneously pay attention to her feet. The other should listen without intervening and try to pay attention to the person speaking. He is also instructed, while listening, to divert part of his attention to the sensations arising from his feet. After about two minutes one therapist sounds the cymbals and asks everybody to stop where they are and be aware of thoughts, emotions and bodily sensations. A pause and then again the cymbals signal the dialogical exercise is starting again. After another two minutes, there is another stop and then another awareness exercise covering the body, and thoughts and emotions provoked by the story. One therapist then sounds the cymbals and asks the couples to switch roles. The procedure is repeated over again.

Meditations on interpersonal schemas are not carried out in pairs. Their interpersonal nature lies in the fact that they are focused on the analysis of schema-correlated relational memories. Therapists evoke these memories in one individual session, happening between the third and fourth stage, immediately before session 7. The therapist asks patients to pick out three schema-correlated memories, each to be worked on in sessions 7–9. The memories are put in an order based on the degree of suffering they generate. The least distressing is tackled first and the most at the end.

Meditation on schemas starts with induction. Then one therapist asks patients to leave their bodies in the background so their distressing interpersonal memory emerges. He then asks patients to inhabit the scene until they stop the individual frame with the highest emotional intensity. Once a scene has been settled on, the therapist helps patients to identify its psychological elements, in line with the schema formulation.

First, patients are asked to identify the wish from which their distressing episode springs. They are then led to explore in detail self's reaction to the other's response: emotional ("What do I feel at this moment?") and cognitive ("What is passing through my mind at this moment?") responses, physical ("What does my body feel at this moment?") and action tendencies ("How do I feel like responding?"; "What do I want to do?").

Note the use therapists make of the present tense, despite referring to reactions not experienced in the here and now, but recalled. The suggestion sounds more or less like: "At this moment, in the scene I am now reliving, what am I feeling?" rather than "At that moment, in that scene, what did I feel?". This is with the aim of getting the patients to more intensely internalize the image, so to let them relive it in the most embodied way possible and simultaneously sidestep reasoning and deductions that would distance them from the experience. Immediately afterwards the patients are asked to identify thoughts, evaluations and emotions emerging in the here and now of their being observers of the distressing scene. Therapists now suggest: "Ask yourself: what do I feel now, when seeing myself again in that scene? What judgements do I tend to express?"

Now the analysis of the scene is over, patients are asked to let go of the image and stay aware, letting the sensations flow. The only instruction therapists give is to let any schema-dependent reaction flow, to identify it in their body and at the present moment, while at the same time avoiding going back to the scene or yielding to the temptation to think it over. Lastly, participants are encouraged to return to the sensation of breathing and combine it with a wider awareness including a perception of the environment and the presence of others. They stay in this state of open awareness until the cymbals sound.

MIMBT builds two meditations on this structure. One of these – session 8 – includes *rescripting*, where a healthy self-part comes on stage and tries to promote the satisfaction of the primary wish. The second – session 9 – contains a section devoted to *self-acceptance*, benevolence and self-kindness. This part starts after letting go of the distressing image and accepting the residual bodily sensations; patients are now asked to let go of their negative emotions and to adopt a stance involving seeking kindness, and benevolent attention towards the self gets promoted.

Attentional and mindfulness techniques in sequence with other techniques: a clinical case

The techniques described here are delivered in combination with the others expounded in this book. As we shall explain in Chapter 11, when therapists deliver techniques in sequence, they anchor themselves to the decision-making procedure (Chapter 4) in order to decide which techniques to select, in what order and according to what rationale. We illustrate their intertwining with a clinical example.

The first is a woman treated in one and the same session with various techniques: induction through repetition of emotionally charged words and two-chairs with anchoring to the body. The second is a girl with a traumatic history, treated with induction through the technique of viewing emotionally charged images and a modified version of the attentional space splitting technique.

In the two cases some techniques get used for the inducing of problematical emotional states, others for emotional self-regulation and yet others for planning adaptive behaviour, in patients having already performed a substantial part of the therapeutic work and completed the joint formulation of functioning stage.

Giorgia

Giorgia was a teacher aged 45 with Dependent and Narcissistic PD. She came for therapy because she had been blocked for a long time in her writing of her doctoral thesis after receiving criticism from one of her tutors. Her interpersonal schema was: wished to be appreciated but considered herself worthless. However, she harboured an alternative, strong self-image; she expected that, if she displayed her skills, others would despise her, thus causing her humiliation. The self's response is: 1) sees the criticism to be unfair, feels angry and reacts aggressively; 2) sees the criticism to be fair – sign of confirmation of the unworthy core self-image, feels despondent and ruminates over its limited worth.

Giorgia described her husband as dominating, socially successful and narcissistic. In their relationship competitive and sado-masochisticic cycles easily got activated (Dimaggio et al., 2007). A typical situation was her husband making veiled, never explicit, comments, oozing contempt and deprecation, which activated her core self-as-unworthy image. Giorgia felt hurt and reacted with anger and verbal aggressions, which made her husband respond by closing up disdainfully. Giorgia now saw herself as mentally ill and felt shame, which made her yielding and suppliant. At the end of these interpersonal cycles Giorgia was dominated by a deep sense of unworthiness.

Once she had grasped her dysfunctional schema and interpersonal cycle, which got repeated especially with her husband, Giorgia felt frustration over her own angry reactions swelling inside her. In one session she asserted she was not capable of responding differently, although she had fully grasped the consequences of her behaviour: "At such moments the words don't come to me. I'd like to hit him and I've done it too in the past. Now I don't do it anymore but I can't manage to speak or communicate what I've grasped and how much he, with his barbed criticism, hits my sore points and wounds me."

The therapist, therefore, proposed she tried talking with her husband in-session using two-chairs (Chapter 6). He asked her to imagine her husband's critical and disdainful face and try to tell him the things she had just said. Giorgia quickly entered the role but felt "a weight on her chest" and got blocked. She could not manage to speak: "All I can do is insult him." At this point the therapist decided to do some role-playing to provoke a powerful activation of her schema, but in a context where she felt freer to express herself. The therapist would play her husband and he forewarned Giorgia he would aim the same criticism and accusation at her, even more explicitly, so as to activate the schema and correlated emotions. Giorgia accepted.

T (*husband*): "Okay, let's start. Giorgia, you're an insubstantial person, with weak nerves. You act just with your guts. You're not able to think but only to

attack blindly and violently [*pause: goes back to talking from the therapist' position*]. Giorgia, how did you feel while I told you these things?"
G: "I felt the weight. I still can. I wanted to yell."

The therapist ensured her emotionality was tolerable and it was.

T: "Okay, Giorgia, we've seen that your schema, with its worthless and harmful self-image, got easily activated and caused you the emotions we know well. Shall we try and do the role-playing again? However, this time I'd ask you, while listening to ne, to pay a share of your attention to a body part. Which is the one you feel most?"
G: "My chest, where I've got the weight."
T: "Let's choose another, because that part is a place where your body displays negative emotion. It is a part very present in you, including when you argue with your husband. If we paid attention to it, your negative emotions would probably grow instead of subsiding. What could be a more neutral part? Breathing, hands, feet?"
G: "Let's try with my hands."
T: "Good. Then I'll say some words to you evoking emotions. Let's start [*playing her husband*]: Giorgia, you're a mediocre and sick person, and with your reactions you make me and our children feel uneasy. As a mother you're worthless. As a person you're worthless [*goes back to adopting the therapist position*]. Okay, Giorgia, how did it go this time? What did you notice?"
G: "Look, I felt the weight, but it was a bit less strong. However, my hands got hot and sweaty and were trembling. In the past I've used them to hit my husband."
T: "Okay, it looks like focusing on your hands on the one hand slightly lessened your emotions, but on the other hand your hands are themselves, like your chest, an area where your emotions nestle. If you agree, I'd try again while taking as a reference point a more neutral body part."

Giorgia accepted and chose her feet. The scene got repeated again and unfolded in the same way as previously. This time Giorgia's emotional response was much more limited: "I felt the harshness of your words again but was like a spectator of what was happening to me rather than participating."

T: "Good, Giorgia. Now let's try two-chairs again, like we did at the start. You expressed the wish to be able to find the right words to tell your husband how he hurts you. You got blocked before. Let's see if you now manage better. Try and address yourself directly to him and tell him what is on your mind and that you usually don't manage to express. Feel free to act as you want, even to scream. My only recommendation: both when you play yourself and when you take on your husband's role, don't lose sight of your feet. Okay?"

Giorgia asked for the instructions to be repeated, to be sure she had understood correctly, and accepted. When she played her husband, she was violent and deprecating and then stayed still waiting for a response. The therapist asked her to change chairs and return to playing herself. Giorgia now replied forcefully but calmly and decisively.

G: "Look Marco, these things you say to me are violent and disdainful. They hurt and grieve me and drive me to react. They're unfair and nasty. Don't do it again. Say it differently or keep quiet, but don't address me like that, because now you know that like that you wound me."
T: "How did you feel during the game? And how do you feel now?"

Giorgia replied she now felt content and not angry with herself. During the scene she reported with a certain surprise that she noticed her emotions were increasing, but she stayed in control. The anger was still there, even more evident than in the past, but it monopolised her mental stage less thanks to the anchoring to her feet.

Alessia

Alessia was 25 and had Narcissistic PD with major depression and PTSD. She sought therapy after being left, six months earlier, by her boyfriend. Her distress was still very strong and got stoked by endless rumination cycles: "Why did he leave me?"; "Was it my fault or his?" She also ruminated angrily, thinking herself to be stupid, superficial and devil-may-care. With a more careful analysis it emerged that her distressing self-image was *unlovable/deserving abandonment*. By association they traced that this was linked to her sister's death several years earlier from leukemia. She reckoned then she had been left alone because she deserved it. Her suffering in the present developed as follows: even trivial stimuli reminded her of her ex and Alessia activated her wishful thinking, dwelt on these memories and savoured the joys of them. As she gradually went on, the feelings of loss and loneliness and the idea of not deserving to be loved increased. Simultaneously she felt she deserved love (*positive self-image*) but faced with another who deceived and cheated her. She now ruminated, which increased her anger and depressed her.

In the first few months the therapist used imagery with rescripting to process the memories linked to her grief for her sister. Alessia got rapidly better and seemed to have almost completely recovered: she no longer thought about her ex. After about eight months the therapy switched to meeting once every 15 days and then once a month. However, after the summer break she had a relapse: she was ruminating again about her ex.

The therapist realised that in the period before the holidays Alessia had shifted to her coping self-image, linked to rank: strong and completely independent. This change in direction could not last long, and in fact on her first encountering of difficulty and loneliness her attachment got reactivated and her non-lovable image re-emerged, with the associated ruminating. Alessia again used dysfunctional coping behaviour: going on social networks to see photos of her ex with his new partner. The photos naturally activated abandonment and competition schemas (she felt inferior). She immediately shifted again to rank, her coping schema: vis-à-vis another deserting her and preferring her rival, she reacted by feeling strong and entitled to react to get herself respected, by subjugating the other.

After a new joint formulation of functioning, the therapist proposed first inducing her schemas through the viewing of emotionally charged images – the photos on social networks – and then the splitting of attentional space. So Alessia went on Facebook, found a picture of her ex with his new girlfriend and, at the therapist's suggestion, concentrated on it. She felt an intense anger and located it in her chest.

T: "On what parts of the photo is your gaze resting on?"
A: "The girl."
T: "What do you feel and what comes to your mind?"
A: "Anger. I ask myself how he could have, what he can have found in her that . . ."
T: "Okay, now shift your gaze to the picture of him. What do you feel?"
A: "I find him handsome. In any case . . . despite everything . . . I like him."
T: "Good. Now let your hands drop down by your seat and pay attention to the sensations coming from there, but without taking your eyes off the girl. Stay for a few seconds with your attention divided between the image and your hands and try to have both of them simultaneously in your field of awareness [*a few seconds of silence*]. Can you?"
A: "Yes . . ."
T [*a few seconds of silence*]: "How's that sensation in your chest going? Do you notice anything?"
A: "Much less. I almost don't feel it any more. I'm generally much less tense."
T: "What relationship do you have now with the image? Are you thinking about it or simply observing it?"
A: "I'm observing it. I'm not moving . . ."
T: "Good. Now shift your gaze to him and then to her, without losing the attention to your hands. Watch if you start ruminating or manage to stay in an observer position [*a few seconds of silence*]. Can you? Do you notice anything?"
A: "Yes, I can. I'm not moving and I'm observing."
T: "What do you notice in your chest? And your body?"
A: "I can't feel anything in my chest. I'm okay."

After the exercise the therapist asked Alessia for her immediate impressions and then discussed the implications of what occurred with her. He concentrated particularly on how much it was in Alessia's power to enter the ruminative/wishful mode and simultaneously exit it. Alessia thus realised empirically she could control her rumination and wishful thinking, and her meta-beliefs about the uncontrollability of her worry were false. She also very clearly realised that the pain, now brief but intense, was the vestige of that she felt for her sister's death but did not indicate she was unlovable.

Attentional techniques in the concluding therapy stages and in preventing relapses

MIT includes various steps, all with their kit of cognitive, imagery, drama and bodily techniques. Nevertheless, at a very advanced treatment stage therapists progressively focus onbehavioural exposure and counteracting IRT (Chapter 11). At such moments the interventions described here, aimed at reducing IRT are fundamental. In the final psychotherapy stages, patients often manage to act healthily, in line with their wishes, but IRT can continue to disturb them. The therapist then asks them to perseveringly apply attentional remodulation and mindfulness techniques to block it, so as to devote time and energy to their own healthy goals and wishes.

CHAPTER 10

Metacognitive Interpersonal Therapy in Group (MIT-G)

PD patients experience interpersonal exchanges problematically. Driven by schemas they act automatically in a way preventing them from satisfying their wishes. Their limited metacognition prevents them from realising what leads them to have relational problems and from changing course. Group therapy could be a safe place for becoming aware of one's schema-related behaviours and functioning (Karterud, 2015) and learning the ability to act under the guidance of a richer mentalistic understanding of self and others.

We describe here a structured psychoeducational/experiential group programme, aimed at helping patients to 1) reflect on what they and others think and feel during social exchanges; 2) adopt new perspectives on social interactions and act more flexibly and adaptively. Group work can be based on ideas that humans are driven by a set of evolutionarily selected motives (Ivaldi, 2017; Prunetti, Bosio, Bateni, & Liotti, 2013), so the programme begins with providing patients with information on the motives underlying social interactions. We then ask them to role-play significant episodes where they were driven by a specific motive. During role-playing participants practise how to use awareness of mental states to tackle relational problems so as to increase the likelihood of fulfilling their wishes. This means increasing metacognitive mastery.

Participants interact with each other and try to identify the elements distinguishing their interpersonal schemas. Feedback received from others about their convictions or the actions they perform helps them to see their functioning from a different perspective. This also helps them to reason about what others think, once free of their negative and schema-dependent attributions. It is therefore possible to slowly open up the other's mind and make it an area to be read with curiosity instead of a place where we delude ourselves that we know everything, or that we consider incomprehensible and dangerous.

During role-playing participants try to handle the situations staged by resorting to their usual methods. Thanks to the dialogue with others, however, they can see things differently, think of new solutions to problems and simultaneously inspire those others with new strategies for handling relational difficulties.

We first manualised Metacognitive Interpersonal Therapy in Group (MIT-G; Popolo et al., 2018, 2019) and then empirically tested it. In initial randomised pilot research (Popolo et al., 2019) the compliance with MIT-G was high (two drop-outs out of 10) and so was the participation (92.19% participation in sessions). At the end of the treatment a significant improvement in symptoms and interpersonally was observed and this was maintained at the next follow-up three months later. The patients displayed a metacognitive improvement: their comprehension of their own mental states and ability to understand mental states and regulate social interactions based on this mentalistic knowledge increased. These were patients with a predominant emotional inhibition (Dimaggio et al., 2018). The results were repeated successfully in pilot research in real-life conditions in a public mental health service (Popolo et al., 2018). Other research in Spain included patients with borderline traits (Inchausti et al., 2020) and results were quite encouraging here too, with participants improving as regards symptoms, functioning and impulsivity.

We present here the general features of MIT-G to show how in groups it is possible to promote awareness of the motivations driving human behaviour, recognise one's interpersonal schemas and use role-play to improve social action thanks to the increase in metacognition.

In this chapter we describe the stand-alone form MIT-G, but it can be flexibly used in parallel to individual MIT, by introducing it at any moment.

MIT-G: general principles

MIT-G includes psychoeducational and experiential aspects. Groups include five to 10 participants. The protocol is addressed particularly to PD patients with inhibited-overcontrolled characteristics, poor metacognition and tendencies swing rigidly and repetitively among a very few mental states when living through relational experiences. As we already said, an adaptation including patients with emotional dysregulation is currently being validated, with sessions starting with mindfulness exercises to promote affect regulation (Inchausti et al., 2020).

MIT-G goals are twofold: promoting metacognition and learning more complex interpersonal relationship handling skills to maximise the odds of fulfilling one's wishes. When patients understand the emotions they feel when others judge them, they court a person they are attracted by and so on, this can help them interpret what is happening without seeing it through their schemas and thus adopt more adaptive and context-appropriate behaviours. Metacognition can be trained (Semerari et al., 2003) and groups are a kind of a relational learning ground. What drives human behaviour can also be learnt.

Everybody experiences difficulties when trying to fulfil one or more motives, as schemas are very often tied to a specific one: some, for example, suffer when driven by social rank, others when driven by attachment, others still because of inhibition of their exploration. When participants are taught these motivations are human, many of their actions acquire more sense to their eyes, in a context where they learn what typically happens to human beings when these motives are switched on. They understand their intentions, thoughts and feelings are normal and discover some of the typical ways people react when facing someone driven by a specific motive.

MIT-G is composed of 16 weekly sessions, lasting two hours each, during which therapists describe basic interpersonal motivations (Chapter 1): 1) competition/social rank, 2) affiliation/belonging, 3) attachment, 4) caregiving, 5) exploratory, 6) sexual and 7) co-operative. Two sessions get devoted to each system – three for the co-operative one, which has shown itself to be the motive patients have most difficulty activating; the last session is devoted to a free debate among participants about their experience during the programme.

Three individual sessions with each patient are foreseen, the first before the start, the second around the middle and the third at the end. With the first there is a collection of the material needed for case formulation. Therapists try to evoke narrative episodes involving the problems reported by patients so as to construct a structured summary of these events (Chapter 4), following the interpersonal schema structure. The middle session is for finding out how patients feel in the group and whether there are obstacles to the therapeutic work or relational problems with other participants. Let us consider, for example, patients displaying poor narrative skills, acting with little spontaneity and having to be directly asked to be involved. In this intermediate session the therapist assesses whether poor communication is the consequence of a self-reflectivity malfunctioning blocking access to personal contents, or of inhibition resulting from feeling excluded and criticised during group sessions.

Generally, in the individual sessions therapists and patients assess how any metacognitive or interpersonal difficulties are influencing group therapy. The goal is to promote engagement and prevent drop-outs. Therapists can attempt to link the episodes related in individual sessions with what patients have related in group or the interaction patterns emerging between them and other members and assess whether maladaptive interpersonal schemas are in course. An example is a participant talking in the intermediate session about feeling excluded during a party.

T: "This sense of exclusion you reported at your friend's party already surfaced in your individual session and was why you sought psychological help. We've seen you feel the need to be with others and suffer loneliness, but when you approach others you sense they are rejecting you and this makes you feel criticised and excluded because you feel inferior. This happens to you not only in social situations like parties, but also in intimate relationships. In this case you feel you get excluded because of the negative judgement you receive. This tears you down, but it also makes you angry as you consider it unfair. You expressed your anger to the extent that your partner threw you out of the house. Now your anger makes you feel strong, but if you follow it, you'll live in a state of constant fighting and this is exhausting, and doesn't help in overcoming loneliness. To find different ways to those you act automatically we need to grasp how you interpret the situation and see yourself and others when you enter a relationship. You told me, for example, referring to the group: 'they were all outside the office waiting to enter as a group and I went past and just kept going'. At that moment what did you think, when you saw them all together? How did you feel?"

The therapist summarised her experience in the various contexts in line with her schema structure, validated her emotional experience and stressed the need to understand the psychological antecedents of her dysfunctional forms of relating. At this moment, once patients have realised they are driven by schemas, one can show how their dysfunctional interpersonal cycles get activated. Patients are simultaneously asked to think there are alternative forms of relating with which they could break up their schemas and exit cycles:

> In a situation where you feel excluded by others, you see them as devaluing and rejecting you. You then tend to implement self-assertion strategies to be able to recover a positive self-image. You want to get revenge and show it: with your mother, your partner and in the group. This form, on the one hand human and understandable, doesn't in the end lead to recovering closeness. The others instead back off more precisely because of the conflict underway. As we've seen in our sessions, this form isn't wrong in itself and can sometimes be useful. But we need to find other strategies too and have the hope they'll be more effective.

During the last individual session patients describe their experience in the group, what they learnt about their interpersonal functioning and what they feel they master better. They also plan how to use what they have learnt from the group in everyday life, to tackle any residual problems.

Session structure

Every session is composed of two parts, 1) psychoeducational and 2) experiential. Therapists need to be MIT-certified. They tend to have distinct roles, one more focused on providing education on the sessions' motivation topics, the other guiding role-play and the subsequent discussion. The roles are not rigid, and they can shift between sessions or intervene while the other is taking the lead, provided they are attuned.

Psychoeducation

Sessions start with "warming-up", during which participants talk freely among themselves for a few minutes, discussing general questions, topics dealt with in the previous session, any difficulties encountered and attempts in daily life to tackle relational problems. This is free time during which the therapists regulate the group's emotional atmosphere by stimulating interpersonal exchanges, and validate experiences reported by participants, with a non-judgemental stance; participants should be encouraged to express themselves freely and overcome fears of being judged for what they say. Warming-up can occur in various ways, as cultural contexts change. For example, colleagues in Norway working with seriously avoidant and socially inhibited patients, start groups with sport to create a playful and relaxed atmosphere, and a sense of belonging (Zahl, 2018).

Now true psychoeducation begins. Therapists take around 10 minutes to describe a motive: what it is, what pushes humans to act, what are its triggers, and what emotions and behaviour emerge when this impulse to act is active. They pay attention to illustrating what someone expects from another when driven by a certain motive and what responses they could typically receive. They then show how humans usually react to the other's behaviour.

Every motivation takes two sessions. During the first the therapists describe motivations generally, the activating conditions and typical emotions associated with them. During the second they go deeper into the relational dynamics typical of that motive, what someone expects from the other in such situations, others' potential responses and how humans react when tackling particular reactions.

Psychoeducation needs to be entertaining and emotionally involving. Patients thus see themselves tackling similar difficulties, experiencing the same distress at feeling neglected when they need care, or expecting to be promoted at work and then seeing the job given to a less qualified colleague.

Therapists can use amusing descriptions for motivations, explaining, for example, social rank with animals challenging each other when courting a partner. We also use video material on animal behaviour, with the aim of creating a playful atmosphere. Therapists later use relational examples close to daily experience and thus easily comprehensible precisely because they are common. They can, for example, describe the submissiveness experienced when receiving an order from one's boss that one feels unfair or the feeling of being an outsider when arriving at a new job.

In the first session devoted to each motivation therapists describe the elements activating it: what drives one to compete, seek attention, explore and so on, and what type of emotions we feel while pursuing this goal and not achieving it. We can feel subjugated and humiliated if we receive an unfair order, embarrassed if we do not know what to say in the presence of strangers or sad if our sweetheart leaves on a long trip.

During the second session about a motive, therapists describe the relational dynamics, behaviour activated and typical interpersonal cycles. One can, talking of group inclusion, use the example of a timid person feeling different from others and fearing being criticised. He tries then to become invisible. This coping leads others to ignore him and think he is not interested in mixing with them. The timid person gets ever more convinced he is light years away from others.

While presenting this illustrative material, Therapists pay attention to participants' non-verbal communication, to adjust their own exposure so as to stimulate greater involvement. They can accordingly prefer narrative examples related verbally or resort to descriptions on the blackboard with diagrams and figures.

Therapists can directly involve participants with simple questions, by asking for comments on the topic being discussed, without embarking on a debate or getting personal contents to emerge. The language also needs to be adjusted to the context, with a preference for expressions like: "It's possible this happened to us . . .", "It may have happened to us . . ." or "It's likely to happen that . . ." to underline the universality of the motivations in question and avoid patients who realise they have problems when driven by a specific motivation feeling negatively judged by others.

In the final sessions therapists underline the differences among the various motivations, what pushes one to switch from one system to another, and the potential links among them. Consider a young man getting sexually excited when meeting an attractive girl. However, he immediately thinks he must win her to demonstrate his worth: the competition system has replaced the sexual one. Showing patients how to shift from one motive to another is particularly beneficial, because it helps them to grasp how they function in real life and how these shifts are typical and normal.

To create a curious and playful atmosphere, therapists use photographs, cartoons, videos, documentaries or animated films to illustrate the dynamics linked to the particular motive: stories with separations and losses, wooing, caregiving or struggles for power. This visual material catches attention, is a quick way to illustrate concepts and involves images that get imprinted on memory. The lights get turned down and, after joking and laughing together before the projection, the participants experience images, sounds and dialogues from scenes selected because they powerfully evoke the motivation being talked about. The projecting of videos consolidates knowledge of the relational dynamics described previously. For this reason, before the viewing, therapists can ask participants to link a video to the features discussed here.

After watching or listening to this video or audio material, lasting about 10 minutes, a group freely expresses its impressions. The purpose of this dialogue is to clarify any doubts and share emotional reactions and thoughts. A video, in fact, stimulates identification processes and the emerging of personal memories and reflections that participants now express. Therapists try to render the links between the theoretical part, videos and narrative episodes as clear and explicit as possible.

To summarise, psychoeducation starts by supplying theoretical material about a specific motivation and then videos and cartoons are displayed. The next step is a free discussion for about 20 minutes. Each patient is able to express his/her impressions of the video and of the material displayed during the theoretical part, re-evoke relational experiences and recall the thoughts and emotions experienced or behaviour implemented in particular situations. Patients can in this way remain in contact with the sensations that the topics presented arouse. It is easier to pinpoint the activating of the belongingness system if one recalls the sensation felt when seeing Al Pacino kindling group spirit in the changing rooms in the film *Any Given Sunday*. One grasps immediately how the competition system works, if, during an argument with a colleague who would like his way of doing things to prevail, one thinks of Derek Zoolander who, in the film of that name, has to deal with Hansel to demonstrate he is still the number one model.

Participants can then express their associations or contribute to reflecting upon the memories re-evoked by the others. Participants then link the psychoeducational information to their own experiences and reflections. During the discussion therapists do not steer participants' responses or pose pre-established questions.

Everyone can take the floor, without any particular order but without occupying the shared space too much. Therapists try to see what the participants have understood. Are their comments apposite to the session topic? Are the personal episodes associated consistent with the motivation described? If this is not so, therapists explain the motivation again and help patients to see that in their narrative there were instead other motivations active and these will be covered in later sessions or have already been in previous ones. Therapists are firm about preventing abstract or moralistic interventions and ask for the narrating of specific episodes. When patients associate personal memories or sensations experienced during the projecting or while they listened to other group members' narratives to, for example, videos, therapists validate the pertinence of their observations without however reasoning about them more than this. After the discussion therapists make a summary helping to recall the links between theory and personal material.

In the earliest sessions, participants can feel awkward and disoriented. They have doubts about what to say: "Can I tell about what happened to me that time?", "In my opinion what he said has nothing to do with what we're saying . . . but who knows if I've got it right?"; "Perhaps we just need to comment on the videos". They do not know when to intervene: "Do we have to wait for the doctors to ask us something?" They can have the idea that the contents of their reflections are inappropriate: "I recall an episode but it's of little interest." This blockage can depend on how patients foresee others' responses: "They'll think I'm an idiot and haven't understood any of it." As sessions proceed, an underlying familiarity builds up among the participants, thanks to which they worry less and express themselves more freely.

Therapists need to let everybody speak and to regulate the emotional atmosphere. They start the discussion with open questions like: "How did this film seem to you? Did it make you think or remember something? What did you feel while the film was being shown?"

If a discussion has difficulty taking off, therapists try to identify the problem. If, for example, it is a question, frequent in early sessions, of embarrassment, therapists can resort to humour, pose generic questions about the video just ended or also express a personal opinion about the video, to explain how it was chosen, express the first impression they had on seeing it or simply say whether they like a particular actor. Practically this involves some self-disclosures as *icebreakers*.

Problems starting a discussion can also be linked to difficulties fully understanding the video's message: "What happened? Why did the character behave like that?" Therapists can summarise scenes by suggesting what the roles performed by the various characters were and the type of exchange unfolding among them, before giving the discussion space back to the group.

Participants can have difficulty linking the video contents with those expounded in the theoretical part: "But what has this video got to do with attachment?" Therapists' response to this is to summarise together with the patients the events in the scene just watched, reminding them of the dynamics typical of the motivation in question and then helping them to make the links between the video and theory.

In the first session on a motive, therapists can ask participants if they recognise the activation, deactivation and typical emotions of a motivation in the characters in a film. In the second session there is a discussion of the relational dynamics among the actors: what happened among them? What did they do and what were they driven by? What impact did they have on the others? Were their attempts successful? With the discussion reactivated, therapists return to intervening only with the purpose of avoiding intellectualising, if, for example, participants tend to act like "movie critics" as regards a video. Therapists return to asking participants whether they have ever had similar experiences to those in the film. In the second session on each motivation they pose questions like: "What do you people feel in such situations? And what do you do to tackle these thoughts and emotions, and these difficulties?"

Sometimes some patients talk simultaneously or do not pay attention to each other. A competition rises and participants try to win territory or make their own ideas prevail. In this case therapists intervene to avoid the discussion becoming a slanging match and refocus attention on linking the personal material with that illustrated with theory and videos. The purpose is to re-establish the group's mentalising functioning (Karterud, 2015).

We repeat that if a patient reports autobiographical memories associated with the topics tackled, therapists do not work them through as in individual sessions. They confine themselves to observing whether they are relevant to the motive at stake. They try to reconstruct the relational dynamics described in these episodes in the light of information supplied previously: "So you were driven by rank and feared criticism, right?" The other participants can comment on the episode and imagine alternative endings. A therapist can now show how one and the same situation lends itself to various interpretations.

The experiential stage: narrative episodes and role-playing

The experiential stage begins after a brief pause. In the first session devoted to each motive the objective is to stimulate knowledge of mental states, both one's own and those of other actors. In the second session, as well as improving the reading of one's own and others' minds, the goal of building strategies to tackle relational problems gets added.

Therapists ask participants to write a brief autobiographical episode where they are actors in an interaction with one or more people, in a scene where they consider they were driven by the motive described during psychoeducation. The explicit goal is to obtain a script that can be staged in the next role-playing.

In reality, already during the writing, patients train their metacognition as they contact emotions and thoughts arising at that moment, and guess what the characters in the story are driven by. Patients need to understand what the story is about, by catching the core elements and then connecting them to personal episodes. Sometimes memories laden with suffering resurface. At other times patients have difficulty recalling rich and detailed autobiographical memories. Many are not used to concentrating on narrative episodes and only manage to recall those linked to their own distressing schemas, often restricted to one motive. They can therefore have difficulty recalling one in the 10 minutes available when talking about motives not at the roots of their schema.

Therapists try not to make patients see this stage as a task and ask for episodes like this: "Try and write an episode from your life in which you think and feel that the motive of which we spoke today got activated. Focus on the wish that was driving you, being appreciated for example (or loved, or included in the group) and on how things went, for example if, instead of being appreciated, you were criticised. If possible, think about an episode during which you experienced some type of difficulty."

Therapists invite participants to describe the scene as clearly as possible, by indicating first the space (where) and time (when) boundaries within which it takes place. They then have to identify the characters present, in as much detail as possible, starting with their age, sex, job and type of relation to the narrator, and the set of actions unfolding. Narrations by PD patients do not always comply with these requirements (Dimaggio et al., 2007): the unfolding of the action may be ill-defined and the time boundaries vague, while characters appear generic and the motives driving them to act unclear. Some relate brief episodes, with a simple plot and poor in thoughts and emotions, while others do not know how to choose one.

Therapists then choose among the written episodes the one seeming most relevant to the topic presented and experienced with the greatest involvement and subjective suffering by the author, even if not completely matching the features sought. In this case, however, before staging the role-playing, therapists ask for further details about when and where it happened, who was present and how the action unfolded.

During role-playing, participants have to face the difficulties they usually meet in relationships but in a safer context. In everyday exchanges there is no time to stop and analyse what is happening and seek optimal solutions to problems. Role-playing offers a protected space where patients can reflect on their own and others' behaviour; doing it with others can facilitate and enrich the understanding of events and also the identifying of new strategies for managing relationships.

At this stage therapists guide the preparation and carrying out of role-playing. In particular, in the role-playing in the first session about each motive they try to draw out self-reflectivity, while in the second session the experiential part has the drawing up of new and more effective strategies, starting with a better understanding of others' minds, as its focus.

Michael was 22 and since his time at middle school he had had few friends. The youngest of four children he was the only one left living at home with his parents. He had Narcissistic PD and sought psychological help because he went out rarely with friends and led an ever more secluded life because he "had to study a lot". When talking about the competition motivation he wrote this autobiographical episode:

> Last summers of my infancy/early youth. My grandmother's and great uncles' country house, with my first and second cousins. "Cops and Robbers", a game on which we spent the majority of our summer days and we could do it not

least because my cousins lived in a big house, with an enormous garden, full of bushes, arable fields and other houses, often uninhabited.

There was also a competition about who was the most athletic, fastest at running, best at hiding, best at finding or most cunning. Being the smallest physically until a few years ago and growing very late, I was always the one most in difficulty and also the easiest target. I remember I looked for ruses, to get away from the cops or trap the robbers, depending on my role. To sum up, I felt inferior and this made me annoyed and sometimes resigned.

Despite a suitable description of an episode centred on competition, Michael did not relate a narrative located in time and space. He only managed to report a general representation of himself as "physically" inadequate and inferior to his cousins, in a recurring situation. Only at the end of this passage did he talk of emotions but vaguely, with terms like "annoyed" and "resigned", not linked in any case to specific moments in an interaction.

The material needed by a clinician was not yet emerging: details on how the action unfolded, the emotions experienced and the thoughts connected to them. In line with the decision-making procedure, the therapist aimed primarily at obtaining a detailed narrative episode. He told Michael he had chosen this passage and asked him to recall a specific moment linked to what he had written:

T: "Well, I've chosen your episode, Michael, but to stage it better I need to ask you a few questions. Can you remember some specific episode, where you hoped to be appreciated but they gave you responses that made you feel inferior?"
M: "There are loads of episodes."

Michael got emotionally activated: he was satisfied about being selected but felt he was being tested, with all eyes on him. He feared criticism and this impaired his ability to remember. The therapist first kept a validating attitude and, when he saw that Michael's embarrassment and fear of criticism had decreased, asked again for a narrative episode located in time and space. In doing so he referred to the emotions the patient had mentioned in his text, to get him closer to his experience but without making him feel obliged to.

T: "If you search in your memories, could you tell us of a specific moment where you felt this sensation of annoyance and resignation in thinking you had no hope of getting the appreciation that you moreover felt you deserved?"
M: "Hmm, it's difficult . . . [*after a few seconds*] I remember that evening. I must have been 10. We were at my grandmother's house. My cousins were getting the teams organised and the two eldest were discussing which of the two teams I should be in and consequently what to do to balance the fact I was the smallest and so the slowest and least good at chasing, which would have put the team at a disadvantage."
T: "And how did you feel?"
M: "Less good. Inferior."

Michael managed to retrieve a precise memory, with time ("I must have been 10") and space ("we were at my grandmother's house") boundaries, in line with the social rank motive. He also described the characters in the scene and the dynamics among them. The therapist now tried to better define the script, by gathering more information about the characters' inner states. He then posed questions stimulating metacognitive monitoring.

Michael replied to the question about what he experienced with talk of "inferiority" and consequently his emotions remained undefined. The therapist asked him to continue dwelling on his memories of the scene.

T: "Let's try and reason together about what emotions we're talking about. Inferiority . . . what could the emotion have been? What do you feel now when you recall it?"

M: "I wouldn't know. I remember I felt very angry and tried to convince my teammates we'd win and I'd play my part like them. I then ran like mad and hid in the most improbable places, once even in the laundry basket. I was glad if they were amazed at my inventiveness. I wanted them to know that even if I was weak physically, I was also the most intelligent."

With these interventions it was possible to obtain a detailed narrative episode where others' emotions and intentions surfaced, even if still described as a "collective other" (his cousins). One could now see that his narcissistic retaliation was his coping regarding his sense of inferiority. On this basis one could launch role-playing.

Let us start from the choice of actors: who shall we involve in the game? Anyone taking part has to feel free to be able to make the experience their own and learn while playing a role. It is important for actors to not be worried about negative criticism. In the earliest sessions it is good to select people offering themselves of their own accord. After the first two/three sessions, however, it should be recalled that all participants should actively take part over the programme's duration, so that they train their metacognition and do not remain prey to coping involving isolation or closing up.

Once the actors have been chosen, therapists summarise the scenes to be played, resuming the episodes chosen and any consolidation conducted subsequently with the authors themselves. Participants are asked to concentrate on where and when the scene took place. The various characters' characteristics and the relationships among them, plus their intentions, emotions, thoughts and action tendencies before, during and after the scene, at least those surfacing, are again described.

The same script gets acted out twice. The first time the narrator plays herself and the episode described gets acted more or less accurately. The second time there is a change in roles and a participant, another group member, now with the "main character" role, gets the chance to add something personal to the script.

During the role-playing participants are not obliged to comply completely with the script. If, during the acting, unexpected changes emerge, these get accepted. The actors therefore keep playing their parts in accordance with what they feel at that moment. In this case, authors called to play themselves are likely to feel there is a discordance between what they experienced during the episode recalled and what they experience during the role-playing. This is an important moment in that it forces patients to exercise their self-reflective skills, in a social exposure context close to the real world.

Let us return to Michael playing at his grandmother's house with his cousins. The therapist briefly summarised the key elements in the scene to be played for the actors.

T: "The scene unfolds in granny's house. It's summer, in the evening and it's time to play cops and robbers. The eldest cousins are organising the teams and, given that they're five in total, start agreeing on who should take Michael in his team."

Role-playing now started. As we shall see, with the first staging where the author again played himself in the past, he was able to more easily access his inner states, which were instead vague and indistinct when he tried to recall them.

Cousin 1: "Let's make two teams, one with three people and one with two. The one with three will obviously take Michael, who's worth a half, given he's the smallest and weakest."
Cousin 2: "Okay, but then we'll have five bonus points, given there are two of us."
Cousin 3: "At most two bonus points. Michael doesn't count. In fact he's lucky we're letting him play."

During the game the participant playing Cousin 3 started laughing and got the other actors laughing too. Michael's face fell and he lowered his gaze.

M: "What jerks you are. Apart from it not being true that I'm weak. In fact I always manage to find some awesome solutions and you no. So I'm anything but a half. I'm worth at least the double of any of you."
Cousin 1: "Okay, dwarfy [*laughing through his teeth*], now you're the best of anyone here . . . okay, you're right. Just let's get started."
Cousin 4: "Okay three extra points and we'll take Michael. Shall we start??!?"
M: "Now I'll show you, bloody bastards."

All the characters seemed to have taken on their roles and the action was consistent with the story: the actors/cousins and their mocking smile, Michael's anger ("bloody bastards"). In the first session for each motivation, the role-playing terminates when the original episode ends and participants are not called to find new and more adaptive solutions for the problem described but only reflect on the psychological elements at the roots of the actions. In this case we have seen how Michael "really" experienced the emotion he had previously only reconstructed by replying to the questions. Now he felt that anger he had experienced in the past.

During role-playing the other patients participate as observers and are called to carefully assess the unfolding of the game and express their thoughts about what the actors are experiencing, on the basis of non-verbal signals and changes made to the original plot during the game. They should also pay attention to their own emotional reactions, provoked by the acting on stage. The observers should in some sense relive the scene with the actors and make the effort to pick up not only the actors' states but also their own. Therapists stress this aspect to avoid those not on stage disengaging. Role-playing should involve everyone, because it represents an experiential moment when they come into contact with their own inner worlds.

Therapists pay attention to the group atmosphere and the dynamics emerging during role-playing, by watching, for example, for anyone pulling out or commenting under their breath. Attention is also paid to anyone seeming intensely involved emotionally. The emerging of defensive relational attitudes or distressing emotions, difficult to handle subjectively, can be linked to the activation of interpersonal schemas, to the unexpected resurfacing of memories connected to the scene or to identifying with characters on stage. When they see patients getting activated emotionally, therapists watch them during a short, informal dialogue and then ask them to go back to the topic either in individual sessions in the programme or their individual therapy.

After role-playing therapists start the discussion, where participants exchange views about their experiences and thoughts during and after the role-playing. Therapists start with general questions: "Have you any comments on what you saw?", "What do you think happened?"

We pose these questions in the first instance to the observers to allow the actors a moment of *debriefing*. After collecting these observations, therapists ask more specific questions to trigger metacognition. To stimulate self-reflectivity they ask participants to focus on the sensations experienced during the role-playing or at that moment: "What did you feel when you saw that scene? What did you notice when X or Y displayed that emotion or they behaved in that way? What do you feel now thinking back over it?"

Other questions explore theory of mind and the reading of emotions in others: "Have you any idea what drove the characters to act like that?"; "What sort of emotion could that character have felt?" The focus needs to be kept on what happened during role-playing; this, for example, is a very valid reply because it is anchored to the role-playing: "Maria said Luisa felt embarrassed during the game and so she closed the conversation as she could not endure the embarrassment. In fact Luisa lowered her gaze, turned her back and spoke more quietly. It seems that Maria understood Luisa's experience pretty well."

The goal is not to decide which reply is right or wrong, but to stimulate participants' mentalistic reasoning so that they discover, perhaps for the first time, that the same situation can have different interpretations. For this reason, therapists have a validating attitude towards participants' contributions, stressing that each interpretation has a meaning, an individual point of view, for that person. Their relational style is inquisitive, empathic, playful and co-operative, aimed at exploring mental states. Simultaneously they try to block intellectualisations, which say nothing about patient' inner worlds, or abstract or excessively vague concepts. *Non-mentalising* replies are therefore avoided (Bateman & Fonagy, 2004; Karterud, 2015). For example, therapists do not accept replies like "not well" or "unease" or theories about human functioning: "People tend to avoid conflicts because they're not in their interest." Participants should attempt to give precise names to their emotions and make specific hypotheses about what drove a character to perform a specific action in a certain situation. Opinions are also immediately pointed out and discouraged.

When the various participants in role-playing are asked the same questions, therapists take advantage of the vibrant memory of the experience, which ought to make access to inner states simpler: "What did you feel at that moment? What were you thinking of doing? Did you feel you wanted to act differently? What stopped you changing your behaviour? Did what the others do or say influence your experience?"

Let us return again to Michael. After the role-playing one therapist started the discussion and further probed Michael's emotions other than the anger he had already pinpointed. The therapist tried to investigate any other emotional states Michael might have experienced, because in the written episode he had referred generically to possible emotions linked to his feeling of inferiority: "resignation".

T: "Together with anger did you feel some other emotion?"
M: "I don't know. . . . I just remember being very pissed off."

During the discussion Michael did not refer to other emotions and resignation did not surface. The therapist asked him to keep thinking about his emotions while remaining in the scene staged, and supported his metacognitive functioning by suggesting certain non-verbal signals could be indicating the surfacing of specific emotions.

T: "Usually, when one feels inferior to others repeatedly and in different situations, one can also feel a bit sad. I noticed that, while you spoke, you lowered your shoulders for a moment and looked down. Could it be you felt sad then?"
M: "Yes, perhaps a bit of sadness, but anger much more so."

As we can see, the questions are simple, aimed solely at probing emotional monitoring (Semerari et al., 2014). The discussion after role-playing does not follow a rigid order, to allow participants to work through their ideas in their own time and feel free to express their own contents or comment on others'. Therapists moreover directly involve any patients with difficulty expressing themselves and not speaking.

In this discussion, as we saw, Michael resolutely asserted that he experienced a profound state of anger at injustice, which now appeared totally clear to him. He seemed able to pick up only this sthenic emotion and not the sadness the therapist believed he had picked up in his non-verbal communications.

Therapists now pose generic questions to all the observers: "What did you notice? How did it seem to you?" They then go on to more directly stimulate the single self-reflective functions, always anchoring them to the specific moment in the episode: "When you replied like that, your face changed. Correct? Did you feel something at that moment?" Or, addressing the participants: "When Y lowered her eyes after you spoke to her like that, what do you think she felt? How did she feel at that moment?"

We always pose questions while trying to not force out replies; if participants have difficulty or just cannot manage to reply, therapists validate their effort and encourage future reflections: "I realise you felt tense but I'm curious to know more about your inner experience. We'll think about it in future sessions. If possible, try and pay attention to what happens during the coming week and try and identify if you feel some specific emotion in situations in your daily life where you're driven by the motive at stake today."

After probing inner states, there is a switch to reflecting on the subjective nature of ideas, which do not necessarily reflect facts, and the existence of different positions and perspectives. This stimulates differentiation.

Let us return to posing questions, starting from the role-playing actors: "You said that while you were in that role, you felt certain emotions and behaved in a certain way because you were driven by specific thoughts. Can we imagine other ways of interpreting this situation? After our reflections together as a group, did your ideas about what happened change in some way? Can you help us to understand if something changed and what made it possible for you to change perspective or impelled you to maintain your previous point of view?"

Therapists then pose the same questions to the patients who observed the role-playing: "You said that, while you were watching the scene, you felt certain emotions and thought particular things. Is this your usual way of thinking about certain situations? Did you notice whether the role-playing led you to seeing the situation from a different perspective? Is what the others in the group say something you can agree with, even if different from what you thought before?"

Therapists welcome all interpretations in order to stimulate greater flexibility in reasoning, so as to realise that different people have different ways not only of observing but also of interpreting human interactions. As always, we do not accept generic considerations and still less moral judgements, which would obstruct exploratory curiosity. Therapists may notice a hypothesis raised by a patient is clearly inconsistent with her non-verbal markers during role-playing: "I realise it's very easy to think one person can want to humiliate another. But this did not seem to involve what participant X expressed with her behaviour or her body during the role-playing, which instead seemed to indicate another emotion, perhaps sadness or disappointment, and this would therefore lead us to think she acted for reasons other than the apparent ones. What do you think about this?" At this stage we need to also investigate the strength of participants' convictions about the ideas they report regarding the scene observed: "How convinced are you that the thought you had previously corresponds to reality?"

In the second session on each motive, the experiential part focuses on the further strengthening of reflective skills and, especially, improving of mastery, and thus the drawing up of new and more effective strategies for handling the interpersonal problems linked to that motivation. The episode staged must clearly show which coping forms the author implemented for handling relational dynamics, the emotions driving him and the results obtained, before role-playing therapists can, for example, help the narrator of an episode to reconstruct the anxiety experienced when meeting the girl he loved with his friends. For example, the narrator may have thought, and perhaps it was true too, that all his friends expected him go up to her, but his anxiety was such that he invented an excuse for leaving: "I'm not up to it. I'll make a fool of myself. I'll disappoint them." Already while returning home he got seized by a miserable idea of failure.

In the next role-playing actors are asked to stage the episode selected, but this time without being necessarily tied to the script proposed. The actors are invited to act the dynamics depicted by the narrator while being free to find different solutions for escaping from a difficult situation. The actors can depict any behaviour during the game they consider useful for reducing the suffering they experience in that situation and pursuing the achievement of their needs, while bearing in mind the other characters' reactions during the scene. In the subsequent discussion the group debates these different forms and tries to pinpoint the probably most effective ones and grasp what impact they had on the role-playing participants.

In the second session on social inclusion a recent, autobiographical episode written by Michael was again chosen.

> A few days ago at university we were asked to form groups of seven people to in the future carry out a job/exam regarding scientific articles about cognitive distress control mechanisms. Already during the lesson some elements plus some girls from the group of university friends, of which I'm part, organised, without telling everyone, a sub-group of seven people, which we only found out about at the end of the lessons that same day. Me and some of the guys excluded from the exam working group but in the same friends' group, pointed this out to the girls, in a not very polite way. Essentially we felt excluded and somewhat offended and betrayed. The guys excluded from the group convinced the members of this working group to split and create a new group, leaving the girls, who had in the first place organised the group, unbeknown to everyone, on their own. In this case I initially felt let down, for the exclusion, but then I got dragged into the other group and witnessed a rather childish retaliation.

In this case too Michael tended to propose a precise but journalistic description of events, writing in an impersonal and detached manner. Only at the end of this passage did he switch to using the first person and manage to report the various components to his feeling of exclusion, even if the emotional one was only hinted at; in this case he seemed to have made the contents presented in the psychoeducational part and the role-playing in the previous session his own.

He did not however appear to be capable of handling the situation. The emotional unease he reported fleetingly did not activate behaviour aiming at reducing it in him, and he thus seemed almost blocked without knowing what to do and apparently letting himself be dragged passively along by the others.

The only passage where Michael seemed to refer to implementing a strategy, even if together with the group, was when he asserted: "We pointed this out to the girls, in a not very polite way." The therapist now tried to get him to watch the scene again from his own perspective to assess how much the strategies ascribed to the group were agreed on by him.

T: "Before switching to role-playing, I wanted to ask you what you mean by "in a not very polite way."
M: "I went and told them they'd been dishonest. We're a group that usually does things together and it would have been correct to at least tell us they wanted to act differently."
T: "While you said that how did you feel?"
M: "I was a bit annoyed because I felt excluded. Immediately afterwards I got angry because they behaved like children."

Thanks to a few direct questions Michael was able to switch from a more general description of the scene to a story in the first person. He had previously described the reactions of the group of which he was part and not his own; we do not know whether this was through a real spirit of belonging or fear of being criticised by the therapeutic group, given that his text would be read by the therapists. If he had initially ascribed the responsibility for the behaviour adopted to his group of friends, getting confused and, as it were, hiding himself among them, when he spoke in the first person he seemed to relive the scene and free himself of the burden of criticism (assisted in this not least by the therapists' validating attitude). He now related the behaviour that he more than anyone had adopted. Now we have the information needed for the script to be enacted!

We construct role-playing in the second session as in the first. Each scene always gets acted twice. After the first enactment, which in any case promotes emotional activation and the understanding of mental states, the main actor is asked to think over what has happened and what he did, and to hypothesise different strategies and solutions for any difficulties emerging. If the actor is unable to formulate a different strategy, the group is asked to make suggestions; from these the main actor chooses those that he considers best fits the case and is closest to his way of behaving or his point of view. Only if nobody formulates alternative hypotheses on how to handle the problematical situation do therapists suggest simple strategies, in line with the participant' skills and plans. One can now switch to role-reversal, with the other actors improvising the scene, given there is no longer a well-defined script.

Let us see how all these steps unfolded in Michael's role-playing.

The therapist summarised the main points of the narrative episode and supplied the actors with the following basic indications:

T: "Let's try and stage this episode, but this time with attention particularly to the strategies implemented by Michael or that could have been implemented to attenuate his feeling of exclusion. We're at the end of the lesson. Michael meets up with his friends, after they've realised they've been excluded by the three girls from the working group."
M: "Hey guys, have you seen those three bitches? They organised everything between them, without even telling us anything."
Friend 1: "Yes, just think. I would never have expected it, not least because we've been hanging around together and doing practically everything together for two years."
Friend 2: "I can't understand why they behaved like this. What's in it for them? Perhaps they think we're too weak for them and we'd risk make them looking stupid."
M: "What??? Us too weak??? Our average marks are much better than theirs. All three of them together can't manage to get one good mark. . . . Let's go and give them a piece of our mind!"

If we reread the episode Michael wrote, we are struck by his difficulty in reconstructing the details of the episodes recalled. This could be linked to a limited access to inner states, but probably also to a conscious wish to hide self-aspects about which he feared criticism. During role-playing he became much more able to involve the audience in the scene and provides many more details of his thoughts, emotions and behaviour. He literally seemed another person and anything but passive!

This is one of the reasons at the root of writing this book: entering episodes narrated on an experiential level and reliving them reduces interference from the, often judgemental, observer position, facilitates access to experience and reactivates thoughts and emotions close to bodily states and behaviour.

In Michael's case we see he experienced a sense of relational effectiveness, albeit while adopting coping involving retaliation. It is important that he accessed self-parts, involving effectiveness and strength, previously in the shadows, instead of the inept and inferior ones leading him to shun criticism, avoid conflicts and get blocked. We notice that as well as the episode now surfacing, Michael displayed important social avoidance patterns, a behaviour also evident when in the group. Attention: we do not want to validate disdainful behaviour or consider it positive! Simply to show beneficial features, like those just stressed, can lurk in maladaptive coping too.

Let us see how the first drafting of the role-playing ended. Michael and his two friends went up to the girls.

M: "I mean I don't understand. How come you didn't tell us anything? Did you think we were weak? Or did you perhaps find somebody better to work with?

Well, now let's see who's better and who gets the best mark. In fact, given that you perhaps feel comfortable with the others, go out with them this evening too, cos we've got better things to do."

Friends 1 and 2 did not speak but nodded, smirked and looked derisively at the girls.

When the first staging was over, the therapist asked Michael how he felt and validated the emotions surfacing. Michael seemed satisfied with the solution he had adopted. The therapist then asked for the roles to be inverted, with Michael and one of the other actors switching parts. This requires more effort from participants and directly stimulates theory of mind and decentring skills.

It is important for the main character to finish the scene, even with the other participants' help. He, and with him the whole group, can thus discover that the script can change significantly when different people play different roles. We underscore that role reversal stimulates theory of mind, but it simultaneously increases self-reflectivity, in that one can see oneself from an observer's perspective.

In the role-playing in the second session we suggest participants hold a "live" discussion with different ways to tackle problematical relational situations, in order to assess together which might be more adaptive. In the case of Michael's role-playing at university it emerged that the strategies he adopted were a direct consequence of the emotional activation linked to his sense of prevarication/injustice, which underlay his sense of group exclusion. This led him to not bestir himself as much for re-establishing closeness and group belonging as seeking social inclusion would have required. Michael instead sought retaliation, while moving within social rank. He thus used a strategy that, as we saw, reactivated a feeling of strength and effectiveness but was dysfunctional as regards the goal of being included in the group.

At the end of the first role-playing the therapist asked the actors and other participants to suggest alternatives to the retaliation strategy:

T: "Now, at the end of the acting, I'd like to ask you to imagine and stage a variant, to use alternative ways for handling the sense of exclusion and humiliation experienced by Michael. We'll do it, as always, not to find the right solution but discover if the same problem can be tackled in different ways and have different effects on the main character and the others."

It was now Michael himself who suggested a potential different behaviour to be implemented afterwards on stage. We describe it exactly as he acted it.

M: "Let's go up to the girls and say, 'Hey girls, that's not how to behave. We felt let down. And what's the point of behaving like that? At the end of the day it's us now excluding you and how do you feel? And imagine if we do a better job than you.'"

Michael seemed to have adopted a decentred perspective of events, by asking himself, even before changing roles, how the girls might feel. He then proposed a retaliation solution, consistent with his prevailing emotion but probably not effective. Stefania, a participant with dependent personality features, proposed an alternative solution:

S: "We could have Michael going up to the girls with his friends – don't know, perhaps they were in class writing – and saying: 'Hey, girls, we felt let down because we were keen to do this thing together, seeing as we're a group. I can't understand why you left us out. However it's important for us to clarify this immediately, to avoid ruining our relationship. Deep down, nothing happened between us.'"

This proposal got accepted and Michael was asked in the role-reverse to play the part of one of the girls. Friend 2 played Michael and, at the end of the role-playing, used the strategy suggested by Stefania. In the girl's role Michael replied as follows:

M: "I'm sorry you've felt let down. We didn't realise. We wanted to finish the job immediately and since we were together at that moment, we set about working without thinking much about it."
Friend 1: "Okay, that's alright. But how shall we carry on now then?"
M: "I don't know . . . by now we've gone ahead. . . . But you tell us. Next time we'll do it together for sure."

The final discussion now focused on the specific relational strategies used by the actors. The main character, particularly, and all the group members opened their minds to the idea that one's behaviour can have effects on others and adopting different behaviour from usual can have a more desirable impact, supporting a relationship and increasing the possibilities of satisfying primary desires.

Therapists first explored the main actor's experience while trying to solve an emotionally challenging situation during the role-playing. They asked him what he thought and felt and if he had found the solution adopted useful and how difficult it had been to adopt it. It was then the other actors' turn to describe their experience dealing with this new behaviour and if, for example, they felt driven by emotions different from those agreed upon in the original script.

The main character can now at this point assess whether his changed behaviour had an, if possible positive, impact on the others and whether changing it could lead to different responses.

Let us see how Michael felt after modifying his behaviour during the role-playing.

T: "Michael, how was it during the first and second ways of dealing with the situation? Did something change?"
M: "The first time I felt excluded and very upset, switching between displeasure and anger. Showing her directly my dissatisfaction made me feel better. Then excluding them, even if on the one hand I knew it wasn't right, made me feel much better, as if I'd got revenge for the wrong suffered."
T: "Instead with the new way of handling the situation how did you feel?"

M: "I tried to regulate my anger a bit and to transmit to her that I was sorry about not being able to be with them. But then, nevertheless, I had to make her understand that I was angry and they shouldn't allow themselves to exclude us."

T: "And how did you feel?"

M: "I felt better. I got myself respected, but simultaneously seeking a minimum of dialogue made me feel the distance from my companions and the exclusion much less. As if telling the girls that I was sorry for what had happened made me feel I'd retrieved the relationship I imagined to be damaged and didn't make me feel humiliated, as I thought would happen. Probably deep down they didn't even intend to keep us out and perhaps they didn't imagine that I'd be offended so much, but I'm happy to have made them understand that their friendship is important."

Therapists now ask the observers if they consider the new forms of behaviour enacted by the actors effective, starting with the reactions they provoked in the other role-playing characters.

We ask participants to observe whether, after changing their relational difficulty handling strategies, the actors appear less or more relaxed, happy, tense, anxious, contented and so on. Therapists can simultaneously provide feedback on which strategies turned out more adaptive and which less, if not positively harmful, but without starting out from a prescriptive position. They should base their comments on the effects the behaviour had on the actors on stage. If a participant adopts a behaviour forming part of a dysfunctional schema, therapists can, with a validating attitude, point to it as one of the possible options; but immediately afterwards they can get the patient, and then the group, to reflect on the relational consequences of the interpersonal cycle getting activated and compare them with those of other solutions introduced by the group.

Encouraged by success in early outcome studies (Inchausti et al., 2020; Popolo et al., 2018, 2019), MIT-G is currently used in Italy, Spain and Norway. In a pilot study in Spain it is used with adolescents too. It is furthermore possible, in a similar way to our adaptation of mindfulness (see Chapter 9), to use it at more advanced stages of therapy. The goal is to stimulate better social relations for patients already achieving some therapeutic progress and needing to put into practice a way of problem solving based on knowledge of mental states together with their peers.

CHAPTER **11**

Technique sequences

The techniques described in this book come from many orientations. We are not claiming originality in this: we have studied, learnt, practised and experienced what others created before us. What, we hope, distinguishes us is the structure in which we apply the techniques and the clarity of the rationale for using them. We have shown how each technique is at the service of metacognitive functions that change and grow as a therapy evolves and is designed around patients' interpersonal schemas.

To summarise, we use the various techniques to: 1) improve the foundations of self-reflectivity; 2) activate arousal and soothe it depending on whether emotions are inhibited or dysregulated; 3) stimulate agency; 4) improve differentiation; 5) access healthy parts and put them into practice in daily life; 6) promote mastery, on various levels; 7) improve understanding of the other's mind.

We orientate ourselves with the decision-making procedure (Chapter 4). The same technique fulfils various functions, and we use several techniques in a sequence. A clinician always has a wide range of interventions available to get a treatment to advance. With these premises, we shall now depict some ideal micro-sequences where therapists synergyically use various techniques one after another.

Experiential techniques in shared formulation of functioning

Gathering narrative episodes and improving metacognitive monitoring

The typical starting point is when patients have difficulty describing their inner state and do not relate specific autobiographical memories but instead use overgeneral memories, abstractions and resorting to moral norms. How can we use the techniques sequentially to improve access to the inner world and stimulate the telling of specific and detailed narrative episodes?

If the problem is a lack of narrative episodes, we resort to early behavioural experiments; we ask patients to pursue a goal while trying to interrupt automatic resorting to behavioural coping. Patients are asked to counteract coping, but not with the goal of dismantling it. While trying to act without letting themselves be overwhelmed by their automatisms, patients concentrate on what is occurring in relationships and what they think and feel. This evokes recent narrative episodes, session after session.

Therapists ask:

> You are often anxious, especially in social situations. You tend to close up, and avoid expressing your opinion because, as you told me, if you exposed yourself you'd feel uneasy. To better grasp this uneasiness and what the thoughts linked to your anxiety are, shall we try over the coming week to expose ourselves more? Could you accept an invitation or decide to say something even if you're tense? Then note what passes through your mind whether you manage to expose yourself or, as is possible, you don't. It's not important you manage to. We don't have this goal. We just need you to pay attention to thoughts and emotions while trying to counteract your protective habits.

What happens most often at the start of therapy is that patients manage, alone or with their therapist's guidance, to relate a narrative episode and report some inner states. When the therapist focuses on the episode structure, she realises it is easier to read the descriptions of the other – cynical, egoistic, neglecting, judgemental – and how the patient adopts coping strategies as a consequence of self's response to other's response. The contents of the latter and the initial wish are however often not clear.

In Chapter 2 we provided a clinical operating description of metacognition as the inability of patients to supply their therapist with information with which to formulate their schemas in their entirety. At this level we therefore have narratives in which only fragments of their schemas can be grasped.

In simple terms, what therapists see is something of this type: "My colleague criticised me and I closed up." This includes the other's response, in terms of critical behaviour, and self's behavioural reaction to other's response. The cognitive-affective motivations leading to closing up when faced with criticism do not surface.

Another example: "When I saw my mother worried, I decided I had to stick by her. After all what can I do? I'm her daughter and she only has me." The other's response surfaces: worried, probably fragile. The coping used is inverted caregiving, but aside from a moralistic assertion, what thoughts and affects drive the patient to care for her mother?

In self's response to other's response there are sometimes emotions associated with a sense of strength surfacing: anger, pride, disdain. Patients however have difficulty identifying the distressing feelings triggering them. In such cases, and still with the goal of improving monitoring, therapists can use guided imagery exercises, aimed exclusively at scanning the episode.

Informal guided imagery, without induction and with the eyes open, is also useful. Patients are asked to describe a scene as if it was happening at that moment, again with the constraint of using the present tense and not reasoning about it. The therapist then draws their attention to their protective behaviour antecedents or, in the case of anger, to the cognitive/affective/somatic state experienced an instant before getting angry.

Sometimes a set of questions is enough for exploring a somatic state: "You told me about tension. In what body part do you feel it? Could you describe it better? A weight? A tightness? A restlessness as if you needed to move? What action would you employ if you could?" (Ogden & Fisher, 2015).

Once contact with sensorial experience has improved, the questions involve cognitions: "So, you feel this tightness in your chest and we've realised it's a sort of worry. What idea is it linked to? In your current thought flow can you manage to pick up what bad thing could happen? Let's try and anchor the worry to this tightness in your chest. Do you feel a weight on your chest at the idea that. . .?"

Again with a view to improving monitoring in the early treatment stages we use bodily interventions (Chapter 7) to regulate distressing states. Thanks to these practices, patients often manage to modulate negative somatic-affective states and to grasp which thoughts and emotions they had before and after the exercise and what has changed thanks to the practice.

To better understand what patients think and feel one can start with brief meditations. Body-scanning (Chapter 9) is precious for this purpose. Patients mindfully observe their body segments and the clinician asks them to take note of the types of thought and emotion surfacing. With these exercises inner world elements emerge very frequently that radically change the schema formulation and render it more accurate, richer in nuances and closer to raw experience.

When patients' tendency to distance themselves from their emotions is massive, memories are deprived of affects. They name some emotions but, when asked to explore them better, they cannot. Here the problem simultaneously regards limited monitoring and low arousal. Against this background understanding and modifying schemas is impossible and therapy would only be a sterile intellectual exercise. It is indispensable to first induce emotions.

Activating emotional arousal

If patients say "If my wife suffers, I feel guilty" in a flat and detached way, it is impossible to change their schema. Similarly, if patients say they fear social exposure situations because they do not want to be criticised but talk in a distant and apparently relaxed way, it means that, from a procedural point of view, avoidance obstructing therapeutic action is underway. At the formulation stage we therefore need to reach an adequate level of arousal before change operations like rescripting.

There are various ways to activate arousal. During guided imagery or two-chairs therapists can point out the most distressing features in patients' experience. For example, if a patient is at the point in a scene where a colleague points out a mistake to her, the therapist asks her to say out loud: "I'm worth nothing. I'm a failure. I've made a terribly bad impression." Patients often realise that what seemed neutral until shortly before is instead emotionally important.

Enactments have the same goal. A patient related a problematic episode but without distress. She felt being left on her own but did not feel any negative emotions: "He's gone but, I don't know, it's not very important. At the end of the day I'm fine on my own too." Here therapists can use the enactment where they turn their back and this makes patients feel the abandonment, loneliness and sadness they previously could not recognise.

The climax of shared formulation: triggering associated memories and formulating the schema; differentiation starts

Thanks to the reactivation of emotional arousal, therapists obtain specific stories where inner states are clear. With these it is easier to draw out associated memories. We recall that emotions are able to make memories of the moments when patients experienced them emerge. However, when these memories do not surface even with sufficient arousal, the use of sequential interventions can solve the problem.

When we talk of associated memories, we do not necessarily mean associations between present and past, developmental, memories. With many patients either developmental memories do not surface or they are not interested in exploring them. Associated memories mean narrative episodes, of any period, that patients identify as being inter-linked.

A patient first analysed a recent episode in detail. The therapist got him to do guided imagery to scan it. Thanks to this and a mindful attention to thoughts and feelings, the patient's inner states have surfaced but associated memories do not appear. The therapist now assigns a behavioural task to assess how thoughts, emotions and behaviour linked to the episode will present themselves in coming weeks.

The task can be of the observational type – "Note when experiences of that type re-emerge" – or involve abstaining from coping – "If you get these tendencies again, try and resist the impulse to enact them and using any strategy you think it might work. While trying to not activate the behaviour we're talking about, pay attention to what you think and feel, on the emotional and somatic levels. We'll thus have more information on how you live certain experiences in relationships."

Multiple narrative episodes, concerning relationships with various significant others, helping patients to grasp they are driven by recurring forms of thinking, feeling and acting, can thus be obtained, session after session.

We now arrive at the point where clinician and patient formulate the schema together. By arriving at this formulation via associated memories patients almost naturally manage an initial type of differentiation, such as: "Before I thought my ideas were true. Now I realise they are the result of learning," or: "Before I thought my ideas were true. Now I realise I tend to react like this to various situations."

In both cases patients can still remain convinced that even if their ideas are the result of something they have learnt during their life history, or are their own personal response style, they nevertheless remain true and it is useful to believe them: "I realise I react angrily to my partners like I did with my father. Is it possible to find a man who's not a shit?" Or: "Yes, it's true I tend to distrust people but I'm right to as they cheat you."

In these cases, other forms of differentiation need to be promoted (Chapter 2) by, for example, asking patients to not focus on others' behaviour but on their own reactions: thoughts and emotions. Mistrusting patients are asked how they feel when faced with a threatening and humiliating other. When we get them to realise they feel weak, fragile, vulnerable or powerless, we get them to remain in this state and ask them how much they feel it to be subjectively true and how much they themselves consider they are inept, inferior or incapable.

When, therefore, patients enter into contact with their core negative self-idea, no matter what the other's opinion, one can get them to differentiate. The problem, therefore, is not getting them to differentiate about the representation of the other, but about their self-representation!

Therapists do not tell patients "Others can be more benevolent then you think" but rather "Others can activate in you the idea of being in danger, but it's you in your mind that feels profoundly weak and vulnerable". It is the core idea of being weak and vulnerable that is the subject of attempts to differentiate.

Apart from the most severe cases, more frequently at this point in the procedures the seed of being able to see one's self-with-others representations from a different perspective and consider them as deeply rooted beliefs and not a mere reflection of reality has been sown. Both when differentiation has started and when, despite associating, it has not been acquired even in an embryonic form, one begins change promoting and here experiential techniques become, if possible, even more invaluable.

Experiential techniques in change promoting

Differentiating and strengthening healthy parts

At this point in therapy patients have reported multiple detailed narrative episodes, the elements of inner experience have emerged, including an initial access to healthy parts and more benign self- and other-representations. It is now a question of promoting or strengthening differentiation, bringing to light healthy parts and supporting the use of new ways of feeling, thinking, acting and regulating inner states outside sessions.

Guided imagery and drama techniques are more or less equivalent for these aims. Some patients are more at ease with the latter, for example, two-chairs, because they do not require closing the eyes and letting go of reality, giving the impression one is still in control. Other patients find guided imagery fascinating. Therapists may have greater familiarity with imagery than with drama techniques or vice-versa, another important factor.

Guided imagery is to be preferred when the scene to be acted is complex, with several characters interacting and not only a dual relationship: for example, a family argument involving parents and siblings. In cases like this it is necessary to understand what patients think and feel towards the various characters and what type of relations exist among them. For example, when faced with an aggressive father, a patient can offer care to her mother and sister, or only the latter, while also being angry with her mother for being submissive and not protecting them.

Rescripting, both in imagery and in dramatechniques is at the roots of differentiation. The core element of this aspect of change is that once a scene has been, so to say, shot for the first time, a therapist invites patients to say new things or act in a different, schema-divergent way. Once patients are able to perform these new imaged or enacted actions and feel them as their own, they realise they were driven by their own perspectives and not by facts.

During rescripting, interventions should rigorously avoid logical-verbal reflection. The therapist must not get patients to reason or pose questions like: "What would he think if you adopted this behaviour? In your opinion, why are you acting like this? How might your father respond?"

Change is to be promoted through actions, behaviour, expressions and new postures; it is embodied change. We propose: "Try and tell your mother: 'I can't bear your criticism any longer.'" Or: "Place your adult self in the scene and put a hand on your child self. Can you? Try and hold his hand"; "Now you're replying to the guy who threatened you, you've got a submissive posture. Try instead to pull up your shoulders, raise your eyes and answer back."

Therapists do not ask "How do you believe your child self is reacting?" or "How do you believe your mother might react to this reply?". They instead always ask patients to observe what happens in a scene: "Watch the child. What expression does he now have after you've put your hand on his shoulder? Can you feel his physical reaction to your gesture?" Or: "What's mum doing now? Has her expression changed? Is it still the same? If it's changed, tell me from close up what you notice that's different."

It is a question in essence of promoting a continuous interweaving between observation of the narrative landscape and internal markers at that moment. In simple words: "Now your mother seems surprised, how do you feel? What are you experiencing and thinking? What parts of your body are getting activated? Can you feel it in your shoulders? On your chest? Can you feel more or less strength in some muscle? Your legs? Your arms?" (Ogden & Fisher, 2015).

Let us return to the intervention sequences. We have got to the change exercises already, after various experiential-type interventions, described at the shared formulation stage. Patients have, for example, reconstructed their schemas with sensory awareness or behavioural exploration exercises. If necessary, they have performed guided imagery exercises aimed at improving metacognitive monitoring, to enrich their knowledge of thoughts and emotions in specific episodes. To better understand their schemas they are engaged in behavioural experiments where their therapist has asked them to abstain from coping, again with the aim of improving monitoring and increasing agency. We now show how this interweaving gets tighter still when we aim at structural change.

During an imagery experience or drama techniques patients are likely to either encounter intense emotions which they have difficulty regulating or, on the contrary, enter states involving hypo-activation and freezing, with micro-dissociative experiences (Ogden & Fisher, 2015). Therapists generally have no reason to worry about these reactions, which are in fact to a certain extent to be expected. Thanks not least to these experiences, patients gain awareness of how much their mental functioning and recurring behaviour depend only up to a certain point on outside factors and are largely forms of action and reaction they have made their own and are rooted in the body.

Patients may however have difficulty at certain moments regulating intense and distressing affectivity and feel overwhelmed by it. Simultaneously they get blocked and numb, remaining spellbound as it were, when faced with problematical scenes. Now, as part of imagery or drama techniques, therapists perform sensorimotor (Chapter 7) or mindfulness (Chapter 9) interventions to regulate the emotions, until they manage to restart rescripting.

Kristoffer was a 55-year-old social worker in a small Danish town. He had Avoidant and Dependent PD with obsessive-compulsive traits. He sought therapy for social anxiety. He was very well regarded at work; they considered him generous, able and an excellent team member. However, he suffered from intense anxiety and embarrassment whenever having to expose himself, for example when talking at team meetings. During his first session his therapist started collecting narrative episodes linked to his present social anxiety. The first part of the session was difficult: Kristoffer was highly embarrassed. The therapist explored whether he felt criticised by her too and, even if with difficulty, he confessed he felt deeply embarrassed when with her. He feared she found his fears ridiculous and thought a social worker not knowing how to speak in public should not do that job.

The therapist validated Kristoffer's fears, by saying they were human and common but, on seeing Kristoffer was still tense, self-disclosed that, when she had to present work at conferences, she was gripped by fear of failure, became perfectionist and was greatly tempted to avoid. Kristoffer smiled and relaxed. As the session ended the therapist taught Kristoffer some simple mindfulness exercises he could use to reduce the impact of worrying before meetings.

Kristoffer started the second session by smiling and telling how mindfulness had helped him, even if there not having been any meetings meant he still had to put himself properly to the test. Then, however, his face changed and he asked permission to talk about another topic, while almost begging the therapist's pardon it was not related to social anxiety. The therapist told him he was free to decide what to talk about.

Kristoffer was in a dispute with a neighbour, who was claiming part of Kristoffer's land adjoining his. He was sure he was right and had land registry documents demonstrating that the neighbour was overstepping the boundary. He was convinced the neighbour's behaviour was arrogant and wrong but feared taking legal action. He felt insecure, had doubts about his ability to defend his arguments and was frightened how the neighbour would react.

On investigating Kristoffer's narrative episodes the therapist realised the problem distressing him was another. The house in fact belonged to his family and he had to get his elder brother to agree on the email to send to their lawyer. The therapist asked him if he had let his brother read it and Kristoffer trembled. He wanted to change the subject. The therapist probed his feelings and thoughts. Kristoffer was frightened to talk about his relationship with his brother.

The therapist showed curiosity, but said she was not bothered if Kristoffer preferred not to talk about it, although she would like to understand what led him to keep the reasons for his distress to himself. She said it calmly, while maintaining an exploratory attitude. The patient reacted well to the therapist's attitude and said he would like to start by trying to relate what he had written in the email. The therapist asked why. Kristoffer replied that, while he was writing it, he found it sensible and he would like to know what the therapist thought about it. She showed her entire agreement.

The email was balanced and described his arguments firmly but calmly. He explained to the neighbour that, if he persisted with his actions, he might take him to court, although maintaining a conciliatory attitude. The therapist praised the email's quality and Kristoffer was visibly satisfied by this appreciation. The therapist asked him what he was planning to do with this email. Kristoffer started getting agitated again: he needed to first discuss it with his brother and was scared. This time he managed to talk about relations between them. He had already told him he wanted to write a formal letter and his brother had reacted by insulting him, calling him a spineless idiot. In his opinion the right strategy was to go straight to the police and smear the neighbour. Kristoffer felt stupid and thought his brother was right. Then a little later he thought his idea was good again, but the idea of being unworthy and the resulting embarrassment dominated: Kristoffer could not defend his own point of view.

The therapist asked him for associated memories about how this relationship, where Kristoffer could not be independent as otherwise his brother threatened, subjugated and despised him, got built. A history of physical and psychological violence suffered at his brother's hands emerged. Moreover, his father was also aggressive and furious and in certain situations his brother had defended him. Kristoffer thus found himself in a cul-de-sac, because he feared the same person that in some circumstances protected him.

The therapist asked him for a specific memory where his brother had mistreated him. Kristoffer's anxiety increased and it almost seemed he wanted to get out of his chair and leave. Sobbing, he said he had had some awful moments. Now, before even recalling the memories, the therapist suggested grounding and this helped him regulate his affects. Kristoffer told about when he was 14 and was with his brother and some friends in a wood, hunting birds with a catapult. At a certain point Kristoffer made a noise, causing the birds to flee. His brother got mad and threatened him in front of everybody. He grabbed his neck and said that, if he acted stupidly like that again, he would strangle him. Remembering this Kristoffer was overwhelmed by fear and shame at the humiliation and anger at the unfairness of the violence he underwent. The therapist asked him to return to grounding and Kristoffer again calmed down.

The therapist summarised the episode:

T: "When you seek to be independent, to express your own point of view, you find yourself facing a powerful, violent and humiliating other. It's something you've learnt painfully, when faced with your father's and brother's attitudes and today it's as if you couldn't manage to think yourself capable of maintaining your own point of view. However, on the one hand you yourself believe yourself an inept and weak person, but simultaneously part of you is tenacious, knows how to express sensible points of view and would like to defend them. You try to stand firm, but you're unable to persist; the idea of being a powerless idiot is still too strong in your mind."

Kristoffer recognised himself fully in this formulation and grasped the therapist supported his impulses towards independence and believed in his worth. She now suggested using guided imagery to go over either the episode with the violence during hunting or where he told his brother he wanted to write the letter to his neighbour. Kristoffer chose the second.

During guided imagery Kristoffer saw his brother's face, expression and posture. He could feel him towering and frightening and he depicted himself as little and stupid. "I can't do anything against him. I'm an idiot. I do everything wrong." Kristoffer now really seemed a worthless child. The therapist encouraged him to breathe mindfully and Kristoffer calmed down.

Rescripting can now be attempted. The therapist suggested replying to his brother. We always recall that the goal is not a sort of skills training, where we prepare patients for replying differently in reality. The goal is to rewrite their schemas, that is, to get Kristoffer to see himself differently and support the valid and active self-image underlying independence and rank, while learning to lend less credence to the idea of being a weakling blocked, subjugated and humiliated by a powerful, violent and intelligent other.

The first reaction was holy terror, but this time a glimpse of rebellion, to which the therapist anchored herself, surfaced.

T: "Do we want to try then?"
K: "Yes."
T: "Is there something you want to try and tell your brother?"
K: [*hesitates, trembles, gets agitated*]: "I don't know . . . perhaps. . . . Yes, that my letter's good."
T: "Try. Tell him: my letter's good."
K: "My letter's written well. We're in the right, but we need to do it gradually."
T: "How do you feel saying it?"
K: "I'm afraid."
T: "Watch your brother. How does he look?"
K: "Really pissed off."
T: "What does he tell you?"
K: "That I'm an idiot and that we should kick the shit out of our neighbour and, if I don't do it, I haven't got balls and have no respect for the family fortune."
T: "How do you feel now?"
K [*lowers his head*]: "I suck. I've no courage, no balls."

The therapist then introduced a sensorimotor component, by asking Kristoffer to adopt a fierce posture, by standing up, pressing his palms against each other and feeling the muscular tension. Kristoffer performed the exercise.

T: "What can you feel now?"
K: "I feel stronger, less at fault."
T: "Excellent! Shall we try and reply to your brother?"
K: "Yes."
T: "What might you tell him?"
K: "I don't know."
T: "Try and tell him 'You can't treat me like this. My idea's sensible.'"
K [*still standing, with his eyes closed. Hesitates. Pauses. Is restless. Doesn't keep his feet still. After about 15 seconds he talks, whispering*]: "You can't treat me like an idiot. I'm right to write this letter."
T: "Good, Kristoffer, you managed!"
K: "I'm tremendously anxious."
T: "Sure, it's normal. You exposed yourself. But let's try again."

The therapist returned to working on his body, while Kristoffer still had his eyes closed and stayed in the imagery scene.

T: "Pull your head up. Press your palms hard together again and breathe by expanding your chest and feeling the air filling and distending it."

Kristoffer tried this and felt a sensation of greater strength and energy.

T: "Excellent. Now repeat what you told your brother, but pushing your voice."

Kristoffer tried it twice and managed to talk louder, although still hesitantly.

T: "Now try and shout 'Don't treat me like this! I'm right.'"

Kristoffer had difficulty and the therapist insisted, saying the message herself ever louder until she shouted. Kristoffer had a moment of intense fear but overcame it by himself and yelled:

K: "Stop treating me like this!"

He gathered his breath – it was almost like a tide building up in him – and in the end snapped.

K: "Arsehole!"

The therapist burst out laughing and Kristoffer joined in. Visibly relieved, he opened his eyes. At the end of the session they planned a behavioural exposure: telling his three siblings, including the abusive one, that he had written the letter to the neighbour. Kristoffer managed to speak with his siblings two weeks later and got a good reaction: without arguing too much his siblings agreed with his strategy. Kristoffer appeared satisfied when he said another brother congratulated him for how he had written the letter. In the following months his inept and submissive self-representation gradually changed.

We have shown how to interweave sensorimotor, mindfulness, guided imagery and rescripting techniques. Naturally, instead of guided imagery, we could use drama techniques, helping patients to regulate themselves during role-play or two-chairs.

The next step is promoting differentiation at the same time as consolidating healthy parts. The sequence we most typically use in this step is: imagery or drama rescripting behavioural experiments.

When we ask patients to respond differently to others, we do not, as explained in Kristoffer's case, aim at changing the relationship with real others, but with their internalised figures. We want to change the self–self relationship. If Kristoffer replied differently to his brother in imagery, he was not replying to his true brother but to his way of representing a tyrannical, humiliating and violent other. What he took home was a new form of experience and an action pattern he was already beginning to perform on a pre-motor level.

Behavioural exercises following rescripting techniques also do not yet have changing behaviour to improve relationships and trigger different responses from others as their prime goal. This is to consolidate the schema change started in-session and involve the motor component, and to place the new ways of thinking and feeling in command of sensorimotor activities, guide action and gain strength.

If the work was limited to in-session rescripting, we would in fact leave patients an easy prey to their automatisms in daily relations. If instead they engage with constancy in behaviour where they counteract pathogenic coping and repeatedly pursue healthy and wished-for goals, maladaptive schemas get broken and new ways of being with others get formed.

For this reason we follow in-session rescripting in the pretend play mode, in the *twin earth* (Lillard, 2001), with behavioural exercises. To this end, after rescripting therapists summarise what has occurred and use it to update the contract, that is, to decide together that patients will try and act in new ways in the coming weeks.

Returning to previous decision-making procedure steps

The decision-making procedure path is not straightforward; MIT has no phases. Therapists help patients to repeat over and over again the same steps until functioning gets consolidated. Have patients differentiated for a certain period but now have difficulty again describing inner states? Their therapy promotes monitoring as long as necessary again. Have patients differentiated, are implementing behaviour aimed at consolidating healthy parts, but have a relapse? Once again, the interweaving of the techniques is a great help in supporting the therapeutic process.

A patient has, for example, already performed guided imagery and rescripting exercises and gone onto behavioural exposure. The exercise is not, however, successful: he does not perform the new action agreed or uses coping again.

At such moments, patients are aware this is a return to malfunctioning. The therapist, as ever, validates the ability to realise that they have had a relapse. She reminds patients that the goal of behavioural exercises is never their success but the effort to try and activate reflexive skills during their performance.

Once a therapist has ascertained patients do not think they have failed or disappointed him, she can return to problematic episode. Here she can again use a guided imagery and rescripting exercise or a drama technique. Patients thus use their relapse to increase their knowledge of their own mental processes and automatisms. Once what emerges during the in-session experience has been processed, one returns to planning new behavioural experiments.

An example drawn from the next part of Matteo's therapy (the businessman aged 39, described in Chapters 5, 6 and 9) will help. Matteo had understood his interpersonal schemas. Here we concentrate on the following: attachment got activated and his core self-representation was *unlovable* and *vulnerable* vis-à-vis an unavailable or judgemental other. His responses were fear, detachment and self-care. Moreover, when he detached, he entered into states of emptiness. To tackle them Matteo used only compulsive seduction as coping. This led him to lose agency and to not plan actions centred on his own wishes and inclinations. He knew that, faced with emptiness, he tended to merely seek women to go out with and have sex to reactivate himself and obtain reward.

The coping also temporarily satisfied his need for attention: he let himself be approached by caregiving-type women, even if he then got bored again and expelled them brusquely. Awareness of his schemas proceeded hand-in-hand with a big reduction in resorting to compulsive seduction. Matteo recovered control over his work too and in many relationships stopped his compliantly submissive behaviour aimed at forestalling others' aggressive and humiliating response. Another part of his schema, relating to independence, was linked to a fragile and suffering picture of other, both his mother and father. When he considered this picture, he felt guilty: an *unworthy* and *disgusting* core self-image emerged and he got blocked. With this other awareness he started to act independently, even if his mother showed she suffered because of this.

In the midst of this wide-ranging progress, Matteo started a session in his seventh therapy month by relating he had met a new woman. At the start his narrative became generalised again, with abstract doubts:

M: "I've been out with a girl, but I can't grasp if the old mechanisms are at work or it's something good."
T: "Do you want to tell me what happened?"
M: "She's Spanish."
T: "What's her name?"
M: "Marisol. I was fine but I don't feel all that sexual attraction. It's weird. But I felt fine with her. We spent the weekend together. She was two days at my house."
T: "How did you meet her?"
M: "Friends. We were drinking something in a bar and they introduced her to me."
T: "What did you like about her? What impression did she make on you?"

M: "She's a tough type. At 19 she's got fed up with her family and has started touring Europe. She's very independent. However, I don't know what I'm doing. I've had sex with her too. It went well but I don't know. I don't feel this great desire. Let's be clear: she's pretty, with a good body, but there's something that doesn't move me very much."
T: "Tell me a bit about what happened when you were together. What you did, so I can understand better."
M: "I like her because I can control her."
T: "Meaning?"
M: "When she left, I told her: 'Okay, return in a week's time and I can do as I like' [*meaning having sex with other women*]. And she said: 'Do as you like.'"
T: "Sorry. I don't understand. How do you control her then?"
M: "She had that: 'Oh yes? Do as you like' attitude."
T: "And so? I still can't understand."
M: "She was playing the role of a girl who couldn't care less."
T: "And you interpreted this as. . .?"
M: "That you could see she did care. But she didn't want to give me satisfaction, and I like that."
T: "Wait. Now I'm beginning to suss. You felt you were in control because you grasped Marisol was caught."
M: "Yes, exactly! But she didn't want to show it."
T: "From your expression it seems this was what you liked, right? In what way?"
M: "Umm. Wait. Perhaps I've realised! It's that I'm used to women who stick to you and don't let you go and, if I do what I like, they complain and I get fed up. She instead is different. She's keen but she knows how to get her act together. She doesn't play the 'You're deserting me. I'm hurt. Why can't you care less about me?'"
T: "Ah. Now it's a little clearer. So you felt the girl was interested in you but wouldn't have forced you to give up your independence because she, poor and fragile, would have suffered."
M: "Exactly!"
T: "Listen Matteo, there's something that occurs to me. In these sessions you talk a lot about characteristics of your mother that are the opposite to this girl. Every time you want to do something off your own bat, Mum ends up suffering and critical and you feel guilty and angry. You'd like Mum to not behave like that because you feel this undermines your independence. Only now are you learning to fight to learn to go on even if Mum does everything possible to make you feel guilty, however . . . I don't know. I reckon this girl has given you a completely different signal, and perhaps you wish to receive this type of new response?"

To be noted: in this case it is the therapist trying to link the recent narrative to other historic ways of relating. This is not contradictory to the decision-making procedure. In the months before the shift from recent memories to links to the past had already been undertaken in line with the procedure and Matteo had linked various types of episodes to his relationships both with his father and his mother. On this basis a therapist can try to link various episodes with each other, with the aim of stimulating patients' integrating skills, while still remembering the principle that he is proffering a hypothesis patients will need to assess.

A therapist should formulate interventions while moving in the therapeutic zone of proximal development (Leiman & Stiles, 2001; Ribeiro, Ribeiro, Gonçalves, Horvath, & Stiles, 2013), that is, by attempting to stimulate the metacognitive skill immediately above the one displayed at that moment. In this case Matteo had already integrated by himself: "Umm. Wait. Perhaps I've realised! It's that I'm used to women who stick to you and don't let you go and if I'm independent, they start to complain and I get fed up," and this justifies the therapist returning to the links therapist and patient reconstructed in previous sessions.

This example helps in showing how in MIT we do not consider an intervention correct *a priori*, even if consistent with the procedure. After any intervention therapists evaluate patients' feedback and gauge their next actions accordingly. The link made by the therapist was consistent and correct and in fact initially Matteo seemed convinced.

M: "Yes, it's true. Golly, I hadn't thought of that! Yes, precisely that, she's exactly my mother's opposite . . ."

Matteo told about how he was untying himself ever more from his mother and described the problematic aspects of this more clear-headedly. In the previous session he had revealed his mother had been anorexic and was still obsessed about being thin and her physical appearance. She was consequently strict and judgemental with herself and with him, of whom she pointed out not only moral imperfections but also every physical one. Matteo realised his mother had very strict critical standards but that was how she functioned. It did not depend on him and he could not do anything to satisfy her. This realisation was accompanied by a growing sense of relief and liberation.

However, immediately afterwards Matteo talked again of his relationship with the girl, again in the form of rumination.

M: "To sum up, I don't know what to do. Should I see her? I like her. I don't like her. I'm confused."

The therapist then realised his intervention involving recalling links between the relationships with Marisol and his mother had on the one hand provided relief to Matteo and made him differentiate, but on the other distracted him from his inner experience and led him to ruminate again. The therapist now returned to the start of *shared formulation* and investigated the narrative episode in depth.

T: "What happened when you said goodbye? What emotions were you left with? What sensation did you have in your mind?"
M: "A total emptiness."

T: "Oh! [*surprised*]. Listen, an emptiness linked to her absence? Or what?"
M: "Emptiness in general. I was seized by a sense of total disquiet, as if I had nothing to do and couldn't bear it."
T: "So you didn't specifically feel her absence and what you'd done together?"
M: "I don't know. I went immediately to my mobile to reply to my messages."
T: "Was it to manage the void? What did you do?"
M: "I replied to a woman who was hassling me [*jokingly*] and started acting silly. I got my evening organised."
T: "And did you see her that evening?"
M: "Yes."

In this dialogue Matteo's monitoring was poor, because of the prior resort to coping. Accordingly the therapist could not then formulate the interpersonal schema activated, because various elements were lacking.

In his schema Matteo identified part of his emotions (*emptiness, boredom*) and self's-response-to-other's-response behavioural reactions (*replying to messages*), but the rest of the information is lacking. What happened when he met Marisol? What led him to attach himself to her? What happened to him in the instant immediately after they split?

The therapist now made a first comment, observing ironically that it was a relapse into compulsive seduction to cope with emptiness.

T: "Matteo, I reckon this happened: you were attached for a short while to Marisol and seemed keen on her. When she left, you saw yourself briefly as lost. You then experienced emptiness, which is a normal part of loss. In this state you were no longer able to plan or recall you had goals, wishes, things you'd like to do. You know that, when you feel this void inside, you tend to compulsively seek women to go out with, to have sex with, as in this case, that arouse and gratify you. In other cases, instead, you seek women you're not keen on but they look after you, even if they then bore you and you turn them away."

Then, given that the narrative episode lacked enough details to reconstruct the schema, he suggested a guided imagery exercise to improve monitoring. A typical step back in the decision-making procedure. The therapist agreed with Matteo he should concentrate on when the girl said goodbye and left. After a brief induction with the simplified grounding (Chapter 7), Matteo returned to the scene. As at other times, he had difficulty entering it, tending to speak in the past – "I was at my place" – and contacting thoughts and emotions of that moment. He referred to one of the women he had mixed with lately that didn't interest him but by whom he let himself be cared for. The therapist interrupted and took him back to the scene:

T: "Matteo, don't reflect. Don't talk in the past. You're there now, at your place. Describe the surroundings to me. The house: look around you. And then describe Marisol to me, what she says and does, how you feel when observing her."

M: "Ok, ok. Well, we're in the sitting room. She comes up and hugs me. She gives me a kiss and we stay like that for a few seconds. Then she says goodbye."
T: "Where are you now?"
M: "On the threshold."
T: "How does Marisol seem to you?"
M: "Pretty. I like her. She's got a nice smile."
T: "And what do you feel?"
M: "I'm fine. Because, if I think about this type of sensation, I tend to feel it . . .".
T: "One moment. We'll reflect later. Tell me how you feel now with Marisol with you."
M: "Ok. No, I'm still fine."
T: "Where do you feel this wellbeing?"
M: "Umm . . . warmth in my chest. I feel lighter too."
T: "Lighter in what sense?"
M: "Like less tension in my muscles."
T: "In some particular place?"
M: "Umm . . . all over my body."
T: "Good. What's Marisol doing now?"
M: "Picking up her suitcase and saying goodbye."
T: "And how do you react?"
M: "I see her go out. I think we were good together. I'm unhappy she's leaving."
T: "Good. What's happening now?"
M: "I'm closing the door. I'm still fine. I go into the garden for a moment, play with the dogs and then return to the house."
T: "How are you now? I can see your face has changed, darkened?"
M: "Yes, now I'm not fine."
T: "What do you notice around you?"
M: "The house empty. I sit in an armchair and look around. I've nothing to do. I get bored. A sense of an enormous void. I pick up my mobile and look at the messages from this woman telling me: 'When are you going to let me see those puppies?' [*he had just got two new dogs*]. I start replying to the messages."
T: "And how are you now?"
M: "More excited. I've woken up. However, it's the usual mechanism."

The therapist now interrupted the exercise. Matteo came out of it with greater awareness. He realised he had experienced sensations he had not integrated into his narrative, particularly warmth, desire for closeness and relaxing. They seem to be linked to the activation of attachment. The sequence reconstruction also makes it possible to hypothesise that emptiness emerges when the other breaks away. Matteo's coping here has a compulsive self-sufficiency value: instead of showing signs of suffering to the figure abandoning him, he seeks gratification and excitement to handle pain and counteract emotional numbing.

The therapist accordingly suggested continuing behavioural exposure with two aims. The first was to see if he experienced states of wellbeing in a romantic relationship. If this was so, Matteo had to assess whether they were linked to the simple fact of a woman caring for him, which had happened to him and he was aware of, or was linked to Marisol's specific presence. The second was to abstain from the coping involving compulsively seeking sex and see what happened in his inner landscape.

Because of his coping, Matteo was unable, except for short moments, to contact his representation of a lovable self vis-à-vis an interested, loving and strong other. The exercises thus served additionally to discover whether, in his relationship with Marisol, Matteo was simply repeating his maladaptive patterns or there were instead the conditions for letting emerge new relationship forms, where he could feel himself lovable vis-à-vis another seen as attentive and loving and whom he could respect. Shortly afterwards he left Marisol and started the first stable relationship in his life, which has now lasted 10 months.

Skill promotion

We shall continue expounding technique sequences in change promoting. A patient differentiates and accesses healthy self-parts. His negative schemas are known and in his consciousness alternative, benevolent self- and other-representations have emerged. He has also tried, with some success, to counteract maladaptive coping and continues to apply himself.

However there is the problem of *how* to act! This is common in patients with chronic agency problems, coming from social withdrawal histories and isolated for years. At this stage in therapy patients have goals and desires, validate them and only marginally fear the consequences of exposure, but their world map is limited. They lack relational procedures for action. A component of experiential work directed at acquiring skills and expertise is now needed.

A typical sequence starts from imagery with rescripting work or a drama technique. Patients know how to reply to a critical, invalidating, suffering and constrictive other. For example, the wish to court a partner, undertake a training programme or start a recreational activity has got reignited after, thanks to experiential exercises, they overcame their feelings of fear, embarrassment or guilt. They know that replying differently in imagery to their father, mother, boss, spouse, colleague or friend is modifying their way of being and is not aimed at generating different replies to that specific person in reality.

If patients see this aspect very clearly, we now use rescripting for affecting reality and building different relationship forms too. This can still be done in-session with various forms of rescripting, or between sessions. We therefore plan behavioural experiments to inclusively enrich patients' cognition and behaviour repertoire; to learn how to do what they wish to achieve.

Thinking in technique sequence terms, patients and therapists may have completed guided imagery with rescripting or a drama technique where the replies to the other are different. There is now an anchoring to the positive feelings emerging during rescripting and a planning of activity directed at acquiring skills. Patients can, for example, repeat a drama technique, to try again and again a new way of acting or responding with a view to training new sensorimotor and behaviour patterns that seem effective. The drama, or imagery, technique will not be tied necessarily to past narrative episodes. Imaginary scenes, where patients act in new ways or contexts, can be enacted.

This time therapists can offer feedback on the reality level, still naturally respecting patients' ideas and especially knowing they are not adopting a prescriptive stance. For example, patient and therapist might enact a university exam, a call to a girlfriend whom the former wishes to date, or advances to a girl or man who attracts him/her. After this simulation patients are asked if the scene is plausible and the actions staged seem sufficiently meaningful to them. The next step is behavioural exposure, with therapists offering their opinion about the functionality of the behaviour.

A specific case of technique sequence is MIT-G (Chapter 10). Patients first perform role-play aimed at improving metacognition. In the next session they perform new role-play, again within a specific motive, but with the goal of mastering their problematic situation differently and more effectively. It is thus a rescripting aimed both at changing schemas and stimulating more developed metacognitive and relational skills. In individual sessions, as in MIT-G, therapists do not indicate the right, prescriptive solution. They suggest adopting an exploratory and flexible approach, attempting new actions and empirically assessing what will make it possible to move towards satisfying wishes, by triggering benevolent responses in others.

With patients not following the MIT-G protocol, one can also therefore use the sequence: 1) guided imagery or drama technique exercise; 2) rescripting directed at schema change; 3) rescripting aimed at building new metacognitive and relational skills. Naturally not all the steps need to be performed in the same session. When we talk of technique sequences, we refer to operations covering periods of therapy from a few weeks to months. What is important is always observing the decision-making procedure.

Therapists can propose behavioural exposure even without simulating the new behaviour in sessions and by limiting themselves to imagining with the patient what might happen, what the latter could do and how he could feel. They now plan the new behaviour and review it in the following session (Chapter 8).

Final therapy stages: persisting with behavioural experiments and modulating interpersonal rumination

A successful therapy with patients suffering from PD typically requires ongoing work, even after the therapy finishes, to support the results and solve residual problems. The logic followed throughout this book is that the most important part of schemas is the embodied one, written in the flesh. Precisely for this reason change needs to be supported with continuing behavioural experiments. Until a therapy is finished, and afterwards too, therapists agree with patients that the latter will act in line with healthy wishes. Patients know that, in doing this, they can relapse into distressing mental states, where their schemas will attempt to retake control. Patients therefore persist with actions consistent with these wishes and interrupt behaviour forms adopting maladaptive coping, like perfectionism, complaisance, self-sacrificing, avoidance and so on.

Many patients however get to advanced therapy stages and say: "I've understood everything, but, when I get certain thoughts, I still don't feel right and I think about it a lot and it's difficult to get these ideas and sensations out of my head and body." In these cases, the last part of therapy focuses mainly on mental regulation of rumination. For example, we can involve patients in MIMBT (Chapter 9). Or we can hold a few individual sessions where they get steered to intercept their distressing schemas, realise they are ruminating and conduct meditation exercises until the distressing state passes and their attention goes back to the world around them.

Lastly, they can continue to practise bodily activities helping to unravel any remaining distressing knots. They can then undertake an in-session sensorimotor work reminder process, and between one session and another apply the exercises making it possible to free themselves from the somatic component of suffering.

The *follow real wishes, don't ruminate and regulate your bodily state* formula is also the recipe we deliver to patients at the end of therapy, serving to forestall relapses. Even in the most successful therapies it can happen that certain life situations reactivate schemas, bodily suffering and dysfunctional coping procedures. It is good for patients to know which road to follow, without necessarily having to resort again to therapy: acting in line with their wishes, even if it scares them, not lingering over repetitive thinking and regulating bodily sensations with the appropriate activities.

In doing this, they use the resources emerging during therapy. To sum up, if we could mould the psychological characteristics an ideal patient should have when therapy ends, we would see him or her as follows: someone preferring to be interested in real experience rather than stay trapped in his or her own mental worlds, capable of sustaining a sense of safety and leaving ample room for exploration, driven by wishes he or she feels strongly and knowing they deserve to be achieved but knowing the real possibilities and limits to their achievement. Someone who, to motivate him or herself to act, has learnt to envisage the wish being achieved rather than go through all the potential negative scenarios, who can allow him or herself to run the risk of undergoing negative experiences, in that he can circumscribe suffering within the time boundaries it deserves, without ruminating about it; a patient knowing how to interpret bodily signals and modulate them, seeing his or her body as a place of energy and activation.

The three practices – behavioural, meditational and sensorimotor – are therefore interweaved. Patients may, for example, identify the activating of their schema, meditate or let their distress flow away from the centre of consciousness and, together with meditating, or as an alternative, perform sensory exercises or engage in activities, like dancing, theatre, sport, yoga or martial arts, with the goal of both enjoying them and experiencing bodily states where they turn their back on suffering.

References

Ackerman, J. M., Nocera, C. C., & Bargh, J. A. (2010). Incidental haptic sensations influence social judgments and decisions. *Science, 328*(5986), 1712–1715. doi:10.1126/science.1189993

Adler, J. M., Chin, E. D., Kolisetty, A. P., & Oltmanss, T. F. (2012). The distinguishing characteristics of narrative identity in adults with features of borderline personality disorder: An empirical investigation. *Journal of Personality Disorders, 26*, 498–512.

American Psychiatric Association. (2013). *Diagnostic and statistical manual of mental disorders (DSM-5)*. Washington, DC: American Psychiatric Association Publishing.

Arntz, A., & Van Genderen, H. (2011). *Schema therapy for borderline personality disorder*. New York, NY: John Wiley & Sons.

Atance, C. M., & O'Neill, D. K. (2001). Episodic future thinking. *Trends in Cognitive Sciences, 5*, 533–539. doi:10.1016/S1364-6613(00)01804-0

Bargh, J. A. (2017). *Before you know it: The unconscious reasons we do what we do*. New York, NY: Simon & Schuster.

Barnow, S., Stopsack, M., Grabe, H. J., Meinke, C., Spitzer, C., Kronmüller, K., & Sieswerda, S. (2009). Interpersonal evaluation bias in borderline personality disorder. *Behavior Research & Therapy, 47*, 359–365. doi:10.1016/j.brat.2009.02.003

Barsalou, L. W. (2008). Grounded cognition. *Annual Review of Psychology, 59*, 617–645. doi:10.1146/annurev.psych.59.103006.093639

Bateman, A. W., & Fonagy, P. (2004). Mentalization-based treatment of BPD. *Journal of Personality Disorders, 18*(1), 36–51.

Beck, A. T. (1976). *Cognitive therapy and the emotional disorders*. New York: International Universities Press.

Beck, A. T., Baruch, E., Balter, J. M., Steer, R. A., & Warman, D. M. (2004). A new instrument for measuring insight: The beck cognitive insight scale. *Schizophrenia Research, 68*, 319–329.

Bender, D. S. (2005). The therapeutic alliance in the treatment of personality disorders. *Journal of Psychiatric Practice, 11*, 73–87.
Bender, D. S., Morey, L. C., & Skodol, A. E. (2011). Toward a model for assessing level of personality functioning in DSM-5, Part I: A review of theory and methods. *Journal of Personality Assessment, 93*, 332–346. doi:10.1080/00223891.2011.583808
Berneiser, J., Jahn, G., Grothe, M., & Lotze, M. (2018). From visual to motor strategies: Training in mental rotation of hands. *NeuroImage, 167*, 247–255. doi:10.1016/j.neuroimage.2016.06.014
Bertsch, K., Krauch, M., Stopfer, K., Haeussler, K., Herpertz, S. C., & Gamer, M. (2017). Interpersonal threat sensitivity in borderline personality disorder: An eye-tracking study. *Journal of Personality Disorders, 31*(5), 647–670. doi:10.1521/pedi_2017_31_273
Bertsch, K., Roelofs, K., Roch, P. J., Ma, B., Hensel, S., Herpertz, S. C., & Volman, I. (2018). Neural correlates of emotional action control in anger-prone women with borderline personality disorder. *Journal of Psychiatry and Neuroscience, 43*(3), 161–170. doi:10.1503/jpn.170102
Bilotta, E., Giacomantonio, M., Leone, L., Mancini, F., & Coriale, G. (2016). Being alexithymic: Necessity or convenience. Negative emotionality × avoidant coping interactions and alexithymia. *Psychology & Psychotherapy: Theory, Research and Practice, 89*, 261–275. doi:10.1111/papt.12079
Bishop, S. R., Lau, M., Shapiro, S., Carlson, L. E., Anderson, N. D., Carmody, J., . . . Devins, G. (2004). Mindfulness: A proposed operational definition. *Clinical Psychology: Science and Practice, 11*, 230–241. doi:10.1093/clipsy.bph077
Blackwell, S. E. (2018). Mental imagery: From basic research to clinical practice. *Journal of Psychotherapy Integration.* doi:10.1037/int0000108
Bohus, M., Dyer, A. S., Priebe, K., Krüger, A., Kleindienst, N., Schmahl, C., . . . Steil, R. (2013). Dialectical behaviour therapy for post-traumatic stress disorder after childhood sexual abuse in patients with and without borderline personality disorder: A randomised controlled trial. *Psychotherapy & Psychosomatics, 82*, 221–233. doi:10.1159/000348451
Bordin, E. S. (1979). The generalizability of the psychoanalytic concept of the working alliance. *Psychotherapy: Theory, Research and Practice, 16*, 252–260.
Borghi, A. M., & Riggio, L. (2015). Stable and variable affordances are both automatic and flexible. *Frontiers in Human Neuroscience, 9*, 351. doi:10.3389/fnhum.2015.00351
Borkovec, T. D., Robinson, E., Pruzinsky, T., & DePree, J. A. (1983). Preliminary exploration of worry: Some characteristics and processes. *Behaviour Research and Therapy, 21*, 9–16. doi:10.1016/0005-7967(83)90121-3
Boswell, J. F., Iles, B. R., Gallagher, M. W., & Farchione, T. J. (2017). Behavioral activation strategies in cognitive-behavioral therapy for anxiety disorders. *Psychotherapy, 54*, 231–236. doi:10.1037/pst0000119
Boterhoven de Haan, K. L., Fassbinder, E., Hayes, C., & Lee, C. W. (2019). A schema therapy approach to the treatment of post-traumatic stress disorder. *Journal of Psychotherapy Integration, 29*, 54–64. doi: 10.1037/int0000120
Bower, G. H. (1981). Mood and memory. *American Psychologist, 36*, 129–148.
Bowlby, J. (1988). *Clinical applications of attachment: A secure base.* London, UK: Routledge.
Bradley, M. M., Codispoti, M., Cuthbert, B. N., & Lang, P. J. (2001). Emotion and motivation I: Defensive and appetitive reactions in picture processing. *Emotion, 1*, 276–298.
Brandon, N. R., Beike, D. R., & Cole, H. E. (2017). The effect of the order in which episodic autobiographical memories versus autobiographical knowledge are shared on feelings of closeness. *Memory, 25*(6), 744–751. doi:10.1080/09658211.2016.1217340
Brewer, J. A., Worhunsky, P. D., Gray, J. R., Tang, Y.-Y., Weber, J., & Kober, H. (2011). Meditation experience is associated with differences in default mode network activity and

connectivity. *Proceedings of the National Academy of Sciences of the United States of America, 108*(50), 20254–20259. doi:10.1073/pnas.1112029108

Brooks, R. (1991). New approaches to robotics. *Science, 253*, 1227–1232.

Brüne, M., Walden, Edel, M-A., & Dimaggio, G. (2016). Mentalisation of complex emotions in Borderline Personality Disorder: The impact of parenting and exposure to trauma on the performance in a novel cartoon-based task. *Comprehensive Psychiatry, 64*, 29–37. http://dx.doi.org/10.1016/j.comppsych.2015.08.003

Bruner, J. S. (1990). *Acts of meaning*. Cambridge, MA: Harvard University Press.

Bryant, F. B. (2003). Savoring beliefs inventory (SBI): A scale for measuring beliefs about savouring. *Journal of Mental Health, 12*, 175–196. doi:10.1080/0963823031000103489

Buccino, G., Binkofski, F., Fink, G. R., Fadiga, L., Fogassi, L., Gallese, V., . . . Freund, H. J. (2001). Action observation activates premotor and parietal areas in a somatotopic manner: An fMRI study. *European Journal of Neuroscience, 13*, 400–404.

Carcione, A., Dimaggio, G., Conti, L., Fiore, D., Nicolò, G., & Semerari, A. (2010). *Metacognition assessment scale-R, scoring manual V.4.0*. Unpublished manuscript.

Carcione, A., Semerari, A., Nicolò, G., Pedone, R., Popolo, R., Conti, L., . . . Dimaggio, G. (2011). Metacognitive mastery dysfunctions in personality disorder psychotherapy. *Psychiatry Research, 190*, 60–71. doi:10.1016/j.psychres.2010.12.032

Carl, J. R., Soskin, D. P., Kerns, C., & Barlow, D. H. (2013). Positive emotion regulation in emotional disorders: A theoretical review. *Clinical Psychology Review, 3*, 343–360. doi:10.1016/j.cpr.2013.01.003

Centonze, A., Inchausti, F., MacBeth, A., & Dimaggio, G. (2020). Changing embodied dialogical pattern in metacognitive interpersonal therapy. *Journal of Constructivist Psychology* https://doi.org/10.1080/10720537.2020.1717117

Chambers, R., Gullone, E., & Allen, N. B. (2009). Mindful emotion regulation: An integrative review. *Clinical Psychology Review, 29*(6), 560–572.

Chapell, M. S. (1994). Inner speech and respiration: Toward a possible mechanism of stress reduction. *Perceptual and Motor Skills, 79*, 803–811.

Cheli, S., Lysaker, P. H., & Dimaggio, G. (2019). Metacognitively oriented psychotherapy for Schizotypal Personality Disorder: A two cases series. *Personality and mental health, 13*, 155–167. https://doi.org/10.1002/pmh.1447

Chiesa, A., & Malinowski, P. (2011). Mindfulness-based approaches: Are they all the same? *Journal of Clinical Psychology, 67*(4), 404–424. doi:10.1002/jclp.20776

Clarkin, J. F., Yeomans, F. E., & Kernberg, O. F. (1999). *Psychotherapy for borderline personality*. New York, NY: John Wiley & Sons Inc.

Cloitre, M., Garvert, D. W., & Weiss, B. J. (2017). Depression as a moderator of STAIR narrative therapy for women with post-traumatic stress disorder related to childhood abuse. *European Journal of Psychotraumatology, 8*(1). doi:10.1080/20008198.2017.1377028

Compas, B. E., Jaser, S. S., Dunbar, J. P., Watson, K. H., Bettis, A. H., Gruhn, M. A., & Williams, E. K. (2014). Coping and emotion regulation from childhood to adulthood. *Australian Journal of Psychology, 66*, 71–81. doi: 10.1111/ajpy.12043

Conway, M. A., & Pleydell-Pearce, C. W. (2000). The construction of autobiographical memories in the self-memory system. *Psychological Review, 107*, 261–288.

Craig, A. D. (2015). *How do you feel? An interoceptive moment with your neurobiological self*. Princeton, NJ: Princeton University Press.

Critchfield, K. L., Dobner-Pereira, J., Panizo, M. T., & Drucker, K. (2019). Beyond the borderline: Expanding our repertoire to address relational patterns and power dynamics attendant to diverse personality disorders. *Journal of Contemporary Psychotherapy, 49*, 61–67. doi:10.1007/s10879-018-9409-8

Damasio, A. R. (1994). *Descartes' error – Emotion and the human brain.* New York, NY: Avon.
Denson, T. F. (2013). The multiple systems model of angry rumination. *Personality and Social Psychology Review, 17,* 103–123. https://doi.org/10.1177%2F1088868312467086
Debeer, E., Raes, F., Williams, J. M. G., & Hermans, D. (2011). Context-dependent activation of reduced autobiographical memory specificity as an avoidant coping style. *Emotion, 11*(6), 1500–1506. doi:10.1037/a0024535
Desmurget, M., & Grafton, S. (2000). Forward modeling allows feedback control for fast reaching movements. *Trends in Cognitive Sciences, 4,* 423–431.
Di Cesare, G., Marchi, M., Errante, A., Fasano, F., & Rizzolatti, G. (2018). Mirroring the social aspects of speech and actions: The role of the insula. *Cerebral Cortex, 4,* 1348–1357. doi:10.1093/cercor/bhx051
Dimaggio, G. (2019). To expose or not to expose? Different roads to similar outcomes in the psychotherapy for Post-Traumatic Stress Disorder. *Journal of Psychotherapy Integration, 29,* 1–5. http://dx.doi.org/10.1037/int0000138
Dimaggio, G., Carcione, A., Conti, M. L., Nicolò, G., Fiore, D., Pedone, R., . . . Semerari, A. (2009). Impaired decentration in personality disorder: An analysis with the metacognition assessment scale. *Clinical Psychology & Psychotherapy, 16,* 450–462. doi:10.1002/cpp.619
Dimaggio, G., Carcione, A., Nicolò, G., Lysaker, P. H., D'Angerio, S., Conti, M. L., . . . Semerari, A. (2013). Differences between axes depend on where you set the bar. Associations among symptoms, interpersonal relationship and alexithymia with number of personality disorder criteria. *Journal of Personality Disorders, 27,* 371–382. doi:10.1521/pedi_2012_26_043
Dimaggio, G., & Lysaker, P. H. (Eds.). (2010). *Metacognition and severe adult mental disorders: From research to treatment.* London, UK: Routledge.
Dimaggio, G., & Lysaker, P. H. (2015a). Commentary: Personality and intentional binding: An exploratory study using the narcissistic personality inventory. *Frontiers in Human Neuroscience, 9,* 325. doi:10.3389/fnhum.2015.00325
Dimaggio, G., & Lysaker, P. H. (2015b). Metacognition and mentalizing in the psychotherapy of patients with psychosis and personality disorders. *Journal of Clinical Psychology: In-Session, 71,* 117–124. doi:10.1002/jclp.22147
Dimaggio, G., & Lysaker, P. H. (2018). A pragmatic view on disturbed self-reflection in personality disorders: Implications for psychotherapy. *Journal of Personality Disorders, 32,* 311–328. doi:10.1521/pedi.2018.32.3.311
Dimaggio, G., Lysaker, P. H., Carcione, A., Nicolò, G., & Semerari, A. (2008). Know yourself and you shall know the other . . . to a certain extent. Multiple paths of influence of self-reflection on mindreading. *Consciousness and Cognition, 17,* 778–789. doi:10.1016/j.concog.2008.02.005
Dimaggio, G., MacBeth, A., Popolo, R., Salvatore, G., Perrini, F., Raouna, A., . . . Montano, A. (2018). The problem of overcontrol: Perfectionism and emotional inhibition as predictors of personality disorder. *Comprehensive Psychiatry, 83,* 71–78. doi:10.1016/j.comppsych.2018.03.005
Dimaggio, G., Montano, A., Popolo, R., & Salvatore, G. (2015). *Metacognitive interpersonal therapy for personality disorders: A treatment manual.* London, UK: Routledge.
Dimaggio, G., Nicolò, G., Semerari, A., & Carcione, A. (2013). Investigating the process in the psychotherapy of personality disorders: The role of symptoms, quality of affects, emotional dysregulation, interpersonal process and mentalizing. *Psychotherapy Research, 23,* 624–632. doi:10.1080/10503307.2013.845921

Dimaggio, G., Popolo, R., Montano, A., Velotti, P., Perrini, F., Buonocore, L., . . . Salvatore, G. (2017). Emotion dysregulation, symptoms and interpersonal problems as independent predictors of a broad range of personality disorders in an outpatient sample. *Psychology and Psychotherapy: Theory, Research and Practice, 90,* 586–599. doi:10.1111/papt.12126

Dimaggio, G., Salvatore, G., Lysaker, P. H., Ottavi, P., & Popolo, R. (2015). Behavioral activation revised as a common mechanism of change for personality disorders psychotherapy. *Journal of Psychotherapy Integration, 25,* 30–38. doi:10.1037/a0038769

Dimaggio, G., Salvatore, G., MacBeth, A., Ottavi, P., Buonocore, L., & Popolo, R. (2017). Metacognitive interpersonal therapy for personality disorders: A case study series. *Journal of Contemporary Psychotherapy, 47,* 11–21. doi:10.1007/s10879-016-9342-7

Dimaggio, G., Semerari, A., Carcione, A., Nicolò, G., & Procacci, M. (2007). *Psychotherapy of personality disorders: Metacognition, states of mind and interpersonal cycles.* London, UK: Routledge.

Dimaggio, G., Semerari, A., Carcione, A., Procacci, M., & Nicolò, G. (2006). Toward a model of self pathology underlying personality disorders: Narratives, metacognition, interpersonal cycles and decision making processes. *Journal of Personality Disorders, 20,* 597–617.

Dimaggio, G., Semerari, A., Falcone, M., Nicolò, G., Carcione, A., & Procacci, M. (2002). Metacognition, states of mind, cognitive biases and interpersonal cycles. Proposal for an integrated model of Narcissism. *Journal of Psychotherapy Integration, 12,* 421–451.

Dimidjian, S., Hollon, S. D., Dobson, K. S., Schmaling, K. B., Kohlenberg, R. J., Addis, M. E., . . . Atkins, D. C. (2006). Randomized trial of behavioral activation, cognitive therapy, and antidepressant medication in the acute treatment of adults with major depression. *Journal of Consulting and Clinical Psychology, 74,* 658–670.

Domsalla, M., Koppe, G., Niedtfeld, I., Vollstadt-Klein, S., Schmahl, C., Bohus, M., & Lis, S. (2014). Cerebral processing of social rejection in patients with borderline personality disorder. *SCAN, 9,* 1789–1797.

Eckberg, M. (2000). *Victims of cruelty: Somatic psychotherapy in the treatment of posttraumatic stress disorder.* Berkeley, CA: North Atlantic Book.

Ecker, B., Ticic, R., & Hulley, L. (2012). *Unlocking the emotional brain: Eliminating symptoms at their roots using memory reconsolidation.* New York, NY: Routledge.

Ehrenreich, J. T., Fairholme, C. P., Buzzella, B. A., Ellard, K. K., & Barlow, D. H. (2007). The role of emotion in psychological therapy. *Clinical Psychology: Science and Practice, 14,* 422–428. doi:10.1111/j.1468-2850.2007.00102.x

Eisenberg, N., Fabes, R. A., & Guthrie, I. K. (1997). Coping with stress. In S. A. Wolchik & I. N. Sandler (Eds.), *Handbook of children's coping. Issues in clinical child psychology.* Boston, MA: Springer.

Elbert, T., Schauer, M., & Neuner, F. (2015). Narrative exposure therapy (NET) – Reorganizing memories of traumatic stress, fear and violence. In U. Schnyder & M. Cloitre (a cura di), *Evidence based treatments for trauma-related psychological disorders: A practical guide for clinicians* (pp. 229–253). Switzerland: Springer.

Ellis, A. (1994). *Reason and emotion in psychotherapy: Revised and updated.* New York, NY: Birch Lane.

Elsner, B., & Hommel, B. (2001). Effect anticipation and action control. *Journal of Experimental Psychology: Human Perception and Performance, 27,* 229–240.

Fassbinder, E., Schweiger, U., Martius, D., Brand-de Wilde, O., & Arntz, A. (2016). Emotion regulation in schema therapy and dialectical behavior therapy. *Frontiers in Psychology, 7,* 1373. doi:10.3389/fpsyg.2016.01373

Foa, E. B., Hembree, E., & Rothbaum, B. O. (2007). *Prolonged exposure therapy for PTSD: Therapist guide.* New York, NY: Oxford University Press.

Fonagy, P. (1991). Thinking about thinking: Some clinical and theoretical considerations in the treatment of a borderline patient. *International Journal of Psycho-Analysis, 72*, 639–656.

Fonagy, P., Gergely, G., Jurist, E. L., & Target, M. (2002). *Affect regulation, mentalization, and the development of the self*. London, UK: Other Press.

Forgas, J. P. (2002). Feeling and doing: The role of affect in interpersonal behavior. *Psychological Inquiry, 9*, 205–210.

Fraley, R. C., & Shaver, P. R. (2000). Adult romantic attachment: Theoretical developments, emerging controversies, and unanswered questions. *Review of General Psychology, 4*, 132–154.

Franzen, N., Hagenhoff, M., Baer, N., Schmidt, A., Mier, D., Sammer, G., . . . Lis, S. (2011). Superior 'theory of mind' in borderline personality disorder: An analysis of interaction behavior in a virtual trust game. *Psychiatry Research, 187*, 224–233.

Fredrickson, B. L. (2001). The role of positive emotions in positive psychology: The broaden-and-build theory of positive emotions. *American Psychologist, 56*, 218–226.

Gaesser, B., Keeler, K., & Young, L. (2018). Moral imagination: Facilitating prosocial decision-making through scene imagery and theory of mind. *Cognition, 171*, 180–193. doi:10.1016/j.cognition.2017.11.004

Garbarini, F., & Adenzato, M. (2004). At the root of embodied cognition: Cognitive science meets neurophysiology. *Brain & Cognition, 56*, 100–106.

Gazzillo, F. (2016). *Fidarsi dei pazienti. Introduzione alla control-mastery theory*. Milano: Raffaello Cortina.

Gazzillo, F., Dimaggio, G., & Curtis, J. T. (2019). Case formulation and treatment planning: How to take care of relationship and symptoms together. *Journal of Psychotherapy Integration*. https://doi.org/10.1037/int0000185

Gazzillo, F., Genova, F., Fedeli, F., Dazzi, N., Bush, M., Curtis, J. T., & Silberschatz, G. (2019). Patients unconscious testing activity in psychotherapy: A theoretical an empirical overview. *Psychoanalytic Psychology, 36*, 173–183. https://doi.org/10.1037/pap0000227.

Gibson, J. J. (1979). *The ecological approach to visual perception*. Hillsdale, NJ: Erlbaum.

Gilbert, P. (Ed.). (2005). *Compassion: Conceptualisations, research and use in psychotherapy*. London, UK: Routledge.

Gjelsvik, B., Lovric, D., & Williams, J. M. G. (2018). Embodied cognition and emotional disorders: Embodiment and abstraction in understanding depression. *Journal of Experimental Psychopathology*. doi:10.5127%2Fpr.035714

Gonçalves, M. M., Ribeiro, A. P., Mendes, I., Alves, D., Silva, J., Rosa, C., . . . Braga, C. (2017). Three narrative-based coding systems: Innovative moments, ambivalence and ambivalence resolution. *Psychotherapy Research, 3*, 270–282. doi:10.1080/10503307.2016.1247216

Gordon-King, K., Schweitzer, R. D., & Dimaggio, G. (2018a). Metacognitive interpersonal therapy for personality disorders: The case of a man with obsessive-compulsive personality disorder and avoidant personality disorder. *Journal of Contemporary Psychotherapy, 49*, 39–47. https://doi.org/10.1007/s10879-018-9404-0

Gordon-King, K., Schweitzer, R. D., & Dimaggio, G. (2018b). Metacognitive interpersonal therapy for personality disorders featuring emotional inhibition: A multiple baseline case series. *Journal of Nervous and Mental Disease, 206*(4), 263–269. doi:10.1097/NMD.0000000000000789

Greenberg, L. S. (2002). *Emotion-focused therapy: Coaching clients to work with their feelings*. Washington, DC: American Psychological Association.

Gross, J. J. (2013). Emotion regulation: Taking stock and moving forward. *Emotion, 13*(3), 359–365. https://doi.org/10.1037/a0032135

Hackmann, A., Bennett-Levy, J., & Holmes, E. A. (2011). *Oxford guide to imagery in cognitive therapy*. Oxford, UK: Oxford University Press.

Hascalovitz, A. C., & Obhi, S. S. (2105). Personality and intentional binding: An exploratory study using the narcissistic personality inventory. *Frontiers in Human Neuroscience, 9*, 13. doi:10.3389/fnhum.2015.00013

Hasson-Ohayon, I., Arnon-Ribenfeld, N., Hamm, J. A., & Lysaker, P. H. (2017). Agency before action: The application of behavioral activation in psychotherapy with persons with psychosis. *Psychotherapy, 54*, 245–251. doi:10.1037/pst0000114

Hayes, S. C., Strosahl, K. D., & Wilson, K. G. (2011). *Acceptance and commitment therapy: The process and practice of mindful change*. Guilford Press.

Hermans, D., De Decker, A., De Peuter, S., Raes, F., Eelen, P., & Williams, J. M. (2008). Autobiographical memory specificity and affect regulation: Coping with a negative life event. *Depression & Anxiety, 25*, 787–792. doi:10.1002/da.20326

Hermans, H. J. M., & Dimaggio, G. (2004). The dialogical self in psychotherapy. In *The dialogical self in psychotherapy* (pp. 17–26). London, UK: Routledge.

Hermans, H. J. M., & Hermans-Konopka, A. (2010). *Dialogical self theory: Positioning and counter-positioning in a globalizing society*. Cambridge: Cambridge University Press.

Hirsch, C. R., & Mathews, A. (2012). A cognitive model of pathological worry. *Behaviour Research and Therapy, 50*, 636–646. https://doi.org/10.1016/j.brat.2012.06.007

Huber, J., Salatsch, C., Ingenerf, K., Schmid, C., Maatouk, I., Weisbrod, M., ... Nikendei, C. (2015). Characteristics of disorder-related autobiographical memory in acute anorexia nervosa patients. *European Eating Disorders Review, 23*, 379–389. doi:10.1002/erv.2379

Hyde, C., Fuelscher, I., Williams, J., Lum, J. A. G., He, J., Barhoun, P., & Enticott, P. G. (2018). Corticospinal excitability during motor imagery is reduced in young adults with developmental coordination disorder. *Research in Developmental Disabilities, 72*, 214–224. doi:10.1016/j.ridd.2017.11.009

Inchausti, F., García-Poveda, N. V., Ballesteros-Prados, A., Ortuño-Sierra, J., Sánchez-Reales, S., Prado-Abril, J., Aldaz-Armendáriz, J. A., Mole, J., Dimaggio, G., Ottavi, P., & Fonseca-Pedrero, E. (2018). The effects of Metacognition-Oriented Social Skills Training (MOSST) on psychosocial outcomes in schizophrenia-spectrum disorders: A randomized controlled trial. *Schizophrenia Bulletin, 44*, 1235–1244. https://doi.org/10.1093/schbul/sbx168

Inchausti, F., Moreno-Campos, L., Prado-Abril, J., Sánchez-Reales, S., Fonseca-Pedrero, E., MacBeth, A., Popolo, R., & Dimaggio, G. (2020). Metacognitive Interpersonal Therapy in Group (MIT-G) for personality disorders: Preliminary results from a pilot study in a public mental health setting. *Journal of Contemporary Psychotherapy*. doi: 10.1007/s10879-020-09453-9

Ivaldi, A. (Ed.). (2017). *Treating dissociative and personality disorders: A motivational systems approach to theory and treatment*. London, UK: Routledge.

James, W. (1890). *The principles of psychology* (Vol. 1). New York, NY: Henry Holt.

Jeannerod, M., & Decety, J. (1995). Mental motor imagery: A window into the representational stages of action. *Current Opinion in Neurobiology, 5*, 727–732.

Jent, J. F., Niec, L. N., & Baker, S. E. (2011). Play and interpersonal processes. In S. W. Russ & L. N. Niec (a cura di), *Play in clinical practice: Evidence-based approaches* (pp. 23–47). New York, NY: Guilford Press.

Jørgensen, C. R. (2010). Invited essay: Identity and borderline personality disorder. *Journal of Personality Disorders, 24*(3), 344–364. doi:10.1521/pedi.2010.24.3.344

Kabat-Zinn, J. (1990). *Full catastrophe living: Using the wisdom of your body and mind to face stress, pain and illness* (1st ed.). New York, NY: Delacorte Press.

Kabat-Zinn, J. (2003). Mindfulness-based interventions in context: Past, present, and future. *Clinical Psychology: Science and Practice, 10*, 144–156. doi:10.1093/clipsy.bpg016

Kanter, J. W., Puspitasari, A. J., Santos, M. M., & Nagy, G. A. (2012). Behavioural activation: History, evidence and promise. *British Journal of Psychiatry, 200*, 361–363. doi:10.1192/bjp.bp.111.103390

Karterud, S. (2015). *Mentalization-based group therapy (MBT-G): A theoretical, clinical, and research manual.* Oxford, UK: Oxford University Press.

Killingsworth, M. A., & Gilbert, D. T. (2010). A wandering mind is an unhappy mind. *Science, 330*(6006), 932. doi:10.1126/science.1192439

Kim, E. H., Crouch, T. B., & Olatunji, B. O. (2017). Adaptation of behavioral activation in the treatment of chronic pain. *Psychotherapy, 54*, 237–244. doi:10.1037/pst0000112

Klein, S. B., & Loftus, J. (1993). The mental representation of trait and autobiographical knowledge about the self. In T. K. Srull & R. S. Wyer (a cura di), *Advances in social cognition* (pp. 1–49). Hillsdale, NJ: Lawrence Erlbaum.

Knowles, M. M., Foden, P., El-Deredy, W., & Wells, A. (2016). A systematic review of efficacy of the attention training technique in clinical and nonclinical samples. *Journal of Clinical Psychology, 72*(10), 999–1025. doi:10.1002/jclp.22312

Knox, J. (2011). *Self-agency in psychotherapy.* New York, NY: W. W. Norton and Company, Inc.

Kohut, H. (1977). *The restoration of the self.* Chicago, IL: University of Chicago Press.

Kok, B. E., & Fredrickson, B. L. (2010). Upward spirals of the heart: Autonomic flexibility, as indexed by vagal tone, reciprocally and prospectively predicts positive emotions and social connectedness. *Biological Psychology, 85*, 432–436. doi:10.1016/j.biopsycho.2010.09.005

Kolb, D. A. (1984). *Experiential learning: Experience as the source of learning and development.* Englewood Cliffs, NJ: Prentice Hall.

Konopka, A., Hermans, H. J. M., & Gonçalves, M. M. (Eds.) (2018). *Handbook of dialogical self theory and psychotherapy: Bridging psychotherapeutic and cultural traditions.* London, UK: Routledge.

Kosslyn, S. M. (1994). *Image and brain: The resolution of the imagery debate.* Cambridge, MA: MIT Press.

Lakoff, M., & Johnson, M. (1980). *Metaphors we live by.* Chicago: University of Chicago Press.

Langston, C. A. (1994). Capitalizing on and coping with daily-life events: Expressive responses to positive events. *Journal of Personality and Social Psychology, 67*, 1112–1125. doi:10.1037/0022-3514.67.6.1112

Lazarus, R. S., & Folkman, S. (1984). *Stress, appraisal and coping.* New York, NY: Springer.

Le Doux, J. (2015). *Anxious: Using the brain to understand and treat fear and anxiety.* New York, NY: Viking.

Lee, M. S., Kim, H. J., & Moon, S. R. (2003). Qigong reduced blood pressure and catecholamine levels of patients with essential hypertension. *International Journal of Neuroscience, 113*, 1691–1701.

Leiman, M., & Stiles, W. B. (2001). Dialogical sequence analysis and the zone of proximal development as conceptual enhancements to the assimilation model: The case of Jan revisited. *Psychotherapy Research, 11*, 311–330.

Levy, K. N., & Scala, J. W. (2015). Psychotherapy integration for personality disorders. *Journal of Psychotherapy Integration, 25*, 49–57. doi:10.1037/a0038771

Lewinsohn, P. M. (1974). A behavioral approach to depression. In R. J. Friedman & M. Katz (Eds.), *The psychology of depression: Contemporary theory and research* (pp. 157–178). Oxford, UK: Wiley.

Lichtenberg, J. D. (1989). *Psychoanalysis and motivation*. Hillsdale, NJ: Analytic Press.

Lillard, A. S. (2001). Pretend play as twin earth: A social-cognitive analysis. *Developmental Review, 21*(4), 495–531. doi:10.1006/drev.2001.0532

Lillard, A. S., Lerner, M. D., Hopkins, E. J., Dore, R. A., Smith, E. D., & Palmquist, C. M. (2013). The impact of pretend play on children's development: A review of the evidence. *Psychological Bulletin, 139*, 1–34. doi:10.1037/a0029321

Linehan, M. M. (1993). *Skills training manual for treating borderline personality disorder*. New York, NY: Guilford Press.

Links, P. S. (2015). Advancing psychotherapy integration for treatment of personality disorders. *Journal of Psychotherapy Integration, 25*, 45–48. doi:10.1037/a0038777

Links, P. S., Mercer, D., & Novick, J. (2016). In W. J. Livesley, G. Dimaggio, & J. F. Clarkin (Eds.), *Integrated treatment for personality disorders: A modular approach* (pp. 282–302). New York, NY: Guilford Press.

Liotti, G., & Gilbert, P. (2011). Mentalizing, motivation, and social mentalities: Theoretical considerations and implications for psychotherapy. *Psychology and Psychotherapy: Theory, Research and Practice, 84*, 9–25.

Livesley, W. J., Dimaggio, G., & Clarkin, J. F. (2016). *Integrated treatment for personality disorder*. New York, NY: Guilford.

Lowen, A. (1975). *Bioenergetics*. London, UK: Penguin.

Lu, W. A., & Kuo, C. D. (2003). The effect of Tai Chi Chuan on the autonomic nervous modulation in older persons. *Medicine and Science in Sports and Exercise, 35*, 1972–1976.

Luborsky, L., & Crits-Christoph, P. (1990). *Capire il transfert*. Tr. It. Milano: Raffaello Cortina, 1992.

Lysaker, P. H., Buck, K. D., & Ringer, J. (2007). The recovery of metacognitive capacity in schizophrenia across thirty-two months of individual psychotherapy: A case study. *Psychotherapy Research, 17*, 713–720.

Lysaker, P. H., George, S., Chaudoin-Patzoldt, K. A., Pec, O., Bob, P., Leonhardt, B. L., . . . Dimaggio, G. (2017). Contrasting metacognitive, social cognitive and alexithymia profiles in adults with borderline personality disorder, schizophrenia and substance use disorder. *Psychiatry Research, 257*, 393–399.

Lysaker, P. H., Gumley, A., Brüne, M., Vanheule, S., Buck, K. D., & Dimaggio, G. (2011). Deficits in the ability to recognize one's own affects and those of others: Associations with neurocognition, symptoms and sexual trauma among persons with schizophrenia. *Consciousness & Cognition, 20*, 1183–1192. doi:10.1016/j.concog.2010.12.018

Lysaker, P. H., Gumley, A., Leudtke, B., Buck, K. D., Ringer, J. M., Olesek, K., . . . Dimaggio, G. (2013). Thinking about oneself and thinking about others: Evidence of the relative independence of deficits in metacognition and social cognition in schizophrenia. *Acta Psychiatrica Scandinavica, 127*, 239–247. doi:10.1111/acps.12012

Lysaker, P. H., & Lysaker, J. T. (2002). Narrative structure in psychosis: Schizophrenia and disruptions in the dialogical self. *Theory & Psychology, 12*, 207–220. doi:10.1177/0959354302012002630

Lysaker, P. H., Olesek, K., Buck, K., Leonhardt, B. L., Vohs, J., Ringer, J., . . . Outcalt, J. (2014). Metacognitive mastery moderates the relationship of alexithymia with cluster C personality disorder traits in adults with substance use disorders. *Addictive Behaviors, 39*(3), 558–561.

Lyubomirsky, S., King, L., & Diener, E. (2005). The benefits of frequent positive affect: Does happiness lead to success? *Psychological Bulletin, 131*, 803–855. doi:10.1037/0033-2909.131.6.803

Maillard, P., Dimaggio, G., de Roten, Y., Despland, J. N., & Kramer, U. (2017). Metacognitive processes and symptom change in a short-term treatment for borderline personality disorder: A pilot study. *Journal of Psychotherapy Integration.* doi:10.1037/int0000090

Mancini, F. (Ed.). (2018). *The obsessive mind: Understanding and treating obsessive-compulsive disorder.* London, UK: Routledge.

Markowitz, J. C., Petkova, E., Neria, Y., Van Meter, P. E., Zhao, Y., Hembree, E., . . . Marshall, R. D. (2015). Is exposure necessary? A randomized clinical trial of interpersonal psychotherapy for PTSD. In *American Journal of Psychiatry, 172,* 430–440.

Martin, A., Wiggs, C., Ungerleider, L., & Haxby, J. V. (1996). Neural correlates of category-specific knowledge. *Nature, 379,* 649–652. https://doi.org/10.1038/379649a0

McAdams, D. P. (1993). *The stories we live by: Personal myths and the making of the self.* New York, NY: Guilford Press.

McNally, R. J., Lasko, N. B., Macklin, M. L., & Pitman, R. K. (1995). Autobiographical memory disturbance in combat-related posttraumatic stress disorder. *Behaviour Research and Therapy, 33*(6), 619–630. doi:10.1016/0005-7967(95)00007-K

Meloy, J. R. (1998). *The psychology of stalking: Clinical and forensic perspectives.* San Diego, CA: Academic Press.

Merlau-Ponty, M. (1945). *Fenomenologia della percezione.* Tr. It. Milano: Bompiani, 2014.

Meyer, V. (1966). Modification of expectations in cases with obsessional rituals. *Behaviour Research and Therapy, 4,* 273–280. https://doi.org/10.1016/0005-7967(66)90023-4

Mitchell, S. A. (2000). *Relationality: From attachment to intersubjectivity.* Hillsdale, NJ: Analytic Press.

Moreno, J. L., & Moreno, Z. T. (1975/2012). *Psychodrama: Action therapy and principles of practice* (Vol. 3). Malvern: The North-West Psychodrama Association.

Morina, N., Lancee, J., & Arntz, A. (2017). Imagery rescripting as a clinical intervention for aversive memories: A meta-analysis. *Journal of Behavior Therapy and Experimental Psychiatry, 55,* 6–15. doi:10.1016/j.jbtep.2016.11.003

Moroni, F., Procacci, M., Pellecchia, G., Semerari, A., Nicolò, G., Carcione, A., & Colle, L. (2016). Mindreading dysfunction in avoidant personality disorder compared with other personality disorders. *Journal of Nervous and Mental Dis*ease, *204,* 752–757. doi:10.1097/NMD.0000000000000536

Nazzaro, M. P., Boldrini, T., Tanzilli, A., Muzi, L., Giovanardi, G., & Lingiardi, V. (2017). Does reflective functioning mediate the relationship between attachment and personality? *Psychiatry Research, 256,* 169–175. doi:10.1016/j.psychres.2017.06.045

Neimeyer, R. A. (2000). Narrative disruptions in the construction of self. In R. A. Neimeyer & J. D. Raskin (a cura di), *Constructions of disorder: Meaning making frameworks for psychotherapy* (pp. 207–241). Washington, DC: American Psychological Association.

Neimeyer, R. A. (2016). Meaning reconstruction in the wake of loss: Evolution of a research program. *Behaviour Change, 33,* 65–79. doi:10.1017/bec.2016.4

Nolen-Hoeksema, S., Wisco, B. E., & Lyubomirsky, S. (2008). Rethinking rumination. *Perspectives on Psychological Science, 3*(5), 400–424. doi:10.1111/j.1745-6924.2008.00088.x.

Ogden, P., & Fisher, J. (2015). *Sensorimotor psychotherapy: Interventions for trauma and attachment.* W. W. Norton and Company, Inc.

Orr, E., & Geva, R. (2015). Symbolic play and language development. *Infant Behavior & Development, 38,* 147–161.

Ottavi, P., D'Alia, D., Lysaker, P. H., Kent, J., Popolo, R., Salvatore, G., & Dimaggio, G. (2014a). Metacognition oriented social skills training for schizophrenia: Theory, method and clinical illustration. *Clinical Psychology and Psychotherapy, 21,* 465–473. doi:10.1002/cpp.1850

Ottavi, P., Pasinetti, M., Popolo, R., Salvatore, G., Lysaker, P. H., & Dimaggio, G. (2014b). Metacognition-oriented social skills training. In P. Lysaker, G. Dimaggio, & M. Brüne (Eds.), *Social cognition and metacognition in schizophrenia: Psychopathology and treatment approaches*. Elsevier Inc.

Ottavi, P., Passarella, T., Pasinetti, M., Salvatore, G., & Dimaggio, G. (2016). Mindfulness for anxious and angry worry about interpersonal events in personality disorders. In W. J. Livesley, G. Dimaggio, & J. F. Clarkin (Eds.), *Integrated treatment for personality disorders: A modular approach* (pp. 282–302). New York, NY: Guilford Press.

Ottavi, P., Passarella, T., Pasinetti, M., MacBeth, A., Velotti, P., Buonocore, L, Popolo, R., Salvatore, G., Velotti, A., & Dimaggio, G. (2019). Metacognitive interpersonal mindfulness-based training for worry about interpersonal events: A pilot feasibility and acceptability study. *Journal of Nervous and Mental Disease, 207*, 944–950. doi: 10.1097/NMD.0000000000001054

Padesky, C. A., & Mooney, K. A. (2012). Strengths-based cognitive-behavioural therapy: A four-step model to build resilience. *Clinical Psychology and Psychotherapy, 19*, 283–290.

Paivio, S. C., & Pascual-Leone, A. (2010). *Emotion focused therapy for complex trauma: An integrative approach*. Washington, DC: American Psychological Association.

Panksepp, J., & Biven, L. (2012). *The archeology of mind: Neuroevolutionary origins of humans emotions*. New York, NY: Norton.

Pascual-Leone, A. (2018). How clients "change emotion with emotion": A programme of research on emotional processing. *Psychotherapy Research, 28*, 165–182. doi:10.1080/10503307.2017.1349350

Pascual-Leone, A., & Greenberg, L. S. (2007). Emotional processing in experiential therapy: Why "the only way out is through." *Journal of Consulting and Clinical Psychology, 75*, 875–887. doi:10.1037/0022-006X.75.6.875

Perls, F., Hefferline, G., & Goodman, P. (1951). *Gestalt therapy*. New York, NY: Gestalt Journal Press.

Pillemer, D. (2003). Directive functions of autobiographical memory: The guiding power of the specific episode. *Memory, 11*(2), 193–202. doi:10.1080/741938208

Popolo, R., MacBeth, A., Brunello, S., Canfora, F., Ozdemir, E., Rebecchi, D., Toselli, C., Venturelle, G., Salvatore, G., & Dimaggio, G. (2018). Metacognitive Interpersonal Therapy in Group (MIT-G): A pilot noncontrolled effectiveness study. *Research in Psychotherapy: Psychopathology, Process and Outcome, 21*, 155–163. doi:10.4081/ripppo.2018.338

Popolo, R., MacBeth, A., Canfora, F., Rebecchi, D., Toselli, C., Salvatore, G., & Dimaggio, G. (2019). Metacognitive interpersonal therapy in group (MIT-G) for young adults personality disorders: A pilot randomized controlled trial. *Psychology and Psychotherapy: Theory, Research & Practice, 92*, 342–358. doi:10.1111/papt.12182

Porges, S. (2011). *The polyvagal theory: Neurophysiological foundations of emotions, attachment, communication, self-regulation*. New York, NY: W. W. Norton and Company, Inc.

Porges, S. (2017). *The pocket guide to the polyvagal theory: The transforming power of feeling safe*. New York, NY: W. W. Norton and Company, Inc.

Pos, A. E. (2014). Emotion focused therapy for avoidant personality disorder: Pragmatic considerations for working with experientially avoidant clients. *Journal of Contemporary Psychotherapy, 44*, 127–139. doi:10.1007/s10879-013-9256-6

Pos, A. E., & Greenberg, L. S. (2012). Organizing awareness and increasing emotion regulation: Revising chair work in emotion focused therapy for borderline personality disorder. *Journal of Personality Disorders, 26*, 84–107. doi:10.1521/pedi.2012.26.1.84

Preißler, S., Dziobek, I., Ritter, K., Heekeren, H. R., & Roepke, S. (2010). Social cognition in borderline personality disorder: Evidence for disturbed recognition of the emotions, thoughts, and intentions of others. *Frontiers in Behavioral Neuroscience, 4*, 182. doi:10.3389/fnbeh.2010.00182

Prunetti, E., Bosio, V., Bateni, M., & Liotti, G. (2013). Three-week inpatient cognitive evolutionary therapy (CET) for patients with personality disorders: Evidence of effectiveness in symptoms reduction and improved treatment adherence. *Psychology and Psychotherapy: Theory, Research and Practice, 86*, 262–279. doi:10.1111/j.2044-8341.2011.02060.x

Pulvermüller, F. (2013). How neurons make meaning: Brain mechanisms for embodied and abstract-symbolic semantics. *Trends in Cognitive Science, 17*, 458–470.

Rabin, S. J., Hasson-Ohayon, I., Moran Avidan, M., Rozencwaig, S., Shalev, H., & Kravetz, S. (2014). Metacognition in schizophrenia and schizotypy: Relation to symptoms of schizophrenia, traits of schizotypy and social quality of life. *The Israel Journal of Psychiatry Related Sciences, 51*(1).

Reich, W. (1933/1980). *Character analysis*. New York, NY: Farrar, Straus & and Giroux.

Ribeiro, E., Ribeiro, A. P., Gonçalves, M. M., Horvath, A. O., & Stiles, W. B. (2013). How collaboration in therapy becomes therapeutic: The therapeutic collaboration coding system. *Psychology and Psychotherapy: Theory, Research and Practice, 86*, 294–314. doi:10.1111/j.2044-8341.2012.02066.x

Rizzolatti, G., Fadiga, L., Gallese, V., & Fogassi, L. (1996). Premotor cortex and the recognition of motor actions. *Cognitive Brain Research, 3*, 131–141.

Rizzolatti, G., & Sinigaglia, C. (2007). *Mirrors in the brain: How our minds share actions, emotions, and experience*. Oxford: Oxford University Press.

Rubin, D. C. (2014). Schema-driven construction of future autobiographical traumatic events: The future is much more troubling than the past. *Journal of Experimental Psychology: General, 143*, 612–630. doi:10.1037/a0032638

Russ, S. W. (2014). *Pretend play in childhood: Foundation of adult creativity*. Washington, DC: American Psychological Association.

Safran, J. D., & Muran, J. C. (2000). *Negotiating the therapeutic alliance: A relational treatment guide*. New York, NY: Guilford Press.

Salvatore, G., Buonocore, L., Ferrigno, A. M., Popolo, R., Proto, M., Sateriale, A., . . . Dimaggio, G. (2016). Metacognitive interpersonal therapy for personality disorders swinging from emotional over-regulation and dysregulation: A case study. *American Journal of Psychotherapy, 70*, 365–381. doi:10.1176/appi.psychotherapy.2016.70.4.365

Salvatore, G., Lysaker, P. H., Procacci, M., Carcione, A., Popolo, R., & Dimaggio, G. (2012). Vulnerable self, poor understanding of others' minds, threat anticipation and cognitive biases as triggers for delusional experience in schizophrenia: A theoretical model. *Clinical Psychology & Psychotherapy, 19*, 247–259. doi:10.1002/cpp.746

Schacter, D. L., Addis, D. R., Hassabis, D., Martin, V. C., Spreng, R. N., & Szpunar, K. K. (2012). The future of memory: Remembering, imagining, and the brain. *Neuron, 76*, 677–694.

Schacter, D. L., Benoit, R. G., De Brigard, F., & Szpunar, K. K. (2015). Episodic future thinking and episodic counterfactual thinking: Intersections between memory and decisions. *Neurobiology of Learning and Memory, 117*, 14–21. doi:10.1016/j.nlm.2013.12.008

Schacter, D. L., & Masore, K. P. (2016). Remembering the past and imagining the future: Identifying and enhancing the contribution of episodic memory. *Memory Studies, 9*(3), 245–255. doi:10.1177/1750698016645230

Schaefer, M., Cherkasskiy, L., Denke, C., Spies, C., Song, H., Malahy, S., . . . Bargh, J. A. (2018). Incidental haptic sensations influence judgment of crimes. *Scientific Reports, 8*, 6039. doi:10.1038/s41598-018-23586-x

Schilling, L., Wingenfeld, K., Lowe, B., Moritz, S., Terfehr, K., Kother, U., & Spitzer, C. (2012). Normal mind-reading capacity but higher response confidence in borderline personality disorder patients. *Psychiatry and Clinical Neurosciences, 66*, 322–327.

Schomers, M. R., & Pulvermüller, F. (2016). Is the sensorimotor cortex relevant for speech perception and understanding? An integrative review. *Frontiers in Human Neuroscience, 10*, 435. doi:10.3389/fnhum.2016.00435

Schulz, A., & Vogele, C. (2015). Interoception and stress. *Frontiers in Psychology, 6*, 993. doi:10.3389/fpsyg.2015.00993

Segal, Z. V., Williams, J. M. G., & Teasdale, J. D. (2002). *Mindfulness-based cognitive therapy for depression: A new approach to preventing relapse.* New York, NY: Guilford Press.

Semerari, A. (2010). The impact of metacognitive dysfunctions in personality disorders on the therapeutic relationship and intervention technique. In G. Dimaggio & P. H. Lysaker (Eds.), *Metacognition and severe adult mental disorders: From research to treatment* (pp. 269–284). London, UK: Routledge.

Semerari, A., Carcione, A., Dimaggio, G., Falcone, M., Nicolò, G., Procacci, M., & Alleva, G. (2003). How to evaluate metacognitive functioning in psychotherapy? The metacognition assessment scale and its applications. *Clinical Psychology and Psychotherapy, 10*, 238–261.

Semerari, A., Colle, L., Pellecchia, G., Buccione, I., Carcione, A., Dimaggio, G., . . . Pedone, R. (2014). Metacognitive dysfunctions in personality disorders: Correlations with disorder severity and personality styles. *Journal of Personality Disorders, 28*, 751–766.

Semerari, A., Colle, L., Pellecchia, G., Carcione, A., Conti, L., Fiore, D., . . . Pedone, R. (2015). Personality disorders and mindreading: Specific impairments in patients with borderline personality disorder compared to other PDs. *The Journal of Nervous and Mental Disease, 203*(8), 626–631. doi:10.1097/NMD.0000000000000339

Shafir, T. (2016). Using movement to regulate emotion: Neurophysiological findings and their application in psychotherapy. *Frontiers in Psychology, 7*, 1451. https://doi.org/10.3389/fpsyg.2016.01451.

Shahar, G., & Govrin, A. (2017). Psychodynamizing and existentializing cognitive – Behavioral interventions: The case of behavioral activation (BA). *Psychotherapy, 54*, 267–272. doi:10.1037/pst0000115

Shapiro, F. (2012). *Getting past your past: Take control of your life with self-help techniques from EMDR therapy.* Emmaus, PA: Rodale.

Sharp, C., Pane, H., Ha, C., Venta, A., Patel, A. B., Sturek, J., & Fonagy, P. (2011). Theory of mind and emotion regulation difficulties in adolescents with borderline traits. *Journal of the American Academy of Child and Adolescent Psychiatry, 50*, 563–573.

Singer, J. A., Blagov, P., Berry, M., & Oost, K. M. (2013). Healthy narrative identity. *Journal of Personality, 81*, 569–582. doi:10.1111/jopy.12005

Spinhoven, P., Bamelis, L., Molendijk, M., Haringsma, R., & Arntz, A. (2009). Reduced specificity of am in cluster C personality disorders and the role of depression, worry and experiential avoidance. *Journal of Abnormal Psychology, 118*, 520–530.

Stern, D. N. (1985). *The interpersonal world of the infant.* London: Routledge.

Stern, D. N. (2010). *Forms of vitality: Exploring dynamic experience in psychology, the arts, psychotherapy, and development.* Oxford, UK: Oxford University Press.

Szpunar, K. K., Spreng, R. N., & Schacter, D. L. (2014). A taxonomy of prospection: Introducing an organizational framework for future-oriented cognition. *Proceedings of* the National Academy of Sciences of the United States of America, 111, 18414–18421. doi:10.1073/pnas.1417144111

Taylor, V. A., Daneault, V., Grant, J., Scavone, G., Breton, E., Roffe-Vidal, S., . . . Beauregard, M. (2013). Impact of meditation training on the default mode network during a restful state. *Social Cognitive and Affective Neuroscience*, 8(1), 4–14. doi:10.1093/scan/nsr087

Tchanturia, K., Doris, E., Mountford, V., & Fleming, C. (2015). Cognitive remediation and emotion skills training (CREST) for anorexia nervosa in individual format: Self-reported outcomes. *BMC Psychiatry*, 20, 15–53. doi:10.1186/s12888-015-0434-9

Teasdale, J. D. (1999). Metacognition, mindfulness and the modification of mood disorders. *Clinical Psychology and Psychotherapy*, 6(2), 146–155. https://doi.org/10.1002/(SICI)1099-0879(199905)6:2%3C146::AID-CPP195%3E3.0.CO;2-E

Tomasello, M. (2016). *A natural history of human morality*. Cambridge, MA: Harvard University Press.

Van der Kolk, B. A. (2014). *The body keeps the score: Brain, mind, and body in the healing of trauma*. London, UK: Penguin.

Van Roekel, E., Heininga, V. E., Vrijen, C., Snippe, E., & Oldehinkel, A. J. (2018). Reciprocal associations between positive emotions and motivation in daily life: Network analyses in anhedonic individuals and healthy controls. *Emotion*. doi:0.1037/emo0000424

Vonk, J., Zeigler-Hill, V., Ewing, D., Mercer, S., & Noserc, A. E. (2015). Mindreading in the dark: Dark personality features and theory of mind. *Personality and Individual Differences*, 87, 50–54.

Wadlinger, H. A., & Isaacowitz, D. M. (2011). Fixing our focus: Training attention to regulate emotion. *Personality and Social Psychology Review: An Official Journal of the Society for Personality and Social Psychology, Inc*, 15(1), 75–102. doi:10.1177/1088868310365565

Wegner, D. M. (2011). Setting free the bears: Escape from thought suppression. *American Psychologist*, 66(8), 671–680. doi:10.1037/a0024985

Weiss, J. (1993). *How psychotherapy works*. New York, NY: Guilford.

Wells, A. (2005). The metacognitive model of GAD: Assessment of meta-worry and relationship with DSM-IV generalized anxiety disorder. *Cognitive Therapy and Research*, 29(1), 107–121. doi:10.1007/s10608-005-1652-0

Wells, A. (2008). *Metacognitive therapy for anxiety and depression*. New York, NY: Guilford Press.

Wells, A., & Matthews, G. (1994). *Attention and emotion: A clinical perspective*. Hove, UK: Erlbaum.

Westen, D., & Shedler, J. (2000). A prototype matching approach to diagnosing personality disorders: Towards the DSM-V. *Journal of Personality Disorders*, 14, 109–126.

White, M., & Epston, D. (1990). *Narrative means to therapeutic ends*. New York, NY: W. W. Norton and Company, Inc.

Wilson, M. (2002). Six views of embodied cognition. *Psychonomic Bulletin & Review*, 9, 625–636.

Wilson, M., & Emmorey, K. (1997). A visuospatial "phonological loop" in working memory: Evidence from American sign language. *Memory & Cognition*, 25, 313–320.

Wolkin, J. R. (2015). Cultivating multiple aspects of attention through mindfulness meditation accounts for psychological well-being through decreased rumination. *Psychology Research and Behavior Management*, 8, 171–180. doi:10.2147/PRBM.S31458

Yeomans, F. E., Delaney, J. C., & Levy, K. N. (2017). Behavioral activation in TFP: The role of the treatment contract in transference-focused psychotherapy. *Psychotherapy*, 54, 260–266. doi:10.1037/pst0000118

Young, J. E., Klosko, J. S., & Weishaar, M. E. (2003). *Schema therapy: A practitioner's guide.* New York, NY: Guilford Press.

Zahl, K.-E. (2018, September 27–29). *Different applications and preliminary outcomes of metacognitive interpersonal therapy in groups in Norway.* Paper presented at the ESSPD, Sitges, Barcelona.

Zheng, S., Kim, C., Lal, S., Meier, P., Sibbritt, D., & Zaslawski, C. (2014). Protocol: The effect of 12 weeks of Tai Chi practice on anxiety in healthy but stressed people compared to exercise and wait-list comparison groups: A randomized controlled trial. *Journal of Acupuncture and Meridian Studies, 7,* 159–165.

Index

agency 10, 16, 28–30, 80–81, 99, 182, 186–188, 228–233
associated memories 87–88, 96, 114–115, 158, 218, 296
autobiographical memories 10–12, 108–109, 114, 143, 279, 293

behavioural exploration 228–246; connecting with healthy part 123; in the differentiation process 95, 122; to improve self-reflectivity 103; to understand interpersonal cycle 127; *see also* behavioural exposure
behavioural exposure 86, 91, 95, 191, 202

change promoting 102, 105, 118, 221, 253, 258, 297, 309
coping strategies 47–56, 61–69, 107, 247–249, 259

differentiation 38, 63, 93, 119, 123, 130, 222, 241, 251
dynamic assessment 80, 89–90, 106–111, 231–232, 252–253

embodied cognition 3, 5, 71–72, 89, 140, 222
emotional regulation 82, 99, 113, 145–150, 207, 213, 228, 247, 260–261

experiential techniques 28, 131–134; in change promoting 297; in shared formulation 293

grounding 80, 87, 207–210, 214–218, 224; using drama techniques 190–191; entering guided imagery 146, 149–151, 154–155, 158, 161, 170; promoting emotion regulation with 87, 158, 161

healthy part 37, 63, 107, 112–113, 119, 123–130; using body interventions 217, 222; using drama techniques 183–184, 188–191, 194–195; using imagery and bodily techniques 89, 97–102, 162–163, 297, 303; promoting behavioural exploration 229, 241–245

interpersonal cycle 59–66, 87, 97, 127–132, 229, 275–276, 292
interpersonal schemas 9–10; dysfunctional interpersonal cycle 61; formulation of 24–25; maladaptive interpersonal schemas 13, 64–65; procedural component of 13–16, 61–62, 69, 76, 158, 228, 253; as a relational test 26–28

joint formulation 206, 214, 216–217, 221, 233, 267, 270

327

metacognition 33–34, 45, 88–95, 106, 253, 272–273, 310
Metacognitive Interpersonal Mindfulness-Based Training (MIMBT) 80, 247, 258, 263–267
mindfulness 80–81, 108, 113, 119, 146, 208, 258–263, 273
motivational system 15–17, 55–56, 59, 143, 192

narrative episode 10–12, 25–26, 108–117, 293–295; assessing coping strategies 248; for body interventions 217–218; for guided imagery 142, 147, 150; in therapy group 279–282

sensorimotor 76, 103, 299, 301, 303, 309, 310–311; using drama techniques 180, 191
shared formulation of functioning 105, 108–109; using body intervention 22; during dynamic assessment 90, 102, 108–109, 231; *see also* joint formulation

therapeutic alliance 135, 228, 249–253
therapeutic contract 133–136, 162–163, 195, 230–231, 238